# The Sharing Economy in Europe

Vida Česnuitytė · Andrzej Klimczuk ·
Cristina Miguel · Gabriela Avram
Editors

# The Sharing Economy in Europe

## Developments, Practices, and Contradictions

palgrave
macmillan

*Editors*
Vida Česnuitytė
Mykolas Romeris University
Vilnius, Lithuania

Cristina Miguel
University of Gothenburg
Gothenburg, Sweden

Andrzej Klimczuk
SGH Warsaw School of Economics
Collegium of Socio-Economics
Warsaw, Poland

Gabriela Avram
Interaction Design Centre
University of Limerick
Limerick, Ireland

ISBN 978-3-030-86896-3 ISBN 978-3-030-86897-0 (eBook)
https://doi.org/10.1007/978-3-030-86897-0



This Palgrave Macmillan imprint is published by the registered company Springer Nature Switzerland AG
The registered company address is: Gewerbestrasse 11, 6330 Cham, Switzerland

Funded by the Horizon 2020 Framework Programme of the European Union

This publication is based upon work from COST Action CA16121, supported by COST (European Cooperation in Science and Technology).

COST (European Cooperation in Science and Technology) is a funding agency for research and innovation networks. Our Actions help connect research initiatives across Europe and enable scientists to grow their ideas by sharing them with their peers. This boosts their research, career and innovation.

www.cost.eu

# Foreword

If we begin with the notion of sharing that ostensibly underlies and precedes the sharing economy, we are faced with two paradoxes. The first paradox noted by Thomas Widlok (2013, p. 11) is 'Why do people share what they value even though they cannot count on a return?' Widlok was talking primarily about hunter-gatherer societies in which the successful hunter allows all those in the hunting party, in the village, or encountered along the way to take what they want from the game she brought down. But we might just as easily be talking about 'borrowing' eggs from a neighbour or a few sheets of paper from a classmate. These are things we value and yet we suspect that once 'lent' we may well never see them or their like again. Nevertheless, we gladly share because it is the neighbourly friendly thing to do.

The second paradox lies in the two components of the phrase, the 'sharing economy':

> "Sharing" implies a moral economy of "sharing in" within a small community of close others..., while "economy" implies a market economy where access-based consumption takes place within a potentially

> large community of distant others. (Belk, Eckhardt and Bardhi 2019, p. 1)

The latter economic component here implies 'sharing without caring' (Belk 2017) or as Bardhi and Eckhardt (2015) put it, the sharing economy is not about sharing at all.

What we are dealing with in these paradoxes are what Miguel et al. in the introductory chapter highlight as the 'contradictions of the sharing economy':

> The sharing economy has been moving away from local and solidarity-based sharing, gifting, bartering, commoning (non-market-based ways of supply), and drifted easily towards commercialised and business-like activities. (Chapter 1, this volume)

In the paradoxes of sharing versus the sharing economy there is a potential for romanticism and an implicit nostalgia for prior days. It is significant in this regard that more than one-third of the authors here are from once-communist Eastern European countries. This fact has some apparent significance. Under communism, although there were widespread shortages of food and consumer goods like appliances and cars, people struggled through together (e.g., Drakulić 1991, 1997). There was sharing within the immediate and extended family, but outside of these close circles the patterns of exchange were instead often coupled with favours, bribes, under-the-table payments, *blat*, *mită*, *podkup*, *kenőpénz*, *łapówka*, etc. (Belk 1997; Makovicky and Henig 2017). Nevertheless, using ingenuity, hoarding, and resourcefulness, for the most part people made it through the tough times alive. Several decades later, there is now a tendency for many to look back fondly on those years of hardship. They are seen by some people through a lens of nostalgia (Boym 2001; Todorov and Gille 2010).

It seems that both the things that some people are nostalgic about from the days of communism in Eastern Europe and what many seem to miss in contrasting small-scale intra-familial 'sharing in' to large scale 'sharing out' with strangers, is a feeling of unity. There's a difference between inviting someone into our home on one hand and contracting online to host a stranger for a fee on the other hand. Likewise, there is a difference between being picked up by a driver while hitchhiking and booking an Uber ride on our smartphone. As Farmaki and Miguel discuss in Chapter 6 of this volume, large-scale sharing economy transactions mediated by digital corporate platforms may be safer, more efficient, and more predictable, but they come at the expense of commodifying what was once social and emotionally driven rather than impersonal and monetarily driven.

We can also note a certain similarity between the 'under-the-table' payments for favours in earlier Eastern European economies and the role of digital platforms in mediating transactions in the contemporary sharing economies of Europe today. Both practises work to hide the mercenary aspects of these transactions and make them feel more like normal ways of behaving in the marketplace. In today's digital sharing economy, because there is no face-to-face exchange of cash it can sometimes feel more like a purely social transaction. The reputation ratings, comments, and tips we may add online after these exchanges take place are also at a digital distance rather than face-to-face. And while a driver who picks up a hitchhiker is apt to turn down an offer of cash at the end of the journey in order to emphasise that the trip was socially rather than monetarily motivated, the Uber driver has no such scruples. Moreover, the Uber driver her- or himself is also caught in a gig economy and can never expect to be promoted, be offered a paid vacation, or receive a raise (see Česnuitytė et al., Chapter 18, this volume; Slee 2015).

So, as the papers in this timely volume emphasise, the sharing economy has many benefits, but for many people these benefits come with a nostalgic feeling that something has been lost. Despite the digital magic that allows these products and services to be exchanged, the exchanges cast a shadow. It is the shadow of earlier non-mediated exchanges that seem, for better or worse, to have been more genuine and authentic. But we will not go back. The chance to work out a moral marketplace lies in the present moment as we shift to digitally mediated exchanges. This book offers some thoughtful analyses of how best to move towards this shared goal of moral sharing economies for all of Europe.

Russell Belk
York University
Toronto, Canada

## References

Bardhi, Fleura, and Giana Eckhardt. 2015. 'The Sharing Economy Isn't About Sharing at All.' *Harvard Business Review*, January 28, https://hbr.org/2015/01/the-sharing-economy-isnt-about-sharing-at-all.

Belk, Russell. 1997. 'Romanian Consumer Desires and Feelings of Deservingness.' In *Romania in Transition*, edited by Lavinia Stan, 191–208. Aldershot, UK: Dartmouth Press.

Belk, Russell. 2017. 'Sharing without Caring.' *Cambridge Journal of Regions, Economy, and Society* 10 (2): 249–261.

Belk, Russell, Giana Eckhardt, and Fleura Bardhi. 2019. 'Introduction to the Handbook of the Sharing Economy: The Paradox of the Sharing Economy.' In *Handbook of the Sharing Economy*, edited by Russell Belk, Giana Eckhardt, and Fleura Bardhi, 1–8. Cheltenham, UK: Edward Elgar.

Boym, Svetlana. 2001. *The Future of Nostalgia*. New York: Basic Books.

Drakulić, Slavenka. 1991. *How We Survived Communism and Even Laughed*. New York: W. W. Norton.

Drakulić, Slavenka. 1997. *Café Europa: Life After Communism*. New York: W. W. Norton.

Makovicky, Nicolette, and David Henig. 2017. 'Introduction—Re-imagining Economies (after Socialism): Ethics, Favours, and Moral Sentiments.' In *Economies of Favor After Socialism*, edited by David Henig and Nicoette Makovicky. Oxford: Oxford University Press.

Slee, Tom. 2015. *What's Yours Is Mine: Against the Sharing Economy*. New York: O/R Books.

Todorov, Maria, and Zsuzsa Gille, eds. 2010. *Post-Communist Nostalgia*. New York: Berghahn.

Widlock, Thomas. 2013. 'Sharing: Allowing Others to Take What Is Valued.' *HAU: Journal of Ethnographic Theory* 3 (2): 11–31.

# Preface

The edited collection *The Sharing Economy in Europe: Developments, Practices, and Contradictions* was initiated by the participants of the COST Action CA16121 'From Sharing to Caring: Examining Socio-Technical Aspects of the Collaborative Economy' supported by the COST (European Cooperation in Science and Technology) Association. The COST Action started in 2017 and provided for participants comprehensive knowledge and experiences on the sharing (collaborative) economy, as well as networking with scholars, professionals, and practitioners working in the area. Approaching the end of the COST Action, the group of editors generated conception of this volume and invited scholars to contribute with the original papers.

In total, over thirty authors from sixteen countries (Albania, Austria, Croatia, Cyprus, Denmark, France, Hungary, Ireland, Italy, Lithuania, North Macedonia, Poland, Portugal, Spain, The Netherlands, and the United Kingdom) created and submitted papers for a deeper understanding of phenomena. The most promising papers that best correspond to the book's goal and objectives and give an integrated vision included in the collection. For better quality, all papers went through a double-blind review.

The book is organised in several parts that consist of eighteen chapters in which authors explore sharing economy, its features, developments, and prospects from the perspective of economy, legislation, Information technologies, communication, and sociology. The studies provide answers to the questions: How is the sharing economy understood nowadays? What roles does the sharing economy play in sharing and redistribution of goods and services across the population in order to maximise their functionality, monetary exchange, and other aspects important to societies? How the contexts of public policies, legislation, digital platforms, and other infrastructure interrelate with the development and function of the sharing economy? What are the contradictions of the development and recent trends in the sharing economy? What experiences and achievements in the sharing economy creation and practising are characteristic to European countries?

The main benefits of this edited collection of papers are the following: the most recent approaches towards the sharing economy conceptualisation, policies, development, and function; the novelty of findings on shifting from the local and solidarity-based sharing to commercialisation and business-like segments, as well as, on trends in sharing economy; interdisciplinary in terms of theoretical approaches, and internationality in terms of countries' dimensions represented in the volume. The authors hope that the book will become a useful tool for scholars, teachers, students, practitioners, and all others who are looking for answers to the phenomena and processes explored in the volume.

The editors of the book express special acknowledgements to the COST Action CA16121 'From Sharing to Caring: Examining Socio-Technical Aspects of the Collaborative Economy' that created a background for collaboration of the editors and contributors and funded the publication of this book in open access. The editors also express acknowledgements to Mijalche Santa from the Ss. Cyril and Methodius

University (Skopje, North Macedonia) for assistance in the preparation of the book.

Vilnius, Lithuania
Warsaw, Poland
Gothenburg, Sweden
Limerick, Ireland
June 2021

Vida Česnuitytė
Andrzej Klimczuk
Cristina Miguel
Gabriela Avram

# Contents

**Part I Introduction**

1 **The Sharing Economy in Europe: From Idea to Reality** 3
*Cristina Miguel, Gabriela Avram, Andrzej Klimczuk, Bori Simonovits, Bálint Balázs, and Vida Česnuitytė*

**Part II Development of the Sharing Economy in Europe**

2 **A Conceptualisation of the Sharing Economy: Towards Theoretical Meaningfulness** 21
*Cristina Miguel, Esther Martos-Carrión, and Mijalche Santa*

3 **The Context of Public Policy on the Sharing Economy** 41
*Błażej Koczetkow and Andrzej Klimczuk*

4 **The Regulatory Context and Legal Evolution: The Cases of Airbnb and Uber** 65
*Kosjenka Dumančić and Natalia-Rozalia Avlona*

**Part III Mapping Sectors of the Sharing Economy in European Countries**

5 **Shared Mobility: A Reflection on Sharing Economy Initiatives in European Transportation Sectors** 89
*Agnieszka Lukasiewicz, Venere Stefania Sanna, Vera Lúcia Alves Pereira Diogo, and Anikó Bernát*

6 **Peer-To-Peer Accommodation in Europe: Trends, Challenges and Opportunities** 115
*Anna Farmaki and Cristina Miguel*

7 **From Uberisation to Commoning: Experiences, Challenges, and Potential Pathways of the Sharing Economy in Food Supply Chains in Europe** 137
*Bori Simonovits and Bálint Balázs*

8 **Unpacking the Financial Services and Crowdfunding Evolution in the Sharing Economy** 163
*Agnieszka Lukasiewicz and Mijalche Santa*

9 **Education, Knowledge and Data in the Context of the Sharing Economy** 181
*Gabriela Avram and Eglantina Hysa*

10 **Solidarity and Care Economy in Times of 'Crisis': A View from Greece and Hungary Between 2015 and 2020** 207
*Penny Travlou and Anikó Bernát*

**Part IV Country-Specific Case Studies**

**11 From a Sharing Economy to a Platform Economy: Public Values in Shared Mobility and Gig Work in the Netherlands** 241
*Martijn de Waal and Martijn Arets*

**12 The Sharing Economy in France: A Favourable Ecosystem for Alternative Platforms Models** 263
*Myriam Lewkowicz and Jean-Pierre Cahier*

**13 A Critical Perspective on the Sharing Economy in Tourism Using Examples of the Accommodation Sector in Austria** 285
*Malte Höfner and Rainer Rosegger*

**14 Unsettled State of Regulation: Italy's Hard Path Towards Effective Rules for the Sharing Economy** 305
*Giulia Priora, Monica Postiglione, Stefano Valerio, Venere Stefania Sanna, and Chiara Bassetti*

**15 Time Banks in the United Kingdom: An Examination of the Evolution** 325
*Rodrigo Perez-Vega and Cristina Miguel*

**16 The Sharing Economy Business Models in Poland: Aspects of Trust, Law, and Initiatives Facing the COVID-19 Pandemic** 343
*Agnieszka Lukasiewicz and Aleksandra Nadolska*

**17 Advances of Sharing Economy in Agriculture and Tourism Sectors of Albania** 365
*Eglantina Hysa and Alba Demneri Kruja*

Part V Conclusions

18 The State and Critical Assessment of the Sharing Economy in Europe 387
*Vida Česnuitytė, Bori Simonovits, Andrzej Klimczuk, Bálint Balázs, Cristina Miguel, and Gabriela Avram*

Index 405

# Notes on Contributors

**Martijn Arets** is an international expert and thinker in the field of the platform economy. As a bridge builder and independent professional outsider, he uses these insights and this network to get stakeholders such as trade unions, government institutions, platforms, and academics together to address relevant issues in a constructive way. Arets' background is in marketing and branding, and previously he has (co-)written the books *Brand Expedition: A Journey Visiting Europe's Most Inspiring Brands* (Utrecht: Eburon); *Crowdfunding: Beyond the Hype* (Utrecht: Eburon); and *Crowdfunding for Dummies* (Amersfoort: BBNC). His most recent book is *De Platformrevolutie* (*The Platform Revolution, Amsterdam: Boom*).

**Natalia-Rozalia Avlona, LL.M.** is a Lawyer and Researcher with expertise in the intersection of open technologies, law, and gender. She is a Marie Skłodowska-Curie Ph.D. Fellow at the Computer Science Department of the University of Copenhagen (DCODE Marie Skłodowska-Curie Innovative Training Network). She has international experience working in several Policy Organisations and European Research Programmes in the UK, Belgium, Greece, and Cyprus. She has been member of the Management Committee of COST Action CA16121–From Sharing to Caring: Examining Socio-Technical Aspects of the Collaborative Economy (2017–2021). Natalia is research co-lead in DisCO Organisation and also the co-founder of the techno-feminist network Restorative Infrastructures.

**Gabriela Avram, Ph.D.** is a Lecturer in Digital Media and Interaction Design and senior researcher at the Interaction Design Centre of the University of Limerick (Ireland). Building on a computer-supported cooperative work background, her research currently focuses on the implications of the collaborative economy on urban communities, with an emphasis on knowledge sharing, civic engagement, and communities' involvement in the preservation of cultural heritage. She has published extensively in Human-Computer Interaction and Computer-Supported Cooperative Work venues. She was the initiator and chair of the COST Action Sharing and Caring.

**Bálint Balázs** is a Senior Researcher and Executive Manager of ESSRG. He has a Ph.D. in environmental sciences, an M.A. in history, and an M.A. in sociology. He has international research experience in the EU projects in the field of sustainable and local food systems, transition to sustainability and policy analysis, as well as public engagement, science-policy dialogues, cooperative research, and participatory action research. He is a board member of the Environment & Society Research Network of the European Sociological Association. He is a secretary of the Editorial Board of the *European Journal of Mental Health: Well-Being in Social and Ecological Context* (since 2018). He is a Member of the Urgenci Community-Supported Agriculture Research Group.

**Chiara Bassetti, Ph.D.** is Senior Assistant Professor at the University of Trento, and a Researcher at the Institute of Cognitive Sciences and Technologies of the Italian National Research Council (CNR). An ethnographer and ethnomethodologist, often working in interdisciplinary teams, her main research focus rests on social interaction, cultural phenomena and workplace practices. Her further research concerns computer-supported collaborative work, grassroots initiatives and socio-economic innovation. Chiara has been Visiting Scholar at the University of California Riverside and the London King's College. Recent publications include Ethnography in and of the age of COVID-19 (Special Issue of Etnografia e Ricerca Qualitativa vol.13 n.2, co-edited with G.A. Fine and C. Chang), and Becoming a Platform in Europe: On the Governance of the Collaborative Economy (now publisher, 2021, co-edited with M. Teli).

**Anikó Bernát** is a sociologist and a research fellow at TARKI Social Research Institute in Budapest, Hungary, since 2002. She is an expert in the social integration of vulnerable social groups and issues related to solidarity, civilian and collaborative action, and participation, which she also researches in the context of sharing or collaborative economy and initiatives. Her research practice applies both qualitative and quantitative methods in an interdisciplinary frame. She has been involved in a wide range of international, European, and domestic research, including large-scale European research programmes and projects of EU bodies.

**Jean-Pierre Cahier** is a member of the Tech-CICO research group at Troyes University of Technology, France, since 2005. As a researcher in knowledge engineering and computer-supported cooperative work (CSCW), he participated in early studies on the 'social-semantic web,' building the infrastructure for a community to dynamically co-construct a pluralist meaning. He is a founding member of the Hypertopic group (http://hypertopic.org) and participated in developing web platforms dedicated to the collaborative representation and participative manipulation of contents and knowledge.

**Vida Česnuitytė, Ph.D.** in sociology, is an Associated Professor, and Head of the Sociological Research Laboratory at the Mykolas Romeris University (Vilnius, Lithuania). Her research fields include life-quality, family sociology, social policy, and methods of social research. She has published four collective monographs, four edited books (at Palgrave Macmillan and Emerald Publishing), three textbooks for university students (one—at Palgrave Macmillan), over fifteen book chapters, and over twenty papers in peer-reviewed national and international journals. Gave over thirty presentations at national and international scientific conferences in Canada, Finland, Greece, Italy, Japan, Poland, Portugal,

Spain, Switzerland, the United Kingdom, etc. Between 2017–2021 she served as Vice-coordinator of the Research Network 'Sociology of Families and Intimate Lives' of the European Sociological Association (ESA RN13). Between 2017–2021, also, was a representative of Lithuania in the COST Action CA16121 Sharing and Caring.

**Vera Lúcia Alves Pereira Diogo, Ph.D.** Professor in the School of Higher Education in the Polytechnic Institute of Porto, Portugal, since 2009. Integrated Researcher at iNED Center for Research and Innovation on Education. She holds a Ph.D. in sociology and has collaborated in research on social exclusion, social economy, social entrepreneurship, social work, socio-professional identification, educational organisations, and student integration in higher education. Currently, she is focussed on the benefits of the educative potential of velomobility for sustainable development under the framework of educating cities. She is a member of the COST Action *from Sharing to Caring: Examining Socio-technical aspects of the collaborative economy* and of the research network *Scientists for Cycling Network* of the European Cyclists Federation and also a collaborator in other international networks in the fields of education and culture.

**Kosjenka Dumančić, Ph.D.** is an Associate Professor of Commercial Law, Vice-Dean for international relations and projects, and the Head of Institute for Euro-Asian Studies at the University of Zagreb, Faculty of Economics and Business. Her research interests are in the fields of European company law, European internal market law, and collaborative economy. Currently, she is actively involved in an EU-funded Erasmus+ COLECO Project, which aims to examine the impacts of the collaborative economy in Europe, focussing on peer-to-peer accommodation platforms.

**Anna Farmaki, Ph.D.** is an Assistant Professor in the Department of Hotel and Tourism Management at the Cyprus University of Technology. Her primary research interests lie in the areas of tourism planning and development and tourist behaviour. Dr. Farmaki has a rich publication record, having published (both as a sole author and a co-author) in several high-ranked peer-reviewed academic journals, including *Tourism*

*Management*, *Annals of Tourism Research*, *Journal of Sustainable Tourism*, *Journal of Business Research*, *International Journal of Hospitality Management*, and *International Journal of Contemporary Hospitality Management*. She is the author of a book titled *Tourism and Society* published by Ion Publishing (in Greek). Dr. Farmaki is a Fellow of the Higher Education Academy (UK) and a Management Committee member in the European Union's COST Actions (CA16121, TU1408).

**Malte Höfner** is a Research Assistant and Ph.D. candidate at the Department of Geography and Regional Research at the University of Graz. After completing his undergraduate degree in geography at the University of Marburg (GER), he worked on the topic of coworking as a collective coping strategy for boundaryless work of creative labour in his master's degree programme in sustainable urban and regional development at the University of Graz. Meanwhile, he was involved in vacancy management and the mediation of temporary interim use at a project called (Raumbasis). He is currently doing research on the project 'Raumteilen' (Sharing Spaces) for his doctoral thesis. Using examples from the City of Graz, he investigates how inclusions and exclusions emerge through social practices of sharing (and dividing) and thus produces new spatial configurations on a local scale in the urban context of everyday realms such as working, housing and public life.

**Eglantina Hysa** is a Lecturer of Economics at Epoka University, Albania, teaching international economy, development and growth, and microeconomics. Her research is focussed on development economics, social aspects, and quality in higher education institutions. She is the author of many scientific publications, including book chapters and technical reports, published in leading international journals and publishing houses, including *Integration of Education*, *Sustainability*, *Journal of Applied Economics*, and Routledge. She is included as a Bologna System expert for higher education in many EU projects.

**Andrzej Klimczuk, Ph.D.** is a sociologist and public policy expert and an assistant professor at the SGH Warsaw School of Economics, Poland. His research focuses on gerontology, labour economics, public management, and social policy. He has published academic articles in both Polish and English in sociology and economics journals as well as contributed chapters to books and encyclopaedias.

**Błażej Koczetkow, Ph.D.** candidate at the SGH Warsaw School of Economics, Poland. He is an attorney-at-law and previously was an attorney. First, he gained experience in international law firms and then started working in his own law firm providing services to entrepreneurs. He established cooperation with a consulting company in the field of business continuity and risk analyses. He acts as a defence lawyer in economic and fiscal penal cases. He was also a member of the management board in a company employing over a thousand people. He is particularly interested in legal responsibility in the economic sphere in terms of behaviourism.

**Alba Demneri Kruja, Ph.D.** is a Lecturer at Epoka University in Albania, Department of Business Administration. She holds an M.B.A. degree from Nebraska University, Lincoln, USA, and a Ph.D. degree in entrepreneurship. At Epoka, she teaches courses of entrepreneurship and management science research at Bachelor, Master, and Ph.D. level. At the same time, she holds the administrative duty of the Academic Coordinator of the Business Informatics Program. Dr. Kruja has been a visiting professor at various universities. She is the author of many research papers and book chapters, where her main research focus is on entrepreneurship and innovation.

**Myriam Lewkowicz** is a full Professor of informatics at Troyes University of Technology, France, where she heads the pluridisciplinary research group Tech-CICO. Her interdisciplinary research in the field of computer-supported cooperative work (CSCW) involves defining digital technologies to support existing collective practices or to design new collective activities. She chairs the European Society for Socially Embedded Technologies (EUSSET). She was the vice-chair of COST Action Sharing and Caring, and she co-chaired its working group focussing on technical platforms.

**Agnieszka Lukasiewicz, Ph.D.** is an associate professor at the Management Systems and Telematic Division, the Road and Bridge Research Institute, Poland. She is an expert in stakeholders' analysis, managing large infrastructure transport projects, together with transport economics and sustainable transportation. Moreover, she has wide experience in various research projects, both on a national and international level. She also has practised in cooperation with different kinds of institutions, local authorities, as well as research documents construction. Agnieszka is a member of the Connected, Cooperative and Automated Mobility Association (CCAM).

**Esther Martos-Carrión, Ph.D.** is a Product Design Lead at eDreams, Spain. She received her Ph.D. in digital sociology from Charles University, the Czech Republic. Her PhD thesis analyses the evolution of the sharing economy in Europe. Covering topics such as digital transformation, the evolution of the semantics of the concept of the sharing economy, and the main drivers for the success of this phenomenon, her Ph.D. dissertation provides a holistic analysis of the sharing economy in Europe. Dr. Martos Carrión has been a sharing economy advisor for HireGo, a private car rental application based on blockchain. Dr. Martos-Carrión has presented her work at different international sharing economy conferences, including the international workshop on the sharing economy and DEPO2015, COMMONism discussion on sharing practices, policies, ownership, and common resources. She has published her research on conference papers and book chapters.

**Cristina Miguel, Ph.D.** is a Senior in Digital Communication at the University of Gothenburg, Sweden. She received her PhD in Media and Communications from the University of Leeds, UK. Her research interests include digital culture (network intimacy, online communities, and online privacy) and digital economy (sharing economy, the political economy of social media, and influencer marketing). Dr. Miguel has published her research in high-ranked peer-reviewed academic journals, including the *International Journal of Hospitality Management*, *Social Media+ Society*, and *Convergence*.

**Aleksandra Nadolska, Ph.D.** attorney-at-law, expert witness, lecturer at the University of Law and Administration in Gdynia. She specialises in financial market law, with particular emphasis on the market supervision institution and its position in the financial safety net. She is also interested in consumer protection of banking services and modern financial technologies.

**Rodrigo Perez-Vega, Ph.D.** is a Senior Lecturer at Kent Business School, UK. He received a Ph.D. in management from Heriot-Watt University. Rodrigo's research interest includes social media marketing, the use of technology in the sharing economy, and applications of artificial intelligence in marketing. Rodrigo is the co-author of the book *Essentials of Digital Marketing*, and he has published in journals such as the *Journal of Business Research*, *Tourism Management*, *The Service Industries Journal*, and *Marketing Review*.

**Monica Postiglione, Ph.D., M.Sc.** is an urban anthropologist at the Turin School of Regulation, Fondazione per l'Ambiente Teobaldo Fenoglio Onlus, in Turin, Italy. She holds a Ph.D. in urban planning from the University of Rome La Sapienza and an M.Sc. from the London School of Economics. She has been visiting student at Harvard University. Her main interests are represented by the social, institutional, and spatial changes, which are transforming urban realities. Since 2017 she has been collaborating with Fondazione per l'Ambiente as Executive Coordinator and International Development.

**Giulia Priora, SJD, LL.M.** is a Assistant Professor at Nova School of Law in Lisbon, Portugal, and Affiliated Researcher at the CEU Center for Media Data and Society in Budapest, Hungary. Her work focuses on intellectual property law, data and consumer protection, platform regulation, social and distributive inequality in digital markets. She has extensively published in these fields, investigating both their EU and comparative legal dimensions. She served as Visiting Scholar at Columbia Law School, Hamburg University, Bournemouth University, and as Visiting Lecturer at Sant'Anna School of Advanced Studies, Bocconi University Milan, Free University of Nuoro, Westfälische Wilhelms University of Münster, CEU School of Public Policy, and the University of Yangon.

**Rainer Rosegger** is a sociologist and has been working in his agency SCAN for 20 years on topics of housing, urban and regional development. From 2008 to 2013, he was actively involved in the organisation of the neighbourhood festival 'Lendwirbel' in Graz. In 2012 he was co-founder of the 'ROSTFEST' in Eisenerz. Both formats deal with the network-like and collaborative implementation of urban development processes. Moreover, he has taught at the University Graz, Graz University of Technology, the University of Applied Sciences and Arts Northwestern Switzerland, and the Stuttgart State Academy of Art and Design. As of 2017, he is represented in the Management Committee of the European research and development network 'From Sharing to Caring: Examining Socio-Technical Aspects of the Collaborative Economy' of the European Science Foundation. He works on societal transformation and the role of social innovation in the context of current challenges in economics, ecology and spatial development.

**Venere Stefania Sanna, Ph.D.** is a researcher in economic and political geography, currently working for the MEMOTEF Department of Sapienza University of Rome and collaborating with Italy's Centre for Politics and International Studies (CeSPI) on a variety of projects. Dr. Sanna also works as a Senior Expert in sustainability and the circular economy for the Ministry for Ecological Transition in Italy (under the auspices of Sogesid S.p.a.). She currently focuses on the analysis and assessment of the social, economic, political, and technological impacts of the transition from the 'linear economy' to a 'circular economy.' She has been involved in many national and international projects, and her research interests include regional economic development, European policies, sustainability issues, social movements, the sharing and collaborative economy, and research methodologies in economic geography. Her research method is based on a strongly interdisciplinary approach that incorporates policy and practice impacts, and her eclectic publication record reflects her diversity in fields of knowledge and study.

**Mijalche Santa, Ph.D.** is an associate professor at the Faculty of Economics-Skopje at Ss. Cyril and Methodius University in Skopje. He received his Ph.D. from University Paris 1, Pantheon, Sorbonne, in 2014. His research focuses on the domains of information systems development and digital innovation. He has published in journals such as *Technology Analysis & Strategic Management*, *Knowledge Management Research & Practice*, and *The Learning Organisation Journal*. He has been part of international research projects such as COST Action 'From Sharing to Caring: Examining Socio-Technical Aspects of the Collaborative Economy' and 'Interactive Narrative Design for Complexity Representations.' He has been the National contact point (NCP) for SME instrument and Access to Risk Finance programmes in the Horizon 2020 programme. He is a member of the Association for Information Systems.

**Bori Simonovits, Ph.D.** in sociology and AMA in social policy analysis, is a Senior Lecturer at Eötvös Loránd University, Budapest Faculty of Education and Psychology, since 2018. Her major research interests include sharing economy, social trust, discrimination, international migration, and attitudes. Besides her teaching activity, she is the principal investigator of a research project titled Trust and Discrimination in the Sharing Economy under the framework of NKFIH FK-127978 project (https://ippi.ppk.elte.hu/en/research). She was a member of the Hungarian team of COST Action titled Sharing to Caring (CA16121) between 2017–2021, taking part actively in collecting short stories and compiling country reports and editing a book on the sharing economy.

**Penny Travlou** is a Lecturer in cultural geography & theory in the Edinburgh School of Architecture & Landscape Architecture at the University of Edinburgh. Her research focuses on social justice, the commons, collaborative practices, emerging networks, feminist methodologies, epistemologies of the South, and ethnography. She has been involved in international research projects in Colombia, the US, and Europe funded by the EU and UK Research Councils. She was the Co-Leader of the Working Group 1 in the COST Action, *From Sharing to Caring: Examining Socio-Technical Aspects of the Collaborative Economy*. She is the Co-Director of the *Feminist Autonomous Centre for Research in Athens*, a non-profit independent research organisation that focuses on feminist and queer studies, participatory education, and activism.

**Stefano Valerio, M.Sc.** is a Research Assistant at Turin School of Regulation, Fondazione per l'Ambiente Teobaldo Fenoglio Onlus, in Turin, Italy. He holds an M.Sc. in environmental policies and economics. He worked as a member of the research team built by Fondazione Claudio

Sabattini to investigate industrial relations, organisational systems, and working conditions in the Italian plants of Fiat Chrysler Automobiles. He then moved to Fondazione per l'Ambiente, where he has been working since 2017, paying special attention to the regulation of digital platforms and the collaborative and sharing economy.

**Martijn de Waal** is a professor of Civic Interaction Design at the Amsterdam University of Applied Sciences. He is a co-author of the book *The Platform Society: Public Values in a Connected World* (Oxford University Press, 2018). In the project Circulate, his research group investigates the design of local platforms for a circular economy. The project explores speculative scenarios around algorithmic governance in local platforms and aims to translate these into design guidelines.

# List of Figures


Fig. 16.1 Individuals using websites or apps for the sharing economy by occupation, comparison of 2018 and 2019 (*Source* Own elaboration based on GUS [2018, 2019]) 351
Fig. 17.1 Strengths, weaknesses, opportunities, and threats analysis of the main sharing economy sectors in Albania (*Source* Own elaboration) 373
Fig. 17.2 Quadruple helix framework for the collaborative economy effectiveness (*Source* Own elaboration) 376

# List of Tables


| | | |
|---|---|---|
| Table 2.1 | List of sources included in the analysis | 27 |
| Table 3.1 | Topics relevant in public policy on the sharing economy | 43 |
| Table 5.1 | EU-28 Performance of modal split by mode (%) | 95 |
| Table 5.2 | EU-28 modal split of passenger transport on land (2017) by country | 96 |
| Table 6.1 | Benefits of P2P accommodation to guests and hosts | 117 |
| Table 7.1 | The three main 'models' of food sharing platforms | 146 |
| Table 7.2 | Modes of urban food sharing (with explanations and examples) | 147 |
| Table 9.1 | Educational Platforms | 187 |
| Table 9.2 | Examples of open education and shared resources in Europe | 190 |
| Table 9.3 | Examples of open and inclusive sharing initiatives in Europe | 196 |
| Table 9.4 | Examples of data sharing initiatives in Europe | 199 |
| Table 16.1 | Usage of websites or apps for the sharing economy in 2018 and 2019 | 348 |
| Table 17.1 | Industry-based examples of the sharing economy in Albania | 370 |

# Part I

## Introduction

# 1

# The Sharing Economy in Europe: From Idea to Reality

Cristina Miguel, Gabriela Avram, Andrzej Klimczuk, Bori Simonovits, Bálint Balázs, and Vida Česnuitytė

## Introduction

The 'collaborative economy' (or 'sharing economy,' as it is widely called) is best known for facilitating peer-to-peer exchanges through the means of digital platforms and mobile communication. As Gansky (2010) put it, the sharing economy is an idealised state characterised by the shift from ownership to renting, bartering, or gifting. Some authors argue for 'collaborative economies,' as this is an umbrella term incorporating many different stakeholder categories, business models, and forms of work,

C. Miguel (✉)
Department of Applied IT, University of Gothenburg, Gothenburg, Sweden
e-mail: cristina.miguel@ait.gu.se

G. Avram
University of Limerick, Limerick, Ireland
e-mail: Gabriela.Avram@ul.ie

A. Klimczuk
SGH Warsaw School of Economics, Warsaw, Poland
e-mail: aklimcz@sgh.waw.pl


V. Česnuitytė et al. (eds.), *The Sharing Economy in Europe*,
https://doi.org/10.1007/978-3-030-86897-0_1

from Airbnb and Uber to urban gardening collectives and online patient communities. According to Avram et al. (2017), two groups of narratives stand out in relation to the collaborative economy, one focussing on social innovation and the aspiration to replace the current paradigm with more sustainable economic and environmental models that favour sharing access to goods and services, and a second, more widely spread one, that centres on the idea of market-focussed digital innovation able to disrupt existing business models and generate new economic activity.

The sharing economy has been described as a disruptive socio-economic system that represents a major challenge to traditional economic models, which generally focus on hyper-consumption and private ownership (Botsman and Rogers 2010; Gansky 2010; Castells et al. 2012; Howard 2015). The sharing economy emerged around the financial crisis of 2007–2008 and related recession period. As Selloni (2017) pointed out, developments in technology and consumers seeking new ways to manage their finances in the context of the global economic downturn that followed the financial crisis came together and facilitated the nascent and emergent sharing economy. The sharing economy allowed cautious and financially constrained consumers to better manage their time, resources, budgets, and experiences. It also allowed those with resources to share and generate an additional and valuable income stream at a time when many incomes were either flat-lining or falling in real terms (Martos-Carrión and Miguel 2021).

The goal of this book is to provide readers with an original and comprehensive approach to the phenomenon of the sharing economy

B. Simonovits
Eötvös Loránd University, Budapest, Hungary
e-mail: simonovits.borbala@ppk.elte.hu

B. Balázs
Environmental Social Science Research Group, Budapest, Hungary
e-mail: balazs.balint@essrg.hu

V. Česnuitytė
Mykolas Romeris University, Vilnius, Lithuania
e-mail: v.cesnuityte@mruni.eu

by covering themes around its conceptualisation, development, mapping across economic sectors, and country-specific case studies. This is an edited collection of chapters on the topic of the sharing economy that is still under discussion. Most of the authors of the chapters are participants in the COST Action CA16121 'From Sharing to Caring: Examining Socio-Technical Aspects of the Collaborative Economy' (abbreviated as 'Sharing and Caring'). The idea for the development of this book emerged as a consequence of the collaboration of researchers from numerous countries in this COST Action. This research network is funded by the European Cooperation in Science and Technology (COST) Association. The main objective of the Action is to develop a European network of actors focussing on the development of collaborative economy models and platforms and on social and technological implications of the collaborative economy through a practice-focussed approach. The 'Sharing and Caring' COST Action started in March 2017 and ended in September 2021. One of the initiatives of this research network was to collect and edit a series of country reports on the state of the art of the collaborative economy in the participating countries that could be useful for the COST Action participants and the general public. The first edition of the country reports collection was initiated in 2017 and published online in May 2018 (Mosconi et al. 2018). A second edition, initiated in 2019, was published on the Action website as an e-book in the autumn of 2021 (Klimczuk et al. 2021). This book builds on information originally included in the country reports. The first nine chapters include original research, further analysis, and synthesis. Also, seven country reports were selected and are expanded as thematic case studies in this edited collection. Therefore, the book was constructed in a way that makes it distinctive and unique in comparison to other publications related to the topic of the sharing economy.

## The Topic and Context

The development of the sharing economy was fostered by the advance of new media technologies (e.g., Web 2.0, GPS) and the 2008 financial crisis (Martos-Carrión and Miguel 2021). Lawrence Lessig (2008) was probably the first author who used the term 'sharing economy' in his book *Remix*, where he defined the sharing economy in terms of the lack of interest in monetary gain to participate. Sharing economy activities may involve monetary exchange (e.g., Airbnb, BlaBlaCar, Car2go), or the exchange can be altruistic (e.g., CouchSurfing, OLIO, TimeBank). Nevertheless, sharing economy platforms mainly function as digital marketplaces where supply and demand are matched, either for economic compensation or for any other type of value exchange. Thus, rather than running in order to foster altruistic sharing, these new business models imply commodity exchange (Belk 2007). As Castells et al. (2012, p. 12) pointed out, the sharing economy is 'an alternative economy sector (not necessarily excluding for-profit production) based on a different set of values about the meaning of life.'

The sharing economy has also been described as the collaborative economy (e.g., Bauwens et al. 2012; Owyang et al. 2013) and collaborative consumption (e.g., Botsman and Rogers 2010; Germann Molz 2014; Hamari et al. 2016; Selloni 2017). According to Owyang et al. (2013, p. 4), 'the collaborative economy is an economic model where ownership and access are shared between corporations, start-ups, and people. This results in market efficiencies that bear new products, services and business growth.' Building on Botsman and Rogers (2010), Germann Molz (2014) explains that collaborative consumption is based on access rather than ownership and highlights the importance of digital platforms to facilitate the exchange of goods and experiences (e.g., ratings and reviews). In a similar vein, Hamari et al. (2016, p. 2047) argue that collaborative consumption is 'a peer-to-peer-based activity of obtaining, giving, or sharing access to goods and services, coordinated through community-based online services' where users can be providers, consumers, or both, the so-called 'prosumers' (Lang et al. 2020).

The fragmentation of the literature in a multitude of disciplines and research traditions most often leans back to one umbrella term, defined by Belk (2007) as 'an alternative to the private ownership that is emphasised in both marketplace exchange and gift-giving. In sharing, two or more people may enjoy the benefits (or costs) that flow from possessing a thing' (p. 127). To get to grips with the fragmentation, Frenken and Schor (2019) argued that the sharing economy has three defining characteristics: consumer-to-consumer interaction, temporary access, and physical goods. Earlier, Frenken et al. (2015) defined the sharing economy as 'consumers granting each other temporary access to under-utilised physical assets ('idle capacity'), possibly for money.' As for the multidimensionality of the term, Habibi et al. (2016) came up with the sharing economy continuum based on Belk (2007), ranging from pure sharing (see Belk's 2007 examples on that, e.g., mothering originally) to pure exchange (e.g., buying bread). While pure sharing can be labelled as non-reciprocal, personal and love and caring are key concepts. The pure exchange can be labelled as reciprocal, impersonal, and money is a key element (for more details, see Habibi et al. 2016, p. 4). Still, the depictions of the sharing economy remain rather contradictory and conceptually vague, especially in defining the purpose.

The main questions that the authors seek to answer in the book are the following:

1. How is the sharing economy understood nowadays? What are the social, business, and political aspects of this concept? What are the occurrences and interpretations of the sharing economy that can be observed in theory and practice?
2. What are the roles played by the sharing economy in the sharing and redistribution of goods and services across the population in order to maximise their functionality, monetary exchange, and other aspects important to societies?
3. What is the place of the sharing economy in connection to various policies? How do the contexts of public policies, legislation, digital platforms, and other infrastructure interrelate with the development and functioning of the sharing economy?
4. What are the contradictions in the development and recent trends in the sharing economy? Which sectors and characteristics of the sharing economy emerge as the most prominent in European countries?
5. What are the experiences and achievements in the sharing economy creation and practice that are characteristic to European countries?

In terms of the scope of the analysis, the unique feature of our project is that our European perspective is based on local information and knowledge gathered through the multidisciplinary team of the COST Action's local researchers coming from 36 countries. However, it is important to note that we apply varied perspectives on a given topic, and our analysis is not comparative in a strict methodological sense. The timeframe of the analysis covers basically the past ten years, and we aim to assess the main trends, issues, and contradictions of the various sharing economy platforms operating since 2010. In geographic terms, we are focussing on the European countries that are members of our COST Action, namely, Albania, Austria, Belgium, Bosnia-Herzegovina, Bulgaria, Czech Republic, Croatia, Cyprus, Denmark, Estonia, Finland, France, Germany, Greece, Hungary, Ireland, Israel, Iceland, Italy, Lithuania, Luxembourg, Malta, Montenegro, the Netherlands, North Macedonia, Norway, Poland, Portugal, Romania, Spain, Slovenia, Slovakia, Sweden, Switzerland, Turkey, and the United Kingdom.

In essence, in this book, we record inherently contradictory tendencies in the sharing economy. From a critical social science point of view, our analysis demonstrates a shift in the motivational basis of the sharing economy. The sharing economy has been moving away from local and solidarity-based sharing, gifting, bartering, commoning (non-market-based ways of supply), and drifted easily towards commercialised and business-like activities. Under the auspices of 'sharing economy business model,' the market-logic has been introduced into ever new spheres of life and therefore—even if unintentionally—led to an extractivist, precarious society based on unsustainable practices, new inequalities, and extraction of human and natural resources (Belk 2014; Schor 2014; Bradley and Pargman 2017). Such inborn contradictions of the sharing economy are also illustrated by the growing differences and tensions in relations between users and providers of goods and services, the motivations for sharing between sectors, and socio-demographic dissimilarity within user groups (Böcker and Meelen 2017). As a main expectation towards the sharing economy, we contend that decoupling from growth could be a critical social promise of the sharing economy so that it could avoid being entirely insensible to socio-ecological problems.

## Outline of the Book

The content of the edited collection consists of eighteen chapters divided into three main parts (Parts II–IV) plus sections containing an Introduction (Part I) and a Conclusion (Part V). The Introduction is dedicated to familiarising the reader with the key topics and issues analysed in the book. The second part of the volume provides a discussion of the concept of the sharing economy as well as a secondary analysis of public policies, programmes, strategies, and legislative documents on the sharing economy. The third part analyses the sharing economy evolutionary practices in selected economic sectors such as mobility or accommodation, among others. The fourth part of this book includes case studies of selected European countries and is based on a selection of best practices, desk research, and the so-called 'short stories' collected within the framework of COST Action. Finally, the Conclusion includes the most significant features, achievements, and issues of the contemporary sharing economy in European countries and future-oriented observations, directions for further research, and recommendations. Each chapter contains an introduction, substantial sections, summary, references, suggested readings, and relevant websites, as well as the author's biographies.

In the first of the three main parts (Part II), the authors focus on the sharing economy conceptualisation, public policies and legislation, and developments that are led by discussions, contradictions, and tensions in European cities.

Chapter 2, authored by Cristina Miguel, Esther Martos-Carrión, and Mijalche Santa, takes up the challenge of conceptual clarification of the sharing economy term. The authors based their chapter on 20 top references, which included definitions of the sharing economy and identified the peculiar core properties of the sharing economy. Ten principles are abstracted: (P1) Redistribution of assets; access over ownership; (P2) The Internet and innovative technologies are the core of the sharing economy; (P3) The sharing economy is a market-based system; (P4) The sharing economy is crowd-based; (P5) The sharing economy is built on decentralised networks; (P6) The sharing economy enables peer-to-peer (P2P) transactions while empowering individuals; (P7) The sharing economy is a socio-economic system that disrupts traditional economic systems; (P8) Trust among strangers enhances social value. Trust is mostly based on reputation systems; (P9) Prosumers play an important role in peer production; and (10) The sharing economy emphasises collective experiences, co-creation, and sustainable lifestyles. Finally, Chapter 2 defines the sharing economy according to these principles.

In Chapter 3, Błażej Koczetkow and Andrzej Klimczuk analyse the sharing economy from a public policy perspective. Firstly, the text focuses the attention on the development of the sharing economy as a driver of both positive economic effects and public problems (e.g., labour market, traditional market sectors). Second, the chapter identifies possible actions for regulating different sharing economy activities. The chapter discusses the role of soft law, stakeholders' networks, self-regulation, and standardisation.

Kosjenka Dumančić and Natalia-Rozalia Avlona, in Chapter 4, address the legal definition of the sharing economy and consider problematic the lack of a general European Union legal framework for the sharing economy, apart from a European Commission Communication from 2016. The main objective of this chapter is to discuss the issues related to the lack of clear regulation of sharing economy activities at the EU level. The chapter analyses the contradictory regulations of some sharing economy activities in various European countries. The lack of harmonisation in the regulation of the sharing economy in different European countries is analysed within the framework of two case studies: Uber and Airbnb.

In the next main part of the volume (Part III), the authors cover analyses of sharing economy evolutionary practices in selected economic sectors: mobility and transportation, peer-to-peer accommodation, food supply chains, financial services, education, knowledge, and data sharing, as well as in the solidarity and care sectors.

In Chapter 5, Agnieszka Lukasiewicz, Anikó Bernát, and Vera Diogo analyse the main shared mobility services in Europe, such as car-based sharing models, bike-sharing, and electric scooter sharing. In particular, Chapter 5 provides a discussion of different car-based sharing models, which include: (1) car-sharing (e.g., public such as Car Sharing Rome, or private such as Share Now); (2) ride-hailing, which parallels taxi services (e.g., Uber), (3) ride-sharing (e.g., BlaBlaCar); and (4) carpooling, where associates and employees of individual companies can select a car from a fleet of vehicles as required. The chapter also examines conflicts in different European countries caused by shared mobility aspects and the possible effects of the COVID-19 pandemic.

Anna Farmaki and Cristina Miguel discuss the evolution of the peer-to-peer (P2P) accommodation market sector in Europe in Chapter 6. First, the chapter distinguishes between free P2P accommodation platforms (e.g., CouchSurfing, BeWelcome); reciprocal P2P accommodation (e.g., HomeExchange, HomeSwap); and paid P2P accommodation platforms (e.g., Airbnb, HomeAway). The case study of Airbnb is introduced here to provide an overview of the platform's origins, evolution, and services. Later, the chapter provides an analysis of both opportunities and challenges that emerge from P2P accommodation activity's rapid growth. The chapter offers insights that may illuminate the understanding of the drivers, inhibitors, and influencers pertinent to the P2P accommodation market sector's development and resilience potential amid the COVID-19 pandemic.

In Chapter 7, Bori Simonovits and Bálint Balázs explore different aspects of the sharing economy within the food supply chains. The chapter offers an analysis of the topic with varied case examples at multiple value chain points (e.g., production, processing, transport, and consumption). Various peer-to-peer production and collaborative consumption initiatives are presented to assess how the idea of the sharing economy entered the food sector. The authors observe that in contrast to the accommodation and transport sectors, the food sector seemed to be probably the quickest-growing area of the sharing economy during the years 2020–2021. In particular, they address how the food delivery sector, the so-called uberisation of food (when contract workers use their personal vehicles to deliver food to customers), has gained even more momentum during the COVID-19 times.

Agnieszka Lukasiewicz and Mijalche Santa cover financial services and crowdfunding evolution within the sharing economy in Chapter 8. Financial services in the sharing economy range from peer-to-peer lending to crowdfunding, with participation from new start-ups and incumbent financial service providers with for-profit or non-profit goals.

The chapter covers different crowdfunding models, namely, donation-based, reward-based, equity-based, royalty-based, and lending-based financial services. It also addresses the value market of alternative financing and the impact of the COVID-19 pandemic in crowdfunding.

Gabriela Avram and Eglantina Hysa address the topics of open education, open design, knowledge, and data sharing in Chapter 9. First, the chapter explores the origins of online peer-to-peer collaborative learning, which can be found in the Open-Source Software movement and in the Wikipedia information production and consumption model. Next, the chapter presents and discusses examples of educational platforms, open education, and shared resources and initiatives in Europe. The text also discusses issues related to platforms facilitating collaborative information production and consumption.

In Chapter 10, Penny Travlou and Anikó Bernát describe the emergence of solidarity actions in two European countries—Greece and Hungary—in response to two recent crises: the arrival of large numbers of refugees in 2015 and the COVID-19 pandemic in 2020. The chapter discusses how the solidarity economy emerged during the 2008 financial crisis and how it was framed not only on monetised value but mostly on care and nurturing. The chapter is based on an ethnographic study that collected data via participant observation, interviews, and focus groups with grassroots solidarity collectives. Penny Travlou and Anikó Bernát embed the solidarity economy within the sharing economy, understood here as a new economic model that includes alternatives to the mainstream capitalist market.

In the third of the main parts of the book (Part IV), the authors' present case studies based on seven selected European country reports that cover best practices in some areas of the sharing economy. For example, the Netherlands case was selected for the country's pioneering initiatives in car-sharing, rental of vehicles, and bike-sharing services; France was selected for car-pooling practices, as well as its private chauffeur services; and the United Kingdom (UK) for its advanced initiatives and experience with time banks.

In Chapter 11, Martijn de Waal and Martijn Arets discuss shared mobility and gig work platforms in the Netherlands, which is one of the pioneer countries in the sharing economy. First, the chapter covers definitions and debates of the sharing economy in the Netherlands. The second part of the chapter focuses on the analysis of three forms of shared mobility that have been debated widely in the Netherlands: bike-sharing, car-sharing, and ride-hailing, covering some local initiatives as well as international players operating in the country, such as Uber. Finally, Chapter 11 critically analyses the gig economy in the Netherlands, which some see as an opportunity for economic growth, while others fear it would lead to the deterioration of workers' rights.

Myriam Lewkowicz and Jean-Pierre Cahier analyse the cooperative platform sector, as an alternative platform model in France, in Chapter 12. First, the chapter provides an overview of the French platform cooperativism ecosystem, highlighting why and how a number of platform cooperatives emerged successfully in France. Secondly, the chapter focuses on platform cooperatives in three domains, namely, meal delivery service, car-pooling, and energy. Finally, the chapter discusses how some identified factors could be considered as characteristics of a 'French touch' in terms of platform cooperativism.

In Chapter 13, Malte Höfner and Rainer Rosegger look at the peer-to-peer accommodation sector in Austria. The chapter covers sharing economy business models, which range from market-based services to platform cooperatives and provides an overview of the sharing economy in Austria. Later, the authors critically analyse the impact of global sharing economy platforms such as Airbnb in the traditional hospitality sector and in the housing market in Austria. They highlight that despite the COVID-19 pandemic has demonstrated the general volatility of the tourism market sector, big market players such as Airbnb have been very quick to adapt to unstable markets in times of crisis. They suggest that peer-to-peer accommodation sustainable business models at the local level, such as Reposée or Schau auf's Land, could provide a good alternative to big platforms and be less disruptive to the traditional accommodation market sector.

In Chapter 14, Giulia Priora, Monica Postiglione, Stefano Valerio, Venere Sanna, and Chiara Bassetti, provide an overview of the development of the sharing economy in Italy, with a special focus on the main legal issues emerging from its consolidation. The authors also reflect on the main implications of the COVID-19 pandemic within the Italian sharing economy sector. The second part of the chapter focuses on analysing specific sharing economy activities, including mobility, accommodation, and food, among others. Furthermore, the chapter offers an account of the legislation related to the sharing economy in Italy and addresses a number of issues in regulating some of the sectors, e.g., accommodation. Finally, the chapter offers some policy recommendations, such as clearly defining the role and obligations of platforms and service providers.

Rodrigo Perez-Vega and Cristina Miguel, in Chapter 15, cover one of the traditional examples of the pure sharing economy: time banks in the UK context. First, the chapter introduces the main definitions and characteristics of timebanks and describes the different typologies, including person-to-person time banks, person-to-agency time banks, and organisation-to-organisation time banks. Later on, the authors discuss the benefits and limitations of time banks. In the last section, the chapter analyses the evolution of time banks in the UK and how the COVID-19 pandemic has fostered the development of new initiatives.

In Chapter 16, Agnieszka Lukasiewicz and Aleksandra Nadolska describe the development of the sharing economy in Poland—from the operation of big players, such as Uber or Airbnb, to smaller local initiatives. The authors also discuss some regulatory issues, such as labour law and competition, which often lead to conflicts between different stakeholders. In addition, the chapter also addresses different aspects of sharing economy initiatives embedded in the COVID-19 pandemic.

Finally, Eglantina Hysa and Alba Demneri Kruja, in Chapter 17, analyse the sharing economy initiatives within the agriculture and tourism sectors in Albania. The authors perform a SWOT (strengths, weaknesses, opportunities, and threats) analysis of the following Albanian sharing economy platforms: Agroquality, MIA (agriculture); and IntoAlbania, Innovation Map Albania, Team Albanians, and Softmogul (tourism). In the second part of the chapter, the authors recommend the use of the quadruple helix collaboration model in order to enhance the collaborative economy in Albania. At the end of the chapter, a discussion is emphasising the main ideas, as well as pointing out some limitations of the development of the sharing economy in Albania.

## Summary

Summing it up, the book provides an innovative and comprehensive presentation of the practices, as well as of the scientific outcomes related to the sharing economy, from the perspectives of different disciplines, including economics, management, organisational studies, sociology, public policy and administration, legal theory, computer, and information science as well as media and communication studies. The book comprehensively discusses the key positive and negative aspects of the sharing economy and best practices that can be disseminated internationally. It also provides new ideas regarding the relations of the sharing economy with the creative industries, solidarity and care sectors, and the COVID-19 pandemic. The book offers a multilevel perspective and combines topics important at the global, European, national, and local level. The book may illuminate the understanding of the future (sharing) economy models, as well as contribute to solving questions of better access to resources and sustainable innovation in the context of degrowth and growing inequalities within and between societies.

## References

Avram, Gabriela, Jaz H. Choi, Stefano de Paoli, Ann Light, Peter Lyle, and Maurizio Teli. 2017. 'Collaborative Economies: From Sharing to Caring.' In *Proceedings of the 8th International Conference on Communities and Technologies*, edited by Douglas Schuler, Myriam Lewkowicz, Markus Rohde, and Ingrid Mulder, 305–7. New York, NY: ACM. https://doi.org/10.1145/3083671.3083712.

Bauwens, Michel, Nicolas Mendoza, and Franco, Iacomella. 2012. *Synthetic Overview of the Collaborative Economy.* Chiang Mai, Thailand: P2P Foundation.

Belk, Russell. 2007. 'Why Not Share Rather Than Own?' *The Annals of the American Academy of Political and Social Science* 611 (1): 126–40. https://doi.org/10.1177/0002716206298483.

Belk, Russell. 2014. 'Sharing Versus Pseudo-Sharing in Web 2.0.' *The Anthropologist* 18 (1): 7–23. https://doi.org/10.1080/09720073.2014.11891518.

Böcker, Lars, and Toon Meelen. 2017. 'Sharing for People, Planet or Profit? Analysing Motivations for Intended Sharing Economy Participation.' *Environmental Innovation and Societal Transitions* 23 (6): 28–39. https://doi.org/10.1016/j.eist.2016.09.004.

Botsman, Rachel, and Roo Rogers. 2010. *What's Mine Is Yours: The Rise of Collaborative Consumption.* New York, NY: Harper Business.

Bradley, Karin, and Daniel Pargman. 2017. 'The Sharing Economy as the Commons of the 21st Century.' *Cambridge Journal of Regions, Economy and Society* 10 (2): 231–47. https://doi.org/10.1093/cjres/rsx001.

Castells, Manuel, João Caraça, and Gustavo Cardoso. 2012. *Aftermath: The Cultures of the Economic Crisis.* Oxford: Oxford University Press.

Codagnone, Cristiano, Federico Biagi, and Fabienne Abadie. 2016. *The Passions and the Interests: Unpacking the 'Sharing Economy'.* Luxembourg: Publications Office of the European Union.

Eurobarometer. 2016. *The Use of Collaborative Platforms: Flash Eurobarometer 438.* Luxembourg: Publications Office of the European Union. Accessed May 20, 2021. https://europa.eu/eurobarometer/surveys/detail/2112.

Eurobarometer. 2018. *Collaborative Economy in the EU: Flash Eurobarometer 467.* Luxembourg: Publications Office of the European Union. Accessed May 20, 2021. https://europa.eu/eurobarometer/surveys/detail/2184.

Frenken, Koen, and Juliet Schor. 2019. 'Putting the Sharing Economy into Perspective.' In *A Research Agenda for Sustainable Consumption Governance*, edited by Oksana Mont, 121–35. Cheltenham, UK: Edward Elgar Publishing.

Frenken, Koen, Toon Meelen, Martijn Arets, and Peter Van de Glind. 2015. 'Smarter Regulation for the Sharing Economy.' *The Guardian* 20 (5). Accessed April 14, 2021. https://www.theguardian.com/science/political-science/2015/may/20/smarter-regulation-for-the-sharing-economy.

Gansky, Lisa. 2010. *The Mesh: Why the Future of Business Is Sharing.* New York, NY: Portfolio.

Germann Molz, Jennie. 2014. 'Toward a Network Hospitality.' *First Monday* 19 (3). https://doi.org/10.5210/fm.v19i3.4824.

Habibi, Mohammad Reza, Andrea Kim, and Michel Laroche. 2016. 'From Sharing to Exchange: An Extended Framework of Dual Modes of Collaborative Nonownership Consumption.' *Journal of the Association for Consumer Research* 1 (2): 277–294. https://doi.org/10.1086/684685.

Hamari, Juho, Mimmi Sjöklint, and Antti Ukkonen. 2016. 'The Sharing Economy: Why People Participate in Collaborative Consumption.' *Journal of the Association for Information Science and Technology* 67 (9): 2047–59. https://doi.org/10.1002/asi.23552.

Howard, Billee. 2015. *We-Commerce: How to Create, Collaborate, and Succeed in the Sharing Economy.* New York, NY: Perigee Books.

ING. 2015. *ING International Survey: Sharing Economy 2015: What's Mine Is Yours—for a Price: Rapid Growth Tipped for the Sharing Economy.* Amsterdam: ING.

Klimczuk, Andrzej, Vida Česnuitytė, and Gabriela Avram, eds. 2021. *The Collaborative Economy in Action: European Perspectives.* Limerick, Ireland: University of Limerick.

Lang, Bodo, Elsamari Botha, Jeandri Robertson, Joya A. Kemper, Rebecca Dolan, and Jan Kietzmann. 2020. 'How to Grow the Sharing Economy? Create Prosumers!.' *Australasian Marketing Journal (AMJ)* 28 (3): 58–66. https://doi.org/10.1016/j.ausmj.2020.06.012.

Lessig, Lawrence. 2008. *Remix: Making Art and Commerce Thrive in the Hybrid Economy.* New York, NY: Penguin Press.

Martos-Carrión, Esther, and Cristina Miguel. 2021. 'Sharing Economy: History, Definitions and Related Concepts.' In *The Sharing Economy: Perspectives, Opportunities and Challenges*, edited by Babak Taheri, Roya Rahimi, and Dimitrios Buhalis. Oxford: Goodfellow Publishers. Forthcoming.

Mosconi, Gaia, Agnieszka Lukasiewicz, and Gabriela Avram, eds. 2018. *Member Countries Report on the Collaborative Economy:* COST Action CA16121. Accessed May 20, 2021. http://sharingandcaring.eu/sites/default/files/files/CountriesReport2018.pdf.

Owyang, Jeremiah, Christine Tran, and Chris Silva. 2013. *The Collaborative Economy: Products, Services, and Market Relationships Have Changed as Sharing Startups Impact Business Models. To Avoid Disruption, Companies Must Adopt the Collaborative Economy Value Chain.* San Mateo, CA: Altimeter Group. Accessed May 20, 2020. http://www.collaboriamo.org/media/2014/04/collabecon-draft16-130531132802-phpapp02-2.pdf.

Schor, Juliet. 2014. 'Debating the Sharing Economy.' Accessed May 20, 2021. https://greattransition.org/publication/debating-the-sharing-economy.

Selloni, Daniela. 2017. *CoDesign for Public-Interest Services.* Cham: Springer International Publishing.

Stephany, Alex. 2015. *Business of Sharing.* Basingstoke, Hampshire: Palgrave Macmillan.

Timbro. 2018. *Timbro Sharing Economy Index*. Stockholm: Timbro.

# Part II

## Development of the Sharing Economy in Europe

# 2

# A Conceptualisation of the Sharing Economy: Towards Theoretical Meaningfulness

Cristina Miguel, Esther Martos-Carrión, and Mijalche Santa

## Introduction

Sharing economy platforms and applications are finding their way into almost every aspect of our lives. There are more than 10,000 companies that can be categorised within the sharing economy, and the 'sharing economy' sector's revenue potential is projected to increase to $335 billion in 2025 (Cho et al. 2019). In terms of services, there are over 20 service areas where the sharing economy has a presence (Ganapati and

C. Miguel (✉)
Applied IT, University of Gothenburg, Gothenburg, Sweden
e-mail: cristina.miguel@ait.gu.se

E. Martos-Carrión
eDreams, Barcelona, Spain

M. Santa
Faculty of Economics, Ss. Cyril and Methodius University, Skopje, North Macedonia
e-mail: mijalche.santa@eccf.ukim.edu.mk


V. Česnuitytė et al. (eds.), *The Sharing Economy in Europe*,
https://doi.org/10.1007/978-3-030-86897-0_2

Reddick 2018). This dramatic emergence of the sharing economy and its impact has attracted scholars from diverse fields to study the practices, implications, culture, meaning and individuals' engagement with the sharing economy. However, one of the rare points scholars agree on in their publication is how hard it is to define the sharing economy and to draw clear conceptual and empirical boundaries (Acquier et al. 2017). Sharing economy as a concept is vague, too broad, and fuzzy (Plewnia and Guenther 2018), and it became a buzzword (Arcidiacono et al. 2018). As a result, there is still a lack of a shared definition of the sharing economy (Botsman 2013; Dillahunt et al. 2017). Lack of conceptual clarity can limit the development of the field because ill-defined concepts can have a negative impact on the propositions and can misguide the efforts of the researcher and practitioners using the same (Wacker 2004). For example, the contrasting and contradictory framings of the sharing economy result in discourse that positions the sharing economy on two extremes as a pathway to sustainability or a nightmarish form of neoliberal capitalism (Martin 2016). As a result, there are calls for conceptual clarification of the sharing economy (Schlagwein et al. 2020).

This chapter takes up this challenge of conceptual clarification of the sharing economy. One possible approach to this is through semantic analysis of sharing economy definitions to identify the common characteristics and structure them in a new definition (Schlagwein et al. 2020). Another approach is to aim for the concept's theoretical meaningfulness. Theoretical meaningfulness of a concept 'refers to the nature and internal consistency of the language used to represent the concept. It addresses the formal adequacy of the logical and theoretical terms comprising one's theory' (Teas and Palan 1997, p. 52). This provides a broader grounding of the concept and enables better drawing of the empirical boundaries of the sharing economy concept. The first section introduces a historical overview of the concept of the sharing economy. The next section presents the theoretical meaningfulness framework methodology through which the literature analysis is structured. Later, the results are presented where the main principles of the sharing economy are identified, and a sharing economy definition based on the analysis is built. Finally, the chapter provides a summary in the Conclusions section.

## Interpretations of the Sharing Economy Over Time

By comparing early definitions and the ones proposed more recently, several differences stand out. Firstly, early understandings identified community building, social relationships, altruism, sustainable lifestyles, and non-monetary exchanges as the main drivers of sharing or collaborative economies (e.g., Felson and Spaeth 1978; Benkler 2004; Lessig 2008). The initial manifestations of the phenomenon were mainly driven by social concerns instead of profitability potential. In fact, it was intended to serve as a participative tool to promote personal relationships by means of shared resources, services, and knowledge. However, as time passed, this aim seems to have shifted: aspects related to sociability, personal experiences or enjoyable lifestyles appear progressively to be used by sharing economy platforms as marketing strategies rather than as part of their true aim (Slee 2015). According to contemporary authors (e.g., Howard 2015; Sundararajan 2016; Slee 2015), the sharing economy is nowadays understood as a global economic system that moves large amounts of capital every year. Indeed, the capitalisation of some sharing economy platforms has led to the redefinition of their own purposes.

Secondly, reputation systems, understood as digital tools that enable users to rate and evaluate other's services, were not considered a main component of the sharing economy until 2010 when Botsman and Rogers published their popular book *What is Mine is Yours*. Although prior to this event, reputation among unknown individuals already played an important role in the sharing economy, it is after the publication of this book when reputation systems begin to draw the attention of diverse authors. As such, Gansky (2010), Owyang et al. (2013), and Stephany (2015) began to explore reputation systems in which users build their own reputation, evaluate the behaviour of others, and report negative/positive experiences. The emergence and use of reputation systems are key features that stand out when comparing traditional digital markets with sharing economy platforms (Sundararajan 2016). Thus, on a broader scope, reliability and trust among strangers are also subject to change and transformation. Personal and direct relationships developed normally at a local scale (Felson and Spaeth 1978; Lessig 2008; Castells et al. 2012) are reshaped by the sharing economy into virtual systems where reputation is based on ratings, comments and feedback provided by multiple users worldwide (Howard 2015; Chase 2015).

Thirdly, it is important to note that some elements have not changed much from the earliest interpretations of the sharing economy to the more contemporary understandings. Fundamentally two elements remain untouched: on the one hand, the Internet is still considered the major pillar upon which the sharing economy rests and, on the other hand, the idea that the main aim of the sharing economy is the efficient access to underused goods and spaces. Drawing a temporal line, it is Benkler who, in 2004, emphasised the collaborative behaviour of large online communities based essentially on open and free sharing of information through decentralised networks. His studies on virtual collaborative systems were rapidly followed by other authors like Tapscott and Williams (2006), Lessig (2008), Bauwens et al. (2012), or Rifkin (2014). Therefore, and excluding the definition proposed by Felson and Spaeth in 1978, which in fact does not mention the Internet, practically all subsequent interpretations of the sharing economy, in one form or another, are linked to the existence of the Internet. The second and most important element applies to the idea that the goal of the sharing economy is efficient access to underused goods and spaces, finds mention in a great number of published definitions. Daily activities such as having lunch, driving to another city or doing laundry were already subject to analysis back in 1978 when Felson and Spaeth observed the benefits of performing these activities collaboratively instead of individually. They described a society where individuals, known or unknown, shared spaces, rides, or equipment among themselves in a way that would become more sustainable as well as enjoyable. This interpretation of the sharing economy has been likewise addressed in the last decade by multiple authors (e.g., Botsman and Rogers 2010; Mason 2015) when explaining the basis of the sharing economy. Therefore, the optimal consumption of underused physical object and spaces, as well as the shared access to knowledge and services, remains, since 1978 to this date, an almost unmodified and major principle of the sharing economy.

## Methodology

Conceptual clarification facilitates theoretical analysis and empirical testing (Teas and Palan 1997). Ill-defined concepts can have a negative impact on the propositions and can misguide the efforts of the researchers and practitioners using the same (Wacker 2004). Furthermore, it can create a situation for everybody to see whatever they want to see in the concept of sharing economy. The sharing economy concept is in the academic focus, and we start to see a proliferation of numerous concepts (collaborative consumption, peer-to-peer, etc.). Thus, it is important to provide an explication of the concept's theoretical meaningfulness. Theoretical meaningfulness of a concept refers to the nature and internal consistency of the language used to represent the concept (Teas and Palan 1997). Usually, the meaningfulness is evaluated after a certain period of time in which there is a proliferation of theoretical explications of the concept. As a result, there is a need to re-evaluate the field and provide a base for its further development. One could say that formalisation can inhibit critical theoretical development (Teas and Palan 1997). However, even the partial formalisation process of the concept and its theorisation can sharpen the discussion of the theory and create an absolutely necessary precondition for meaningful analysis (Hunt 1990). Thus, formalising the sharing economy concept and explicating the meaning of the terms can provide a base for the concept's development.

The determination of the meaning of a concept involves three realms: linguistic, conceptual, and physical realm (Bunge 1967; Teas and Palan 1997). The linguistic realm, through terms and definitions, designates a concept that can be referred to in the physical realm. Each concept has an intention, a list of properties possessed by the concept (Teas and Palan 1997). The extension, or denotation or domain of applicability, of the concept, is the set of all objects in the physical realm embodying the concept's intentional properties. Thus, the answer to 'What is meant by 'sharing economy'?' must be made by giving a definition, listing the properties of sharing economy and by listing typical examples of sharing economy. To identify the content that will be analysed through the prism of the theoretical meaningfulness framework, the authors performed an extensive literature review to identify the semantic transformation of the sharing economy concept and identify the core principles of the sharing economy. After that, a more focused literature analysis of 20 sources (books and journal articles) was performed. These sources are presented in Table 2.1.

Two authors coded the papers in order to identify the concept's intention, i.e., a list of properties possessed by the concept, and denotation, e.g., a set of all objects in the physical realm embodying the concept's intentional properties. These properties and objects were generalised and used as a base for the development of a definition of the sharing economy concept. This definition was evaluated based on the rules 'good' formal, conceptual definition (Wacker 2004). The seven rules provide a guideline that can be used to evaluate if the definition provides sufficient ground for structuring and measuring the concept, and based on that, make the concept distinct from other similar concepts.

**Rule 1**: Requires the formal, conceptual definition to follow the rule of exchangeability (Bunge 1967, p. 134). That is when the 'definiendum' (the term being defined, i.e., sharing economy) can be substituted with the 'definiens' (terms used to define a concept) in any sentence without changing the sentence's meaning (Wacker 2004).

**Rule 2**: Requires each concept to be uniquely defined. To avoid 'concept stretching,' the definition should include earmarks (core properties) that combined provide precise delimitation of the concept of seemingly similar concepts (i.e., existing general economy). For example, by including the term 'platform,' the definition clearly delimitates it from other places of exchange. This is additionally constrained by the term 'self-determined.'

**Rule 3**: Include only unambiguous and clear terms. To achieve this, the definition first does not include connector terms such as 'and' as well as 'or' that make the definition vague since they indicate two concepts (Wacker 2004). Instead, modifiers next to terms are used to promote the concept's clarity by differentiating it from other similar concepts, i.e., 'closed,' 'unique,' and 'scalable.'

**Rule 4**: The definition should have as few as possible terms. The proposed definition violates this criterion, and there is a need in the future to find options to shorten the definition.

**Table 2.1** List of sources included in the analysis

| No. | Author(s) | Source title |
|---|---|---|
| 1 | Bauwens et al. (2012) | *Synthetic Overview of the Collaborative Economy*. Chiang Mai: P2P Foundation |
| 2 | Benkler, Yochai (2004) | 'Sharing Nicely: On Shareable Goods and the Emergence of Sharing as a Modality of Economic Production.' *The Yale Law Journal* 114 (2): 273–358 |
| 3 | Belk, Russell (2014a) | 'You Are What You Can Access: Sharing and Collaborative Consumption Online.' *Journal of Business Research* 67 (8): 1595–1600 |
| 4 | Belk, Russell (2014b) | 'Sharing versus Pseudo-sharing in Web 2.0.' *The Anthropologist* 18 (1): 7–23 |
| 5 | Botsman et al. (2010) | *What is Mine is Yours: The Rise of Collaborative Consumption*. New York, NY: HarperCollins |
| 6 | Chase, Robin (2015) | *Peers Inc.: How People and Platforms are Inventing the Collaborative economy and reinventing capitalism*. London: Headline Book Publishing |
| 7 | Ert et al. (2016) | 'Trust and Reputation in the Sharing Economy: The Role of Personal Photos in Airbnb.' *Tourism Management* 55: 62–73 |
| 8 | Guttentag, Daniel (2015) | 'Airbnb: Disruptive Innovation and the Rise of an Informal Tourism Accommodation Sector.' *Current Issues in Tourism* 18 (12): 1192–1217 |
| 9 | Hamari et al. (2016) | 'The Sharing Economy: Why People Participate in Collaborative Consumption.' *Journal of the Association for Information Science and Technology* 67 (9): 2047–2059 |

(continued)

**Table 2.1** (continued)

| No. | Author(s) | Source title |
|---|---|---|
| 10 | Lamberton, Cait Poynor, and Randall L. Rose (2012) | 'When is Ours Better Than Mine? A Framework for Understanding and Altering Participation in Commercial Sharing Systems.' *Journal of Marketing* 76 (4): 109–125 |
| 11 | Lessig, Lawrence (2008) | *Remix. Making Art and Commerce Thrive in the Hybrid Economy*. New York: Penguin Press |
| 12 | Martin, Chris J. (2016) | 'The Sharing Economy: A Pathway to Sustainability or a Nightmarish Form of Neoliberal Capitalism?' *Ecological economics* 121: 149–159 |
| 13 | Mason, Paul (2015) | *Post-Capitalism: A Guide to our Future*. London: Allen Lane |
| 14 | Rifkin, Jeremy (2014) | *The Zero Marginal Cost Society: The Internet of Things, the Collaborative Commons and the Eclipse of Capitalism*. New York, NY: Palgrave Macmillan |
| 15 | Slee, Tom (2015) | *What is Yours is Mine: Against the Sharing Economy*. New York, NY: OR Books |
| 16 | Stephany, Alex (2015) | *The Business of Sharing: Making it in the New Sharing Economy*. Basingstoke, Hampshire: Palgrave Macmillan |
| 17 | Sundararajan, Arun (2016) | *The Sharing Economy: The End of Employment and the Rise of the Crowd-based Capitalism*. Cambridge: The MIT Press |
| 18 | Tapscott, Don, and Anthony D. Williams (2006) | *Wikinomics: How Mass Collaborations Changes Everything*. New York, NY: Portfolio |
| 19 | Wirtz et al. (2019) | 'Platforms in the Peer-to-peer Sharing Economy.' *Journal of Service Management* 30 (4): 452–483 |

(continued)

Table 2.1 (continued)

| No. | Author(s) | Source title |
|---|---|---|
| 20 | Zervas et al. (2017) | 'The Rise of the Sharing Economy: Estimating the Impact of Airbnb on the Hotel Industry.' *Journal of Marketing Research* 54 (5): 687–705 |

*Source* Own elaboration

**Rule 5**: Be consistent with the field. Ideally, the 'definiendum' (the term being defined) would completely signify what the defined term is (Wacker 2004). The term 'sharing economy' shows that it is about the economy, thus making a link with the field of general economic practices that the sharing economy influences. Furthermore, adding the modifier 'sharing' shows that it is an economy where the main practice is sharing.

**Rule 6**: Not make any term broader. The definition does not enlarge the meaning of economy, but it reduces the generalised concept of the economy to a narrower one. For example, by limiting it to the technological platform, the concept is limited only to one element of the total economy where value exchange can happen.

**Rule 7**: Not introduce new hypotheses, i.e., if a 'definition' is necessary to prove a statement, then it is not a definition (Bunge 1967, p. 130). The proposed definition does not introduce hypotheses by suggesting what should the output be of the sharing economy.

The starting point of a conceptualisation of the sharing economy research is to identify the peculiar core properties of the sharing economy. Bunge (1967) calls them earmarks. A set of earmarks makes up the core intention of a concept. The core intention is both necessary and sufficient for determining the domain of application of the concept (Bunge 1967). As a result, their identification will provide a guide for establishing an empirical boundary of the sharing economy concept or will at least ensure an unambiguous application of the concept. These properties in the conceptual and theoretical discussions are presented through terms and phrases in the linguistic realm. Thus, the next section presents the sharing economy properties identified in the broader literature and later a definition that we map on the analysed papers (Table 2.1).

## The Principles of the Sharing Economy Concept

This study can broadly state that the sharing economy is 'essentially' characterised by the following ten principles:

**Principle 1: Redistribution of assets. It promotes access over ownership**. The sharing economy aims to redistribute existing goods across the population in order to maximise their functionality (Howard 2015). Sharing economy platforms allow users to share (not necessarily for free) their possession with others, thus developing new patterns of consumption. Goods are owned by few but enjoyed by many; the sharing economy highlights the need to make use or dispose of the overproduced goods of large capitalist enterprises (Botsman and Rogers 2010; Rifkin 2014). Accordingly, a considerable number of everyday goods such as toys, digital devices, construction tools and sports equipment pass from user to user, thus reducing the need to buy the same product as a new brand. As Martin (2016, p. 150) observed, 'the sharing economy enables a shift away from a culture where consumers own assets (from cars to drills), toward a culture where consumers share access to assets.' Placing access over ownership considerably reduces costs, given that consumers pay solely for the needed time.

**Principle 2: The Internet and innovative technologies are the core of the sharing economy**. The emergence of the sharing economy has been made possible by the development of certain innovative digital devices combined with online networks (Tapscott and William 2006). Activities such as swap, exchange, rent or trade constitute a quite antique form of consumption. Nevertheless, when referring to the sharing economy, it is essential to frame the concept within a technological and digital environment (Sundararajan 2016). The evolution of the website and the subsequent advent of the smartphone have greatly contributed to creating new ways of commerce in which large communities are digitally connected (Benkler 2004). The majority of sharing economy initiatives are based on high-tech platforms which enable the combination of multiple features such as location by Global Positioning System (GPS), instant messaging, online payments, rating systems and the integration of social networks, among others. The technology aspect is present in all the analysed sources. It is clearly noted that the sharing economy is seen 'primarily through the lens of the information technology' (Hamari et al. 2016, p. 2048) and that it is through these technological platforms through which the sharing is facilitated. The rise of the Internet-enabled expansion of these systems of networks (Guttentag 2015). However, the presence of technology raises the issue of access. Access can be seen from a general perspective of internet access (Belk 2014a) but also from a perspective of platform access.

**Principle 3: The sharing economy is a market-based system.** It is important to remark that the sharing economy also relates to its own term 'economy,' in that it produces, distributes and consumers goods and services (Slee 2015). Sharing economy platforms mainly function as a digital marketplace where supply and demand are matched, either for economic compensation or for any other type of value exchange. The sharing economy is being applied to a considerable range of different niche markets, thus creating new opportunities for commerce. Purpose-driven networks, also referred to as 'pure sharing,' represent a minor part of the whole system in which there normally is not any monetary exchange (e.g., time banks). Zervas et al. (2017, p. 687) emphasise the intervention of monetary exchange within the sharing economy in their definition: 'The emergence of peer-to-peer platforms, collectively known as the 'sharing economy,' has enabled people to collaboratively make use of underutilised inventory through fee-based sharing.'

**Principle 4: The sharing economy is crowd-based.** The sharing economy is conceived as an enormous network of connectivity in which users can easily participate (Sundararajan 2016). This statement directly stems from the fact that sharing platforms are coded on the Internet. In other words, due to the widespread use of the Internet, local sharing initiatives such as second-hand markets or hitch-hiking have evolved into global initiatives. This was not possible before the Internet. On-demand services operating under the umbrella of the sharing economy depend on crowds; that is, the bigger the network is, the better. This type of platform requires immediacy, which means that services and goods must be exchanged at anytime and anywhere.

**Principle 5: The sharing economy is built on decentralised networks.** As opposed to hierarchical and pyramidal structures, sharing economy platforms are designed as decentralised and often distributed networks (Bauwens et al. 2012). A decentralised network is intended to spread decision-making power among its nodes in order to avoid superior control (Botsman and Rogers 2010). By doing so, the figure of the middleman loses importance; nonetheless, it is relevant to point out that in a certain way, platforms function as a sort of middleman. Even though sharing economy workers are allowed to decide their own schedule, price, settings, etc., the platform owners are ultimately the ones who decide the basic rules and obligations, being able to change them at any time. For this, it is important to clarify that just a minor part of the sharing economy is executed through purely distributed networks (Slee 2015).

**Principle 6: The sharing economy enables peer-to-peer (p2p) transactions while empowering individuals.** Sharing economy applications allow individuals to trade, exchange, share or swap from p2p while avoiding any external middleman except the platform itself (Wirtz et al. 2019). In terms of labour, p2p platforms empower individuals because: (1) there is no need for previous payments or investments, and users can easily raise capital by uploading content to the net; (2) in terms of bureaucracy, extensive legal forms are replaced by simple online sign-ups; and, (3) it allows users to capitalise on their own possessions, knowledge or time; for many, sharing economy platforms function as a secondary source of income. The sharing economy offers commercial opportunity, fosters micro-entrepreneurship and economic empowerment (Martin 2016). On these platforms, mechanisms that enable the p2p matching are available. The goal of the platform participants is to access and use the goods or services when they need them (Belk 2014a). This creates a need for real-time matching (Ert et al. 2016). This is where the technological platforms distinguish themselves from one another and try to enable this matching (Lamberton and Rose 2012; Hamari et al. 2016).

**Principle 7: The sharing economy is a socio-economic system that disrupts traditional economic systems.** The emergence of digital economies, in which the sharing economy is included, has disrupted common trade practices, traditional regulations, policy systems, city legislations, consumer behaviour and other socio-economic habits (Mason 2015). Theoretically, the sharing economy, compared to for-profit organisations, promote access over ownership, collaborative consumption over hyper-consumption, openness over privacy, cooperation over competition, self-organisation over hierarchy and control, peer-to-peer (p2p) over business-to-business (b2b), networked structures over top-down structures, prosumers over passive consumers and customisation over standardisation. As Martin (2016, p. 154) observed: 'Digital innovations with the potential to disrupt the consumption-production, finance and education regimes (amongst many others) are considered part of the sharing economy.' However, in practice, many sharing platforms are becoming increasingly corporate and profit-driven, contradicting their original guiding principles (Slee 2015). Regardless, it is remarkable to notice how different manners of consumption and production are being developed through digital environments, in apparent contradiction with capitalist principles. When referring to the system, the following terms are used: socio-economic system, economic-technological system, socio-digital experiment. According to Ert et al. (2016, p. 62), the sociability created via direct interactions that follow the online transaction 'comprises perhaps the most distinct difference between the early P2P markets and the new sharing economy markets.'

**Principle 8: Trust among strangers enhances social value. Trust is mostly created from reputation systems**. Although trust between peers fosters successful exchanges within sharing economy communities, a lack of trust greatly discourages individuals from sharing their own goods or spaces with others (Stephany 2015). The emergence of reputation systems, which fundamentally enable people to evaluate each other's services by means of comments and ratings, marked the transition from early digital marketplaces (e.g., Craigslist) to the current sharing economy (Ert et al. 2016; Sundararajan 2016). Sharing economy participants usually consider comments and ratings as trustworthy and reliable proof to base their final decision when accessing a service. In terms of trust-building, large communities will generate fairer systems than smaller ones. Statistically, an asset valued by many will be more reliable than the same one rated by a few.

**Principle 9: Prosumers play an important role in peer production**. The term prosumer must be understood with a digital framework. Authors (e.g., Benkler 2004; Tapscott and Williams 2006) use the term prosumer in reference to digital producers and consumers: users who actively create digital content while consuming other's information, as for instance is the case with open-source coders or wiki writers. Secondly, prosumers are also defined as active citizens who play reciprocal roles in sharing economy platforms, not only by allowing others to use their possessions but also by actively accessing and using others' assets. For example, 'couchsurfers' are intended to be guests and hosts at any time in order to be part of the community. As such, prosumers share physical goods.

**Principle 10: The sharing economy emphasises collective experiences, co-creation and sustainable lifestyles.** The sharing economy fosters cooperation and collaboration among community members enabling them to collectively consume goods and services. The sharing economy aims to create a collaborative atmosphere driven by trust, altruism, transparency, openness and common goods (Lessig 2008). The sharing economy is framed as 'a more sustainable form of consumption' (Martin 2016, p. 149). The values that the sharing economy stands for are one of the most debated aspects of the literature. According to Martin (2016, p. 154), the sharing economy is 'built around concern for people and the environment; and is driven by the values of liberty, democracy, social justice and environmental justice.' The integration of these factors into communities leads to both personal and collective positive feelings. On each individual platform, the participants accept, share and, to a certain point, co-create the rules and culture of the platform. The individuals (micro) level, through their agency, develops and influence the rules and culture of each particular platform. Thus, some platforms can be closer to neoliberal capitalism and others to sustainability, but it is the peers who are sharing this culture. As observed by Martin (2016, p. 149), despite a critique of hyper-consumption as a core element in the emergence of the sharing economy, 'it has been successfully reframed by regime actors as purely an economic opportunity.' Therefore, when sharing economy companies follow this pathway of corporate co-option, it is unlikely that they would drive a transition to sustainability.

After carefully deconstructing the concept of the sharing economy into specific principles, the following definition is proposed: 'The sharing economy is a closed socio-economic system facilitated by digital platforms which match peer-to-peer service demand and offer based on the rules and culture of the platform actors.' This definition, through its earmarks, enables the creation of frameworks using the core properties as dimensions through which different explications of the sharing economy can be evaluated and categorised. This will help scholars, researchers and policymakers to make structured and justified decisions on what can be included in the sharing economy and whatnot. The aim of this definition is to specify the meaning of terms and reduce the ambiguity and vagueness of the concept. The working definition supplies the peculiar properties of the sharing economy concept.

## Summary

The sharing economy is a ubiquitous feature of contemporary society. The sharing economy aims to redistribute existing goods (e.g., tools, cars) across the population in order to maximise their functionality (Howard 2015). It seeks fairer and more sustainable means of consumption of products and services through digital platforms (Hamari et al. 2016). As originally indicated by Felson and Spaeth (1978), when analysing collaborative consumption, current sharing platforms continue to attract new members by highlighting the meaningfulness of experiencing sharing practices with strangers. This chapter has explored the definitions of the concept of the sharing economy, also known as collaborative consumption (Botsman and Rogers 2010; Hamari et al. 2016) or collaborative economy (Owyang et al. 2013), among several other names. Purpose-driven networks also referred to as 'pure sharing,' where there is not any monetary exchange (e.g., timebanks), represent a minor part of the whole ecosystem. Thus, most of these new business models imply commodity exchange (Belk 2014b). The sharing economy, therefore, also addresses the economy term in that it produces and distributes goods and services (Slee 2015).

This chapter aimed to offer a conceptual clarification of the sharing economy concept. This is an endeavouring challenge due to the continuous and unrestrained global innovation that resulted in ever-growing applications, models, and domains where the sharing economy is developed or recognised. This is followed by a plethora of academic publications. To overcome this challenge, a simplified theoretical meaningfulness framework and two independent analyses were used. First, we conducted a general literature review to provide a historical overview of the evolution of the sharing economy concept and later a semantic development of the concept. The result is a definition for the sharing economy concept that is value-neutral and provides a hierarchical structuring to accommodate the diversity of the sharing economy phenomena. The definition provides lenses through which other scholars and policymakers can classify different types of economies and provide a conceptual mapping of the sharing economy instances.

## References

Acquier, Aurélien, Thibault Daudigeos, and Jonatan Pinkse. 2017. 'Promises and Paradoxes of the Sharing Economy: An Organising Framework.' *Technological Forecasting and Social Change* 125: 1–10. https://doi.org/10.1016/j.techfore.2017.07.006.

Arcidiacono, Davide, Alessandro Gandini, and Ivana Pais. 2018. 'Sharing What? The 'Sharing Economy' in the Sociological Debate.' *The Sociological Review* 66 (2): 275–288. https://doi.org/10.1177/0038026118758529.

Bauwens, Michel, Nicolas Mendoza, and Franco, Iacomella. 2012. *Synthetic Overview of the Collaborative Economy.* Chiang Mai: P2P Foundation.

Belk, Russell. 2014a. 'You Are What You Can Access: Sharing and Collaborative Consumption Online.' *Journal of Business Research* 67 (8): 1595–1600. https://doi.org/10.1016/j.jbusres.2013.10.001.

Belk, Russell. 2014b. 'Sharing Versus Pseudo-Sharing in Web 2.0.' *The Anthropologist* 18 (1): 7–23. https://doi.org/10.1080/09720073.2014.11891518.

Benkler, Yochai. 2004. 'Sharing Nicely: On Shareable Goods and the Emergence of Sharing as a Modality of Economic Production.' *The Yale Law Journal* 114 (2): 273–358.

Botsman, Rachel. 2013. 'The Sharing Economy Lacks a Shared Definition.' *Fast Company*, November 21. https://www.fastcompany.com/3022028/the-sharing-economy-lacks-a-shared-definition.

Botsman, Rachel, and Roo Rogers. 2010. *What is Mine is Yours: The Rise of Collaborative Consumption.* New York, NY: HarperCollins.

Bunge, Mario. 1967. *Scientific Research I: The Search for System* (1st ed.). Heidelberg: Springer-Verlag.

Castells, Manuel, João Caraça, and Gustavo Cardoso. 2012. *Aftermath: The Cultures of the Economic Crisis.* Oxford: Oxford University Press.

Chase, Robin. 2015. *Peers Inc.: How People and Platforms are Inventing the Collaborative Economy and Reinventing Capitalism.* London: Headline Book Publishing.

Cho, Sunyoung, Park ChongWoo, and Kim Junghwan. 2019. 'Leveraging Consumption Intention with Identity Information on Sharing Economy Platforms.' *Journal of Computer Information Systems* 59 (2): 178–187. https://doi.org/10.1080/08874417.2017.1326295.

Dillahunt, Tawanna R., Xinyi Wang, Earnest Wheeler, Hao Fei Cheng, Brent Hecht, and Haiyi Zhu. 2017. 'The Sharing Economy in Computing: A Systematic Literature Review.' *Proceedings of the ACM on Human-Computer Interaction* 1, art. 38: 1–26. https://doi.org/10.1145/3134673.

Ert, Eyal, Aliza Fleischer, and Nathan Magen. 2016. 'Trust and Reputation in the Sharing Economy: The Role of Personal Photos in Airbnb.' *Tourism Management* 55: 62–73. https://doi.org/10.1016/j.tourman.2016.01.013.

Felson, Marcu, and Joe L. Spaeth. 1978. 'Community Structure and Collaborative Consumption: A Routine Activity Approach.' *American Behavioral Scientist* 21 (4): 614–624.

Ganapati, Sukumar, and Christopher G. Reddick. 2018. 'Prospects and Challenges of Sharing Economy for the Public Sector.' *Government Information Quarterly* 35 (1): 77–87.

Gansky, Lisa. 2010. *The Mesh, Why the Future of Business is Sharing.* New York, NY: Portfolio.

Guttentag, Daniel. 2015. 'Airbnb: Disruptive Innovation and the Rise of an Informal Tourism Accommodation Sector.' *Current Issues in Tourism* 18 (12): 1192–1217. https://doi.org/10.1080/13683500.2013.827159.

Hamari, Juho, Mimmi Sjöklint, and Ukkonen, Antti. 2016. 'The Sharing Economy: Why People Participate in Collaborative Consumption.' *Journal of the Association for Information Science and Technology* 67 (9): 2047–2059. https://doi.org/10.1002/asi.23552.

Howard, Billee. 2015. *We-Commerce: How to Create, Collaborate, and Succeed in the Sharing Economy.* New York, NY: Perigee Books.

Hunt, Shelby D. 1990. *Modern Marketing Theory: Critical Issues in the Philosophy of Marketing Science*. Southampton: South-Western Pub.
Lamberton, Cait Poynor, and Randall L. Rose. 2012. 'When Is ours Better Than Mine? A Framework for Understanding and Altering Participation in Commercial Sharing Systems.' *Journal of Marketing* 76 (4): 109–125. https://doi.org/10.2139/ssrn.1939289.
Lessig, Lawrence. 2008. *Remix: Making Art and Commerce Thrive in the Hybrid Economy.* New York, NY: Penguin Press.
Martin, Chris J. 2016. 'The Sharing Economy: A Pathway to Sustainability or a Nightmarish Form of Neoliberal Capitalism?' *Ecological Economics* 121: 149–159. https://doi.org/10.1016/j.ecolecon.2015.11.027.
Mason, Paul. 2015. *Post-Capitalism: A Guide to our Future.* London: Allen Lane.
Owyang, Jeremiah, Christine Tran, and Chris Silva. 2013. *The Collaborative Economy: Products, Services, and Market Relationships Have Changed as Sharing Startups Impact Business Models. To Avoid Disruption, Companies Must Adopt the Collaborative Economy Value Chain.* San Mateo, CA: Altimeter Group. Accessed May 20, 2020. http://www.collaboriamo.org/media/2014/04/collabecon-draft16-130531132802-phpapp02-2.pdf.
Plewnia, Frederik, and Edeltraud Guenther. 2018. 'Mapping the Sharing Economy for Sustainability Research.' *Management Decision* 56 (3): 570–583. https://doi.org/10.1108/MD-11-2016-0766.
Rifkin, Jeremy. 2014. *The Zero Marginal Cost Society: The Internet of Things, the Collaborative Commons and the Eclipse of Capitalism.* New York, NY: Palgrave Macmillan.
Schlagwein, Daniel, Detlef Schoder, and Kai Spindeldreher. 2020. 'Consolidated, Systemic Conceptualization, and Definition of the 'Sharing Economy.' *Journal of the Association for Information Science and Technology* 71 (7): 817–838. https://doi.org/10.1002/asi.24300.
Slee, Tom. 2015. *What is Yours is Mine: Against the Sharing Economy.* New York, NY: OR Books.
Stephany, Alex. 2015. *The Business of Sharing: Making it in the New Sharing Economy.* Basingstoke, Hampshire: Palgrave Macmillan.
Sundararajan, Arun. 2016. *The Sharing Economy: The End of Employment and the Rise of the Crowd-based Capitalism.* Cambridge: The MIT Press.
Tapscott, Don, and Anthony D. Williams. 2006. *Wikinomics: How Mass Collaborations Changes Everything.* New York, NY: Portfolio.
Teas, R. Kenneth, and Key M. Palan. 1997. 'The Realms of Scientific Meaning Framework for Constructing Theoretically Meaningful Nominal Definitions

of Marketing Concepts.' *The Journal of Marketing* 61 (2): 52–67. https://doi.org/10.2307/1251830.

Wacker, John G. 2004. 'A Theory of Formal Conceptual Definitions: Developing Theory-Building Measurement Instruments.' *Journal of Operations Management* 22 (6): 629–650. https://doi.org/10.1016/j.jom.2004.08.002.

Wirtz, Jochen, Kevin Kam Fung So, Makarand Amrish Mody, Stephanie Q. Liu, and HaeEun Helen Chun. 2019. 'Platforms in the Peer-to-Peer Sharing Economy.' *Journal of Service Management* 30 (4): 452–483. https://doi.org/10.1108/JOSM-11-2018-0369.

Zervas, Georgios, Davide Proserpio, and John W. Byers. 2017. 'The Rise of the Sharing Economy: Estimating the Impact of Airbnb on the Hotel Industry.' *Journal of Marketing Research* 54 (5): 687–705. https://doi.org/10.1509/jmr.15.0204.

## Suggested Readings

Martos-Carrión, Esther, and Cristina Miguel. 2021. 'Sharing Economy: History, Definitions and Related Concepts.' In *The Sharing Economy: Perspectives, Opportunities and Challenges*, edited by Babak Taheri, Roya Rahimi, and Dimitrios Buhalis. Oxford: Goodfellow Publishers.

Marvin, Henry, Daan Schraven, Nancy Bocken, Koen Frenken, Marko Hekkert, and Julian Kirchherr. 2021. 'The Battle of the Buzzwords: A Comparative Review of the Circular Economy and the Sharing Economy Concepts.' *Environmental Innovation and Societal Transitions* 38: 1–21.

## Relevant Websites

Sharing Economy UK: https://www.sharingeconomyuk.com.
Sharing Economy Spain: https://www.sharingespana.es.
OuiShare: https://www.ouishare.net.

# 3

# The Context of Public Policy on the Sharing Economy

Błażej Koczetkow and Andrzej Klimczuk

## Introduction

It is much easier to talk about public policy—in general or in relation to some aspects of it—when it is viewed not as an abstract idea but as a phenomenon embedded in a given historical context. Therefore, it seems appropriate and necessary to present the (future) regulation of the sharing economy, not only as a set of possible practical solutions but also—in the spirit of the French school of Michel Aglietta (1979)—as an element characterising a given stage of capitalism. Looking at this issue from a broader perspective, not limited to specific solutions, also allows taking into account modern technologies as a factor that increasingly determines the shape of contemporary politics.

B. Koczetkow · A. Klimczuk (✉)
SGH Warsaw School of Economics, Warsaw, Poland
e-mail: aklimcz@sgh.waw.pl

B. Koczetkow
e-mail: bk85885@doktorant.sgh.waw.pl


V. Česnuitytė et al. (eds.), *The Sharing Economy in Europe*,
https://doi.org/10.1007/978-3-030-86897-0_3

This chapter begins with a theoretical introduction in which, in addition to shedding light on the phenomenon of regulation related to the dominant capitalist model at a given time, we also outline contemporary features of 'digital governance.' This governance transforms political practice through changes in the regulatory activity of the state and, as such, deserves attention. On this basis, we take up the issue of what and why can be the subject of normalisation within the sharing economy and how the modern states can deal with the problems and challenges emerging in this context. At this point, it is impossible to ignore the concept of the so-called 'Regulation 2.0' and the *Lex Informatica* phenomenon, in which we will consider the 'esteem-based regulation' promoted by the sharing economy platforms.

Let us also emphasise that a legal regulation can be conceptualised in two ways: once as a regulation in narrow meaning, that is establishing norms; another time as its opposite, that is, deregulation. Let us assume that a key aspect of 'regulatory capitalism' is the relationship between rulemaking and commodification, which is understood as the transformation of purely social relations into market relations, with a measurable value (e.g., the commodification of education, social security, forms of neighbour help; see Esping-Andersen 1990). Moreover, although regulation in the sense of standardisation may bring to mind primarily the activities of the entities of the nation-state, there is no reason not to see it either in conflict or in agreement with regulatory activities at the global, national, regional, or local level undertaken and conducted by other entities, such as federations of non-governmental organisations (NGOs) or business associations. The subsequent sections of the chapter discuss three categories of issues relevant to public policy on the sharing economy (Table 3.1).

**Table 3.1** Topics relevant in public policy on the sharing economy

| The potential of the concept of digital governance and new regulatory approaches | Positive and negative effects of the sharing economy | Selected regulatory instruments towards the sharing economy |
|---|---|---|
| Relations of the digital governance and regulations | Heterogeneous approaches in regulation of the sharing economy | Soft law |
| Open texture, relational regulation, and regulation 2.0 | The challenge of algorithmic regulation | Rules and standards |
| Self-regulation in the sharing economy | Directions of regulating the sharing economy | Individual normativity and esteem-based regulation |

*Source* Own elaboration

# The Potential of the Concept of Digital Governance and New Regulatory Approaches

## Relations of the Digital Governance and Regulations

The current considerations about possible regulatory solutions should be placed in the broader context of digital governance or digital co-management. It should be noted that governance—due to the suggested logic of intervention—is taking into account the network of actors going beyond the narrow understanding of 'government' (Oramus 2015). Within the concept of digital governance, public problems (e.g., changes in forms of employment and unemployment; commodification of cooperation and favours among the inhabitants of the municipality or local community; changes in ownership) are seen more through the prism of their consequences rather than their causes (the causal links that led to them). Nowadays, there is a widespread opinion that global dependencies and processes speak against ambitious intervention plans, conceived as a top-down attempt to reach the causes of problems or find solutions by means of socio-political engineering. By focusing on effects rather than cause-effect chains, the forms and practice of intervention policies are distinct from those that are at the root of the problem.

The presented approach is considered to be a type of depoliticisation activity (Chandler 2019). Meanwhile, discussions that have so far dominated the issue of causation could not ignore socio-political analyses and ways of making political choices. In such cases, decision-making inherent in sovereign power and political responsibility came to the fore. The critical issue of causality is connected with the assumption that power operates hierarchically (and is not networked, as it is proclaimed in the governance approach) and that the results of politics are the result of well-thought-out choices, games of power, and possibilities. While controlling cause-and-effect relationships is—as Giorgio Agamben (2014) writes—the essence of politics, controlling effects is its opposite. The philosophical dimension of such a vector shift should not escape our attention: it reveals an epochal change in the very idea of governance. If it is difficult to control the causes, it is safer and more beneficial to try to control the effects. 'Consequence management' can therefore be seen as breaking ties with the modernist or causal understanding of governance.

Additionally, the shift from causality to effects is reflected in a corresponding shift in the conceptualisation of governance as such. Digital governance—understood as an attempt to improve social responses to effects—shifts the focus from the formal (legal) and public political sphere to the ability of systems or entire societies to respond to changes in their environment (Chandler 2019). Exercising power over the effects means transformations in the redistribution of agency, understood precisely as the ability to react, and thus allows governments to avoid the problem of responsibility for problems and the need to make decisions, which are an element of political decision-making. Political interventions are now taking the form of digital governance, as governments perceive the effects of indeterminism and risk as inherent in the complex and interdependent contemporary world. This kind of attitude seems to break with the current understanding of problems in line with the modernist logic of solutionism and progress.

The example of studies on German administrative law shows how the modern regulatory approach is oriented towards behavioural regulation, and the law is considered as a means to achieve goals appropriate in a given context, set taking into account organisational and procedural issues (Burgi 2020). The shift towards the results that comes from certain regulatory choices is largely due to the fact that the modern welfare state—with its ambition of social engineering through law—has led to the application of the law to many areas of social life (e.g., education, health protection, labour market, municipal housing). However, despite this intense activity, the law proved incapable of ensuring the implementation of these goals. The discourse around law-making, changes in the perception of the role of the state and the ineffectiveness of traditional legal tools have called into question the usefulness of the traditional approach to the current challenges of public administration and administrative law. However, whatever we are saying about the mechanics of law-making as they are prevalent at a given moment, one should bear in mind that the question of whether consumer-friendly laws really work or just deepen the incompetence of consumers is rarely asked. There is no law that could replace common sense and basic financial knowledge. Nevertheless, one possible effect of introducing consumer-friendly laws is that the consumer gains more consciousness of minimum standards that should be expected from financial providers. Another effect can be the implementation of minimum levels of protection (Kawiński 2009).

Let us add after Antoine Garapon and Jean Lassègue (2018) that in the case of digitalisation, which is central in the context of sharing economy platforms, the core is a radical project aimed at a new world order, grounded in new ways of empowering, manufacturing and authentication that builds trust. The economy and digital technology are presented as means by which social life could do without a political foundation. In this way, a new being arises *homo numericus*, the variation of which is *homo œconomicus*. While in the classical model, it is assumed that the public authority communicates with the society by means of obligations (i.e., the law), the new type of social solidarity, shaped with the progress of modern technologies, allows the authority to express itself in digital interactions. Therefore, it cannot break away from them because it is based on the commodification of personal data ('surveillance capitalism;' see Zuboff 2019). The control of individuals is organised similarly: no longer from the outside, but from the inside; no longer vertically, but horizontally; not by orders, but by interactions; not in a narrower context, but on the web; and not through forms, but performatively—despite the risk that the mediation of forms is an indispensable condition of freedom.

## Open Texture, Relational Regulation, and Regulation 2.0

Bronwen Morgan (2015) writes that there is a shift from hierarchy to network; from a regulatory agency to regulatory space; and from sovereignty to remote governance. All these features characterise new public governance, digital co-management, and digital governance. According to the post-structural position, the essence of this transformation is not so much the reduction of the regulatory power as its dispersion. Therefore, it refers with a distance to the claims about the prospects for individual emancipation. He also questions the thesis that regulatory solutions in the spirit of 'open texture' should relieve tensions between the market and the state. This is due, in part, to the idea that power should be more productive than punitive, and the emphasis should shift from formal state power to how indirect regulation of social activity fosters the emergence of self-disciplined entities.

Moreover, referring to the findings of Ruthanne Huising and Susan S. Silbey (2011), Morgan (2015) also points to 'relational regulation,' a characteristic of dynamic interdependence in relationships between 'sociological citizens.' This peculiarity, or sociological character, means in a regulatory context that individuals who are characterised by it go beyond their customary assigned tasks, formal roles, and professional group duties. What they undertake (either in return or in addition) is participation in alliances aimed at achieving regulatory goals. Entities become sociological actors because they develop an awareness of regulatory categories and the possibility of applying them in multiple social and political circumstances.

Relational regulation in terms of Huising and Silbey (2011) undermines the claim that it is necessary to eliminate the difference between 'the law on paper' and 'the law in action.' Rather, the focus is on the problem of how and what means a practically observed departure from the current model that can not only be approved as a daily practice but also acquire the attribute of legality—on the sole principle of persistence and prevalence of a given phenomenon—practice.

Moreover, another innovative approach to the contemporary understanding of regulation was presented by Abbey Stemler (2017). This scholar assumes that due to profound changes in technology, traditional regulation methods ('Regulation 1.0') are not able to satisfy the public interest. The 'Regulation 2.0' comes in handy, the essence of which includes three basic assumptions: (1) reliance on results (and not performance) standards; (2) privileging private (e.g., non-state) actors in setting standards; and (3) giving priority to audited self-regulation. Regulation 2.0 is complemented by public policy instruments encapsulated in the *Lex Informatica* formula, i.e., technical solutions (architecture of computer software) which define the scope of their users' activities.

## Self-Regulation in the Sharing Economy

Self-regulation brings to mind the category of corporate social responsibility (CSR), although—as Renginee G. Pillay (2014) shows—its contemporary understanding is radically different from that which, several decades ago, equated the obligations of enterprises towards society (stakeholders) with those that they had with their shareholders. We pay attention to CSR here because its essential features include, among others, focus and reliance on corporate self-regulation and voluntary action as mechanisms organising specific areas of social life. The discussed concept focuses on the bottom-up norm-creating activity of private actors (e.g., enterprises), positioning itself in opposition to top-down legislation, i.e., legislation originating from the state and sanctioned by it. An expression of such activity is, for example, adopting 'binding corporate rules' as part of corporate governance. Thus, CSR supports the postulate that the state should play the smallest possible role in the economy. The arguments behind this position emphasise that unjustified state interventions in the economy may disrupt the beneficial processes of increasing efficiency and maximising profits.

However, in the context of regulatory actions, it is worth noting that in recent years, the concept of CSR has been criticised, which has not bypassed the mechanisms of voluntary self-regulation used by corporations, expressed in individual regulatory actions. The effectiveness of corporate responsibility in which accountability and transparency are to be self-regulated rather than subject to state regulation has been denied. As Peter Newell (2002) writes, the reason for the critical position is the existence of two limitations of business responsibility: (1) which concerns its scope (object), and (2) which relates to the practice of sanctioning infringements.

Those who raise concerns about corporate responsibility fall into two groups. The first, less radical, advocates state sanctioning of 'private regulations' and non-regulatory instruments. This would reduce the risk that non-state solutions do not go beyond the declarations. The second group, going further, takes the position that under the guise of CSR based on voluntary actions and self-regulation, enterprises play a game of appearances. Its aim is, on the one hand, to convince that corporations are interested in moderating external costs (e.g., environmental pollution, destroying local cultures, 'digital disruption' of traditional sectors), and—on the other hand—to prevent proper, i.e., state-derived regulation. According to critics, even if social activity—including the activity of strong NGOs—can make a significant contribution to mitigating irregularities related to economic activity, it will never replace state regulation.

## Positive and Negative Effects of the Sharing Economy as a Regulatory Challenge

### Heterogeneous Approaches in Regulation of the Sharing Economy

According to Kathleen Thelen (2018), the literature on the political economy of advanced capitalism basically formulates two views on the causes of heterogeneous regulation of new phenomena. The first view, with an evident liberal character, explains this heterogeneity in such a way that the advent of new business models entails deregulation because the rapid pace of technological development allows some companies, such as Uber, to exploit loopholes in existing legal systems. These types of companies can use grey zones to establish robust operational structures, supported by enthusiastic consumers, and thus—through the accomplished fact method—to 'regulate' the area they have annexed before the state actors react (see Dumančić and Čeh Časni 2021). As a consequence of such action, pressure is put on the legislators to approve established practices in advance.

On the other hand, the second view sees the reasons for the various regulatory policies and refers to the existence of capitalist variations, showing the differences between the liberal market economies (e.g., United States) and coordinated market economies (concentrated in countries of continental Europe, e.g., France) (Hall and Soskice 2001). Briefly saying the liberal market economies include features such as competitive market arrangements and inter-firm relations; equilibrium achieved through the demand/supply and hierarchy; direct product competition; complete and formal contracting; freer movement of inputs; full-time employment in case of general skill and short-term employment in specific skills; wage bargain at the firm level; focus on formal education from high schools and colleges; low rate of unionisation; unequal income distribution; radical innovation; comparative advantages in high-tech and service and policies aimed at deregulation, antitrust and tax breaks. On the other hand, the coordinated market economies are characterised by the non-market relations; equilibrium achieved through the strategic interaction between firms and other actors; collaborative inter-firm ties; differentiated and niche production; incomplete legal system and informal contracting, monitoring and sanctioning institutions; shorter hours of employment in case of specific skills and long term for immobile jobs; wage bargain at the industry level; apprenticeship imparting industry-specific skills; high rate of unionisation; equal income distribution; incremental innovation; comparative advantage in manufacturing and policies focused on encouraging collaboration of firms. However, the perspective of varieties of capitalism fails to explain the lack of a homogeneous approach to regulation in case of the differences within the coordinated model. The research conducted by Thelen (2018) led her to conclude that the directions that individual countries such as Germany and Sweden take in the approach to the sharing economy (e.g., regarding Uber) are determined by local conditions. Of particular importance here are the balance of power and the ability to mobilise the opponents of the triumphal march of the sharing economy in given countries (e.g., traditional taxi drivers and hotel industry workers).

Using the generalisable example of the United States (with which the emergence of the sharing economy itself should be associated), let us note that the difficulty in optimally regulating the sharing economy is determined primarily by an incomplete understanding of its essence on the side of regulators and its participants (Dyal-Chand 2015). These leads, among others, to attempts to force new institutions into the old legal frameworks, which seems doomed to failure. The aforementioned confusion as to the nature of the sharing economy is problematic primarily because it shows a failure to recognise the central issue here—that the 'platform capitalism' (Srnicek 2016) has emerged as a new form of capitalism with different mechanisms for the production, distribution and redistribution of goods and services that go beyond the digital realm. As a consequence, not everything that was in line with the current model of this system is compatible with this new quality.

The sharing economy is usually associated with the activities of digital platforms, including the most popular such as Uber or Airbnb. As Vanessa Katz (2015) writes, in most cases, the activities of these platforms do not introduce new risks. After all, the same events can take place both in traditional hotels and in apartments rented via the Internet; the same events can take place in traditional taxis as in cars running under the Uber brand. At first glance, this seems to support the statement that service providers should be subject to the same obligations as traditional companies. However, in the sharing economy, the balance of power is different: service providers who use platform intermediation do not have any 'special relationship' with their service users that would justify imposing any specific obligations on them. The thesis that lawmakers hold platforms indirectly liable for the consequences of irregularities that occurred (only) in connection with their activities (e.g., relations under labour law, insurance law, or property law) also seems not obvious.

As far as service providers are concerned, the sharing economy obsoletes a number of assumptions that so far justified specific obligations on the part of service providers. These concerns, in particular, the weaker position of consumers and assigning service providers the role of 'least-cost avoiders,' which traditionally, due to the endangered interests of consumers, justified burdensome regulations. In addition, service providers using platforms tend to be small-scale and self-employed, which distinguishes them from organised business activities. Finally, many of the services they provide are standardised by platforms, which calls into question the thesis about a stronger market position of service providers, allowing for harmful shaping of contract terms. Taken together, this puts into question the need to regulate what they do, just as they do with companies.

On the other hand, in the case of platforms, it should first of all be noted that in many cases, they are either really the least-cost avoider (while *Lex Informatica* may serve to prevent unfavourable phenomena), or simply the easiest 'target' of legislators. However, most often, they function (or claim to function) as intermediaries whose role is exhausted in associating the parties to a given transaction. Therefore, their possible liability would, in principle, be indirect.

## The Challenge of Algorithmic Regulation

According to Tom Slee (2017), the sharing economy is at the forefront of 'algorithmic regulation,' with computer algorithms taking the place of consumer protection laws. Proponents of such a solution believe that in a world where each service provider is assessed, the existence of legally regulated control and remedial mechanisms is losing importance because consumers themselves maintain order in the market. However, this scholar also notes that this position ignores the fact that most traditional regulations concern matters that the consumer does not see (e.g., fire protection, the way in which meals are stored and prepared, or the technical condition of cars). On the other hand, a reputation that can be built or lost based on consumer judgements matters in the context of the popular Silicon Valley's view that service providers on digital platforms are micro-entrepreneurs. As such, they are a variety of companies, so their reputation is a kind of brand.

Many governments have raised concerns about the sharing economy in various areas, not least with regard to consumer protection. After Thelen (2018), we may notice that there are also other questionable issues: competition and consumer protection, employment conditions, relations with social policy, and taxation of sharing economy entities. On the other hand, despite the reservations signalled, states see the sharing economy as a way to increase budget revenues and enable people to obtain additional benefits, including earnings. An expression of a more sympathetic attitude to the sharing economy will be, for example, the work that the French Senate has undertaken on the draft solutions in the field of tax law, aimed at introducing a 'simple, uniform and fair' order in the sphere of the sharing economy (SFR 2017).

## Directions of Regulating the Sharing Economy

Regarding the most general approaches to regulating the sharing economy, Cristiano Codagnone et al. (2016) indicate four directions: (1) repression against illegally operating service providers; (2) regulation; (3) deregulation; and (4) tacit acceptance (tolerance) of new practices. Nevertheless, for example, Gabriel Doménech-Pascual (2016) considers a range of other possibilities. He begins with a variant, the sense of which is expressed in the assessment of how well the current standards work in the case of new phenomena. It emphasises the importance of collecting information, without which it is impossible to take deliberate action. Subsequently, this scholar analysed the idea of introducing new regulations, individual ones that were designed specifically to manage issues related to the sharing economy. Another idea presented by Doménech-Pascual is a temporary regulation, somewhat on a trial basis and also allowing the collection of new information. Later this expert also considers the concept of the coexistence of various regulatory regimes, that is, 'old' and 'new', so that—on the one hand—those who are threatened by the sharing economy can remain subject to the current regulation. On the other hand, there are prospects of introducing a new regulation better suited to changed circumstances. Thanks to this, there is also a kind of competition between the 'old' and 'new,' so the interested parties, on the basis of the collected information, can choose the best solutions. Finally, there are proposals for experimental legislation and the payment of compensation to those whose financial situation has suffered as a result of the expansion of the sharing economy.

Some authors, such as Diego Zuluaga (2016), questions whether the sharing economy—as such—could constitute a separate category of European regulation. Companies operating in accordance with the business models of this economic system operate in many sectors, competing both with traditional service providers and other companies. According to this scholar, there is no apparent justification for companies (platforms) to be subject to any separate regulations. In any event, new developments should not restrict the opportunities that the sharing economy presents to consumers and service providers. Especially given the fact that this economy already has an established place in many European Union (EU) countries, and it would be undesirable for EU legislation to slow down its development. Rather, regulation should further strengthen the advantages of the sharing economy rather than reduce them (e.g., flexibility, cost containment, employing those who would otherwise be unemployed). Burdensome employment regulations may contribute to reducing the number of employees and adversely affect the position of consumers. Instead, the sharing economy shows the need to liberalise existing norms. Thanks to it, companies existing on the market even before this economy began to feel competitive pressure, and regulations in the field of price regulation or consumer protection became redundant.

In the case of EU Member States, the choice between the generally outlined directions is free because—as indicated in the literature on the subject—due to the subsidiarity principle in force in the EU, solutions adopted at the local level should be the norm, and EU regulations should apply only when regulation at the regional or national level cannot meet its goals (Frenken et al. 2020). Meanwhile, many issues that may be considered requiring regulation in the sphere of the sharing economy are often resolved at the local level (e.g., the rules of short-term rental apartments or transport). Under such conditions, tension may arise between the expectations formulated at the EU level regarding the sharing economy and the sector policies of a given country or region. The European Commission (EC) states in its communication that in order for Europe to fully reap the benefits of the sharing economy and stimulate the growth of European start-up platforms, there must not be 28 (before the United Kingdom's withdrawal from the EU—author's note) sets of rules related to online platforms. Divergent national or even local regulations in this regard create uncertainty for economic operators, limit the availability of digital services and cause confusion for consumers and enterprises (EC 2016). Harmonisation of regulations at the EU level, such as the adoption of the Directive on Security of Network and Information Systems (the NIS Directive) in 2016 and the General Data Protection Regulation (GDPR) in 2018, is essential to facilitate the rapid growth and intensification of innovative platforms. Finally, according to the EC, principles-based self-regulatory or co-regulatory measures, including industry tools for ensuring the application of legal requirements and appropriate monitoring mechanisms, can play a role. Underpinned by appropriate monitoring mechanisms, they can strike the right balance between predictability, flexibility, efficiency, and the need to develop future-proof solutions.

## Selected Regulatory Instruments Towards the Sharing Economy

### Soft Law

The division into 'soft law' and 'hard law' has attracted the interest of researchers since the 1990s. Soft law is a set of quasi-legal instruments that demonstrate the possibility of achieving regulatory policy goals—both on a national and transnational scale—with the help of soft and even informal solutions and incentives that can be effective as when the 'hard' ones that are sanctioned by law used. Francis Snyder (1993) defines soft law as rules of solutions that, although generally not legally binding, have practical effects. As Anna Di Robilant (2006) writes, 'softness' is a defining feature of postmodern epistemology. The softness formula includes—on the one hand—regulatory instruments, and on the other—governance mechanisms, which in both cases, despite being referred to as a kind of normative obligation, are not based on binding provisions or the regime of formalised sanctions. The concept of soft law reflects two fundamental trends in the process of globalisation of law: the multiplication of norms and the privatisation of law. On the negative side, soft law is understood as an expression of criticism against the vertical, hierarchical, and state-oriented model of law-making. A negative definition is easier to formulate, as the term soft law from the positive side turns out to be difficult due to the multiplicity and complexity of soft law systems.

Study of Kenneth W. Abbott et al. (2000) characterised the legal norm as a composition of three elements: 'duty,' 'precision,' and 'delegation.' By 'duty' they mean an order to behave in a certain way or to refrain from acting in a certain way. By 'precision' they understand—not so much the command as its content and essence. On the other hand, by 'delegation'—authorising certain entities to lay down the content of legal norms, apply them, and settle disputes arising from them. Therefore, it is assumed that if even one of these components is missing, a given norm may still be considered legal, but it cannot be classified as hard law—it is connected with the assumption that soft law does not include all elements of hard law.

With reference to Fabien Terpan (2015), let us modify the above assumptions only to such an extent that precision will cease to be a necessary component, and instead of delegation, we will talk about 'execution.' On the one hand, to speak of an obligation, two elements are indispensable: the source and the content. The softness of duty results from *soft instrumentum* or *soft negotium*, but both may be included alternatively or cumulatively. On the other hand, duty is hard when both its source and content are hard. However, the dividing line between hard law and soft law is also determined by the way in which a given obligation is executed. The following possibilities can be distinguished here: hard execution, soft execution and no execution. The first of these options essentially covers those cases where the performance of duties is subject to judicial review (e.g., financial penalty for illegal competitive practices of taxi companies, prohibition of activity for short-term rentals at the local level). On the other hand, soft enforcement applies to situations in which punishing or limiting mechanisms are not applied (e.g., publication of local guidelines or education measures for capacity building). Where no execution is foreseen, in principle, there is no law, even understood as soft law. The two moments highlighted above: source and sanction—allow soft law to be defined as an autonomous normative category. Regulations are considered to be soft law when at least one of the above elements (source and sanction) is not hard.

## Rules and Standards

Let us note that regardless of what model of regulation is used to regulate a given social phenomenon, rules can be divided into 'rules' and 'standards.' The rules are precise and formulated *ex-ante*, and their role is to indicate to the addressees whether a given behaviour will be legal or not. When it comes to rules, it is important that they are recorded as detailed as possible; otherwise, their addressees will not know how to proceed with certainty. On the other hand, the standards at the time of their establishment remain largely general (e.g., 'due diligence'). These general formulas are filled with content only when the addressee of the standard has already behaved in some way—then it is for the authority applying the law to determine whether the behaviour complied with the standard or not.

When it comes to standards, the following are distinguished: purposeful standards, result-oriented standards, and specification-oriented standards (Surdej 2014). The first type of standards set out only goals that the regulated entities should meet but do not indicate the ways in which it should be done. The result and specification standards define the conditions that must be met by a given product, service, or enterprise. However, the result-oriented standards do not specify how these conditions are to be met, and the specification-oriented standards do so in detail.

It is sometimes said that the application of standards in regulation promotes innovation and leads to increased rationality and consistency within individual industries, types of services and organisations (Blind 2016). Setting standards gives rise to disputes between numerous actors in complicated power systems, including international corporations, organised interest groups or state regulators (e.g., in the electronic communications sector, radio and television sector, energy sector, and financial markets). Regardless of the results of these conflicts, it can generally be said that the existence of standards is often attributed to granting significant power to entities located between the policy area and the strictly economic sphere, which is an alternative solution to traditional state regulation (Graz 2019).

In the literature that deals with the choice between principles and standards, it is usually assumed that standards perform better in those cases where the normalised behaviour is less frequent than more frequent, and at the same time is heterogeneous (not all cases are homogeneous) (Korobkin 2000). Since these cases are rather rare, the costs of designing detailed standards are omitted. Principles reduce the cost of making decisions in the specific cases to which they apply, and these cases are generally frequent and homogeneous. The economy of scale is at work here: it is enough to adopt the rule once, and there is no need to check every time whether the behaviour was within the standard. So far, we may risk the hypothesis that there are no clear examples of already advanced and bottom-up standardisation initiatives in the sharing economy.

## Individual Normativity and Esteem-Based Regulation

In the context of regulating the sharing economy, there is also the issue of the so-called 'individual normativity,' understood as one of the ways of regulating the considered phenomenon. Admittedly, regulation is associated with the activity of an external entity towards persons whose behaviour is subject to regulation. As Vincent Gautrais (2018) notes, in today's increasingly complex society, it is difficult to lay down general abstract standards with universal application, using general clauses, expressed, for example, in the slogans such as 'appropriate' or 'reasonable.' Therefore, it is necessary to consider the procedural law, the meaning of which is expressed in focusing on the bottom-up evaluation of the activities of regulated actors. The author also points to the possibility of a specific regulation through 'documentation,' which basically means creating one's own rules—those based on formal law, those based on less formal standards generally accepted by standardisation institutions or customarily followed in a given branch of the economy or community. In addition, as part of the process-oriented approach, there may also be control (auditing) instruments, the essence of which includes—depending on the model chosen: (1) actions essentially aimed at detecting irregularities or (2) enabling an overview of the entire institution or phenomenon under consideration.

The issue of regulation related to the concern for 'respect' and 'esteem' deserves a special mention in the context of assessing the participants of digital platforms. Richard H. McAdams (1997) writes that in the 1980s, rational choice theorists drew attention to the fact that members of some social groups living in Asia (with a homogeneous ethnic structure) as a rule fulfilled their contracts, despite the lack of a particular enforcement apparatus. Under these conditions, this tendency to keep one's word was explained thanks to the social ties that gave members of these groups the possibility of informally punishing violations. Using considerations about the individual costs of execution that discourage individuals from engaging in sanctioning norms, Richard H. McAdams advances the importance of respect as the soil from which norms grow. Thus, people have the opportunity to punish violators at no cost, and the punishment is to refuse to show respect to someone who wants to enjoy it. According to the cited scholar, it is the desire for respect—when it manifests itself under appropriate conditions—that creates the norm.

Therefore, let us discuss the conditions for the formation of a norm. There must be an agreement among a certain group of people as to how, right, or wrong, a given behaviour is assessed. Then there is a risk of detecting abnormal behaviour. Finally, both the agreement itself and the risk of breaches being detected must be widely known in a given environment. Where respect is desired, and all the above-mentioned conditions have been met, the violator must take into account the cost of violating the norm, and the standard itself arises when, for a sufficient number of people in a given population, the (image) cost of such violation exceeds the cost of complying with the norm. According to Richard H. McAdams (1997), what limits the scale of normalisation is the expected high cost of their enforcement. However, where anyone can get either reward someone for following the rules or punish them for breaking them, there is no incentive to break the rules. Nevertheless, it cannot be assumed that respecting or denying respect is norm-setting in itself. Whether this will happen depends, among others, on the importance attached to the estimate, the power of understanding between the interested parties, and whether the knowledge of these matters has been sufficiently disseminated, and the cost of compliance with the standards itself.

## Summary

It will not be an exaggeration to suppose that as the sharing economy develops, the law will undergo fundamental changes. It is not just that radical technological progress leaves law far behind socio-economic challenges. Furthermore, it seems equally important that the development of the sharing economy heralds a change in the perspective from which not only the law itself is perceived but also the state as the organiser of social life. It ceases to be invariably linked to the hierarchy associated with the traditional law-making activity of the state. In more and more digital times, hierarchical structures are beginning to give way to self-organising networks, and in their case, the impact of law-making is not obvious.

Therefore, it seems desirable that, instead of trying to force the sharing economy into the framework of traditional law (which—apart from the purposefulness and effectiveness of such activities—is possible), we should consider keeping pace with the rather irreversible changes. As a result, however, there is a fear of moving from one extreme to the other—from a conservative approach in which it is appropriate to seek to harness novelty with well-known tools or to take no action, to a revolutionary zeal for change in which it is easy to overlook the threats to citizens states.

The search for intermediate solutions—perhaps imperfect but amenable to revision—should protect those responsible for specific public policies from the risk of facing an accomplished fact. This task will be all the more difficult as the sharing economy is not homogeneous, and the perception of digital platforms through the prism of commonly known (e.g., Airbnb and Uber)—although understandable—obscures the picture and threatens the selection of inappropriate resources to the challenges.

It is worth pointing to a number of further directions of research. First of all, it is crucial to analyse the possibility of using various instruments regulating entities and practices of the sharing economy in individual sectors. It is evident that solutions specific to some areas may not be applicable to others (e.g., regulations on sharing in the area of hospitality and mobility and the exchange of goods and services in neighbourhood groups). Secondly, it makes sense to build a set of good practices to regulate the sharing economy at various levels (local, regional and national). Thirdly, it is legitimate to try to interpret the regulation of the sharing economy through the prism of assumptions of various theories of public policy (e.g., group theories, class analysis, and analysis of transaction costs).

## References

Abbott, Kenneth W., Robert O. Keohane, Andrew Moravcsik, Anne-Marie Slaughter, and Duncan Snidal. 2000. 'The Concept of Legalization.' *International Organization* 54 (3): 401–419. https://doi.org/10.1162/002081800551271.

Agamben, Giorgio. 2014. 'For a Theory of Destituent Power.' *Chronos.* Accessed September 20, 2020. http://www.chronosmag.eu/index.php/g-agamben-for-a-theory-of-destituent-power.html.

Aglietta, Michel. 1979. *A Theory of Capitalist Regulation: The US Experience.* London: NLB.

Blind, Knut. 2016. 'The Impact of Standardisation and Standards on Innovation.' In *Handbook of Innovation Policy Impact*, edited by Jakob Edler, Paul Cunningham, Abdullah Gök, and Philip Shapira, 423–449. Cheltenham, UK, Northampton, MA: Edward Elgar Publishing. https://doi.org/10.4337/9781784711856.00021.

Burgi, Martin. 2020. 'Public Administration and Law.' In *European Perspectives for Public Administration: The Way Forward*, edited by Geert Bouckaert and Werner Jann, 147–161. Leuven: Leuven University Press. https://doi.org/10.2307/j.ctvv417th.12.

Chandler, David. 2019. 'Digital Governance in the Anthropocene: The Rise of the Correlational Machine.' In *Digital Objects, Digital Subjects: Interdisciplinary Perspectives on Capitalism, Labour and Politics in the Age of Big Data*, edited by David Chandler and Christian Fuchs, 23–42. London, UK: University of Westminster Press. https://doi.org/10.25969/mediarep/11926.

Codagnone, Cristiano, Federico Biagi, and Fabienne Abadie. 2016. *The Passions and the Interests: Unpacking the 'Sharing Economy.'* Luxembourg: Publications Office of the European Union.

Di Robilant, Anna. 2006. 'Genealogies of Soft Law.' *The American Journal of Comparative Law* 54 (3): 499–554. https://doi.org/10.1093/ajcl/54.3.499.

Doménech-Pascual, Gabriel. 2016. 'Sharing Economy and Regulatory Strategies Towards Legal Change.' *European Journal of Risk Regulation* 7 (4): 717–727. https://doi.org/10.1017/S1867299X0001014X.

Dumančić, Kosjenka, and Anita Čeh Časni. 2021. 'The State of the Sharing Economy in Croatia: Legal Framework and Impact on Various Economic Sectors.' In *The Collaborative Economy in Action: European Perspectives*, edited by Andrzej Klimczuk, Vida Česnuitytė, and Gabriela Avram, 90–99. Limerick, Ireland: University of Limerick.

Dyal-Chand, Rashmi. 2015. 'Regulating Sharing: The Sharing Economy as an Alternative Capitalist System.' *Tulane Law Review* 90 (2): 241–309.

EC (European Commission). 2016. *Communication from the Commission to the European Parliament, the Council, the European Economic and Social Committee and the Committee of the Regions: Online Platforms and the Digital Single Market Opportunities and Challenges for Europe. Swd(2016) 172 Final.* Brussels: European Commission.

Esping-Andersen, Gøsta. 1990. *The Three Worlds of Welfare Capitalism.* Princeton, NJ: Princeton University Press.

Frenken, Koen, Arnoud van Waes, Peter Pelzer, Magda Smink, and Rinie van Est. 2020. 'Safeguarding Public Interests in the Platform Economy.' *Policy & Internet* 12 (3): 400–425. https://doi.org/10.1002/poi3.217.

Garapon, Antoine, and Jean Lassègue. 2018. *Justice digitale: révolution graphique et rupture anthropologique.* Paris: Presses Universitaires de France/Humensis.

Gautrais, Vincent. 2018. 'The Normative Ecology of Disruptive Technology.' In *Law and the 'Sharing Economy': Regulating Online Market Platforms*, edited by Derek McKee, Finn Makela, and Teresa Scassa, 115–147. Ottawa: University of Ottawa Press. https://doi.org/10.2307/j.ctv5vdczv.8.

Graz, Jean-Christophe. 2019. *The Power of Standards: Hybrid Authority and the Globalisation of Services.* Cambridge: Cambridge University Press. https://doi.org/10.1017/9781108759038.

Hall, Peter A., and David Soskice, eds. 2001. *Varieties of Capitalism: The Institutional Foundations of Comparative Advantage.* Oxford: Oxford University Press.

Huising, Ruthanne, and Susan S. Silbey. 2011. 'Governing the Gap: Forging Safe Science Through Relational Regulation.' *Regulation & Governance* 5 (1): 14–42. https://doi.org/10.1111/j.1748-5991.2010.01100.x.

Katz, Vanessa. 2015. 'Regulating the Sharing Economy.' *Berkeley Technology Law Journal* 30 (4): 1067–1126. https://doi.org/10.15779/Z38HG45.

Kawiński, Marcin. 2009. 'Consumer Protection and Dispute Resolution within the EU Financial Sector.' *PROGRES* 49 (6): 1–6.

Korobkin, Russell B. 2000. 'Behavioral Analysis and Legal Form: Rules vs. Standards Revisited.' *Oregon Law Review* 79 (1): 23–60.

McAdams, Richard H. 1997. 'The Origin, Development, and Regulation of Norms.' *Michigan Law Review* 96 (2): 338. https://doi.org/10.2307/129 0070.

Morgan, Bronwen. 2015. 'Upside Down and Inside Out: Regulators and Regulatory Processes in Contemporary Perspective.' In *The Handbook of Law and Society*, edited by Austin Sarat and Patricia. Ewick, 150–167. Chichester: Wiley Blackwell. https://doi.org/10.1002/9781118701430.ch10.

Newell, Peter. 2002. 'From Responsibility to Citizenship? Corporate Accountability for Development.' *IDS Bulletin* 33 (2): 1–12. https://doi.org/10.1111/j.1759-5436.2002.tb00025.x.

Oramus, Marek. 2015. 'Model współzarządzania (governance) i problemy dotyczące jego wdrażania w administracji publicznej.' *Rocznik Administracji Publicznej* (1): 179–195.

Pillay, Renginee G. 2014. 'The Limits to Self-Regulation and Voluntarism: From Corporate Social Responsibility to Corporate Accountability.' *Amicus Curiae* 99: 10–13.

SFR (Senate of the French Republic). 2017. *Rapport D'information Fait Au Nom De La Commission Des Finances (1) Relatif À L'adaptation De La Fiscalité À L'économie Collaborative, No. 481.* Paris: Senate of the French Republic.

Slee, Tom. 2017. *What's Yours Is Mine: Against the Sharing Economy.* Brunswick, Vic. Scribe Publications. https://doi.org/10.2307/j.ctt1bkm65n.

Snyder, Francis. 1993. 'The Effectiveness of European Community Law: Institutions, Processes, Tools and Techniques.' *The Modern Law Review* 56 (1): 19–54. https://doi.org/10.1111/j.1468-2230.1993.tb02852.x.

Srnicek, Nick. 2016. *Platform Capitalism.* Oxford: Polity Press.

Stemler, Abbey. 2017. 'Regulation 2.0: The Marriage of New Governance and Lex Informatica.' *Vanderbilt Journal of Entertainment & Technology Law* 19 (1): 87–131. https://doi.org/10.2139/ssrn.2746229.

Surdej, Aleksander. 2014. 'Regulacyjne instrumenty w polityce publicznej.' *Studia z Polityki Publicznej* 1 (4): 69–85. https://doi.org/10.33119/KSzPP.2014.4.4.

Terpan, Fabien. 2015. 'Soft Law in the European Union-the Changing Nature of EU Law.' *European Law Journal* 21 (1): 68–96. https://doi.org/10.1111/eulj.12090.

Thelen, Kathleen. 2018. 'Regulating Uber: The Politics of the Platform Economy in Europe and the United States.' *Perspectives on Politics* 16 (4): 938–53. https://doi.org/10.1017/S1537592718001081.

Zuboff, Shoshana. 2019. *The Age of Surveillance Capitalism: The Fight for Human Future at the New Frontier of Power.* New York, NY: PublicAffairs.

Zuluaga, Diego. 2016. *Regulatory Approaches to the Sharing Economy: A Briefing.* London, UK: Institute of Economic Affairs. Accessed September 20, 2020. https://iea.org.uk/wp-content/uploads/2016/07/Regulating%20the%20sharing%20economy%20Briefing%202016.pdf.

## Suggested Readings

Corrales Compagnucci, Marcelo, Nikolaus Forgó, Toshiyuki Kono, Shinto Teramoto, and Erik P. M. Vermeulen, eds. 2020. *Legal Tech and the New Sharing Economy.* Singapore: Springer Singapore. https://doi.org/10.1007/978-981-15-1350-3.

Daugareilh, Isabelle, Christophe Degryse, and Philippe Pochet. 2019. *The Platform Economy and Social Law: Key Issues in Comparative Perspective.* Brussels: European Trade Union Institute.

Davidson, Nestor M., John Infranca, and Michèle Finck, eds. 2018. *The Cambridge Handbook of the Law of the Sharing Economy.* New York, NY: Cambridge University Press. https://doi.org/10.1017/9781108255882.

Inglese, Marco. 2019. *Regulating the Collaborative Economy in the European Union Digital Single Market.* Cham: Springer International Publishing. https://doi.org/10.1007/978-3-030-30040-1.
Orsi, Janelle. 2014. *Practicing Law in the Sharing Economy: Helping People Build Cooperatives, Social Enterprise, and Local Sustainable Economies.* Lanham: American Bar Association.
Sundararajan, Arun. 2017. *The Collaborative Economy: Socioeconomic, Regulatory and Labor Issues.* Brussels: European Parliament.

## Relevant Websites

Davidson, Nestor M., and John J. Infranca. 2021. 'Regulatory Challenges in the Sharing Economy.' Accessed September 20, 2020. https://www.americanbar.org/groups/government_public/publications/public_lawyer_articles/regulatory-challenges-in-the-sharing-economy/.
Erickson, Kristofer, and Inge Sørensen. 2016. 'Regulating the Sharing Economy.' *Internet Policy Review* 5 (2). Accessed September 20, 2020. https://policyreview.info/articles/analysis/regulating-sharing-economy.

# 4

# The Regulatory Context and Legal Evolution: The Cases of Airbnb and Uber

Kosjenka Dumančić and Natalia-Rozalia Avlona

## Introduction

The collaborative economy as a phenomenon emerged in 1995 and has been widespread across the globe and started to disrupt the traditional business market (Cohen and Munoz 2016). The confusion (Murillo et al. 2017) around the diversity of terms that have been employed in order to describe this emerged economic model was mostly a result of the peer-to-peer (P2P) (Wirtz et al. 2019) activity of these platforms. The model of acquiring, providing, or sharing access to goods and services

K. Dumančić (✉)
Faculty of Economics and Business, University of Zagreb, Zagreb, Croatia
e-mail: kdumancic@efzg.hr

N.-R. Avlona
Department of Computer Science, University of Copenhagen, Copenhagen, Denmark
e-mail: naav@di.ku.dk


V. Česnuitytė et al. (eds.), *The Sharing Economy in Europe*,
https://doi.org/10.1007/978-3-030-86897-0_4

instead of owning (Menor Campos et al. 2019) them that were facilitated by a community-based online platform has created ambiguity about its novelty (Ertz et al. 2016) and its nature (Murillo et al. 2017). Terms such as gig economy (Fisk 2017), platform economy (Cohen 2017), sharing economy (Schor 2016), peer-to-peer economy (Selloni 2017), and collaborative economy (Vaughan and Daverio 2016) have been used widely as an attempt to classify this economic model. The EU Commission has chosen to use the term 'collaborative economy' in its papers, as an umbrella definition, though the term itself can be deceptive since it is evoking the values of altruism and solidarity (Frenken and Schor 2019), while these platforms and their extractive nature are a continuation of the market mechanism.

While there have been many attempts to define and classify this economic activity so as to determine the way of regulating it (Drahokoupil and Fabo 2016), there has been confusion in the effort to pin down this phenomenon. The distinction between the collaborative economy and the commons-based peer production (Bauwens and Pantazis 2018) is crucial in its historicity since it expresses the different economic models with which these two seemingly similar networked and decentralised models of transacting are operating, and why regulation is crucial for the second one.

The primary role of the online platform primarily is to connect providers and users and facilitate the transactions between them (Wirtz et al. 2019). Besides the role of connecting, the platform is also providing the service by itself. In such a scenario, the platform should be deemed a business entity and, specifically, a trader (Busch 2016). According to the European Commission (2016), a case-by-case analysis ought to be performed in order to set the legal nature of the platform's activities. It is now well established from a variety of studies that the collaborative economy employs a diversity of online platforms that can be classified into typologies in accordance with the type of services provided, the labour engaged (Benjaafar et al. 2021) and the idle resources that are utilised. For example, Uber involves local services (Guda and Subramanian 2019) and physical skills (Tomassetti 2016), whereas Airbnb offers global services using local property (Coyle 2016), whilst Mechanical Turk (Drahokoupil and Fabo 2016) offers global services and uses online global labour force. These platforms have moved away from the initial model of the 'on-demand economy' (Frenken and Schor 2019) that matches demand and supply amongst peers and have evolved into a disruptive business model which aimed purely at profit-seeking (Inglese 2019). That said, the diversity of the platforms in the collaborative economy is at the same time implying a variety of impacts in the labour sector (Berins Collier et al. 2017), re-organising the employment relationships (Degryse 2016), the local labour market and the conditions of self-employment (Echikson 2020).

This chapter will give an overview of the regulatory concept of the collaborative economy in the European Union's law. Regulation of the collaborative economy is developing in the light of the Court of Justice of the European Union case law in the field of transport and accommodation. This raised the need for the analysis of the judgement in the cases of Airbnb and Uber. As a basis for the different approach in these two judgements services and information society services analysis is presented.

## Regulatory Development in the European Union's Law

In the midst of these technological innovations and less than a decade after the invention of the Internet, in 1999, the EU attempted to regulate the transnational economic exchanges that were based on the Internet. This regulation effort was twofold. Addressing the collaborative economy from the one hand as an online platform forced the EU to apply the Directive 2000/31/EC on certain legal aspects of information society services, in particular, electronic commerce in the Internal Market (E-Commerce Directive), setting clear limits on liability for digital platforms and in particular electronic commerce in the Internal Market. Platforms were not to be held responsible for illegal material uploaded to their sites; only for taking it down when informed (Echikson 2020). Particularly, Articles 12–15 of the E-Commerce Directive restrict the liability of providers in respect of the assumed functions. Article 15 of the E-Commerce Directive states that providers do not have any obligation 'to monitor the information which they transmit or store, nor a general obligation actively to seek facts or circumstances indicating illegal activity (Spindler 2017, p. 290). The second Directive that the EU selected as the most applicable for the regulation of the online platforms is the Directive (EU) 2015/1535 laying down a procedure for the provision of information in the field of technical regulations and rules on information society services (Information Society Services Directive). This Directive defined information society services as services provided upon a user's request, supplied through an information society service, at a distance and for remuneration.

When it comes to what kind of regulation (if any) is essential for these platforms, the most answered that the best solution for the legal problems would be a combination of regulatory and self-regulatory measures (Cohen and Sundararajan 2015), a key issue in all replies relates to platforms' responsibility and liability (Eurobarometer 2018). To address these issues, the EU Commission had in 2016 promulgated its Communication: 'A European Agenda for the Collaborative Economy' where it has advised, i.e., to monitor the regulatory and economic environment of the P2P economy, that would enable following pricing trends as well as to identify obstacles, especially arising from various national regulations. The Commission pointed out the following main tools: Periodic surveys of consumers and businesses on the use of the collaborative economy; Ongoing mapping of regulatory developments in the Member States; Stakeholder dialogue in the framework of the Single Market Forum, with twice-yearly forums to assess sector development on the ground and to identify good practices; and the results of the monitoring of the collaborative economy will be summarised in the Single Market Scoreboard.

The rapid growth of the collaborative economy tourism accommodation sector within less than a decade has bought with its diverse impacts prompting a range of responses from governments across Europe. Cultural attitudes, traditional institutional approaches to regulation, the nature and extent of impacts, and the level of public debate in each city have undoubtedly influenced government responses. The diversity of responses across Europe are challenging the consolidation of the Single Market and has prompted the European Commission to propose the development of guidance with the aim of fostering competitiveness, maximising the positive effects of growth and jobs, and securing opportunities for innovation in sharing (EU Parliament Report 2015).

Given that in 2015 the EU Commission admitted that 'the rise of the sharing economy also offers opportunities for increased efficiency, growth and jobs, through improved consumer choice, but also potentially raises new regulatory questions' (COM (2015) 550 final, par. 3.3.1.) it was no surprise that the intention was to boost the single market and modernise the legislation through the European Commission Digital Market Strategy. Despite this concrete intention, the European Union (EU) has not provided an ad hoc EU legal framework for the collaborative economy. What has been issued so far, after consultations with various groups and individual stakeholders (Cauffman and Smits 2016), was the policy guidance in the form of a Communication by the European Commission dated June 2016. The document, which was not legally binding, expressed a favourable position towards the new platform-based business models in the hope they may fix some market failures.

The policy agenda sketched by the EU Commission aims to persuade Member States to apply existing EU law to the collaborative economy in a uniform and balanced way. The sought balance is between, on the one side, the protection of consumers and, on the other, an inclusive and prosperous single market. In particular, the Commission emphasised the free access to the market granted to providers of information society services under EU law (E-commerce directive, Article 4) and suggested loosening the grip of the market access requirements also for collaborative economy players for a more inclusive and dynamic digital economy. The aspiration towards market inclusivity and dynamism, which reflected in the Communication, is to be read for the benefit of both online platforms and private users, as the latter—the Communication suggests—should not fall under the category of 'professional service providers'. At the same time, the Commission appeared to be fully aware of the risks and the needed precaution, which come together with the collaborative economy evolutions in the market to guarantee the safety of the public. In this vein, the Communication included reflections on the liability regime to be applied to the collaborative economy platforms

(European Commission 2016a, p. 8) and on the protection of consumers (European Commission 2016a, p. 9), often highlighting the complexity of the legal questions involved and suggesting a case-by-case responsive approach.

As a result, the 'Agenda on Collaborative Economy' of 2016 has one great limit, which is represented by the effort of providing guidance to regulate the collaborative economy phenomenon by applying provisions already existing within the EU legal framework (Cauffman 2016). This means that in addition to its non-binding nature, the Communication left many legal issues unanswered and, thus, broad room for the Member States to develop specific normative responses to the collaborative economy. At the same time, the collaborative economy often raises issues with regard to the application of existing legal frameworks, blurring established lines between consumer and provider, employee and self-employed, or the professional and non-professional provision of services.

Since the beginning of the development of the regulation at the EU level and enacting of the EC Agenda for the collaborative economy, there were no other regulatory activities (Rousseau 2017) in the area of the collaborative economy at the EU level. This is why the impact of the Court of Justice of the European Union (CJEU) is, at the moment, the only legal source (Hacker 2018) for future analysis. The CJEU acted in two sectors: transportation (Colangelo and Maggiolino 2018) and accommodation (Van Cleynenbreugel 2020) since these sectors were highly disrupted (Menegus 2019) by the collaborative economy platforms, and reaction from the EU level was needed.

## Case C-434/15 Uber

### Uber's Business Model

Uber started as a technology platform (Thelen 2018). Their application is made for smartphones, and it works as an intermediary between partner drivers and users. After the registration, the user is able to order a taxi on a location-service basis, and the nearest partner-driver should accept a ride and come to the exact location. The user application also displays information on partner-driver, including the name, car brand and the number of the registration table (Hacker 2018).

Uber has implemented strict rules when it comes to their rights and responsibilities towards partner drivers based on the contractual agreement that regulates terms of use, collection and use of personal data. Uber services are only available for personal, non-commercial use. It is explicitly stated in the contract agreement that Uber Technologies Inc. does not provide transport or logistic services and does not serve as any transport provider and that all services of transport or logistics are provided by an independent Third party who is not employed in Uber or its subsidiaries (Uber 2021).

## Taxi-Service Providers vs Uber

Despite its huge popularity among users, other taxi service providers (Berger et al. 2018) were not that welcoming toward the new market competitor. Functioning of the Uber caused legal dispute (Seidl 2020) started by the traditional taxi companies which publicly protested against Uber (e.g., Paris, Torino, Milan, Genova, Napoli, London, Hong Kong, Johannesburg (Sao Paolo, Rio de Janeiro, and Zagreb) (Pollio 2019). The main problem was that Uber is considered to be unfair competition, as in many countries, service was provided by an individual carrier, an Uber partner, who was not required to possess any licenses nor permission that is legally required from traditional taxi service providers (Berger et al. 2018). When providers are not required to possess any licences, it decreases their barriers to entry into the market and enables them to set lower prices for customers. They became a serious competition to traditional taxi-service providers who are not able to set low prices due to all conditions they have to satisfy in order to enter the market. This is the reason why most of the EU Member States' national regulatory (bodies prohibited Uber from cooperating with individual taxi drivers who do not have licences (Rauch and Schleicher 2015; Thelen 2018).

Regarding all issues that competitors in this market segment have with Uber and the way in which it operates, it is not strange that Uber faced several lawsuits (Ferro 2019) in various countries, which finally ended at the CJEU (Case C-526/15 Uber Belgium, C-434/15 Association Professional Elite Taxi).

In 2014 the Asociacion Profesional Elite Taxi, which is a professional organisation that represents taxi drivers in the city of Barcelona, Spain, brought an action before the national court of the first instance, asking the court to impose penalties on the Spanish company Uber Systems Spain SL. This is the company that belongs to a group managing the Uber platform. Penalties were aimed against the unfair competition toward Elite Taxi's drivers. Elite Taxi maintained that Uber Spain is not entitled to provide UberPop, a non-professional service in the city of Barcelona. Neither Uber Spain nor the owners or drivers of the vehicles concerned have the licence and authorisations required under the city of Barcelona's regulations on taxi services (Case C-434/15 Asociacion Profesional Elite Taxi).

## Uber: A Transportation Service or an Internet Service Provider?

In Uber judgement, the CJEU showed a great impact on determining the nature and definition of service that is provided by Uber and the way in which this kind of services should be regulated in the future (Rauch and Schleicher 2015). Decisions made by the CJEU have great importance when it comes to the way in which legal arrangements are made as well as the providing auto taxi services in the EU Member States.

In order to decide whether Uber is solely a technology platform or a transport company, it is needed to represent two different relationships. The most important question that should be answered in order to bring a valuable and legally correct decision is whether Uber provides an 'information society service' in the sense of the Directive 98/34/EC laying down a procedure for the provision of information in the field of technical standards and regulations and rules on Information Society services, which falls under the principle of the freedom to provide services or if it is a transport service that is regulated by the national law according to the Directive 2016/123EC on services in the internal market. The dilemma was posed in the sense that on the one hand, if the CJEU decides that Uber is an Information Society service provider, Barcelona's license and authorisation requirements may contradict the principle to provide services, while on the other hand, if CJEU decides that Uber is a transport service provider, each Member State would be free in regulating Uber's activity.

According to the definition that is set out in Article 1(2) of Directive 98/34 to which an Article 2(a) of Directive 2000/31/EC of the European Parliament and of the Council of 8 June 2000 on certain legal aspects of information society services, in particular electronic commerce, in the Internal Market (Directive on electronic commerce), is that the 'service' is any Information Society service, that is to say, any service normally provided for remuneration, at a distance, by electronic means and at the individual request of the recipient of services. Or, in another case, as a transport service or service in the field of transport for the purposes of Article 58(1) the Treaty on Functioning of the European Union (further: TFEU) and Article 2(2)(d) of Directive 2006/123/EC, 'this Directive shall not apply to the following activities: '(...) (d) services in the field of transport. Including port services, falling within the scope of Title V of the Treaty'.

As Uber makes it possible to locate a driver via a smartphone application and serves as an intermediary between a driver who supplies urban service and a consumer who demands it, it can be seen as a composite service (Thelen 2018). Composite service is a service whereas one part of it is provided by electronic means, and the other one, by definition, is not. General Advocate examined Uber's activity in the light of the considerations related to the composite service to be able to bring the clear proposition in front of the CJEU (Case C-434/15 Asociacion Profesional Elite Taxi).

Furthermore, according to the Advocate General, Uber should not be referred to as an Information Society service as it does not operate independently from the transport service and transport services are not provided via electronic means. If Uber is to fall within Article 2(a) of Directive 2000/31, it would mean that it serves as an intermediary that connects supply and demand via the mobile application, while all Terms and Conditions of performing transport service are set by the exact service provider. But, as is stated before, Uber exercise high control.

The main question is whether the collaborative economy is part of the information society services and, if so, whether such activities are protected under EU law to provide services freely or under the national law of a specific sector of the Member State in which they operate. For the decision on this issue, it is necessary to analyse the activity of the platform and the connection of the electronic and non-electronic elements of their business. In the case of composite services, services involving electronic and non-electronic elements, it can be considered that the service is entirely provided by electronic means when the supply which is not provided by electronic means is economically independent of the service provided by such means. This is particularly the case when the intermediary service provider facilitates commercial relations between users and independent service providers. An example of this case may be the platforms for airline tickets or hotel reservations. In those cases, the intermediary service has real value-added for the consumer and trader but remains economically independent as the trader independently pursues out his business activity (Szpunar 2017).

## Case C-390/18 Airbnb Ireland

When the case Airbnb was brought in front of the CJEU, the general public thought that the reasoning would follow the reasoning from the Uber cases. The Opinion was given by the same Advocate General (AG) Szpunar. It was a surprise when he, in his Opinion of Airbnb Ireland, concluded that Airbnb provides an information technology service in accordance with Article 2(a) of the E-Commerce Directive, read in conjunction with Article 1(b) of Information Society Services Directive. Para 41 of the Opinion to illustrate his point, AG Szpunar highlights that, 'AIRBNB Ireland does not physically meet the recipients of its services: neither the hosts nor the guests. As is apparent from the preliminary observations concerning AIRBNB Ireland's activities, hosts are not required to approach AIRBNB Ireland in person in order to publish their accommodation on the platform. Furthermore, a user of the platform managed by AIRBNB Ireland may rent accommodation at a distance without having to be physically in contact with that service provider. However, it is clear that the connection of users of the platform managed by AIRBNB Ireland results in the use of an accommodation, which may be regarded as a non-electronic component of the service provided by that company'. In its Opinion para. 53 AG Szpunar quotes the conclusion from the judgements in Asociación Profesional Elite Taxi and Uber France where the CJEU established two criteria to be applied in order to determine whether a service provided by electronic means that, taken separately, *prima facie* meets the definition of an 'information society service' is separable from other services having material content (Busch 2018), namely the criteria relating to the fact that the service provider offers services having a material content and to the fact that the service provider exercises decisive influence on the conditions under which such services are provided (Dredge et al. 2016). The grounds for the analysis of the AIRBNB Ireland case lies in satisfying these two criteria.

Regarding the first criteria, AG Szpunar concludes that AIRBNB does not create an offer in the meaning of the Elite Taxi and Uber France case. He explains that the accommodation services are not inseparably linked to the service provided by AIRBNB Ireland by electronic means, in the sense that they can be provided independently of that service. Those services retain their economic interest and remain independent of AIRBNB Ireland's electronic service. Regarding the second criteria of the relationship between the creation of an offer of services and the exercise of control over those services, AG Szpunar para. 65 of his Opinion concludes that service provider not only has to create a new supply of services that are not provided by electronic means but that the creation of those services must be followed by the maintenance, under the control of that provider, of the conditions under which they are provided. AG Szpunar analyses the determination of whether AIRBNB Ireland exercises control over the conditions governing the provision of short-term accommodation services. As the result of his analysis para 87, he concludes that 'consider that the services having a material content, which is not inseparably linked to the service provided by electronic means, are not capable of affecting the nature of that service. The service provided by electronic means does not lose its economic interest and remains independent of the services having a material content'.

Motivating his interpretation, he explained that the service provided by Airbnb has to be interpreted as an 'information society service' as explained para 89 of his Opinion 'that a service consisting in connecting, via an electronic platform, potential guests with hosts offering short-term accommodation, in a situation where the provider of that service does not exercise control over the essential procedures of the provision of those services, constitutes an information society service within the meaning of those provisions'.

According to the European Union's legislation, platforms are exempted from liability (European Parliament Research Service 2021) for the information they are storing under certain circumstances. The applicability of this exemption will depend on legal and factual circumstances, and according to Article 14 of the EU E-Commerce Directive, platforms will be exempt from liability when providing hosting services. Hosting services are services whose activities are passive, technical and automatic, which implies that the information society service provider has neither knowledge of nor control over the information which is transmitted or stored. The Commission, at the same time, encourages responsible behaviour and voluntary action by all types of online platforms, for example, to help tackle the important issue of fake or misleading reviews. Such voluntary measures are taken to strengthen trust and to offer a more competitive service (European Commission 2016).

In order to analyse whether the established relationship falls within the scope of EU consumer protection law, another relevant aspect is the distinction between freedom of establishment and free provision of services. Generally speaking, the establishment of a business is considered as something permanent, while the provision of a service is rather deemed a temporary activity. Both are provided by professionals who pursue an economic purpose. While analysing the collaborative economy phenomenon, these criteria may help to distinguish the professional trader, as a provider of the collaborative economy service, from the non-trader. This seems to reflect the European Commission's approach from its 'Agenda on Collaborative Economy' supporting analysis, inasmuch it differentiates the long-term profit-seeking business activity from the occasional service, which could also be without remuneration. Highlighting the enduring legal uncertainty surrounding such definition is the case of Airbnb, an online platform that does not provide a service by itself but is, however, deemed a professional trader (Codagnone et al. 2018).

## Summary

Despite all the advantages and facilitation the collaborative economy has created, and despite being openly embraced by society, the rise of platforms such as Uber and Airbnb (Coyle 2016), allowing non-professionals to offer their services, has given rise to some legal and social issues. In many European cities, taxi drivers have engaged in various protests against Uber, arguing its legality. The reason for that is obvious internet companies that only exist online are subject to one set of regulations, while transportation companies such as taxis are subject to other, much more demanding laws. Hence, the governments may not remain indifferent on all the issues collaborative consumption has developed. In Europe, since the very beginning of the sharing apps' functioning, the policies for Uber and Airbnb have been vigorously discussed and been subject to various rulings of the CJEU, as well as member states courts (Grotkowska 2020).

In the case of Uber, the CJEU clearly distinguished digital platforms and transportation service providers, This reaffirmed the solid basis for the application of national rules instead of voicing the need for developments of EU law addressing the CE phenomenon. In case of a reversed judgement, in fact, thus meaning if Uber had been deemed a digital platform and not a transportation service provider, the Service Directive, as well as the E-commerce Directive, would have found application.

Returning to the question posed at the beginning of this chapter, of whether the top-down EU regulatory approach towards the collaborative economy, along with the CJEU diverse judgements in the case of Airbnb and Uber, consists of the best applicable regulation for this disruptive economic phenomenon. As it was analysed above, the first EU response to the expansive phenomenon of the collaborative economy was an effort to create an inclusive definition that would cover the diversity of the online platforms. For the legal problems that a wide range of online platforms, from Uber to Airbnb and Amazon Turk, that fall under the umbrella term collaborative economy, the EU initially applied the E-Commerce Directive 2000/31/EC and the information Services Directive (EU) 2015/1535. In 2016 the European Commission published a Communication on the collaborative economy, policy guidance that is not legally binding and is leaning towards the revival of the European Single market through these new business platforms. An implication of the EU response was that it did not classify the platforms as professional service providers, nor did it clarify the issues around the liability regime, the consumer rights, and the employment condition specifics.

The second regulatory evolution that defined the European landscape of collaborative economy was CJEU judgements on the cases of Uber and Airbnb. In the case of Uber, the CJEU asserted the platform is providing transportation service and is not an intermediate providing an information society service. Airbnb, on the other hand, was classified as an information technology service in accordance with Article 2(a) of the E-Commerce Directive. These contradictory CJEU judgements based on the two EU Directives the E-Commerce and the Information Services, respectively, illustrated the necessity for applying the national legislation instead of the EU directives that attempt to foster the Digital Single Market, as a core part of the EU's Agenda for the digital economy, helping European companies to grow globally.

Several questions and legal implications still remain to be answered. Nevertheless, the common denominator of the disruptive effect that collaborative economy has brought is the transformation of the work and the very definition of employment. The structure of employment that been re-organised and the labour is brought into a blurry state of self-employment, while it has created unfair completion to licensed professions, is one of the main, yet the only one, issues that require further regulation. The national employment law and the casualisation of work are at stake, particularly in the post-covid era. If these platforms have managed to bypass the International Labour Organisation conventions, then it is crucial for the EU to re-open a pan-European, consultation that will engage the national legislators, the trade unions, and the workers' collectives in order to respond to this crisis.

Lastly, the two very recent legislative initiatives of the European Commission to upgrade the rules governing digital services in the EU, the Digital Services Act (DSA) and the Digital Markets Act (DMA), create a consultation space for the consumers' protection as users of the digital service implications, and the data protection in a collaborative economy that becomes more and more a data-driven one.

## References

Bauwens, Michel, and Alekos Pantazis. 2018. 'The Ecosystem of Commons-Based Peer Production and Its Transformative Dynamics.' *The Sociological Review* 66 (2): 302–319. https://doi.org/10.1177/0038026118758532.

Benjaafar, Saif, Jian-Ya Ding, Guangwen Kong, and Terry Taylor. 2021. 'Labor Welfare in On-Demand Service Platforms. Manufacturing & Service.' *Operations Management* 0 (0). https://doi.org/10.1287/msom.2020.0964.

Berger, Thor, Chinchih Chen, and Carl Benedikt Frey. 2018. 'Drivers of Disruption? Estimating the Uber Effect.' *European Economic Review* 110: 197–210. https://doi.org/10.1016/j.euroecorev.2018.05.00.

Busch, Christoph. 2016. 'The Rise of the Platform Economy: A New Challenge for EU Consumer Law?' *Journal of European Consumer and Market Law* 5 (1): 3–10.

Busch, Christoph. 2018. 'The Sharing Economy at the CJEU: Does Airbnb Pass the "Uber Test"?—Some Observations on the Pending Case C-390/18—Airbnb Ireland.' *Journal of European Consumer and Market Law* 4: 172–174.

Case C-390/18 AIRBNB Ireland delivered on 30 April 2019, ECLI:EU:C:2019:336.

Case C-434/15 Asociacion Profesional Elite Taxi v Uber Systems Spain, ECLI:EU:C:2017:364.

Case C-526/15 Uber Belgium BVA v Taxi Radio Bruxellois NV, ECLI:EU:C:2016:830.

Cauffman, Caroline. 2016. 'The Commission's European Agenda for the Collaborative Economy (Too) Platform and Service Provider Friendly?' *EuCML* 6: 235–243. https://doi.org/10.2139/ssrn.2883845.

Cauffman, Caroline, and Jan Smits. 2016. 'The Sharing Economy and the Law. Food for European Lawyers.' *Maastricht Journal of European and Comparative Law* 23 (6): 903–907. https://doi.org/10.1177/1023263X1602300601.

Codagnone, Cristiano, Athina Karatzogianni, and Jacob Matthews. 2018. "Index", Platform Economics: Rhetoric and Reality in the "Sharing Economy" (Digital Activism and Society: Politics, Economy and Culture in Network Communication). Bingley: Emerald Publishing Limited. https://doi.org/10.1108/978-1-78743-809-520181007.

Cohen, Boyd, and Pablo Munoz. 2016. 'Sharing Cities and Sustainable Consumption and Production: Towards an Integrated Framework.' *Journal of Cleaner Production* 134, part A: 87–97. https://doi.org/10.1016/j.jclepro.2015.07.133.

Cohen, Julie E. 2017. 'Law for the Platform Economy.' *UCD Law Review* 51: 133–204.

Cohen, Molly, and Arun Sundararajan. 2015. 'Self-Regulation and Innovation in the Peer-to-Peer Sharing Economy.' *University of Chicago Law Review Online* 82 (1) Article 8: 116–133. Available at: https://chicagounbound.uchicago.edu/uclrev_online/vol82/iss1/8.

Colangelo, Margherita, and Mariateresa Maggiolino. 2018. 'Uber in Europe: Are There Still Judges in Luxembourg?' *CPI Antitrust Chronicle*. Available at: https://ssrn.com/abstract=3192086.

Collier, Ruth Berins, V. B. Dubal, and Christopher Carter. 2017. 'Labor Platforms and Gig Work: The Failure to Regulate.' *IRLE Working Paper No. 106–17*, UC Hastings Research Paper 251: 1–32. https://doi.org/10.2139/ssrn.3039742.

Communication from the Commission to the European Parliament, the Council, the European Economic and Social Committee and the Committee of the Regions, Upgrading the Single Market: more opportunities for people and business. COM (2015) 550 final.

Communication from the Commission to the European Parliament, the Council, the European Economic and Social Committee and the Committee of the Regions 'A Digital Single Market Strategy for Europe.' COM (2015) 192 final.

Coyle, Diane, Yu-Cheong Yeung. 2016. 'Understanding AirBnB in Fourteen European Cities.' *The Jean-Jacques Laffont Digital Chair*. Working papers.

Degryse, Christophe. 2016. 'Digitalization of the Economy and Its Impact on Labour Markets.' *WP 2016.02*. ETUI, Brussels.

Directive (EU) 2015/1535 of the European Parliament and of the Council of 9 September 2015 laying down a procedure for the provision of information in the field of technical regulations and rules on information society services (codified text), OJ L 241, 17.9.2015, pp. 1–15.
Directive 2000/31/EC of the European Parliament and of the Council of 8 June 2000 on certain legal aspects of information society services, in particular electronic commerce, in the Internal Market ('Directive on electronic commerce'), OJ L 178, 17.7.2000, pp. 1–16.
Directive 2006/123/EC of the European Parliament and of the Council of 12 December 2006 on services in the internal market, OJ L 376, 27.12.2006, pp. 36–68.
Directive 98/34/EC of the European Parliament and of the Council of 22 June 1998 laying down a procedure for the provision of information in the field of technical standards and regulations and of rules on Information Society services, OJ L204 of 21 July 1998 Directive 98/48/EC of the European Parliament and of the Council of 20 July 1998.
Drahokoupil, Jan and Brian Fabo. 2016. 'The Platform Economy and the Disruption of the Employment Relationship.' ETUI Policy Brief No. 5.
Dredge, Dianne, Szilvia Gyimóthy, Andreas Birkbak, T. E. Jensen, and A. K. Madsen. 2016. 'The Impact of Regulatory Approaches Targeting Collaborative Economy in the Tourism Accommodation Sector: Barcelona, Berlin, Amsterdam and Paris.' Impulse Paper No 9 prepared for the European Commission DG GROWTH. Aalborg University, Copenhagen. Available at: http://ec.europa.eu/growth/tools-databases/newsroom/cf/itemdetail.cfm?item_id=8961&lang=en.
Echikson, William. 2020. 'Europe's Collaborative Economy Charting a Constructive Path Forward.' Centre for European Policy Studies (CEPS), CEPS Task Force Report, Brussels.
Ertz, Myriam, Fabien Durif, and Manon Arcand. 2016. 'Collaborative Consumption or the Rise of the Two-Sided Consumer.' *The International Journal of Business & Management* 4 (6): 195–209.
Eurobarometer. 2018. *Collaborative Economy in the EU. Flash Eurobarometer 467*. Luxembourg: Publications Office of the European Union. Accessed May 20, 2021. https://europa.eu/eurobarometer/surveys/detail/2184.
European Commission. 2015. Press Release 'A Deeper and Fairer Single Market: Commission Boosts Opportunities for Citizens and Business.' Accessed October 28, 2015. http://europa.eu/rapid/press-release_IP-15-5909_en.htm.

European Commission. 2016a. Communication to the European Parliament, the Council, the European Economic and Social Council and the Council of Regions: European Agenda for the Collaborative Economy, 356, Brussels.
European Commission. 2016b. Staff Working Document 'European Agenda for the Collaborative Economy—Supporting Analysis,' SWD (2016) 184 final.
European Commission. 2016c. Staff Working Document 'Guidance on the Implementation/Application of Directive 2005/29/EC on Unfair Commercial practices' SWD (2016) 163 final, 124.
European Parliament. 2015. 'Report on Towards a Digital Single Market Act' (2015/2147(INI)). Committee on Industry, Research and Energy Committee on the Internal Market and Consumer Protection.
European Parliamentary Research Service. 2021. 'Liability of Online Platforms.' Available at: https://www.europarl.europa.eu/RegData/etudes/STUD/2021/656318/EPRS_STU(2021)656318_EN.pdf.
Ferro, Miguel Soussa. 2019. 'Uber Court: A Look at Recent Sharing Economy Cases before the CJEU.' *EU Law Journal* 5 (1): 68–75. https://doi.org/10.21814/unio.5.1.251.
Fisk, Catherine. 2017. 'Hollywood Writers and the Gig Economy.' *Legal Studies Research Paper Series. University of Chicago Legal Forum.* Vol. 2017, Article 8. UC Irvine School of Law Research Paper No. 2016-55. Available at: https://chicagounbound.uchicago.edu/uclf/vol2017/iss1/8.
Frenken, Koen, and Juliet Schor. 2019. 'Putting The Sharing Economy Into Perspective.' In *A Research Agenda for Sustainable Consumption Governance*, edited by Oksana Mont. UK: Edward Elgar Publishing: 121–135. https://doi.org/10.4337/9781788117814.00017.
Grotkowska, Wiktoria. 2020. 'Challenges and Legal Issues of Modern Sharing Economy.' *Fundamental and Applied Researches in Practice of Leading Scientific Schools* 40 (4): 34–40. https://doi.org/10.33531/farplss.2020.4.5.
Guda, Harish, and Upender Subramanian. 2019. 'Your Uber Is Arriving: Managing Independent Workers through Surge Pricing, Forecast Communication and Worker Incentives.' *Management Science* 65 (5). https://doi.org/10.1287/mnsc.2018.3050.
Hacker, Philipp. 2018. 'UberPop, UberBlack, and the Regulation of Digital Platforms after the Asociación Profesional Elite Taxi Judgment of the CJEU.' *European Review of Contract Law* 14 (1): 80–96. https://doi.org/10.1515/ercl-2018-1005.

Inglese, Marco. 2019. *Regulating the Collaborative Economy in the European Union Digital Single Market.* Switzerland: Springer Nature Switzerland AG. https://doi.org/10.1007/978-3-030-30040-1.

Menegus, Giacomo. 2019. 'Uber Test' Revised? Remarks on Opinion of AG Szpunar in Case Airbnb Ireland.' *European Papers* 4 (2): 603–614.

Menor-campos, Antonio P., Hidalgo-fernández, Amalia, and Valverde-roda, José M. 2019. 'La economia collaborativa: Analysis conceptual.' *Revista Espacios* 40 (3): 30.

Murillo, David, Heloise Buskland, Val Esther. 2017. 'When the Sharing Economy becomes Neoliberalism on Steroids: Unravelling the Controversies.' *Technological Forecasting and Social Change.* Elsevier 125: 66–76.https://doi.org/10.1016/j.techfore.2017.05.024.

Szpunar. 2017. Case C-434/15 Asociación Profesional Elite Taxi v. *Uber Systems Spain*, ECLI: ECLI:EU:C:2017:981

Pollio, Andrea. 2019. 'Forefronts of the Sharing Economy: Uber in Cape Town.' *International Journal of Urban and Regional Research* 43 (4): 760–775. https://doi.org/10.1111/1468-2427.12788.

Rauch, Daniel E., and David Schleicher. 2015. 'Like Uber, but for Local Government Law: The Future of Local Regulation of the Sharing Economy.' *Ohio State Law Journal* 76 (4): 901–963. http://hdl.handle.net/1811/75456.

Rousseau, Stephane. 2017. 'L'économie collaborative: quels modeles de régulation envisager?' In *Quelles régulations pour l'économie collabortive*? edited by Parachkevova, Irina, Teller, Marina, Nice, France: Dalloz.

Schor, Juliet. 2016. 'Debating the Sharing Economy.' *Journal of Self-Governance and Management Economics* 4 (3): 7–22. https://doi.org/10.22381/JSME4320161.

Seidl, Timo. 2020. *The Politics of Platform Capitalism: A Case Study on the Regulation of Uber in New York.* Center for Open Science. https://doi.org/10.31219/osf.io/up9qz.

Selloni, Daniela. 2017. 'New Forms of Economies: Sharing Economy, Collaborative Consumption, Peer-to-Peer Economy.' In *CoDesign for Public-Interest Services*, edited by Daniela Selloni. Springer International Publishing. https://doi.org/10.1007/978-3-319-53243-1.

Spindler, Gerald. 2017. 'Responsibility and Liability of Internet Intermediaries: Status Quo in the EU and Potential Reforms.' In *EU Internet Law. Regulation and Enforcement*, edited by Tatiana-Eleni Synodinou, Philippe Jougleux,

Christiana Markou, and Thalia Prastitou, 289–314. Cham. Switzerland: Springer International Publishing AG. https://doi.org/10.1007/978-3-030-25579-4.
Thelen, Kathleen. 2018. 'Regulating Uber: The Politics of the Platform Economy in Europe and the United States.' *Perspectives on Politics* 16 (4): 938–953. https://doi.org/10.1017/S1537592718001081.
Tomassetti, Julia. 2016. 'Does Uber Redefine the Firm? The Postindustrial Corporation and Advanced Information Technology.' *Hofstra Labor & Employment Law Journal* 34 (1), Article 3: 1–78.
Uber. 2021. https://www.uber.com.
Van Cleynenbreugel, Pieter. 2020. 'Accommodating the Freedom of Online Platforms to Provide Services Through the Incidental Direct Effect Back Door: Airbnb Ireland.' *Common Market Law* Review 57 (4): 1201–1228.
Vaughan, Robert, and Raphael Daverio. 2016. (PWC) 'Assessing the Size and Presence of the Collaborative Economy in Europe.' European Commission. Brussels. https://doi.org/10.2873/971404.
Wirtz, Jochen, Kevin Kam Fung So, Makarand Amrish Mody, Stephanie Q. Liu, and HaeEun Helen Chun. 2019. 'Platforms in the Peer to Peer Sharing Economy.' *Journal of Service Management* 30 (4): 452–483. https://doi.org/10.1108/JOSM-11-2018-0369.

## Relevant Websites

Data & Society: https://datasociety.net/library/the-end-of-the-job-and-the-future-of-work/.
Foundation for European Progressive Studies: https://www.feps-europe.eu/resources/publications/686-the-platformisation-of-work-in-europe.html.
Library of Congress: https://blogs.loc.gov/law/2018/03/uber-at-the-ecj-the-legal-saga-in-europe-continues/.
Quartz: https://qz.com/548137/all-the-names-for-the-new-digital-economy-and-why-none-of-them-fits/.

# Part III

## Mapping Sectors of the Sharing Economy in European Countries

# 5

# Shared Mobility: A Reflection on Sharing Economy Initiatives in European Transportation Sectors

Agnieszka Lukasiewicz, Venere Stefania Sanna, Vera Lúcia Alves Pereira Diogo, and Anikó Bernát

## Introduction

Mobility is an inherent component of human life, and thus there is no need to underline its importance. Sharing mobility systems have become a common feature of the modern urban landscape in many cities worldwide (Shaheen et al. 2015), providing residents and visitors with a new mode of transportation. Such a substantial change in people's thinking and behaviours resulted in triggering a mobility ecosystem which is favouring a model more focused on 'accesses' to a means of transportation rather than ownership. This attitude has a great influence on mobility pattern changing, especially in urban space,

A. Lukasiewicz (✉)
Management Systems and Telematics Division, Road and Bridge Research Institute, Warsaw, Poland
e-mail: alukas@ibdim.edu.pl

V. S. Sanna
Centre for Politics and International Studies (CeSPI), Department of MEMOTEF, Sapienza University, Rome, Italy



V. Česnuitytė et al. (eds.), *The Sharing Economy in Europe*,
https://doi.org/10.1007/978-3-030-86897-0_5

where sharing can assume a number of forms: (1) purchase a service—pay for a ride (ride-sharing); (2) exchange a service (car-pooling); (3) renting—a vehicle can be rented rather than purchased (car-sharing); (4) lending—a vehicle can be borrowed or loaned (car-sharing); (5) subscribing—people can become members of a car-sharing scheme (car-sharing); and (6) donating—people can give free rides in their vehicle (car-pooling) (Standing et al. 2019).

The concept of shared-use mobility systems dates back to the 1960s in Europe. The idea has spread over the years, contributing both to a substantial reduction in the individual use of private vehicles and by integrating itself into urban public transportation systems. Some European public entities also have experience with a wide range of public–private partnership arrangements in this sphere. Various definitions of shared mobility can be found in the literature. Machado et al. (2018) widely define shared mobility as trip alternatives aiming to maximise the utilisation of the mobility resources that society can pragmatically afford, disconnecting their usage from ownership. Thus, shared mobility is the short-term access to shared vehicles related to the user's needs and convenience. The majority of authors agree that shared mobility is characterised by the sharing of a vehicle, therefore 'access' instead of ownership, and the use of technology to connect users and providers (Crozet et al. 2019; Santos 2018). Such access is typically facilitated by a digital platform.

This chapter adopts the definition suggested by Shaheen and co-authors (2015), who affirm that shared mobility is 'the shared use of a vehicle, bicycle, or another mode—enabling users to gain short-term access to transportation modes on an 'as-needed' basis. New forms of

V. L. A. P. Diogo
Department Polytechnic Institute of Porto, iNED Center for Research and Innovation On Education, Porto, Portugal
e-mail: veradiogo@ese.ipp.pt

A. Bernát
TÁRKI Social Research Institute, Budapest, Hungary
e-mail: bernat@tarki.hu

'mobility 2.0' range from the more traditional bike and car, scooter, van and on-demand ride services—used for both person transport and for goods and urban freight deliveries—to more innovative solutions such as e-scooter services and car park sharing. The shared mobility sector is part of the wider 'collaborative and sharing economy' defined in the European agenda (European Commission 2016). The question arises how the sharing and collaborative economy and, in particular, the shared mobility systems influence the path towards sustainable development.

In 2016 the CIVITAS Forum Network published a *Policy Note* in which the most relevant impacts that shared mobility services have on cities have been identified and related to the three main pillars of sustainability: environmental, social and economic. Moreover, the study claims that there is an increase in mobility services coordination, leading to the generation of a 'mobility ecosystem', which means that mobility is considered as a single, consistent service, rather than a series of different and separate set of services (CIVITAS 2016). That indicates its relationship with the concept of 'mobility as a service' (MaaS).

Nevertheless, sustainability in the transport sector is hard to achieve because different stakeholders, characterised by contrasting interests, are involved—and this is particularly the case of some sharing services such as Uber, which caused a number of conflicts among stakeholders and therefore raised criticisms. Moreover, the infrastructure for different, and new forms of transport, such as electric scooters, is limited, and that can generate additional competition.

Certainly, 2020 will be remembered as the year of the outbreak of the COVID-19 virus in Europe. Because of the risk of infection, the need for social distance, and lockdown, the pandemic has triggered a shift in users' priorities in relation to mobility. A change in travel behaviour and the use of shared mobility was observed, with travellers inclined to put more trust in private transport. Inevitably, the changeability and uncertainty of the current situation suggest there will be a further evolution of mobility habits, including rethinking the use of shared mobility altogether. As a matter of fact, users that want to avoid COVID-19 transmission might eventually come to view ride-sharing as a good alternative to more congested forms of mobility that make social distance difficult, such as public transportation (Andersson et al. 2020).

## Applying the Stakeholder Approach to Shared Mobility

The World Commission on Environment and Development of the United Nations (1987) set the foundation for the sustainability concept by stating that, in its broadest sense, a sustainable development strategy aims at promoting harmony among human beings and between humanity and nature, entailing that for sustainability, society and environment are crucial elements, in addition to the economy. Building on this, a first sustainability concept was developed by Elkington (1999) as the 'triple bottom line' or 'Triple-P (People, Planet, Profit)' model, regarding sustainability as the balance between economic, social, and environmental issues.

In 2015, all the member states of the United Nations approved the 2030 Agenda for Sustainable Development. This broad action program aims to end poverty, protect the planet and ensure prosperity for all, and includes 17 Sustainable Development Goals (SDGs), for a total of 169 'targets' or milestones to be met by 2030 with the intention of leaving no one behind (UNPF 2015). Sustainable transport is a theme that crosses numerous development objectives; it is a prerequisite to progress in realising the promise of the Agenda and is fundamental to achieve those targets related, for example, to healthy living, air quality and the reduction of air pollution. Transport is therefore causally linked with Goals such as number 3 (health and well-being), 9 (industry, innovation and infrastructures), 11 (sustainable cities and communities), and 13 (fight against climate change). Of big significance is the shift from a focus on providing mobility based on individual motorised transport and improved traffic speed to the idea of access to transport, prioritising people and their quality of life, with strong attention to safety and social equity (United Nations 2016). According to the High-Level Advisory Group created by the UN, sustainable transport is 'the provision of services and infrastructure for the mobility of people and goods—economic and social development to benefit today's and future generations—in a manner that is safe, affordable, accessible, efficient and resilient, while minimising carbon and other emissions and environmental impacts'. As Litman (2021) states, common sustainable transport objectives include:

1. Improved transport system diversity. This generally means improving walking, cycling, ride-sharing, public transportation, car-sharing, telework and local delivery services, and creating more walkable and transit-oriented communities.
2. Smart growth of land use development. This includes land-use policies that create more compact, mixed, connected, multi-modal development and provide more affordable housing in accessible, multi-modal locations.
3. Energy conservation and emission reductions. This may include more fuel-efficient vehicles, shifts to alternative fuels, and reductions in total motor vehicle travel. This includes improving the quality of energy-efficient modes, including walking, cycling, ride-sharing, public transit and telework, and increasing land use accessibility.
4. Efficient transport pricing. This includes more cost-based pricing of roads, parking, insurance, fuel, and vehicles.

Demographic trends—including the rising number of older people, as well as the young generation, which increasingly make use of, and are familiar with, the internet, mobile devices and social media—have consequences for transport (Mitrović Dankulov et al. 2020). In particular, accessibility and proximity are crucial for older people, while younger generations are driving trends, including the one favouring the sharing economy. Nevertheless, those trends vary according to the geographical location and their level of development (Crozet et al. 2019). Such attitudes towards sharing and on-demand transport, joining public transport services and shared transport can allow, especially in cities, to move away from the conventional models of car-centric development.

Shared transport is characterised by the involvement of many different stakeholders and complex relationships. Stakeholder theory was first described by R. Edward Freeman (1984) in his landmark book *Strategic Management: A Stakeholder Approach*. Freeman suggests that shareholders are merely one of many stakeholder groups in a company. According to the theory, the stakeholders' setting includes anyone invested and involved in or affected by the company: employees, environmentalists near the company's plants, vendors, governmental agencies and more. Presented theory suggests that a company's real success lies in satisfying all its stakeholders, not just those who might profit from its stock. So, it is about creating value for stakeholders (Freeman et al. 2010). Similarly, sustainable transport should create good value for many of the present, as well as the future stakeholders. In the description of sustainable development included in Agenda 2030, prosperity and attention for all stakeholders are assumed. Those who are affected and who affect—thus all involved in the process of creating new business models in shared mobility—should be satisfied, which often is not possible. In addition, different views and aims make stakeholders take opposite stances. It can be observed in the sharing economy transport sector. Additionally, new emerging means of transport such as electric scooters joining already crowded streets, where the present infrastructure is not enough for the existing traffic, can create conflict between different kinds of users. Different kinds of conflicts are distinguished; however, while taking into consideration shared mobility, the conflict concentrates on the competition between groups within society over limited resources, as well as different interests. There are opposite groups, such as in the case of Uber—taxi drivers that do not accept inequalities and their interests are in opposition. Conflict can take different forms, from hidden antagonism to open fights.

## The European Mobility Ecosystem in Data

According to the European Commission (2019, p. 3), 'transport's activity across Europe is high and set to continue growing, estimates suggest that passenger transport will increase by 42% by 2050, and freight transport by 60%'. In particular, over the past few decades, passenger transport has grown rapidly, and it is expected to follow a similar trend for the future (Eurostat 2020a, b). This unbalanced and rapid growth has resulted in a multitude of effects on people and the environment, including traffic congestion, pollution, and health-related issues, which in the absence of a radical shift towards more sustainable (and maybe shared) means of transportation, will worsen even further in the immediate future.

In order to assess the possible contribution of shared mobility to the transition towards a more sustainable European mobility ecosystem, it is relevant to understand which sectors contribute the most to the current modal split scenario. Considering the EU-28 modal split by mode (Table 5.1), data shows that overall, the car is the most used mode of transportation, accommodating more than 70% of the total trips in 2017. From a historical perspective (last row of Table 5.1), air transport (72.3%) is the sector that grew the most over the last 23 years. Public transport experienced a significant increase for tram and metro (14.3%) and railway (6.2%), while sea transport (−33.3%) and bus and coach (−23.7%) have decreased. As a result, even though the share of the tram, metro and railway (15.8% in 2017) transport is growing over time, public transport is still perceived to be a poor alternative to car use (70.9% in 2017).

In a more detailed way (Table 5.2), in 2017, data about a modal split of passenger transport on land by country shows that overall, the EU-28 passenger relies for 80.9% on cars, while public transport counts for less than 20% in total (with the following shares: 11.7% buses and coaches,

**Table 5.1** EU-28 Performance of modal split by mode (%)

| Year | Passenger cars | P2W | Bus and Coach | Railway | Tram and Metro | Air | Sea |
|---|---|---|---|---|---|---|---|
| 1995 | 73.3 | 2.1 | 9.7 | 6.4 | 1.4 | 6.5 | 0.6 |
| 2000 | 72.9 | 1.8 | 9.2 | 6.4 | 1.4 | 7.8 | 0.5 |
| 2005 | 72.7 | 1.9 | 8.7 | 6.2 | 1.4 | 8.5 | 0.5 |
| 2010 | 72.9 | 1.9 | 8.3 | 6.5 | 1.5 | 8.4 | 0.4 |
| 2015 | 71.6 | 1.9 | 8.0 | 6.8 | 1.6 | 9.7 | 0.3 |
| 2017 | 70.9 | 1.8 | 7.4 | 6.8 | 1.6 | 11.2 | 0.4 |
| ***Variation 1995–2017*** | ***−3.8%*** | ***−14.3%*** | ***−23.7%*** | ***6.2%*** | ***14.3%*** | ***72.3%*** | ***−33.3%*** |

*Notes* Modal split by mode: indicator defined as the percentage share of each mode of transport in total inland transport
*Air and Sea* only domestic and intra EU-28 transport; provisional estimates
*P2W* powered two-wheelers
*Source* Own elaboration based on (EC 2019)

**Table 5.2** EU-28 modal split of passenger transport on land (2017) by country

| | Passenger cars | Buses and coaches | Railways | Trams and metro |
|---|---|---|---|---|
| **EU-28** | **80.9** | **11.7** | **5.7** | **1.7** |
| BE | 81.1 | 10.1 | 7.7 | 1.1 |
| BG | 81.5 | 14.9 | 2.0 | 1.5 |
| CZ | 66.2 | 15.7 | 8.4 | 9.7 |
| DK | 81.2 | 9.9 | 8.5 | 0.5 |
| DE | 84.2 | 5.6 | 8.6 | 1.5 |
| EE | 79.9 | 17.2 | 2.2 | 0.7 |
| IE | 82.3 | 14.3 | 3.1 | 0.3 |
| EL | 81.4 | 16.4 | 0.9 | 1.3 |
| ES | 83.5 | 7.7 | 6.9 | 1.9 |
| FR | 81.0 | 6.2 | 10.9 | 1.8 |
| HR | 82.7 | 13.1 | 2.3 | 1.9 |
| IT | 82.0 | 11.4 | 5.9 | 0.7 |
| CY | 81.0 | 19.0 | – | – |
| LV | 83.8 | 12.1 | 3.3 | 0.7 |
| LT | 91.1 | 8.0 | 0.9 | – |
| LU | 82.9 | 12.4 | 4.7 | – |
| HU | 67.6 | 20.4 | 8.6 | 3.4 |
| MT | 82.5 | 17.5 | – | – |
| NL | 85.3 | 2.8 | 11.3 | 0.5 |
| AT | 72.7 | 9.7 | 11.2 | 6.4 |
| PL | 77.2 | 13.5 | 7.6 | 1.6 |
| PT | 87.6 | 7.0 | 4.3 | 1.1 |
| RO | 75.4 | 14.1 | 4.4 | 6.1 |
| SI | 86.5 | 11.7 | 1.8 | – |
| SK | 73.8 | 15.6 | 9.9 | 0.7 |
| FI | 83.6 | 10.3 | 5.4 | 0.7 |
| SE | 81.7 | 7.0 | 9.4 | 1.9 |
| UK | 84.5 | 5.0 | 8.7 | 1.8 |

*Source* Own elaboration based on (EC 2019)

5.7% railways, 1.7% trams and metro). There are no countries where means of transportation other than cars count for the majority of the modal shift-share. Nevertheless, there are a few countries which show a better distribution among the analysed means, such as Hungary (67.6% passenger cars, 20.4% buses and coaches, 8.6% railways, and 3.4% trams and metro) and the Czech Republic (66.2% passenger cars, 15.7% buses and coaches, 8.4% railways and 9.7% trams and metro).

Overall, these figures reveal that the dependence on the car has accelerated dramatically in most European cities between 1995 and 2017, whereas public transport has remained at very low levels, with some modest success stories (e.g., Hungary, Malta, Estonia, Slovakia for bus and coaches; the Netherlands, Austria, and France for railways and the Czech Republic, Austria; and Romania for trams and metro). Clearly, car dependence has a series of implications for the future sustainability of cities, and shared mobility can play a key role in a transition towards a more sustainable European mobility ecosystem.

The access to actual figures of shared mobility services is still limited and what can be presented in this chapter represents a non-exhaustive overview. Nevertheless, some data about the principal sharing schemes available in Europe can help to understand this fast-evolving sector and might contribute to highlight possible synergies with other transport modes—especially with public transport.

## Car-Based Sharing Models: Evolution and Recent Trends

The car-based sharing landscape in Europe is evolving rapidly. Systems can vary from: vehicles available for self-drive (e.g., public such as Car Sharing Rome, or private such as Share Now); services provided by private car owners, who provide for-hire rides such as ride-hailing—to parallel a taxi service (e.g., Uber or Lyft), or ride-sharing—individuals offering to share their vehicle on usually longer journeys (e.g., BlaBlaCar); to car-pooling where associates and employees of individual companies can select a car from a fleet of vehicles as required.

About services where people 'pay for a ride' such as Uber or BlaBlaCar—stressing that the first one is more similar to taxi service—the landscape of these services in Europe is very varied. In some countries such as Italy, Germany, Hungary, France, Finland, and the Netherlands, the strict regulation in the taxi industry makes it difficult for concepts such as Uber to penetrate while ride-sharing is allowed. In countries such as the United Kingdom, apps, e.g., Uber and Gett, can operate because they have been properly regulated, and BlaBlaCar is becoming increasingly popular (Schiller et al. 2017).

About the use of car-sharing, the EU-funded project *Shared mobility opportunities And challenges foR European citieS* (STARS) in 2018 reported and assessed different aspects of the majority of European car-sharing services (about 90% of the total), with 186 analysed car-sharing services spread over 25 countries (Rodenbach et al. 2018). According to this research, the most diverse selection of car-sharing services is found in Germany—with 155 available at the time of publication. They found that Belgium, France, Italy, the Netherlands and the UK also offered a large number of car-sharing services. Furthermore, some of the schemes are cross-border, operating in a number of national territories. The researchers identified Share Now, Zipcar, Communauto, Snappcar and Carmigo as enjoying a more dominant market position due to their more 'international approach' (Rodenbach et al. 2018).

In the past few years, car-sharing has gained popularity due to several positive factors, such as reduced travel costs, traffic congestion and emissions. Before the pandemic, almost 1000 cities worldwide have offered car-sharing services (Movmi 2019). However, the COVID-19 outbreak's impact on the sector is huge, and 'the car-sharing market is estimated to lose its share by 50–60% during 2020' (MarketsandMarkets Research Private Ltd. 2020). Even though evidence-based research on the impact of COVID-19 measures on a modal share of private and public transport are still scarce (Bucsky 2020), some study argues that private car usage increased dramatically during the pandemic while car-sharing lost its shared as a 'result of the WHO recommendations to maintain social distancing and avoid sharing the same space with multiple people' (Articonf 2020).

## Bike-Sharing: A Fast-Growing Sector

Bike-sharing systems (BSS) have experienced a significant evolution over time. From a technological point of view, BSS available in Europe today belong mainly to (i) the third generation systems, where bicycles can be borrowed or rented from an automated station or 'docking stations' (bike racks) that lock the vehicle and only release it by computer control (in this system the bike can be returned at any station belonging to the same system) and (ii) the fourth-generation systems where: free-floating bikes (dockless bikes) are available on-demand using mobile phone apps and Global Positioning System (GPS) technologies.

Due to the rapid changes in BSS systems, and the dynamic of the market providers, it is almost impossible to quantify the number of bikes available in Europe. There are some estimates based on a variety of sources that cannot be considered definitive numbers. A Bike Share World Map has been made available by Google (Meddin et al. 2020) in order to localise bike-sharing schemes all over the world. At the date of publishing, according to Wikipedia, Europe counts 190,000 bicycles available for sharing (Wikipedia 2020).

Countries such as Spain, France, the United Kingdom and Italy have the largest number of such schemes, which are all but absent in 'cycling countries' such as the Netherlands and Denmark. Bike-sharing schemes, therefore, seem to be most relevant where bicycle ownership is not (yet) peaking (European Commission 2020).

The sector has been affected by the COVID-19 pandemic. Interestingly, recent research (a case study about Budapest in Hungary, for the limited period of March 2020) shows that bike-sharing became more popular due to rapid virus containment measures, while other shared mobility systems saw a lower-than-average decrease. The restrictions to people's mobility due to the pandemic caused, in fact, the lowest decrease of every mean of transport for cycling and bike-sharing in particular (23 and 2%, respectively) (Bucsky 2020).

## Electric Scooter Sharing: A New-Born Means of Shared Mobility

Similar to what happened in 2018 across the United States, within the past two years, a wave of electric scooter (e-scooter) operators has emerged in European cities. As of March 2020, Paris and Berlin appear to be the hub of e-scooter sharing in Europe, followed by Madrid and Stockholm. At the end of 2019, e-scooter sharing in Europe was available in 112 cities (Mobility Foresights 2020). The rapid explosion of companies offering electric scooters in Europe presumably took advantage of a reluctance of people to use public transport during the COVID-19 pandemic, when, in fact, almost '93% of the new riders were turned into regular riders, i.e., more than four rides per week, which is a greater conversion than pre-COVID times' (Mobility Foresights 2020). Due to the increased demand for sustainable transport, many cities promoted e-scooters by both investing in cities' infrastructures (e.g., renovating bicycle paths and/or increasing their length) and in terms of monetary subsidies provided by the government (e.g., subsidies or tax discounts for the purchase of bikes and/or e-scooters).

The increased use and availability of e-scooters in European cities brings opportunities for sustainable transport, but at the same time, the cycling infrastructure needs significant improvement in order to accommodate both bicycles and e-scooters; adequate parking areas are necessary to provide a safer environment for e-scooter use and, at a more general level, the e-scooter invasion on the streets imposes a series of challenges for those managing the public space. As a consequence, a series of regulation challenges have emerged. These are mainly related to the following topics: (i) the spaces where e-scooters can be used (e.g., roads, bike lanes, pavements, pedestrian areas); (ii) their compliance with safety rules (e.g., helmet, lights and turn signals); (iii) age requirements for their users; (iv) the need to re-establish local government competencies in micro-mobility management; and (v) training requirements (e.g., driving licence) (Eltis 2020).

## Conflicts and Tensions Around Shared Mobility Uses

This section presents the challenges that stem from shared mobility experiences identified within the COST Action *From Sharing to Caring: Examining Socio-Technical Aspects of the Collaborative Economy* gathered from twenty-six country reports on the main trends in the sharing economy regulation and practices by 2019 (Klimczuk et al. 2021) and twenty-eight short stories (Sharing and Caring 2020) that presented shared mobility practices from all over Europe in a concise format.

Two main types of challenge, one at the micro-level and another at the macro-level, have been uncovered by the meta-analysis of the country reports and short stories with regard to the shared mobility ecosystem in Europe. At the micro-level, conflicts derived from the uses of sharing mobility schemes are referring to bike-sharing or e-scooter sharing and ride-sourcing (platforms to book a ride/taxi), while at the macro level, inadequate regulations are the source of tensions linked either directly or indirectly to the collaborative economy in general, and to the shared mobility in particular. However, tensions at both levels stem from two questions: (1) who has the right of way, i.e., 'who is the dominant or preferential user of public spaces – including roads, streets, pavements, and parking areas (motor vehicles vs micro-mobility, i.e., passengers, cyclists, or e-scooters)?' and (2) 'how are responsibilities allocated in terms of liability, taxation, and social contribution?'.

The micro-level conflicts emerge due to the rapid growth of bike and e-scooter sharing schemes in a general situation where dockless vehicles are left disorderly on the sidewalks. This exasperates locals in many ways across Europe, from Lisbon, where an urgent need for more thorough legislation is requested by the public (Bettega et al. 2021) through Prague, where these businesses triggered a number of conflicts in connection to issues ranging from parking and safety to legislation, taxation and liability issues (Munzarova 2019), to Oslo, where e-scooters generated particular concerns for the safety of the blind pedestrians and also for the limitations of e-scooter use in winter (Halvorsen et al. 2021).

The conflicts triggered by the new taxi service platforms, such as Uber, Cabify, Taxify (Bolt) and others, are related to the revendications of unfair competition between these new services and the traditional taxi services. In many European cities, taxi drivers' professional associations have organised protests that have led the governments to change transportation regulations. The tensions between collaborative and traditional taxi services followed diverse trends:

1. 'The unification', which can lead to two different directions: either opening the market for taxi drivers to operate without being subordinated to a central office and requiring taxi licences, such as in Norway and Slovenia, where it is legislated but not applied yet (Halvorsen et al. 2021; Završnik et al. 2021); or making it compulsory for new forms of on-demand ride-services to acquire taxi licenses, as in Poland (Lukasiewicz and Nadolska 2021) and in Finland, where after the transportation deregulation reform, taxi companies and Uber were addressed by the same law and thus can operate under the same conditions (Lanamaki 2018).
2. 'The prohibition of platforms', e.g., in Hungary or Serbia (Simonovits et al. 2021; Ćirić et al. 2021), which often opens a market niche for new players which was left by the prohibited service (e.g., Uber), or, in some cases, had no effective results since the activity is still provided illegally.
3. 'Introducing various forms of specific regulation', even within a country, such as in Germany, where the federal car-sharing law has not yet been fully implemented, while some states and municipalities allowed the designation of public parking areas for car-sharing vehicles (BCS 2019). In 2017, the Spanish government's regulation established the obligation to communicate every transport route that a platform provides, and in 2018, limited their services to interurban routes. Different autonomous regions applied specific restrictions to the use of P2P transport platforms, for instance, the Balearic Islands and Catalonia, in 2019, limiting these services to 'a minimum period of 15 minutes to contract the transportation services' (Garcia-Teruel 2021). In Portugal, in 2018, the new law regulated Uber and similar services by imposing three conditions: drivers must hold driving licences for at least three years and are required to obtain a certificate of a driver of a vehicle operating through digital platforms; cars must be no older than seven years (Bettega et al. 2021).
4. 'Adaptation of the service providers' either by the new or the old actor in the specific market is another way to relieve the tension. In Italy, for example, after being banned for its standard service, Uber withdrew the service for which it had become famous (private drivers with no taxi licence) in favour of its business-class services (Uber Black

and Uber Lux), which recruits only licenced drivers. The new strategy involves adaptation to local regulations, and cooperation with other market actors, offering them a scheme that increases their income by optimising bookings and working times (Valerio et al. 2021). On the contrary, in Iceland, the traditional taxi company had to adapt to the new situation when their monopoly was abolished by the state due to the increasing demand, which the one and only official taxi company was unable to meet. As new service providers entered the market, the taxi company had to adapt by using a digital platform similar to Uber as an alternative to the traditional phone-based call system (Karlsson 2019).

In some cities, the tensions between new and traditional taxi service providers eventually led to protests and civil conflicts, including physical violence incidents between taxi drivers and platform drivers, and sometimes even with their customers, for example, in Hungary or Portugal (Bettega et al. 2021; Simonovits et al. 2021). Tensions on similar grounds also emerged in some German federal states or municipalities where taxi drivers' associations have tried to stall the expansion of such services both through the courts and on the streets, organising public protests against the new ride-sharing services, driven by the assumption that these new providers with lower rates could be cross-subsidised across locations, marginalising fixed-rate (and more regulated) local services, that work on a traditional, established business model (Zehle et al. 2021).

The macro-level issues around shared mobility derived from inadequate legal frameworks existing in many countries (e.g., in Albania, Bulgaria, Czech Republic, France, Georgia, Hungary, Italy or Lithuania, among others, see Klimczuk et al. 2021), which directly or indirectly affect both shared mobility providers and users. One typical issue for the lack of proper regulation is the vulnerable situation of the platform workers in ride-sharing services. The weak labour market position of the platform workers, their unclear rights and obligations are open issues in some countries, such as Bulgaria or Hungary (Baltova and Vutsova 2021; Simonovits et al. 2021). Closely connected to the field of informal and undeclared work, these can have negative effects at micro and macro levels: it is disadvantageous at the micro-level for the platform workers due to insecurity and long-term losses (e.g., unemployment benefit, pension), although it might be beneficial on the short run due to tax and social security contributions avoidance.

On the other hand, the possible macro-level losses derive from the unregulated sharing economy sector burdens on the economy and society. The example from the Czech Republic demonstrates how current taxation, social security and health insurance regulations and visa obligations can be breached by ride-sharing companies to employ third-country nationals. Drivers from the former Soviet Union countries were recruited, via online ads in Russian, to come to Prague on a tourist visa and work as drivers in ride-hailing companies (Tetrevova 2021). France deals with two main issues regarding regulations affecting platforms and platform workers, but mainly from the macro-economic aspect (Barbezieux and Herody 2019): one is to ensure the tax contribution of platforms to national/local budgets, while the other is to clarify the position of tax authorities on the distinction between income and cost-sharing and that of the social administration on the notion of professional activity (Lewkowicz 2021). The latter issue is embedded into the general discussion in France on the ambiguous status of workers in the collaborative economy who are considered 'legally independent' but 'economically dependent' (Institut Montaigne 2019).

## Shared Mobility in the Time of COVID-19

Before the pandemic, shared mobility, vehicle sharing schemes and trip sharing gained in popularity. However, the situation has been changing since the World Health Organization (WHO) officially declared the outbreak of the COVID-19 virus in March 2020. The general idea during the crisis has been to significantly reduce movement, as well as keep a social distance, but these indications do not match the sharing mobility model, especially in the cases of car and trip sharing schemes. As a consequence, a significant drop in the use of shared modes of transportation has been observed, and real-time ride-sharing and the industry has very quickly lost both passengers and profits (Andersson et al. 2020). According to Andersson et al. (2020), only 5–8% of respondents think that car-sharing, ride-sharing, or shared micro-mobility are safe from a health standpoint. Subsequently, 7% feel public transportation is safe, and 81% consider private vehicles safe. Concerning those safety issues, people have changed their mobility patterns greatly. Furthermore, ride-hailing companies in multiple geographies have experienced a 60–70% decline in passengers during the COVID-19 crisis.

Supposedly, the post-lockdown world will impose significant challenges in developing shared modes usage. Mobility solutions will have to tackle critical aspects, in particular, ensuring safe and healthy commuting modes. In this scenario, cycling and walking might be favoured as they make it easier to maintain physical distance. Additionally, by strengthening multi-modal and complementary integration with public transport, shared mobility service markets could be significantly revived.

So far, many Europe-wide local authorities have begun to encourage this trend well before the outbreak of the pandemic (Lozzi et al. 2020). In fact, these services require careful integration into the local transport system, thus avoiding risks such as the increase of unnecessary travel. Given the need for more flexible public transport, shared vehicles, such as electric cars, bicycles, e-scooters, can become part of the offer, providing more integrated transport solutions.

An efficient and more sustainable transportation system needs, in fact, increasing the diversity of transportation means (Litman 2021) while diminishing the use and circulation of vehicles, as well as moving towards more efficient modes of transportation such as public transport, walking, cycling and shared modes. Although private cars often represent users' preferred options for reasons of flexibility and comfort, a main social and environmental goal is to reduce traffic, congestion and air emissions while improving people's health and well-being. Shared mobility, promoting the use of fewer vehicles to move the same number of users, can contribute to reaching these goals.

## Summary

Shared mobility systems have become a common feature of the modern urban landscape in many European cities (Shaheen et al. 2015), providing residents and visitors with a new mode of sustainable transportation. Shared systems have gained popularity, especially among young generations, while this is not always true for older people or disadvantaged groups for whom technological issues, accessibility and geographical locations can represent significant barriers to the access and/or use of such services. Indeed, usage of smartphone apps aggregating information about real-time travel, options, in addition to optimisation of routes for travellers, have occurred as an important component of shared mobility but can constitute exclusion factors for 'some' potential users.

Recently, holistic transport system approaches for providing more integrated transport solutions, in the framework of the sharing economy, namely the Mobility as a Service (MaaS) concept, have been developed. The most important of these, as in collaborative consumption, are based on services that promote the shift away from personally owned modes of transportation, especially cars.

Nevertheless, unbalanced and rapid socio-economic growth has resulted in a multitude of effects on society, as well as the environment—including traffic congestion, pollution and health-related issues—which in the absence of a radical shift towards more sustainable (and possibly shared) means of transportation, might worsen even further in the immediate future.

In this scenario, shared mobility might play a key role in a transition towards a more sustainable European mobility system. However, sustainability in the transport sector is hard to achieve, as a variety of stakeholders are involved. The shortage of resources, the unwillingness to share benefits and opposite interests can lead to conflicts. Also, the appearance of new services such as electric scooters sharing—adding pressure on the existing, limited infrastructure and in the absence of clear regulations—can generate additional frictions.

The assumptions of sustainable development depicted in Agenda 2030 are aimed at prosperity and attention for all stakeholders. Thus, all parts involved in the process of creating new business models in shared mobility should be considered and possibly satisfied.

The COVID-19 pandemic exacerbated some issues and limitations to the achievement of sustainable development goals connected to the transport sector and mobility in particular, and because of the many restrictions introduced in order to limit the spread of the diseases, a factual shift away from personally owned modes of transportation and towards mobility provided as a service might be compromised. The general indication to significantly reduce movements as well as keep social distance, in particular, does not match the assumptions of sharing mobility, especially in the case of car-sharing, trip sharing schemes. That is why there has been a big drop in using shared modes of transportation, real-time ride-sharing has significantly diminished, and the industry has very quickly lost both passengers and profits (Andersson et al. 2020).

The dynamic and uncertainty of the current situation indicate, therefore, a further transition. Notwithstanding, by strengthening multimodal and complementary integration with public transport, shared mobility service markets could be significantly revived. The main goal is to reduce the production of pollution and traffic congestion while increasing health and well-being. Sharing mobility, using fewer vehicles to move the same number of users can equally contribute to reaching these goals.

## References

Andersson, Lennart, Andreas Gläfke, Timo Möller, and Tobias Schneiderbauer. 2020. *Why Shared Mobility Is Poised to Make a Comeback after the Crisis*. Atlanta: McKinsey & Co. Accessed November 15, 2020. https://www.mckinsey.com/~/media/McKinsey/Industries/AutomotiveandAssembly/OurInsights/Whysharedmobilityispoisedtomakeacomebackafterthecrisis/Why-shared-mobility-is-poised-to-make-a-comeback-after-the-crisis-vF.pdf?shouldIndex=false.

Articonf. 2020. 'How COVID-19 Affects Carsharing? Ridesharing Business Post-Pandemic.' Accessed November 15, 2020. https://articonf.eu/how-covid-19-affects-carsharing/.

Baltova, Stela, and Albena Vutsova. 2021. 'Setting the Stage of the Sharing Economy: The Case of Bulgaria.' In *The Collaborative Economy in Action: European Perspectives*, edited by Andrzej Klimczuk, Vida Česnuitytė, and Gabriela Avram. Limerick, Ireland: University of Limerick.

Barbezieux, Philippe, and Camille Herody. 2019. 'Rapport Au Premier Ministre Sur l'économie Collaborative. Mission Confiée à Pascal Terrasse Député de l'Ardeche.' Hôtel de Matignon. Accessed March 15, 2021. https://www.gouvernement.fr/sites/default/files/document/document/2016/02/08.02.2016_rapport_au_premier_ministre_sur_leconomie_collaborative.pdf.

BCS (Bundesverband CarSharing). 2019. *CarSharing in Deutschland Jahresbericht [Annual Report] 2018/19*. Berlin: Bundesverband CarSharing e.V.

Bettega, Mela, Raul Masu, and Alves Pereira Diogo, Vera Lúcia. 2021. 'Collaborative Economy in Portugal: The Recent Evolution.' In *The Collaborative Economy in Action: European Perspectives*, edited by Andrzej Klimczuk, Vida Česnuitytė, and Gabriela Avram. Limerick, Ireland: University of Limerick.

Bucsky, Péter. 2020. 'Modal Share Changes Due to COVID-19: The Case of Budapest.' *Transportation Research Interdisciplinary Perspectives* vol. 8: 100141. Accessed May 10, 2021. https://doi.org/10.1016/j.trip.2020.100141.

Ćirić, Maja, Svetlana Ignjatijević, Aleksandra Fedajev, Marija Panić, Dejan Sekulić, Tanja Stanišić, Miljan Leković, and Sanela Arsić. 2021. 'Serbia: Sharing Economy as a New Market Trend and Business Model.' In *The Collaborative Economy in Action: European Perspectives*, edited by Andrzej Klimczuk, Vida Česnuitytė, and Gabriela Avram. Limerick, Ireland: University of Limerick.

CIVITAS (Cleaner and Better Transport in Cities). 2016. *Smart Choices for Cities. Cities towards Mobility 2.0: Connect, Share and Go!* Porto: CIVITAS Initiative.

Crozet, Yves, Georgina Santos, and Jean Coldefy. 2019. *Shared Mobility, MaaS and the Regulatory Challenges of Urban Mobility*. Brussels: Centre on Regulation in Europe CERRE. Accessed March 8, 2021. https://cerre.eu/wp-content/uploads/2020/07/190827_CERRE_MaaS_FinalReport.pdf.

Elkington, John Brett. 1999. *Cannibals with Forks: The Triple Bottom Line of Sustainability. New Society Publishers*. Oxford: Capstone Publishing.https://doi.org/10.1002/tqem.3310080106.

Eltis. 2020. 'Overview of Policy Relating to E-Scooters in European Countries.' 2020. https://www.eltis.org/resources/case-studies/overview-policy-relating-e-scooters-european-countries.

European Commission. 2016. 'A European Agenda for the Collaborative Economy.' COM(2016) 356 final. *Communication from the Commission to the European Parliament, the European Economic and Social Committee of the Regions*. Accessed November 15, 2020. Brussels: European Commission. https://ec.europa.eu/docsroom/documents/16881/attachments/2/translations/en/renditions/pdf.

European Commission. 2019. *Transport in the European Union Current Trends and Issues*. Brussels: European Commission, Directorate-General Mobility and Transport. Accessed November 15, 2020. https://ec.europa.eu/transport/sites/transport/files/2019-transport-in-the-eu-current-trends-and-issues.pdf.

European Commission. 2020. 'Walking and Cycling as Transport Modes | Mobility and Transport.' Accessed November 15, 2020. https://ec.europa.eu/transport/road_safety/specialist/knowledge/pedestrians/pedestrians_and_cyclists_unprotected_road_users/walking_and_cycling_as_transport_modes_en.

Eurostat. 2020a. *Eurostat Regional Yearbook*. Luxembourg: Publications Office of the European Union. Accessed March 8, 2021. https://doi.org/10.2785/98733.

Eurostat. 2020b. 'Transport Statistics at Regional Level.' Statistics Explained. Accessed March 8, 2021. https://ec.europa.eu/eurostat/statisticsexplained/.

Freeman, R. Edward. 1984. *Strategic Management: A Stakeholder Approach*. Boston: Pitman.

Freeman, R. Edward, Jeffrey S. Harrison, Andrew C. Wicks, Bidhan L. Parmar, and Simon de Colle. 2010. *Stakeholder Theory: The State of the Art*. Cambridge: Cambridge University Press.

Garcia-Teruel, Rosa M. 2021. 'An Introduction to the Collaborative Economy in Spain.' In *The Collaborative Economy in Action: European Perspectives*, edited by Andrzej Klimczuk, Vida Česnuitytė, and Gabriela Avram. Limerick, Ireland: University of Limerick.

Halvorsen, Trond, Christoph Lutz, and Johan Barstad. 2021. 'The Sharing Economy in Norway: Emerging Trends and Debates.' In *The Collaborative Economy in Action: European Perspectives*, edited by Andrzej Klimczuk, Vida Česnuitytė, and Gabriela Avram. Limerick, Ireland: University of Limerick.

Institut Montaigne. 2019. 'Travailleurs Des Plateformes: Liberté Oui, Protection Aussi.' Paris: Institut Montaigne. Accessed March 8, 2021. https://www.institutmontaigne.org/ressources/pdfs/publications/travailleurs-des-plateformes-liberte-oui-protection-aussi-rapport.pdf.

Karlsson, Emil. 2019. 'Transforming the 'Uber-Model' into a Cooperative.' COST Action Sharing and Caring, Short Stories. Accessed March 8, 2021. http://sharingandcaring.eu/case-study/transforming-uber-model-cooperative.

Klimczuk, Andrzej, Vida Česnuitytė, and Gabriela Avram, eds. 2021. *The Collaborative Economy in Action: European Perspectives.* Limerick, Ireland: University of Limerick.

Lanamaki, Arto. 2018. 'Uber in Helsinki, Finland, after the Deregulation in July 2018.' COST Action Sharing and Caring, Short Stories. Accessed March 8, 2021. http://sharingandcaring.eu/case-study/uber-helsinki-finland-after-deregulation-july-2018.

Lewkowicz, Myriam. 2021. 'France: An Ecosystem Favourable to the Development of the Sharing Economy.' In *The Collaborative Economy in Action: European Perspectives*, edited by Andrzej Klimczuk, Vida Česnuitytė, and Gabriela Avram. Limerick, Ireland: University of Limerick.

Litman, Todd. 2021. 'Developing Indicators for Sustainable and Livable Transport Planning.' Victoria Transport Policy Institute. Accessed March 8, 2021. http://www.vtpi.org/wellmeas.pdf.

Lozzi, Giacomo, Maria Rodrigues, Edoardo Marcucci, Tharsis Teoh, Valerio Gatta, and Valerio Pacelli. 2020. *Research for TRAN Committee: COVID-19 and Urban Mobility: Impacts and Perspectives.* Brussels: European Parliament, Policy Department for Structural and Cohesion Policies. Accessed November 15, 2020. https://www.europarl.europa.eu/thinktank/en/document.html?reference=IPOL_IDA(2020)652213.

Lukasiewicz, Agnieszka, and Aleksandra Nadolska. 2021. 'Poland: Country Report on the Sharing Economy.' In *The Collaborative Economy in Action: European Perspectives*, edited by Andrzej Klimczuk, Vida Česnuitytė, and Gabriela Avram. Limerick, Ireland: University of Limerick.

Machado, Cláudia A. Soares, Nicolas Patrick Marie de Salles Hue, Fernando Tobal Berssaneti, and José Alberto Quintanilha. 2018. 'An Overview of Shared Mobility.' *Sustainability (Switzerland)* 10 (12): 1–21. https://doi.org/10.3390/su10124342.

MarketsandMarkets Research Private Ltd. 2020 'COVID-19 Impact on Ride Sharing Market by Service Type, Data Service, and Region: Forecast to

2021.' Accessed November 15, 2020. https://www.marketsandmarkets.com/Market-Reports/covid-19-impact-on-ride-sharing-market-15098676.html.

Meddin, Russell, Paul DeMaio, Oliver O'Brien, Renata Rabello, Chumin Yu, Jess Seamon, Thiago Benicchio, Deng Han, and Jacob Mason. 2020. 'The Meddin Bike-Sharing World Map.' Accessed November 15, 2020. http://bikesharingworldmap.com/.

Mitrović Dankulov, Marija, Maria Del Mar Alonso-Almeida, Fariya Sharmeen, and Agnieszka Lukasiewicz. 2020. 'Social Networks Theory: Definitions and Practice.' In *Digital Social Networks and Travel Behaviour in Urban Environments*, edited by Pnina O. Plaut and Dalit Shach-Pinsly, 7–26. Milton Park, Abingdon, Oxon; New York, NY: Routledge. https://doi.org/10.4324/9780429488719.

Mobility Foresights. 2020. 'E Scooter Sharing Market 2019–2024.' Accessed December 15, 2020. https://mobilityforesights.com/product/scooter-sharing-market-report/.

Movmi. 2019. 'Car-Sharing Industry: Carsharing Market & Growth 2019.' 2019. Accessed December 15, 2020. https://movmi.net/carsharing-market-growth-2019/.

Munzarova, Simona. 2019. 'Electric Scooter Sharing: LIME in the Czech Republic.' COST Action Sharing and Caring, Short Stories. 2019. Accessed December 15, 2020. http://sharingandcaring.eu/case-study/electric-scooter-sharing-lime-czech-republic.

Rodenbach, Johannes, Jeffrey Mathis, Andrea Chicco, Marco Diana, Johannes Rodenbach Marco Diana, Peter Wells, and Stefano Beccaria. 2018. 'Car Sharing in Europe: A Multidimensional Classification and Inventory.' Deliverable D2.1, Research and Innovation action H2020-MG-2016–2017, *Shared Mobility Opportunities and Challenges foR European Cities.* Torino. Accessed March 8, 2021. http://stars-h2020.eu/wp-content/uploads/2019/06/STARS-D2.1.pdf.

Santos, Georgina. 2018. 'Sustainability and Shared Mobility Models.' *Sustainability* 10 (3194): 1–13. https://doi.org/10.3390/su10093194.

Schiller, Thomas, Julia Scheidl, and Thomas Pottebaum. 2017. 'Car Sharing in Europe: Business Models, National Variations and Upcoming Disruptions.' *Monitor Deloitte*, no. 6: 1–8. Accessed March 15, 2021. https://www2.deloitte.com/content/dam/Deloitte/de/Documents/consumer-industrial-products/CIP-Automotive-Car-Sharing-in-Europe.pdf.

Shaheen, Susan, Nelson Chan, Apaar Bansal, and Adam Cohen. 2015. *Shared Mobility: A Sustainability & Technologies Workshop: Definitions, Industry*

*Developments, and Early Understanding*. Berkley, CA: University of California. Accessed March 15, 2021. https://escholarship.org/content/qt2f61q30s/qt2f61q30s.pdf.
Sharing and Caring COST Action CA16121. 2020. 'Short Stories.' Accessed November 15, 2020. http://sharingandcaring.eu/short-stories.
Simonovits, Bori, Anikó Bernát, and Bálint Balázs. 2021. 'The Fragile Landscape of the Sharing Economy in Hungary.' In *The Collaborative Economy in Action: European Perspectives*, edited by Andrzej Klimczuk, Vida Česnuitytė, and Gabriela Avram. Limerick, Ireland: University of Limerick.
Standing, Craig, Susan Standing, and Sharon Biermann. 2019. 'The Implications of the Sharing Economy Fortransport.' *Transport Reviews* 39 (2): 226–42. https://doi.org/10.1080/01441647.2018.1450307.
Tetrevova, Libena. 2021. 'The Sharing Economy in Practice in the Czech Republic: A Small Post-Communist Economy.' In *The Collaborative Economy in Action: European Perspectives*, edited by Andrzej Klimczuk, Vida Česnuitytė, and Gabriela Avram. Limerick, Ireland: University of Limerick.
United Nations. 2016. *Mobilising Sustainable Transport for Development. Analysis and Policy Recommendations from the United Nations Secretary-General's High-Level Advisory Group on Sustainable Transport.* New York, NY: United Nations. https://doi.org/10.18356/2c1884f4-en.
UNPF (United Nations Population Fund). 2015. *Transforming Our World: The 2030 Agenda for Sustainable Development. A/RES/70/1.* New York: United Nations Population Fund. Accessed November 15, 2020. https://www.unfpa.org/sites/default/files/resource-pdf/Resolution_A_RES_70_1_EN.pdf.
Valerio, Stefano, Monica Postiglione, Venere Stefania Sanna, Chiara Bassetti, and Giulia Priora. 2021. 'Italian Style: Legislative Developments in Accommodation, Mobility, Food, Delivery, and Transport in Italy's Collaborative and Sharing Economy.' In *The Collaborative Economy in Action: European Perspectives*, edited by Andrzej Klimczuk, Vida Česnuitytė, and Gabriela Avram. Limerick, Ireland: University of Limerick. Forthcoming.
Wikipedia. 2020. 'List of Bicycle-Sharing Systems.' Accessed November 15, 2020. https://en.wikipedia.org/wiki/List_of_bicycle-sharing_systems.
World Commission on Environment and Development. 1987. *Our Common Future*. New York: United Nations. Accessed February 7, 2021. https://sustainabledevelopment.un.org/content/documents/5987our-common-future.pdf.

Završnik, Aleš, Katja Simončič, Manja Kitek Kuzman, and Tomaž Kušar. 2021. 'A Snapshot of Slovenia's Collaborative Economy.' In *The Collaborative Economy in Action: European Perspectives*, edited by Andrzej Klimczuk, Vida Česnuitytė, and Gabriela Avram. Limerick, Ireland: University of Limerick.

Zehle, Soenke, Hannes Käfer, Julia Hartnik, and Michael Schmitz. 2021. 'Germany: Co-creating Cooperative and Sharing Economies.' In *The Collaborative Economy in Action: European Perspectives*, edited by Andrzej Klimczuk, Vida Česnuitytė, and Gabriela Avram. Limerick, Ireland: University of Limerick.

## Suggested Readings

Cohen, Boyd, and Jan Kietzmann. 2014. 'Ride On! Mobility Business Models for the Sharing Economy.' *Organization & Environment* 27 (3): 279–296.

Nail, Thomas. 2018. *The Ontology of Motion*. Edinburgh: Edinburgh University Press. https://doi.org/10.1215/10418385-438298.

Sassen, Saskia. 2014. *Expulsions: Brutality and Complexity in the Global Economy*. Cambridge, MA: Harvard University Press.

Vaughan, Robert, and Raphael Daverio. 2017. *Assessing the Size and Presence of the Collaborative Economy in Europe*. Brussels: European Commission, Directorate-General for Internal Market, Industry, Entrepreneurship and SMEs. https://doi.org/10.2873/971404.

## Relevant Websites

CIVITAS (Cleaner and Better Transport in Cities): https://civitas-initiative.eu.

European Commission webpage about the urban mobility issues. https://ec.europa.eu/transport/themes/urban/urban_mobility_en.

The European Cyclists' Federation (ECF): https://ecf.com/topics/bike-sharing.

World Transit Research: https://www.worldtransitresearch.info.

# 6

# Peer-To-Peer Accommodation in Europe: Trends, Challenges and Opportunities

Anna Farmaki and Cristina Miguel

## Introduction

Supported by the principles of the sharing economy (Belk 2014) and enabled by technological advances (Gupta et al. 2019), peer-to-peer (P2P) accommodation platforms emerge as new marketplaces to exchange unused accommodation capacity. While there are non-for-profit P2P accommodation platforms such as CouchSurfing (Chen 2018; Miguel 2018) and HomeExchange (Sdrali et al. 2015; Chung 2017), online paid P2P accommodation (Dolnicar 2019), which includes P2P rental platforms and vacation rental platforms, represents the largest

A. Farmaki (✉)
Faculty of Management and Economics, Cyprus University of Technology, Limassol, Cyprus
e-mail: anna.farmaki@cut.ac.cy

C. Miguel
Department of Applied IT, Gothenburg University, Gothenburg, Sweden
e-mail: cristina.miguel@ait.gu.se



V. Česnuitytė et al. (eds.), *The Sharing Economy in Europe*,
https://doi.org/10.1007/978-3-030-86897-0_6

sector of the sharing economy in terms of the transaction value (PwC 2016). Companies such as Airbnb, HomeAway and 9Flats have been able to generate a new output of rooms for people to stay in, without the need to create new assets or increase the number of human resources in the company. P2P accommodation occurs when individuals offer a room or an entire property for short-term accommodation. The annual growth rate for global P2P accommodation is estimated at 31% between 2013 and 2025, six times the growth rate of traditional bed-and-breakfasts and hostels (Bakker and Twining-Ward 2018). The World Economic Forum (2017) predicts that by 2025, the global hotel sector's annual revenue from short-term rentals will increase from 7 to 17%, resulting in the migration of $8 billion in annual profits from the hotel industry to the P2P accommodation market sector. Nevertheless, these growth figures have been highly impacted by the effects of the COVID-19 pandemic on tourism and hospitality (AllTheRooms 2020; Hall et al. 2020).

Several attempts were made by researchers to understand the drivers of the P2P accommodation phenomenon. Relevant studies point towards a range of benefits offered to both tourists (guests) and service providers (hosts), which in essence explain the rapid growth of P2P accommodation in Europe (Sthapit and Jimenez-Barreto 2018; Sung et al. 2018). Table 6.1 illustrates the main benefits offered by P2P accommodation to both guests and hosts.

In the case of hospitality exchange platforms, such as CouchSurfing and HomeExchange, the motivation to use these services revolve around saving money (Sdrali et al. 2015; Decrop et al. 2018); building relationships and/or make new friends (Kim et al. 2018; Aydin and Duyan 2019); finding (sexual) partners (Miguel 2018); sharing experiences, intimate information, knowledge and skills (Aydin and Duyan 2019); enjoying helping others (Kim et al. 2018); living 'like a local' (Sdrali et al. 2015; Chung 2017) and sustainability (Forno and Garibaldi 2015).

P2P accommodation platforms offer a number of opportunities, mainly related to the empowerment of individuals in generating revenue using existing assets. This is argued to be a sustainable business model that further democratises tourism by improving the amount and type of accommodation offered and by reducing hotels prices, which is ultimately beneficial for the end-user (Guttentag 2015; Forgacs and

**Table 6.1** Benefits of P2P accommodation to guests and hosts

| | Relevant studies |
|---|---|
| Guests | |
| Value for money | Chen and Chang (2018), Tussyadiah and Pesonen (2018), Tran and Filimonau (2020) |
| Seeking authentic experiences | Bucher et al. (2018), Paulauskaite et al. (2017), Shuqair et al. (2019) |
| Interaction with locals | Guttentag et al. (2018), Moon et al. (2019), Zhu et al. (2019) |
| Attributes of the properties | Belarmino et al. (2019), Tran and Filimonau (2020) |
| Environmental motives | Agag (2019), Böcker and Meelen (2017) |
| Hosts | |
| Income generation | Fang et al. (2016), Lutz and Newlands (2018), Sung et al. (2018), Stienmetz et al. (2020) |
| Social interaction | Karlsson and Dolnicar (2016), Farmaki and Stergiou (2019) |

*Source* Own elaboration

Dolnicar 2017; Hajibaba and Dolnicar 2018). On the other hand, P2P accommodation platforms may introduce some challenges resulting from their contribution to the gentrification of cities, regulatory issues and taking over market share from the hospitality industry (Slee 2015; Codagnone and Martens 2016; seen such rapid growth in Europe, with urban areas experiencing a concentration of P2P accommodation units (Gurran and Phibbs 2017), that concerns have been voiced over the associated impacts on local communities and economies. Indeed, there are numerous media reports that draw attention to the problems caused by P2P accommodation growth in relation to the well-being and resilience capacity of Europe's local communities (Williams 2017; Greig 2020). Impacts have also been noticed in the European hotel sector, with Sigala (2017) arguing that P2P accommodation has emerged as one of the greatest disruptors in the hospitality industry.

As a result, there is an ongoing debate over the benefits and costs brought by the P2P accommodation sector in European cities, wherein the phenomenon is more noticeable (Ranchordas et al. 2016). While the emphasis was placed by European intergovernmental organisations on the need to regulate the sector (Hatzopoulos and Roma 2017), this has proven to be a difficult task to accomplish considering the varying legal frameworks across European countries (EC 2018). Therefore, this chapter aims to contribute to the continuing debate on the P2P accommodation phenomenon and the implications it carries by examining the key trends influencing the sector's operation and future development while identifying the challenges and opportunities the sector faces in the COVID-19 pandemic era. The rest of the chapter is organised as follows. First, the definition and types of P2P accommodation are explained. Then, the opportunities generated by P2P accommodation in European cities are analysed in order to explain the reasons for driving the rapid growth of P2P accommodation in Europe. Moving on, the negative impacts of P2P accommodation are outlined. Last, the key trends, challenges and opportunities are discussed as conclusions.

## P2P Accommodation: Definition and Types

The growth of the P2P accommodation phenomenon has led to a reordering of resources, skills, and meanings (Richards 2014) within the hospitality sector. P2P accommodation is defined as online networking platforms that allow people to rent out for a short period of time available space within their property and/or the entire property (Belk 2014). In essence, it refers to short-term rental units that are typically offered to prospective guests by their owners who function as hosts and, as such, may additionally offer hospitality services including cooked meals, airport pick-ups and so on. Although accommodation in the form of commercialised homes (e.g., bed & breakfasts, guesthouses) existed long before the rise of P2P accommodation, the popularisation of the sharing economy business model in the hospitality sector led to the development of a distinct form of the accommodation offered from peer-to-peer. Sweeney et al. (2018) argued that, at the outset, P2P accommodation might offer services similar to those provided in commercialised homes; yet commercialised homes have been primarily operating on a small scale (Lyu et al. 2019). Contrary, P2P accommodation has arisen due to technology enabling users to share information globally and, in turn, encouraging individuals who would not have previously considered renting a room in a private residence to prefer such accommodation options to mainstream ones (Cohen and Kietzmann 2014). The business model of P2P accommodation consists mainly of a service provider (platform), which acts as an intermediary between the supplier (host) and the customer (guest) who will pay for underutilised products and/or services (Kumar et al. 2018). Even though these three parties are a commonality in all P2P accommodation platforms, there are three distinct forms of P2P accommodation.

First, there is P2P accommodation offered for free from hosts to guests via platforms such as Couchsurfing or BeWelcome (Chen 2018; Miguel 2018), where there is no monetary exchange between the parties involved but social and cultural capital exchange (Spitz 2017). As Schuckert et al. (2018) pointed out, these platforms emphasise the social component over the material one. CouchSurfing is often used as an example of the 'pure sharing economy' since there is no monetary exchange between the parties involved (Belk 2014). Geiger and Germelmann (2015), who investigated sharing practices in the context of Couchsurfing, identified that sharing is viewed as a non-profit act, where there is mutual reciprocity between the host and the couchsurfer. At the same time, CouchSurfing can be considered as an 'anti-consumerist' reaction with sharing values (Decrop et al. 2018). According to Kocher et al. (2014), CouchSurfing members are motivated to participate in the service by the sharing of experiences while material sharing (the property) acts as a catalyst. CouchSurfing worked as a charity and was run mainly by volunteers until 2011 when it received $7 million from venture capitalists and became a corporation (Miguel 2018). Since 2015, CouchSurfing incorporated advertising in the site for users who are not verified, and they also promoted the verification system, which costs $25 as another source of revenue (Miguel 2017, 2018). In her study, Miguel (2018) identified that CouchSurfing users found the commercial turn of CouchSurfing controversial as, even though the hospitality exchange service is based on the altruism of its users, some people aim to gain money from couchsurfers' hospitality.

Second, there is reciprocal P2P accommodation such as that found in platforms such as HomeExchange or LoveHomeSwap where houses are swapped between two parties with no monetary exchange taking place between host and guest despite home swappers paying a fee to the platform (Grit and Lynch 2011; Andriotis and Agiomirgianakis 2014). For instance, in the HomeExchange platform, users either pay a membership fee of €120 per year or pay a €10 rate per night of stay at someone else's home (HomeExchange 2020). Most platforms offer either reciprocal exchange (which can be simultaneous or non-simultaneous exchange) or exchange with guest points which users collect by previously offering their homes to other users.

Third, there is profit-based P2P accommodation such as that endorsed by the Airbnb, Booking.com or HomeAway platforms whereby a guest pays the host for the service provided. Although Airbnb popularising the P2P accommodation practice (Camilleri and Neuhofer 2017), which consists of either shared property in which the host stays with the guest or the entire property is rented to the guest without the host sharing the same space (Farmaki and Kaniadakis 2020), according to the World Bank Group report (2018) the most successful P2P accommodation platform to date is Booking.com. With almost 5 million listings classified as alternative or non-hotel accommodation, Booking.com emerges as the leader of the P2P accommodation market, followed by Airbnb with 4.85 million listings and HomeAway with 2 million listings (World Bank Group 2018). In different European countries, local paid P2P accommodation platforms have been launched, for instance, Flatio and Mojechaty (Czech Republic), Gloveler and 9flats (Germany), Rentalia, Hundredrooms and Intercambiocasas (Spain), Trumpam (Lithuania), or Realitica and Sobe-Smestaj (Serbia). Some of these platforms operate in different European cities or at a global level (e.g., Hundredrooms, Flatio).

**The Case of Airbnb**

Airbnb was first established in 2008 and has quickly expanded in over 191 countries, including more than 200 million members. Around 650,000 Airbnb members are hosts who have approximately 6 million listings worldwide (Airbnb 2020). Such was the rapid growth of the platform that its current estimated value of $30 billion exceeds most of the hospitality groups (Cheng and Jin 2019). It is, thus, not surprising that scholars suggested that the platform is emerging as a potential threat to the hotel sector (e.g., Guttentag and Smith 2017)

For example, the Airbnb platform opened up its space to commercial hospitality providers such as traditional B&Bs and boutique hotels through its initiative called 'Airbnb for Everyone'. Accordingly, Airbnb seems to be attracting a group of customers (e.g., business travellers) who would not have previously considered using P2P platforms (Guttentag and Smith 2017). In particular, Airbnb set up a business travel portal with customised search results and introduced a 'business badge' similar to its 'superhost' and 'superguest' badges that are analogous to hotel loyalty schemes and award benefits (e.g., discounts) to dedicated users (Liang et al. 2017)

The platform also introduced 'Airbnb Plus', which refers to an elite selection of properties that have 'exceptional hosts' and 'Airbnb Luxe' that comes with the services of a dedicated concierge in a bid to extend its inventory to more luxurious properties. Airbnb's most recent addition is 'Airbnb Experiences' which refers to tours and activities designed and offered by locals to Airbnb guests with the aim of allowing the visitor to immerse in the local life. Indeed, in recent years, there is a noticeable change in Airbnb's strategies towards more traditional accommodation services, which adds to the debate on whether it may even be regarded as a P2P accommodation platform embracing the sharing economy philosophy (Crommelin et al. 2018)

## Opportunities Generated by P2P Accommodation in European Cities

The impact of the adoption of the sharing economy model on hospitality has also had a wider effect on society. While there are no statistics about the economic impact of home exchange (Andriotis and Agiomirgianakis 2014), it is recognised that users of this type of platform contribute to the economy of several destinations, despite the scale of contribution being marginal compared to paid online P2P accommodation platforms such as Booking or AirBnb (Gössling and Hall 2019). According to a study conducted by Eurostat (2020) about participation in P2P accommodation in the EU, Luxembourg is the country with the most individual hosts (46%), followed by Ireland (34%) and Malta (30%). Conversely, there were some countries with less than 10% of the population being hosts: Cyprus and the Czech Republic (both 5%), Latvia (8%) and Bulgaria (9%).

Peer-to-peer accommodation involves a number of positive side effects (Forgacs and Dolnicar 2017; Hajibaba and Dolnicar 2018) including: extra income for individuals; micro-entrepreneurship opportunities on services for hosts (cleaning services, key-handling etc.); generation of new jobs since tourism increases as a result of affordable accommodation, increased tax revenues and covering temporarily spiking accommodation needs associated with big events (e.g., Mobile World Congress in Barcelona) or natural disasters. For hosts, P2P accommodation has emerged as a potential arena for micro-entrepreneurship (Stabrowski 2017; Zhang et al. 2019), allowing individuals to gain additional income by using idle assets (Lutz and Newlands 2018; Sung et al. 2018). Generally speaking, it allows hosts to make a living from renting their properties on a short-term basis, thus constitutes their main source of income (Portolan 2012) or additional income (Stienmetz et al. 2020). Correspondingly, through hosting, individuals can improve their standard of living. Nevertheless, some studies (e.g., Heo et al. 2019) show that the profitability for a host is dropping due to the saturation of the market. For example, Heo et al.'s (2019) study about the impact of Airbnb in the hotel industry in Paris found that 'the average occupancy has reached a plateau' and 'profitability for hosts is dropping' (p. 87). In addition to financial gain, social benefits were identified as driving people to participate as hosts in P2P accommodation when renting rooms in their properties (Farmaki and Stergiou 2019). For example, Farmaki and Stergiou (2019), in their study about Airbnb hosts in Europe, found that several individuals engage in P2P accommodation hosting to combat feelings of loneliness.

In terms of positive effects for consumers, P2P accommodation services, which have been used by 12% of European citizens (Eurobarometer 2018), provide several competitive advantages against traditional hospitality alternatives. The first one is related to cost. For example, Airbnb hosts are able to provide competitive pricing due to having limited additional labour costs since the platform facilitates the booking and payment process (Guttentag 2015). According to Airbnb (2019), their P2P business model is also democratising tourism since 'thirty-one percent of the people who travel on Airbnb say they would have stayed home or would not have stayed as long but for Airbnb'. Nevertheless, Guttentag (2016) found in his study that actually from the low-budget users, only 2% of users would not have travelled if Airbnb did not exist, while 4% would have stayed with family and friends or CouchSurfing; 17% would have substituted Airbnb for a hostel, and 10% for a B&B. Visitors who choose P2P accommodation benefit from lower prices, and they can spend more money on the tourism sector. As a result, local neighbourhoods have been transformed by spending from increasing numbers of visitors (Fang et al. 2016).

## Challenges Generated by P2P Accommodation in European Cities

Despite the benefits generated by P2P accommodation, at the same time, the activity produces several negative impacts in the cities where this activity is popular. Local people may encounter some difficulties: increase in their rents; overcrowding by tourists and noise-related issues (Slee 2015; Lee 2016). Slee (2015) highlights that Airbnb is contributing to the massive flow of tourists in cities, preventing them from finding the balance they need between tourism and the other needs of a healthy, sustainable city. In addition, Hajibaba and Dolnicar (2018) point out that the character of neighbourhoods' changes with large numbers of non-residents and inconsiderate short-term visitors can also negatively affect residents' quality of life. Several studies provide evidence that the proliferation of house rentals under this model negatively impact the housing market in European cities (e.g., Sans and Quaglieri 2016; Gutiérrez et al. 2017; Dogru et al. 2019; Cocola-Gant and Gago 2019). Cocola-Gant and Gago (2019) in their study about the impact of Airbnb in Lisbon, Seville, and Barcelona, identified a 'buy-to-let investment process' that increases prices in the centric neighbourhoods and runs away from the sharing economy ethos. Nevertheless, research on this topic is inconsistent, with some studies reporting an increase in pricing when Airbnb listing increase (e.g., Lee 2016) while others do not find any relationship between the two factors (Ranchordas et al. 2016).

Likewise, scholars expressed concerns over the spatial implications of the phenomenon (Gutiérrez et al. 2017; Ioannides et al. 2019), which enhances the touristification of residential areas. Indeed, as the supply of Airbnb-type rentals intensifies, tourist overcrowding in central areas increases (Ioannides et al. 2019), threatening residents' well-being (Sans and Quaglieri 2016; Stergiou and Farmaki 2020). Additionally, the research highlighted the adverse effects of the growth of P2P accommodation on the hotel sector (Hajibaba and Dolnicar 2017). Nevertheless, evidence from the study conducted by Heo et al. (2019) in the Parisian accommodation market that Airbnb and hotels are not in direct competition. In addition, the (de)regulation of the P2P activity has been discussed by different scholars (e.g., Koolhoven et al. 2016; Ferreri and Sanyal 2018). For instance, Koolhoven et al. (2016) highlight specific liability issues raised by the P2P accommodation sector in analysing the P2P accommodation regulatory framework in Amsterdam, Barcelona, and Paris since these are the cities with the biggest P2P accommodation activity. Correspondingly, there are increasing pressures placed by industry practitioners and local communities on governments that are called to establish relevant regulatory controls (Farmaki and Kaniadakis 2020).

Nevertheless, Dolnicar and Zare (2020) argue that the problems that some cities experienced with regulating the P2P accommodation market would disappear with the reduced number of P2P accommodation properties. The COVID-19 pandemic has changed the impact of P2P accommodation since travel restrictions have reduced, to a great extent, the number of travellers during 2020. The P2P accommodation market sector has suffered as a result of a large number of cancellations due to *force majeure* and falls in reservations during the summer season (Farmaki et al. 2020). In the European market of Airbnb, the cities which have lost the most revenue from the pandemic so far are Barcelona, Berlin, Madrid, Paris, Milan and Rome (AirDNA 2020). As explained by Dolnicar and Zare (2020), COVID-19 has stopped the exponential growth of Airbnb, which has been increasingly incorporating commercial actors and lost its original P2P idea and sharing economy ethos.

## Summary

This chapter aimed at discussing the evolution of P2P accommodation in Europe in order to identify key trends that shape the sector as well as related operations and practices. In addition, the chapter focused on identifying the various opportunities and challenges brought about by the growth of the P2P accommodation sector in Europe. To start with, the chapter distinguished between different types of P2P accommodation platforms ranging from paid (e.g., Airbnb, Booking.com) to not-for-profit (e.g., Couchsurfing, BeWelcome) as well as platforms based on home exchanges (e.g., HomeExchange, LoveHomeSwap), explaining the key characteristics and differences among them. The chapter also explored the reasons driving the growth of these platforms, identifying benefits to both hosts and guests as integral for the continuous expansion of the sector in Europe. Although some variation was noticed in the key motives driving P2P accommodation demand and supply depending on the type of platform, total economic and social reasons were found to motivate participation in P2P accommodation exchanges. For instance, individuals rent available space in their properties through P2P accommodation platforms in order to make a living or supplement their income as well as meet new people from different cultures (Karlsson and Dolnicar 2016; Lutz and Newlands 2018; Stienmetz et al. 2020). Similarly, convenience, value for money and the search for more authentic and localised tourist experience seem to drive demand for P2P accommodation (Bucher et al. 2018; Shuqair et al. 2019; Tran and Filimonau 2020; Zhu et al. 2019).

Evidently, P2P accommodation platforms offer numerous opportunities to both hosts and guests as they represent a tool of empowerment that allows individuals to make more suitable choices regarding their accommodation as well as generate revenue using existing assets and relatively low capital. In turn, P2P accommodation platforms have been argued to contribute to a more sustainable economic development as they advocate business models that democratise the tourism industry (Forgacs and Dolnicar 2017; Hajibaba and Dolnicar 2018) while extending accommodation options and forcing the traditional accommodation sector (e.g., hotels) to respond with more appealing offerings. Despite such promising prospects, P2P accommodation has been found to yield several negative impacts on local economies and communities in Europe. The immense growth of the sector in European cities, where the phenomenon is most noticeable, has brought along a range of problems, including overcrowding from the influx of tourists in residential areas, higher pollution levels and increased rent prices, among others (Gurran and Phibbs 2017; Ioannides et al. 2019). In addition to these impacts, the P2P accommodation sector has been argued to inflict great effects on the performance, occupancy levels and revenue of hotels (Sigala 2017), forcing them to respond to the increasing competition and adapt their product by incorporating characteristics of P2P accommodation (e.g., home feeling) in their offering (Zhu et al. 2019).

Within this context, European intergovernmental organisations have been pressurising national governments of European countries to establish a regulatory framework in order to monitor the associated impacts of P2P accommodation growth. The regulation of the sector, nonetheless, is not an easy task as there are varied legal and regulatory systems among European countries. Regulatory attempts are further problematised by the fact that European destinations face varying tourism development levels, forms, and strategies. The COVID-19 pandemic has further highlighted the need for regulation in the sector. The pandemic has had great adverse effects on P2P accommodation leading not only to hosts exiting the platforms but also to guests questioning the level of hygiene and safety standards implemented by individuals in the rented properties. Undoubtedly, the pandemic has exposed the vulnerable aspects of the P2P accommodation sector (Farmaki et al. 2020), calling for greater consolidation of policymaking and regulatory attempts in order to ensure that the interests of users (hosts and guests) and local communities are safeguarded in the foreseeable future. By discussing the key trends pertinent to the growth of the P2P accommodation sector as well as the emerging opportunities and challenges brought about by the phenomenon in Europe, this chapter has contributed to the ongoing debate on the merits and disadvantages of P2P accommodation, which has changed the tourism and hospitality landscape indefinitely.

## References

Agag, Gooma. 2019. "Understanding the determinants of guests' behaviour to use green P2P accommodation.' *International Journal of Contemporary Hospitality Management* 39 (9): 3417–3446. https://doi.org/10.1108/IJCHM-09-2018-0755.

Airbnb. 'Airbnb Fast Facts.' Accessed March 23, 2020. https://press.atairbnb.com/app/uploads/2017/08/4-Million-Listings-Announcement-1.pdf.

AirDNA. 'Impact of Coronavirus on the STR Market.' Accessed May 5, 2020. https://www.airdna.co/blog/coronavirus-impact-on-global-short-term-rental-markets.

Alltherooms. 2020. Airbnb Statistics. Available at: https://www.alltherooms.com/analytics/airbnb-statistics/.

Andriotis, Konstantinos, and George Agiomirgianakis. 2014. Market escape through exchange: Home swap as a form of noncommercial hospitality. *Current Issues in Tourism* 17 (7): 576–591.

Aydin, Serhat, and Emin Cihan Duyan. 2019. 'Post-modern tanrı misafiri: Couchsurfing deneyim süreci.' *Journal of Economy Culture and Society* 60 (1): 227–243. https://doi.org/10.26650/JECS2019-0003.

Bakker, Martine, and Louise Twining-Ward. 2018. *Tourism and the Sharing Economy: Policy and Potential of Sustainable Peer-To-Peer Accommodation.* Washington, USA: World Bank.

Belarmino, Amanda, Elizabeth Whalen, Yoon Koh, and John T. Bowen. 2019. 'Comparing Guests' Key Attributes of Peer-To-Peer Accommodations and Hotels: Mixed-Methods Approach.' *Current Issues in Tourism* 22 (1): 1–7. https://doi.org/10.1080/13683500.2017.1293623.

Belk, Russell. 2014. 'You Are What You Can Access: Sharing and Collaborative Consumption Online.' *Journal of Business Research* 67 (8): 1595–1600. https://doi.org/10.1016/j.jbusres.2013.10.001.

Böcker, Lars, and Toon Meelen. 2017. 'Sharing for People, Planet or Profit? Analysing Motivations for Intended Sharing Economy Participation.' *Environmental Innovation and Societal Transitions* 23: 28–39. https://doi.org/10.1016/j.eist.2016.09.004.

Bucher, Eliane, Christian Fieseler, Matthes Fleck, and Christoph Lutz. 2018. 'Authenticity and the Sharing Economy.' *Academy of Management Discoveries* 4 (3): 294–313. https://doi.org/10.5465/amd.2016.0161.

Camilleri, Jeannette, and Barbara Neuhofer. 2017. 'Value Co-creation and Co-destruction in the Airbnb Sharing Economy.' *International Journal of*

*Contemporary Hospitality Management* 29 (9): 2322–2340. https://doi.org/10.1108/IJCHM-09-2016-0492.

Chen, De-Jung. 2018. 'Couchsurfing: Performing the Travel Style Through Hospitality Exchange.' *Tourist Studies* 18 (1): 105–122. https://doi.org/10.1177/1468797617710597

Chen, Chia-Chen, and Ya-Ching Chang. 2018. 'What Drives Purchase Intention on Airbnb? Perspectives of Consumer Reviews, Information Quality, and Media Richness.' *Telematics and Informatics* 35 (5): 1512–1523. https://doi.org/10.1016/j.tele.2018.03.019.

Chung, Jin Young. 2017. 'Online Friendships in a Hospitality Exchange Network: A sharing Economy Perspective.' *International Journal of Contemporary Hospitality Management* 29 (12): 3177–3190. https://doi.org/10.1108/IJCHM-08-2016-0475.

Cocola-Gant, Agustin, and Ana Gago. 2019. Airbnb, buy to let investment and tourism-driven displacement: A case study in Lisbon. *Environment and Planning A: Economy and Space*.

Codagnone, Cristiano, and Bertin Martens. 2016. Scoping the sharing economy: Origins, definitions, impact and regulatory issues. *Institute for Prospective Technological Studies Digital Economy Working Paper, 1*.

Cohen, Boyd, and Jan Kietzmann. 2014. 'Ride on! Mobility Business Models for the Sharing Economy.' *Organization & Environment* 27 (3): 279–296. https://doi.org/10.1177/1086026614546199.

Crommelin, Laura, Laurence Troy, Chris Martin, and Chris Pettit. 2018. 'Is Airbnb a Sharing Economy Superstar? Evidence from Five Global Cities.' *Urban Policy and Research* 36 (4): 429–444. https://doi.org/10.1080/08111146.2018.1460722.

Decrop, Alain, Giacomo Del Chiappa, Jérôme Mallargé, and Pietro Zidda. 2018. "Couchsurfing has Made Me a Better Person and the World a Better Place': The Transformative Power of Collaborative Tourism Experiences.' *Journal of Travel & Tourism Marketing* 35 (1): 57–72. https://doi.org/10.1080/10548408.2017.1307159.

Dogru, Tarik, Makarand Mody, and Courtney Suess. 2019. Adding evidence to the debate: Quantifying Airbnb's disruptive impact on ten key hotel markets. *Tourism Management, 72*: 27–38.

Dolnicar, Sara. 2019. 'A Review of Research into Paid Online Peer-To-Peer Accommodation: Launching the Annals of Tourism Research Curated Collection on Peer-To-Peer Accommodation.' *Annals of Tourism Research* 75: 248–264. https://doi.org/10.1016/j.annals.2019.02.003.

Dolnicar, Sara, and Samira Zare. 2020. 'COVID19 and Airbnb–Disrupting the Disruptor.' *Annals of Tourism Research* 83: 102961. https://doi.org/10.1016/j.annals.2020.102961.

Eurobarometer. 2018. Collaborative economy in Europe. Available at: https://europa.eu/eurobarometer/surveys/detail/2184.

Eurostat. '*Individuals: use of collaborative economy*.' Accessed October 3, 2020. https://ec.europa.eu/eurostat/web/products-eurostat-news/-/DDN-20200205-1.

Fang, Bin, Qiang Ye, and Rob Law. 2016. 'Effect of Sharing Economy on Tourism Industry Employment.' *Annals of Tourism Research* 57: 264–267. https://doi.org/10.1016/j.annals.2015.11.018.

Farmaki, Anna, Cristina Miguel, Maria Hadjielia Drotarova, Ana Aleksić, Anita Čeh Časni, and Fani Efthymiadou. 2020. 'Impacts of Covid-19 on Peer-To-Peer Accommodation Platforms: Host Perceptions and Responses.' *International Journal of Hospitality Management* 91: 102663. https://doi.org/10.1016/j.ijhm.2020.102663.

Farmaki, Anna, and Dimitrios P. Stergiou. 2019. 'Escaping Loneliness Through Airbnb Host–Guest Interactions.' *Tourism Management* 74: 331–333. https://doi.org/10.1016/j.tourman.2019.04.006.

Farmaki, Anna, and Antonios Kaniadakis. 2020. 'Power Dynamics in Peer-To-Peer Accommodation: Insights from Airbnb Hosts.' *International Journal of Hospitality Management* 89: 102571. https://doi.org/10.1016/j.ijhm.2020.102571.

Farmaki, Anna, Dimitrios P. Stergiou, and Prokopis Christou. 2020. 'Sharing Economy: Peer-To-Peer Accommodation as a Foucauldian Heterotopia.' *Tourism Review*. https://doi.org/10.1108/TR-08-2019-0354.

Ferreri, Mara, and Romola Sanyal. 2018. 'Platform Economies and Urban Planning: Airbnb and Regulated Deregulation in London.' *Urban Studies* 55 (15): 3353–3368. https://doi.org/10.1177/0042098017751982.

Forno, Francesca, and Roberta Garibaldi. 2015. 'Sharing Economy in Travel and Tourism: The Case of Home-Swapping in Italy.' *Journal of Quality Assurance in Hospitality & Tourism* 16 (2): 202–220. https://doi.org/10.1080/1528008X.2015.1013409.

Garau-Vadell, Joan B., Desiderio Gutiérrez-Taño, and Ricardo Díaz-Armas. 2019. "Residents' Support for P2P Accommodation in Mass Tourism Destinations.' *Journal of Travel Research* 58 (4): 549–565. https://doi.org/10.1177/0047287518767067.

Geiger, Alina, and Claas Germelmann. 2015. Reciprocal Couchsurfing versus sharing's non-reciprocity principle. *In Proceeding of the 44th EMAC Conference.*
Gössling, Stefan, and C. Michael Hall. 2019. 'Sharing Versus Collaborative Economy: How to Align ICT Developments and the SDGs in Tourism?' *Journal of Sustainable Tourism* 27 (1): 74–96. https://doi.org/10.1080/09669582.2018.1560455.
Greig, Jim. 2020. 'European cities Taking Action Against Airbnb.' VICE. Accessed October 30, 2020. https://www.vice.com/en/article/wx8qz5/airbnb-blocked-europe-lisbon-paris-berlin.
Grit, Alexander, and Paul Lynch. 2011. 'An Analysis of the Development of Home Exchange Organisations.' *Research in Hospitality Management* 1 (1): 19–24. https://doi.org/10.1080/22243534.2011.11828271.
Gupta, Manjul, Pouyan Esmaeilzadeh, Irem Uz, and Vanesa M. Tennant. 2019. 'The Effects of National Cultural Values on Individuals' Intention to Participate in Peer-To-Peer Sharing Economy.' *Journal of Business Research* 97: 20–29. https://doi.org/10.1016/j.jbusres.2018.12.018.
Gurran, Nicole, and Peter Phibbs. 2017. 'When Tourists Move in: How Should Urban Planners Respond to Airbnb?' *Journal of the American Planning Association* 83 (1): 80–92. https://doi.org/10.1080/01944363.2016.1249011.
Guttentag, Daniel. 2015. 'Airbnb: Disruptive Innovation and the Rise of an Informal Tourism Accommodation Sector.' *Current Issues in Tourism* 18 (12): 1192–1217. https://doi.org/10.1080/13683500.2013.827159.
Guttentag, Daniel. 2016. Why tourists choose Airbnb: A motivation-based segmentation study underpinned by innovation concepts (Doctoral Dissertation, University of Waterloo). https://uwspace.uwaterloo.ca/bitstream/handle/10012/10684/Guttentag_Daniel.pdf.
Guttentag, Daniel A., and Stephen LJ Smith. 2017. 'Assessing Airbnb as a Disruptive Innovation Relative to Hotels: Substitution and Comparative Performance Expectations.' *International Journal of Hospitality Management* 64: 1–10. https://doi.org/10.1016/j.ijhm.2017.02.003.
Guttentag, Daniel, Stephen Smith, Luke Potwarka, and Mark Havitz. 2018. 'Why Tourists Choose Airbnb: A Motivation-Based Segmentation Study.' *Journal of Travel Research* 57 (3): 342–359. https://doi.org/10.1177/0047287517696980.
Gutiérrez, Javier, Juan Carlos García-Palomares, Gustavo Romanillos, and María Henar Salas-Olmedo. 2017. 'The Eruption of Airbnb in Tourist

Cities: Comparing Spatial Patterns of Hotels and Peer-To-Peer Accommodation in Barcelona.' *Tourism Management* 62: 278–291. https://doi.org/10.1016/j.tourman.2017.05.003.

Hajibaba, Homa, and Dolnicar, Sara. 2018. 'Helping When Disaster Hits.' In *Peer-to-Peer Accommodation Networks: Pushing the boundaries*, edited by Sara Dolnicar, 237–245. Oxford: Goodfellow Publishers.

Hajibaba, Homa, and Sara Dolnicar. 2017. 'Substitutable by Peer-To-Peer Accommodation Networks.' *Annals of Tourism Research* 66 (C): 185–188. https://doi.org/10.1016/j.annals.2017.05.013.

Hall, C. Michael, Daniel Scott, and Stefan Gössling. 2020. 'Pandemics, Transformations and Tourism: Be Careful What You Wish for.' *Tourism Geographies* 22 (3): 577–598. https://doi.org/10.1080/14616688.2020.1759131.

Hatzopoulos, Vassilis, and Sofia Roma. 2017. 'Caring for sharing? The collaborative economy under EU law.' *Common Market Law Review* 54 (1): 81-127.

Heo, Cindy Yoonjoung, Inès Blal, and Miju Choi. 2019. 'What is Happening in Paris? Airbnb, Hotels, and the Parisian Market: A Case Study.' *Tourism Management* 70: 78–88. https://doi.org/10.1016/j.tourman.2018.04.003.

HomeExchange. 'Home exchange: How does it work?' Accessed June 13, 2020. https://www.homeexchange.com/p/how-it-works-en.

Ioannides, Dimitri, Michael Röslmaier, and Egbert Van Der Zee. 2019. 'Airbnb as an Instigator of 'tourism bubble' Expansion in Utrecht's Lombok Neighbourhood.' *Tourism Geographies* 21 (5): 822–840. https://doi.org/10.1080/14616688.2018.1454505.

Karlsson, Logi, and Sara Dolnicar. 2016. 'Someone's Been Sleeping in My Bed.' *Annals of Tourism Research* 58: 159–162. https://doi.org/10.1016/j.annals.2016.02.006.

Kim, Sodam, Kyung Young Lee, Chulmo Koo, and Sung-Byung Yang. 2018. 'Examining the Influencing Factors of Intention to Share Accommodations in Online Hospitality Exchange Networks.' *Journal of Travel & Tourism Marketing* 35 (1): 16–31. https://doi.org/10.1080/10548408.2016.1244024.

Koolhoven, R., E. D. C. Neppelenbroek, O. E. Santamaría Echeverria, and P. L. Verdi. 2016. *Impulse Paper on Specific Liability Issues Raised by the Collaborative Economy in the Accommodation Sector*. Groningen: University of Groningen Faculty of Law.

Kumar, Vinnet, Avishek Lahiri, and Orhan Bahadir Dogan. 2018. 'A Strategic Framework for a Profitable Business Model in the Sharing Economy.' *Industrial Marketing Management* 69: 147–160. https://doi.org/10.1016/j.indmarman.2017.08.021.

Lee, Dayne. 2016. 'How Airbnb Short-Term Rentals Exacerbate Los Angeles's Affordable Housing Crisis: Analysis and Policy Recommendations.' *Harvard Law & Policy Review* 10: 229–255.

Liang, Sai, Markus Schuckert, Rob Law, and Chih-Chien Chen. 2017. 'Be a 'Superhost': The Importance of Badge Systems for Peer-To-Peer Rental Accommodations.' *Tourism Management* 60: 454–465. https://doi.org/10.1016/j.tourman.2017.01.007.

Lutz, Christoph, and Gemma Newlands. 2018. 'Consumer Segmentation within the Sharing Economy: The Case of Airbnb.' *Journal of Business Research* 88: 187–196. https://doi.org/10.1016/j.jbusres.2018.03.019.

Lyu, Jing, Mimi Li, and Rob Law. 2019. 'Experiencing P2P Accommodations: Anecdotes from Chinese Customers.' *International Journal of Hospitality Management* 77: 323–332. https://doi.org/10.1016/j.ijhm.2018.07.012.

Miguel, Cristina. 2017. Beyond engineered intimacy: Navigating social media platforms to manage intimate relationships. In *Mediated Intimacies* (pp. 130–142). Routledge.

Miguel, Cristina. 2018. *Personal relationships and intimacy in the age of social media*. London: Palgrave.

Moon, Hyoungeun, Li Miao, Lydia Hanks, and Nathaniel D. Line. 2019. 'Peer-To-Peer Interactions: Perspectives of Airbnb Guests and Hosts.' *International Journal of Hospitality Management* 77: 405–414. https://doi.org/10.1016/j.ijhm.2018.08.004.

Paulauskaite, Dominyka, Raymond Powell, J. Andres Coca-Stefaniak, and Alastair M. Morrison. 2017. Living like a local: Authentic tourism experiences and the sharing economy. *International Journal of Tourism Research, 19* 6: 619–628.

Portolan, Ana. 2012. 'The Impact of Private Accommodation on Economic Development of Tourist Destination—the Case of Dubrovnik-Neretva County.' *Oeconomica Jadertina* 2 (1): 35–45.

PwC. 2016. 'Sharing or paring? Growth of the sharing economy.' Accessed October 25, 2020. https://www.pwc.com/hu/en/kiadvanyok/assets/pdf/sharing-economy-en.pdf.

Ranchordas, Sofia, Gedeon, Zusanna, and Zurek, Karolina, 2016. *Home-sharing in the digital economy: The cases of Brussels, Stockholm, and Budapest*. Brussels: European Commission.

Richards, Greg. 2014. 'The New Geographies of Tourism: Space, Place and Locality.' *Paper Presented at the Wageningen Geography Lectures,* January 13, 2014.

Sans, Albert Arias, and Alan Quaglieri. 2016. 'Unravelling Airbnb: Urban Perspectives from Barcelona.' In *Reinventing the Local in Tourism: Producing, Consuming and Negotiating Place,* edited by Antonio Paolo Russo and Greg Richards, 209–228.

Schuckert, Markus, Mike Peters, and Gerhard Pilz. 2018. The co-creation of host–guest relationships via couchsurfing: A qualitative study. *Tourism recreation research,* 43 (2): 220–234.

Sdrali, Despina, Maria Goussia-Rizou, Panagiota Giannouli, and Michalis Kokkinis. 2015. 'Exploring Home Exchange in Greece: An Alternative Choice of Vacation.' *Almatourism: Journal of Tourism, Culture and Territorial Development* 6 (12): 211–214.

Shuqair, Saleh, Diego Costa Pinto, and Anna S. Mattila. 2019. 'Benefits of Authenticity: Post-failure Loyalty in the Sharing Economy.' *Annals of Tourism Research* 78: 102741. https://doi.org/10.1016/j.annals.2019.06.008.

Sigala, Marianna. 2017. 'Collaborative Commerce in Tourism: Implications for Research and Industry.' *Current Issues in Tourism* 20 (4): 346–355. https://doi.org/10.1080/13683500.2014.982522.

Slee, Tom, 2015. *What's yours is mine: Against the sharing economy.* New York: O/R Books

Spitz, Tara. 2017. '*The Commodification of Hospitality: An Analysis of Tourism Encounters between Interculturality and Difference in Regard to Turkish Couchsurfing Experiences.*' Master of Arts in Transcultural Communication, Turkey: Kadir Has University.

Stabrowski, F. (2017). "People as businesses': Airbnb and Urban Micro-entrepreneurialism in New York City.' *Cambridge Journal of Regions, Economy and Society* 10 (2), 327–347. https://doi.org/10.1093/cjres/rsx004.

Stergiou, Dimitrios P., and Anna Farmaki. 2020. 'Resident Perceptions of the Impacts of P2P Accommodation: Implications for Neighbourhoods.' *International Journal of Hospitality Management* 91: 102411. https://doi.org/10.1016/j.ijhm.2019.102411.

Sthapit, Erose, and Jano Jimenez-Barreto. 2018. "Exploring tourists' Memorable Hospitality Experiences: An Airbnb Perspective.' *Tourism Management Perspectives* 28: 83–92. https://doi.org/10.1016/j.tmp.2018.08.006.

Stienmetz, J. L., Liu, A., and Tussyadiah, I. P. (2020). 'Impact of Perceived Peer To Peer Accommodation Development on Community Residents' Well-Being.' *Current Issues in Tourism*, 1–19. https://doi.org/10.1080/13683500.2020.1797644.

Sung, Eunsuk, Hongbum Kim, and Daeho Lee. 2018. 'Why Do People Consume and Provide Sharing Economy Accommodation? A Sustainability Perspective.' *Sustainability* 10 (6): 2072. https://doi.org/10.3390/su10062072.

Sweeney, Majella, John Docherty-Hughes, and Paul Lynch. 2018. "Lifestyling entrepreneurs' Sociological Expressionism.' *Annals of Tourism Research* 69: 90–100. https://doi.org/10.1016/j.annals.2018.01.006.

Tran, Trang Ha, and Viachaslau Filimonau. 2020. 'The (de) Motivation Factors in Choosing Airbnb Amongst Vietnamese Consumers.' *Journal of Hospitality and Tourism Management* 42: 130–140. https://doi.org/10.1016/j.jhtm.2019.10.011.

Tussyadiah, Iis P., and Juho Pesonen. 2018. 'Drivers and Barriers of Peer-To-Peer Accommodation Stay—An Exploratory Study with American and Finnish Travellers.' *Current Issues in Tourism* 21 (6): 703–720. https://doi.org/10.1080/13683500.2016.1141180.

Williams, Lara. 2017. 'When Airbnb Rentals Turn into Nuisance Neighbours.' *The Guardian*. Accessed June 11, 2017. https://www.theguardian.com/technology/2016/sep/17/airbnb-nuisance-neighbours-tribunal-ruling.

World Bank Group. 2018. '*Tourism and the Sharing Economy: Policy & Potential of Sustainable P2P Accommodation*.' Washington, DC: World Bank.

World Economic Forum. 2017. 'Collaboration in Cities: From Sharing to 'Sharing Economy.' *World Economic Forum*. Accessed December 2, 2017. http://www3.weforum.org/docs/White_Paper_Collaboration_in_Cities_report_2017.pdf.

Zhang, Tingting, Diego Bufquin, and Can Lu. 2019. 'A Qualitative Investigation of Microentrepreneurship in the Sharing Economy.' *International Journal of Hospitality Management* 79: 148–157. https://doi.org/10.1016/j.ijhm.2019.01.010.

Zhu, Yunxia, Mingming Cheng, Jie Wang, Laikun Ma, and Ruochen Jiang. 2019. 'The Construction of Home Feeling by Airbnb Guests in the Sharing Economy: A Semantics Perspective.' *Annals of Tourism Research* 75: 308–321. https://doi.org/10.1016/j.annals.2018.12.013.

## Suggested Readings

Hardy, Anne, Dolnicar, Sara and Vorobjovas-Pinta, Oscar. 2021. 'The Formation and Functioning of the Airbnb Neo-Tribe. Exploring Peer-To-Peer Accommodation Host Groups.' *Tourism Management Perspectives* 37: 100760.

Liang, Sai, Xiaoxia Zhang, Chunxiao Li, Hui Li, and Xiaoyu Yu. 2021. 'Tit for Tat: Understanding the Responding Behavior of Property Hosts on Peer-To-Peer Rental Platforms.' *International Journal of Contemporary Hospitality Management* 33 (3): 1105–1126. https://doi.org/10.1108/IJCHM-07-2020-0705.

Reinhold, Stephan, and Dolnicar, Sara. 2021. 'Sharing Economy, Collaborative Consumption, Peer-To-Peer Accommodation or Trading of Space?' In *Airbnb Before, During and After COVID-19*, edited by Sara Dolnicar. University of Queensland. https://doi.org/10.6084/m9.figshare.14195945.

Zhu, Jingjie, Cheng, Mingming, and Li, Zhiyong. 2021. 'Peer-To-Peer Accommodation Experience and Guest Actual Recommendations: A Novel Mixed-Method Approach.' *Tourism Management Perspectives* 38: 100816.

## Relevant Websites

Are you part of the collaborative economy? https://ec.europa.eu/eurostat/web/products-eurostat-news/-/ddn-20200205-1

European Holiday Home Association. https://ehha.eu.

Exploratory Study of consumer issues in peer-to-peer platform markets. https://ec.europa.eu/info/publications/exploratory-study-consumer-issues-peer-peer-platform-markets_en.

Short-term Accommodation Association UK. https://www.ukstaa.org/#welcome.

# 7

# From Uberisation to Commoning: Experiences, Challenges, and Potential Pathways of the Sharing Economy in Food Supply Chains in Europe

Bori Simonovits and Bálint Balázs

## Introduction

Sharing, commoning, and collaborative solidarity systems in food provisioning are gaining more recognition of 'from farm to fork' and beyond chain, which is constituting now a consolidating field of experimentation. The policy prospect of food sharing economies is the capability to internalise some negative externalities of agriculture production and food supply. For consumers, it carries the hope of personalised nutrition and health. For industry, the primary driver is the digitalisation in

B. Simonovits (✉)
Faculty of Education and Psychology, Eötvös Loránd University, Budapest, Hungary
e-mail: simonovits.borbala@ppk.elte.hu

B. Balázs
Environmental Social Science Research Group, Budapest, Hungary


V. Česnuitytė et al. (eds.), *The Sharing Economy in Europe*,
https://doi.org/10.1007/978-3-030-86897-0_7

the agri-food sector, often criticised for the data-driven approach from a responsible innovation point of view.

Food sharing as an ancient and universal human behaviour is at the core of our social life since the hunter-gatherer societies (Hunt 2000). Recently sharing food re-emerged as a mediated exchange in the form of sharing economy. For most analysts, originally, it carried the potential and hope about creating an alternative to the productivist-consumerist paradigm in food provisioning (Heinrichs 2013) by radically decreasing the resource use and creating less waste and more sustainable food. While the informal (non-monetised) forms of sharing and commoning are still dominant in human food provisioning, the sharing economy certainly created new opportunities for sophisticated platform-based and profit-maximising global enterprises (Martin 2016). It undoubtedly made its mark on the food markets and created new opportunities in the life cycle of our food from farm to fork. Although sharing economy research lacks overarching theoretical perspectives, it became a crowded field of study that builds on diverse intellectual traditions.

This chapter presents intersections of the research on sharing economy and food, including various market and non-market arrangements. Both authors are sociologists and grew up in Budapest and got to know each other after the political regime transformation in the 1990s when food commoning, sharing and exchange was an inherent part of our everyday life and much less organised through commodity market channels. To provide meaningful evidence of sharing economy mechanisms, its Janus-faced characteristics in the food supply, we turn to the review of the literature and empirical evidence from our own research and preliminary data gathering within the COST Action 'From Sharing to Caring: Examining Socio-Technical Aspects of the Collaborative Economy' (Sharing and Caring 2020a). Based on our literature review, we present our overview on the transformational potential and the multiple benefits it allegedly offers in the food sector, and then we summarise the attempts to define the sharing economies in the food sector. Section three is based on desk research to show various typologies of food sharing models and analyses multiple benefits of the food sharing economy. This is followed by our illustrative examples of food sharing economies from Europe and beyond, then some hopeful, inspirational cases. In conclusion, we reflect on the scholarly and policy narratives around the food sharing economy. The empirical basis of this chapter relies on the meta-analysis of the 26 country reports with a special focus on food initiatives and the short stories—collecting practices from all over Europe in a concise format—within the framework of COST Action 'Sharing and Caring' provided by country experts in the area of food-related initiatives and re-organised them according to our categorisation provided further in Table 7.2.

## Definition of Sharing in Relation to Food

The term sharing economy is usually related to a socio-economic ecosystem created around the sharing of resources. Since the literature on sharing economy research is becoming overwhelming, definitions are also proliferating. Google Scholar finds 42,700 search results for potentially pertinent papers with reports of sharing economy only in 2020; one-tenth is based on food examples.

On the one hand, it is characterised as a pathway to sustainability by inspiring a more sustainable and collaborative form of consumption (Fitzmaurice et al. 2020). Botsman and Rogers (2010) understand sharing as a possible way to liberate underutilised assets (either in the market or on a solidarity basis). In food sharing, this means the use of food surplus via online communities or donating vulnerable groups via food banks. On the other hand, the sharing economy is also characterised as a neoliberal nightmare with corporate co-optation that promotes overconsumption and drives us away from sustainability transition. As an example, Martin (2016) raises the complexity of sharing economy services, as its certain forms and aspects could be seen as pathways to sustainability while others may rather be labelled as 'nightmarish forms of neoliberal capitalism'. He argues that within the new economic frameworks created by the sharing economy business model, more sustainable forms of consumption and a decentralised, more equitable and sustainable economy could be created. Food sharing initiatives can be seen as good examples for unregulated marketplaces—enabling innovations in multiple respects. Pottinger (2018) and many scholars also observed a sheer bias in the literature that tends to prioritise novel, digitally mediated and often for-profit iterations of the 'on-demand' economy over the lived experience of sharing and its relationship with activist praxis. The informal, non-market form of food sharing economy encompasses gardening by households and other food self-provisioning and sharing practices that in the Central and Eastern European countries reached a high rate of self-sufficiency and unintentional environmental practices (Jehlička et al. 2020).

In food and consumption studies, the descriptions of sharing economies have two main focal points: 'access' and 'collaboration'. Sharing economy is understood most often and primarily as access-based consumption where consumers access to usage of a garden or produce- instead of buying and owning means of food production, consumers pay for access to the produce. Notable examples are the sharing economies performed by community-supported agriculture or community gardens, or consumer groups. Within this category, Miralles et al. (2017) analysed five sharing economy models: consumer groups, commercial community gardens, network-based community gardens, privately owned community gardens, and publicly owned self-consumption community gardens.

Another distinctive type of sharing economy in the food scholarship is (food-based) collaborative consumption. This, in essence, goes beyond the markets by bartering, swapping. Notable examples are seed swap events, potlucks, tapas eating. In these settings, individuals actively engage in the production of service offerings to benefit others (Perren and Grauerholz 2015). Therefore, a different aspect of food is becoming visible: the non-commodity aspect. Several initiatives are promoting food sharing and, in this sense, promote a non-commodity meaning of food (food is a right), such as in the case of Incredible Edible Todmorden (Incredible 2021). Market-oriented novelty creation also happens by involving the users of food. Many small-scale companies invite their stakeholders, including consumers as innovation participants, to co-create food concepts, products, or services by providing their own work and ideas for free.

The two main focal points of access and collaboration create a broad dimensionality of the food sharing economies that range from non-profit to for-profit initiatives. The uniqueness of the sharing economies in the agri-food sector is that their intersections present a full spectrum of these initiatives and that also provides exciting ground for exploring the emergence of food commons and multiple ways in which food can be valued, governed, and shared (Vivero-Pol et al. 2018). In our understanding, food as 'commons' means the value in use (feeding people) prevails over the value in exchange (market profit). Food sharing in non-market food systems is rather customary in human societies and mainly means self-provisioning or bartering, foraging.

## Multiple Benefits of Food Sharing Economies

As the sharing economy became a battlefield of actors with different capacities and power to transform markets, analysts recorded that the debate is mostly about the normative conceptualisation of the 'true sharing economy'. Public perceptions of the realities of the sharing economy have a pivotal role in such definitions: Cherry and Pidgeon (2018) uncovered broader social values of equality, communities, fairness that are underpinning expectations towards a true sharing economy. Hofmann et al. (2019) investigated how the sharing economy triggered the public sector (also by completely disrupting its regulatory role) to act more like a professional, efficient, service-oriented, and engaging actor. The sharing economy can push the public sector away from regulation towards the role of customer, service, and platform provider. Ciulli and Kolk (2019) argued that the main market players could easily reap the emerging market opportunities and diminish newcomers' competition. The COVID-19 pandemics largely changed these emerging trends, and recently Hossain (2020) recorded a precarious situation in the sharing economy. It all seems that in the accommodation and transport sectors, the sharing economy does not prove to be resilient. In contrast, the food sector is probably the quickest-growing areas of the sharing economy.

A recent bibliographic analysis (Kraus et al. 2020) contended that studies on the sharing economy are from the start quite multidisciplinary and interdisciplinary. The organisational aspects (community vs commercial orientation) and behavioural aspects (consumers vs citizen) protruded from the studies. Within food studies, food waste is the most prominent research theme for the research on sharing economy. Sharing economies can present multiple benefits in the food sectors ranging from the ecological through the social to the economic. The agri-food system opened up its idle components to the sharing economy by offering its food communities to deal with food system failures and inefficiencies, such as food waste, food delivery, food swapping, and food commoning.

As for the ecological 'benefits,' it is questionable how sharing economy initiatives can help a transition towards sustainability of our food—by, e.g., radically reducing food waste. Morone et al. (2016) found in their experimental study that adoption of food sharing practices does not translate automatically into food waste reduction in households. Laukkanen and Tura (2020) explored the value creation element and found that sharing economy initiatives via their choice of business models do not advance sustainability by default. Dabbous and Tarhini (2020) further depicted the key factors that ensure sustainable consumption through the sharing economy. They found that knowledge and technology have indirect and significant effects on engaging in sustainable consumption through trust. Platforms for surplus food exchange are gaining new ground as companies perceive sufficient incentives to manage surplus food more efficiently.

In their study on 'imperfect produce', Richards and Hamilton (2018) show that user demand rises in the number of growers shipping to the platform, and grower demand for distribution rises in the number of users. Their findings indicate that secondary markets have the key elements needed. The uncertainty about the ecological benefits is also illustrated by Davies et al. (2017), and Davies and Evans (2019). They gathered into a database more than 4000 technology-assisted urban food sharing activities operating across 100 cities in six continents. To conclude, food sharing practices—especially information and communications technology (ICT)-mediated forms—are still empirically understudied in their potential ecological benefits. It all seems that the sharing economy can underperform in terms of sustainability. Still, any improvement is highly dependent on business models that are often changing during the implementation. Therefore, strategic and deliberate efforts would be necessary from researchers, practitioners, advocacy organisations and policymakers to increase the sustainability performance of sharing platforms (e.g., Curtis and Mont 2020).

The 'economic' viability of sharing economy initiatives is still uncertain whether they can disrupt (redefine or reorient) the economy. The value proposition, creation, and appropriation in the sector would be key in understanding the resilience of sharing economies. The industry giants maintain a top-secret and continuous management of the synergies between (1) the value they enable and create and (2) the value they appropriate. The business modelling of sharing economies is consequently diverse. Ritter and Schanz (2019) explicate four segments of the singular transaction, subscription-based, commission-based platforms, and unlimited platforms (for more details on the four models, see the Figure presented by Ritter and Schanz 2019, p. 18).

'Social' achievements of the sharing economy are not less contradictory. Instead of building new communities, Schor et al. (2016) clearly explained how inequality is reproduced within micro-level interactions during a food swap. While the social benefits of sharing economies are dynamically evolving, the meaning of work in this sector is emphasised. For example, in the food delivery sector, Lin et al. (2020) found a remarkably diverse relationship between food delivery workers' meaning of work and their career commitment. The expectation for social benefits in the sector is high: the food sharing economy workers have a more meaningful concept of their work, and their intrinsic work goals generate work engagement and career commitment the most. Nica-Avram et al. (2021) identified a particular profile of network usage of OLIO (a popular P2P food sharing platform, founded in 2015) users that point to food insecurity, acute food need. As for creating more social equity in consumption, Harvey et al. (2020) studied OLIO and found that instead of reciprocity, kin selection, tolerated scrounging, and costly signalling, donor-recipient reciprocity and balance are rare, but also show that genuinely novel social relations have formed between organisations and consumers which depart from traditional linear supply chains. Asian et al. (2019) studied the sharing economy's potential to enable organic smallholders to overcome social challenges by sharing resources and aggregating peer-to-peer activities using a sharing economy-based collaborative platform.

Sharing food is a universal human social trait that coevolved with human cooperation. However, is there a potential to solve problems of poverty, inequality, and democratic accountability via sharing economies? Critiques of the mainstream sharing economy argue that via renting of cars, couches, bedrooms, spaces, labour time etc., platforms are building markets by simply assigning a monetary value to previously non-commodified and idle capacities of our life worlds. While this is true, the market created from these underutilised assets is a home-based, communal, intimate market, a morally attuned market that sellers and buyers often see as artisanal, domestic, and homey (Fitzmaurice et al. 2020). From the point of view of sustainable consumption and production, the sharing economy has become regarded as a revolutionary area within the broader 'new economics' that regards capitalist market production from a critical stance, pointing out its structural inequalities. It seeks alternatives to its inequalities' growth and GDP obsession (Rifkin 2014) and therefore presents hope for handling environmental problems through fundamental changes in the economic system. This moves turn attention from the centralised state and traditional business solutions to grassroots initiatives, decentralised services, and de-growth. Structural change-makers are already existing locally, and their uniqueness is that they are about sharing, not selling. One could argue that when monetary transactions are excluded, then calling it 'sharing economy' is a misnomer. The added value is created via sharing skills, knowledge, assets. Other times it is rather about swapping, bartering, or exchanging.

In sum, the sharing economy in the food sector has created different (and simpler) ways of allocating food along the whole value chain from producing through transforming to accessing and distributing. The role of ICT in mediating food sharing is pivotal. Still, it does not help avoid recreating existing inequalities and does not translate to more sustainable food by default either. Sharing economies encompass for-profit and not-for-profit allocation mechanisms via the market, the state, the community, and the third sector. A typical market-based solution is any short food supply chain that, by creating the direct link between consumers and producers, shapes new niche markets that challenge traditional food distribution. Initiatives by the state actors, such as in public food procurement or state food programmes, allocate food to varied social groups and render food independent from market mechanisms. Community-based sharing economies link households, family, and friends into food communities by letting them informal food provisioning via gifting or bartering. In the third sector, food-focused associations, foundations, non-governmental organisations (NGOs) seek opportunities to organise different stakeholders into civic food networks. All these modalities enable to make different meanings of food visible, not merely a tradeable commodity but also conviviality, human right, and public good.

## Possible Typologies of Food Sharing Models

Based on our literature review, we found various typologies summarising food sharing models. Michelini et al. (2018), in their study on food waste, identified three faces of sharing economy initiatives: for charity, for money, for the community. Table 7.1 summarises the three basic models of the sharing platforms based on Michelini et al. (2018) analysis focusing on food sharing initiatives.

Davies and Legg (2018) focused on urban food sharing initiatives and developed a two-dimensional typology to create a framework for a food sharing database from all around the world (from 43 countries from 6 continents). Table 7.2 shows Davies and Legg's typology as a suitable and quite complex starting point for our analytical framework, completed with examples from Europe, based on the collection of COST short stories, country reports, and our desk research (Sharing and Caring 2021b; Klimczuk et al. 2021).

## Sharing the Harvest, Meal, and Leftover: Illustrative Cases from Europe

Firstly, it is important to note that our data collection does not offer a representative overview of the food sharing initiatives across Europe, only

**Table 7.1** The three main 'models' of food sharing platforms

| Model | Features |
|---|---|
| Food sharing for money<br>B2C<br>For-profit | The sharing economy in food is mostly understood as part of the market-based supply or provisioning of food. Market services create new markets. Typical examples are short food supply chains with intermediaries; initiatives that resell unused food (to reduce waste and generate revenue); food (and drink) delivery services such as Uber Eats, Farmigo, Bortársaság; or business enterprises that engage their consumers in product development |
| Food sharing for charity<br>B2B<br>Non-profit | Surplus food is most often collected and distributed via non-profit social enterprises, charities, food banks to vulnerable groups, typically organised by food justice organisations, such as Budapest Bike Maffia or Food.Cloud |
| Food sharing for the community<br>P2P<br>Peer learning and co-creation | Community garden members mutually help each other and share the means of production. Urban consumer groups often help local farmers sell their produce by collective ordering and sharing. Typically operated through apps where curators or chefs recommend food (http://www.chefsfeed.com), or consumers themselves build hubs and recruit local farmers via online platforms (http://www.thefoodassembly.com), or DIY restauranteurs offer home-cooked food (Restaurant Day) |

*Source* Own elaboration based on the classification of Michelini et al. (2018)

a selection of illustrative cases based on desk research and the collections and working materials of the COST project. Short stories were defined as examples from the mostly European countries participating in the COST Action, with some illustrative multidimensional cases. Altogether 12 cases were collected from the food sector, with a wide variety of examples ranging from seed bank projects to food waste projects. The meta-analysis of the country reports revealed that most countries highlighted at least one (i) food production or distribution (ii) home delivery

Table 7.2 Modes of urban food sharing (with explanations and examples)

| Modes | Stuff (e.g., seeds, food, food waste, compost) | Spaces (shared growing, food preparation, or eating spaces) | Skills (knowledge and/or experiences about food sharing, growing or waste disposal) |
|---|---|---|---|
| Collecting | sharing food that has been 'liberated' foraged or gleaned | guerrilla gardening of public open spaces | identifying places where gleaning or foraging might occur |
| Gifting | providing food for free<br>SeedBank (Czech Rep, France)<br>Leftovers (Czech Rep)<br>Budapest Bike Maffia (Hungary)<br>'A social plate for all' (Greece, Bulgaria)<br>Waste not want not: Redistribution of surplus food (Denmark) | providing spaces for growing for free | providing skills around growing |
| Bartering | swapping food and food services<br>e.g., SeedBank (Czech Rep, France) | providing spaces where food can be exchanged for labour | providing opportunities to gain experience in growing food, swap seeds, and produce |
| Selling (not for profit) | providing affordable food on a non-profit basis, Bios Coop: farm-to-table social initiative (Greece)<br>Foodbank (Albania)<br>Foodsavers (Belgium) | providing spaces for people to grow food on a not-for-profit basis<br>e.g., Celebrate food (Hungary) | providing workshops around nutrition<br>e.g., Let's bake a loaf!<br>the Czech Republic |

(continued)

Table 7.2 (continued)

| Modes | Stuff (e.g., seeds, food, food waste, compost) | Spaces (shared growing, food preparation, or eating spaces) | Skills (knowledge and/or experiences about food sharing, growing or waste disposal) |
|---|---|---|---|
| For-Profit | selling home-cooked food that generates income beyond the costs of production<br>Munch.hu: fighting food waste (Hungary<br>Brlog-women cooperative is a brewery (Croatia) | providing spaces for supper clubs or dining experiences | providing opportunities for travellers to experience home-cooked meals with locals, e.g., |

*Source* Own elaboration based on case study examples rendered into the classification developed by Davies and Legg (2018)

systems and (iii) food waste initiative at the national level, as relevant examples of sharing initiatives dedicated to the fight against poverty and food waste. We organised the examples along with these three categories.

## Harvest Sharing

Many country reports include examples of food production and/or distribution, such as the regional example from Belgium called Puur Limburg (2021), founded in 2016. Puur Limburg is a local food initiative encouraging local producers and volunteering citizens to share their efforts in advertising, selling, and distributing their goods. It is 'a cooperative of more than 30 Limburg farmers and producers. We believe in fair and sustainable products, and we proudly show who makes the product. By working together, we strengthen each other, and we offer a delicious assortment from our own soil!' (Sharing and Caring 2021b; Klimczuk et al. 2021). This Belgian initiative is a good example of how professional food producers, citizen volunteers, and the regional government cooperate to generate more sustainable local food chains and to boost the local food market. Another example is the so-called 'potato trust' Kartoffelkombinat (2021), a cooperative (of 1500 households, as of 2020) committed to the creation of a regional, commons-based sustainable food supply in Germany.

In France, there were also several food cooperatives reported aiming at shortening the supply chains, mostly based on local networks, such as AMAP (2021), LaLouve (2021), and Plantezcheznous (2021). These initiatives are less platform-oriented and often related to time-banking services. In Hungary there several 'box-based' initiatives were collected, mostly working on a for-profit basis. Some of these 'farm-to-table' shortened food chain models offer a home delivery system in Budapest, and its surroundings, such as Nekedterem ('Grownforyou') (2021) others rely mostly on a pick up-point-system, primarily for sustainability and ecological reasons (Szatyorbolt, 'Bagshop' 2021). However, most recently, due to the COVID-19 related restrictions, Szatyorbolt has also offered contactless home delivery in Budapest, especially for those who are in official quarantine. In certain European countries, food is distributed directly from farmers to consumers through Facebook groups, e.g., REKO networks in Norway. As of early 2020, approx. 80 REKO networks distributed throughout Norway, primarily in urban, more densely populated areas. Rather similar examples may be found in Portugal, such as 'Prove' (2021) and in Poland Future Farms (2021), creating networks of local farmers that sell vegetables and fruits to the urban population through an online platform.

Furthermore, we found 'special initiatives' in the area of food distribution may be highlighted as good practices: The idea of the German-based 'cow-sharing' Kauf ne Kuh (2021) is that the animal is not slaughtered until its meat is 100% pre-sold. The Hungarian Youtyúk (YourHen) (2021) is a small platform-based 'farm-to-table' shortened food chain system, focusing solely on the distribution of fresh farm eggs. Customers may pick up the ordered eggs in boxes through a flexible network of various local stores acting as pick up points.

Summing it up, some of these food production and distribution initiatives define themselves as 'shopping communities' or 'social enterprises', others are closer to platform-based home delivery for-profit businesses. Their common values are strong sustainability and ecology focus.

## Food Delivery

Several companies' in-home delivery help restaurants deliver what, when, and where diners want to be served. Wolt, Uber Eats, Deliveroo, Just Eat Takeaway, Delivery Hero, and others provide platforms that allow consumers to explore more takeout dining options than ever before. Food delivery from commercial kitchens (or virtual restaurants) is gaining important roles in provisioning food. EatWith offers immersive culinary experiences with locals in more than 130 countries by bringing together food communities of foodies, home cooking entrepreneurs, food lovers or chefs as hosts. Online groceries, logistics sharing platforms are also fast-growing. Coop Danmark allows its buyers to order online and get deliveries by private bicycle messengers within minutes. Any cyclist can register to make money by delivering groceries. The crowd-farming models help sustainable human-scale farms with unsubsidised funding by letting their customers invest in them directly.

Most recently, food 'home delivery systems' have gained special significance with the COVID-19 crisis. As most European countries have already experienced the second wave of COVID-19 and its related lockdown regulations, the relevance of home delivery from restaurants increased, especially when restaurants had to restrict their services to pick up and delivery. As the country reports rely on 2019 empirical data, we have only anecdotic evidence based on desk research on this issue. Major international actors in this field are Wolt and UberEats, and the German company called Foodora, which have been active in Nordic countries (Norway, Finland, and Sweden) as well as in Italy and Portugal.

Foodora faced certain difficulties, as their riders demanded higher wages and better working conditions in Norway and Italy in the past years. In Norway, 85 bike riders demanded higher wages in September 2019, claiming that their platform provider should cover expenses for maintaining their bikes. After five weeks, Foodora finally agreed to sign a collective agreement with the labour union (see, e.g., country reports of Italy and Norway in Stories (Sharing and Caring 2021b; Klimczuk et al. 2021).

From a strict 'sharing and caring' point of view, it is questionable whether these highly profit-oriented and platform-based companies (such as UberEats and Wolt) should be discussed in this chapter at all, their platform provider should cover expenses for maintaining their bikes, arguing that market-mediated sharing is not sharing anymore. However, the Uberisation of food provisioning has become a significant issue in various regards and undoubtedly transformed the mainstream markets. The term uberisation in itself carries this vagueness. While the Cambridge Dictionary (2021) defines uberisation as 'the act or process of changing the market for a service by introducing a different way of buying or using it, especially using mobile technology'. According to the Collins Dictionary (2021), uberisation is the 'conversion of existing jobs and services into discrete tasks that can be requested on-demand; the adoption of the business model used by the taxi service Uber'.

From a sustainability point of view, 'restaurants without seats' (or more precisely, commercial kitchens dedicated solely for meal delivery) have special relevance. These businesses can be physically smaller, as no seats and parking lots are required and also cheaper as they have their premises in lower rent neighbourhoods (IFCO 2017). Further special examples from Portugal are 'Eat Tasty' and 'Portuguese Table' which can be labelled as meal intermediation services. The Lisbon-based 'Eat Tasty' connects home cooks, riders, and people who want to receive a home-cooked meal at their workplace. 'Portuguese Table' is active in nine Portuguese cities, developing a platform that allows hosts to receive (paying) guests for a shared meal at their place.

Other examples derived from desk research are examples of 'cooperation between hypermarkets and their customers'. Since 2017 Carrefour, the French hypermarket and most recently the Danish Coop company, have offered a collaborative delivery service called 'Thanks Neighbor;' i.e., shoppers register to provide shopping and delivery services to other nearby customers, for which they receive compensation. These are illustrative examples of how neighbourhoods and hypermarkets can cooperate easily and cheaply based on a suitable platform (IFCO 2017) to reach resource efficiency. From an economic point of view, food delivery initiatives share platforms that grow the fastest economically and financially. In light of this, it is worth monitoring systematically the activity of platforms operating in this sector, as their impacts are essential from a labour market point of view.

## Leftover Sharing

According to a recent study, food waste along the supply chain has been estimated at approximately 88 million tonnes in 2013, or 173 kg per capita per year, and is expected to rise to about 126 million tonnes per year by 2020 in the European Union (Stenmarck et al., 2016). According to this study, the highest food waste generators are the Netherlands (541 kg/capita), Belgium (345 kg/capita), Cyprus (327 kg/capita), and Estonia (265 kg/capita) yearly. Therefore, several organisations are working in European countries on reducing food waste.

Food sharing is transforming from an ancient customary practice into a trend to avoid food waste. As a practice, it builds on physical distribution points and linked ICT platforms connecting food savers in non-monetary exchange in several European regions in Belgium, Germany, Austria, and Switzerland. Most of these initiatives operate in a non-profit way; we found examples in less and more developed countries, e.g., Food Bank (2021) in Albania or Foodsavers (2021) in Belgium. The basic idea of these initiatives is to manage food surpluses by collaborating with restaurants, institutions, and individuals to collect food donations and raise awareness about food waste. Generally, the aims of these initiatives are manifold: eradicating poverty by utilising the food waste based on a complex network and ICT generated platform. Moreover, these initiatives often employ people with difficulties as staff members (e.g., Foodsavers in Belgium) to further help re-integrate disadvantaged people into the labour market.

## Decommodifying Food: Inspirational Examples from Hungary

Concerning the life cycle of our food and the farm to fork perspective, it is unclear how sharing economy can meaningfully redefine the roles of food chain actors, especially those who have most to lose but least power to influence the value chain characteristics, farmers, and consumers. In the recent decade, Hungary presented several exciting food sharing economy examples inspired by and inspiring others locally and beyond.

They help explain the dilemmas and confusion related to access-based vs collaborative consumption and how these practices render certain food provisioning characteristics visible. The transition towards a resilience-enhancing, commons-based food system would need such collaborative and access-based forms as allies in creating momentum. The examples also demonstrate the rising political recognition and growing popular consciousness around food justice, preventing food waste, or seeking food sovereignty.

As for for-profit companies, Budapest Makery is an exciting example of the 'DIY restaurant model', where guests are invited to cook their own meals in an inexpensive downtown eatery from a weekly changing menu. The recipes are developed by top-notch Hungarian gastronomy figures and cooked from scratch following the instructions from a tablet. It is not only that the food can be shared with a colleague or friend but also that the cooking and eating spaces are transformed into a convivial community experience. Although this DIY kitchen concept is free from being a cooking school, the skills and food knowledge are also shared, promoting the decommodification of eating out and a community feeling around sharing food from preparation to consumption. This redefinition of the consumer role into a more active and playful food chain actor carries the potential that consumers turn those regarding more attention to the origin of their food, the ecological diets and climate-friendly food preparations.

The Budapest Bike Maffia is an 'active civic food hub' founded by voluntary bikers in 2011 to feed vulnerable social groups, homeless people in the downtown of Budapest via food donations. In a few years, several other towns followed this concept of food as a human right, such as Debrecen, Miskolc, Pécs, Szeged, Székesfehérvár, and now the team also provides regular school programs and community building events around food justice issues, promoting the radical decrease of food waste. The initiative combines redistribution of food with solidarity and also works as a social enterprise. Also, it takes the valuation of food out of the commodity interpretation and enables the food as a common's framework.

Instead of selling and purchasing seeds, Magház (i.e., seed house), as a 'grassroots seed organisation,' has organised seed exchange events in

Hungary since the 2010s. The initiative connects people who maintain seeds of old varieties, landraces (vegetables, ornamentals, herbs, fruits) and share both the seeds and knowledge about these plants. Magház enables seeds as commons by promoting agricultural biodiversity in Hungary through seed exchanges, other related events, and online social media platforms. Their primary target group and seed swap visitors are smallholders, hobby gardeners, vegetable growers, subsistence farmers and anybody interested in chemical-free cultivation of love seeds. Therefore, seed swaps are particularly exciting events for the knowledge commons, with a range of non-reciprocal and non-obligatory interactions: disseminating information about sustainable agricultural methods, food sovereignty and exchanging know-how or experiences about seeds or saving seeds.

These food system innovations have the potential to lead to 'sustainability transitions' if they manage to radically change our mainstream practices around the existing food system failures. Food justice, convivial community, seed sovereignty, home-grown food sharing are all emergent components of our actually existing sharing economy. This sector comprises a varied network of for-profits, non-profits, and social enterprises operating in various segments of the food system that all promote urban food sharing practices. As the main motive, they are driven by the desire to transform our food system—mainly to decommodify food and enable food or seeds as commons. The food system transformation would require innovation of the food governance (how we organise food provisioning) and also a much wider popularisation and acknowledgement of actually existing food sharing practices.

## Summary

The food sharing economy does not automatically translate into more equitable and sustainable practices; therefore, its meaningful contribution to a new economic paradigm (Frenken and Schor 2019) is rather questionable. As a for-profit arrangement relying on ICT platforms, it often disguises consumers by hiding the negative outcomes (extreme market concentration, precarious jobs, unfair labour practices, disinvestments of social goods, generating overconsumption, hiding ecological externalities, greenwashing). In practice, the trend of blurring the line between grocery shopping, cooking, and eating at home or eating out becomes even more clear during the COVID-19 times. The inherent unsustainability of our global agri-food system resulted in various failures in recent decades. This chapter examined a broad spectrum of actually existing food sharing economies that have been opened up recently from food production through foodservice to consumption to counteract these systemic failures. We pictured the expansion and sporadic lessons learned from food sharing economies, some of their immediate challenges and opportunities. In the agri-food sector, numerous new sharing economy initiatives have been created as unregulated marketplaces—enabling innovations or beyond-the-market solutions for food system failures.

Similarly, to Pottinger (2018), we argue that it is not only the media-hyped digitally mediated, for-profit arrangements that would need more attention but also the less visible, quiet sustainability (Jehlička and Danek 2017), which has already been a lived experience for many. The transformation towards a more democratic, just, and sustainable food system will rely on these small-scale but growing urban food sharing economies. Still, much more empirical evidence would be desirable to understand the sharing economy in food and how seemingly marginal initiatives enact reform or alternative-building strategies in food governance. Either treating food as a commodity or a public good, sharing economy models (service or community-oriented) require grass rooting and decentralised forms to fight food injustices and create better food democracies via sharing unused or underutilised food-related skills, knowledge, and assets.

## References

AMAP-Assosiacitons pour le maintien d'une agriculture paysanne. 2021. Accessed April 14, 2021. http://www.reseau-amap.org.

Asian, Sobhan, Ashkan Hafezi Alkotob, and Jubin Jacob John. 2019. 'Sharing Economy in Organic Food Supply Chains: A Pathway to Sustainable Development.' *International Journal of Production Economics* 218: 322–338. https://doi.org/10.1016/j.ijpe.2019.06.010.

Botsman, Rachel, and Roo Rogers. 2010. 'Beyond Zipcar: Collaborative Consumption.' *Harvard Business Review* 88(10): 30.

Cambridge Dictionary. 2021. '*Uberisation*.' Accessed April 14, 2021. https://dictionary.cambridge.org/dictionary/english/uberization.

Cherry, Catherine E., and Nick F. Pidgeon. 2018 'Is Sharing the Solution? Exploring Public Acceptability of the Sharing Economy.' *Journal of Cleaner Production* 195: 939–948. https://doi.org/10.1016/j.jclepro.2018.05.278.

Ciulli, Francesca, and Ans Kolk. 2019. 'Incumbents and Business Model Innovation for the Sharing Economy: Implications for Sustainability.' *Journal of Cleaner Production* 214: 995–1010. https://doi.org/10.1016/j.jclepro.2018.12.295.

Collins Dictionary. 2021. '*Uberisation*.' Accessed April 14, 2021. https://www.collinsdictionary.com/submission/17695/Uberization.

Curtis, Steven K., and Oksana Mont. 2020. 'Sharing Economy Business Models for Sustainability.' *Journal of Cleaner Production* 266: 121519. https://doi.org/10.1016/j.jclepro.2020.121519.

Dabbous, Amal, and Abbas Tarhini. 2020. 'Does Sharing Economy Promote Sustainable Economic Development and Energy Efficiency? Evidence from OECD Countries.' *Journal of Innovation & Knowledge* 6 (1): 58–68. https://doi.org/10.1016/j.jik.2020.11.001.

Davies, Anna R., and Legg, Robert 2018. 'Fare Sharing: Interrogating the Nexus of ICT, Urban Food Sharing, and Sustainability.' *Food, Culture & Society* 21 (2): 233–254. https://doi.org/10.1080/15528014.2018.1427924.

Davies, Anna, and David Evans. 2019. 'Urban Food Sharing: Emerging Geographies of Production, Consumption and Exchange.' *Geoforum* 99: 154–159. https://doi.org/10.1016/j.geoforum.2018.11.015.

Davies, Anna R., Ferne Edwards, Brigida Marovelli, Oona Morrow, Monika Rut, and Marion Weymes. 2017. Making Visible: Interrogating the Performance of Food Sharing Across 100 Urban Areas. *Geoforum* 86: 136–149. https://doi.org/10.1016/j.geoforum.2017.09.007.

Fitzmaurice, Connor J., Isak Ladegaard, William Attwood-Charles, Mehmet Cansoy, Lindsey B Carfagna, Juliet B Schor, Robert Wengronowitz. 2020. 'Domesticating the Market: Moral Exchange and the Sharing Economy.' *Socio-Economic Review* 18 (1): 81–102. https://doi.org/10.1093/ser/mwy003.

Food Bank Albania. 2021. Accessed April 14, 2021. https://foodbank.al.

Foodsavers Belgium. 2021. Accessed April 14, 2021. https://foodsavers.be.

Frenken, Koen, and Juliet Schor. 2019. 'Putting the Sharing Economy into Perspective.' *A Research Agenda for Sustainable Consumption Governance*. Edward Elgar Publishing.

Future Farms. 2021. Accessed April 14, 2021. https://www.startupgrind.com/events/details/startup-grind-warsaw-presents-future-farms-starakiewicz-szydelko-mazuryk-czech-satagro-rolnikon-fundingbox-sggw/.

Harvey, John, Andrew Smith, James Goulding, Ines Branco Illodo. 2020. 'Food Sharing, Redistribution, and Waste Reduction via Mobile Applications: A Social Network Analysis.' *Industrial Marketing Management* 88: 437–448. https://doi.org/10.1016/j.indmarman.2019.02.019.

Heinrichs, Harald. 2013. 'Sharing Economy: A Potential New Pathway to Sustainability.' *Gaia* 22(4): 228–231. https://doi.org/10.14512/gaia.22.4.5.

Hofmann, Sara, Øystein Sæbø, Alessio Maria Braccini, Stefano Za. 2019. 'The Public Sector's Roles in the Sharing Economy and the Implications for Public Values.' *Government Information Quarterly* 36 (4): 101399. https://doi.org/10.1016/j.giq.2019.101399.

Hossain, Mokter. 2020. 'The Effect of the Covid-19 on Sharing Economy Activities.' *Journal of Cleaner Production* 280: 124782. https://doi.org/10.1016/j.jclepro.2020.124782.

Hunt, Robert C. 2000. 'Forager Food Sharing Economy: Transfers and Exchanges.' *Senri Ethnological Studies* 53: 7–26.

IFCO. 2017. '*The Uberization of Food: How the Sharing Economy is Transforming the Supply Chain for the Better*.' Published by IFCO Systems, 9 November 2017. Accessed April 14, 2021. https://www.ifco.com/the-uberization-of-food-how-the-sharing-economy-is-transforming-the-supply-chain-for-the-better.

Incredible Edible Todmorden. 2021. Accessed April 14, 2021. https://www.incredible-edible-todmorden.co.uk/home.

Jehlička, Petr, and Petr Daněk. 2017. 'Rendering the Actually Existing Sharing Economy Visible: Home-Grown Food and the Pleasure of Sharing.' *Sociologia Ruralis* 57 (3): 274–296. https://doi.org/10.1111/soru.12160.

Jehlička, Petr, Miķelis Grīviņš, Oane Visser, and Bálint Balázs. 2020. 'Thinking Food like an East European: A Critical Reflection on the Framing of Food Systems.' *Journal of Rural Studies* 76: 286–295. https://doi.org/10.1016/j.jrurstud.2020.04.015.

Kartoffelkombinat. 2021. Accessed April 14, 2021. https://www.kartoffelkombinat.de.

Kauf ne Kuh. 2021. Accessed April 14, 2021. https://www.grutto.com/global/.
Klimczuk, Andrzej, Vida Česnuitytė, and Gabriela Avram, eds. 2021. '*The Collaborative Economy in Action: European Perspectives.*' Limerick, Ireland: University of Limerick.
Kraus, Sascha, Hongbo Li, Qi Kang, Paul Westhead, and Victor Tiberius. 2020. 'The Sharing Economy: A Bibliometric Analysis of the State-of-the-Art.' *International Journal of Entrepreneurial Behavior & Research* 26 (8): 1769–1786. https://doi.org/10.1108/IJEBR-06-2020-0438.
LaLouve. 2021. Accessed April 14, 2021. https://cooplalouve.fr.
Laukkanen, Minttu, and Nina Tura. 2020. 'The Potential of Sharing Economy Business Models for Sustainable Value Creation.' *Journal of Cleaner Production* 253: 120004. https://doi.org/10.1016/j.jclepro.2020.120004.
Lin, Pearl M.C., Wai Ching Au, Vicky T.Y. Leung, and Kang-Lin Peng. 2020. 'Exploring the Meaning of Work Within the Sharing Economy: A Case of Food-Delivery Workers.' *International Journal of Hospitality Management* 91: 102686. https://doi.org/10.1016/j.ijhm.2020.102686.
Martin, Chris J. 2016. 'The Sharing Economy: a Pathway to Sustainability or a Nightmarish Form of Neoliberal Capitalism?' *Ecological Economics* 121: 149–159. https://doi.org/10.1016/j.ecolecon.2015.11.027.
Michelini, Laura, Ludovica Principato, and Gennaro Iasevoli. 2018. 'Understanding Food Sharing Models to Tackle Sustainability Challenges.' *Ecological Economics* 145: 205–217. https://doi.org/10.1016/j.ecolecon.2017.09.009.
Miralles, Isabel, Domenico Dentoni, and Stefano Pascucci. 2017. 'Understanding the Organisation of Sharing Economy in Agri-Food Systems: Evidence from Alternative Food Networks in Valencia.' *Agriculture and Human Values* 34 (4): 833–854. https://doi.org/10.1007/s10460-017-9778-8.
Morone, Piergiuseppe, Pasquale Marcello Falcone, Enrica Imbert, Marcello Morone, and Andrea Morone. 2016. '*New Consumers Behaviours in the Sharing Economy: an Experimental Analysis on Food Waste Reduction.*' Economics Department, Universitat Jaume I, Castellón (Spain). Working Papers (11): 1–12. http://www.doctreballeco.uji.es/wpficheros/Morone_et_al_11_2016.pdf.
Nekedterem ('Grownforyou'). 2021. Accessed April 14, 2021. https://nekedterem.hu.
Nica-Avram, Georgiana, John Harvey, Gavin Smith, Andrew Smith, and James Goulding. 2021. 'Identifying Food Insecurity in Food Sharing Networks via

Machine Learning.' *Journal of Business Research* 131:469–484. https://doi.org/10.1016/j.jbusres.2020.09.028.

OLIO. 2021. '*Share more, waste less.*' Accessed April 14, 2021. https://olioex.com/about/.

Perren, Rebeca, and Liz Grauerholz. 2015. 'Collaborative Consumption.' In: James D. Wright (ed). *International Encyclopedia of the Social & Behavioral Sciences* 4: 139–144.

Plantezcheznous. 2021. Accessed April 14, 2021. https://www.plantezcheznous.com.

Pottinger, Laura. 2018. 'Growing, Guarding and Generous Exchange in an Analogue Sharing Economy.' *Geoforum* 96: 108–118. https://doi.org/10.1016/j.geoforum.2018.07.007.

Prove. 2021. Accessed April 14, 2021. https://tasteportugal.com.

Puur Limburg. 2021. Accessed April 14, 2021. https://www.puurlimburg.be.

Richards, Timothy J., and Stephen F. Hamilton. 2018. 'Food Waste in the Sharing Economy.' *Food Policy* 75: 109–123. https://doi.org/10.1016/j.foodpol.2018.01.008.

Rifkin, Jeremy. 2014. '*The Zero Marginal Cost Society: The Internet of Things, the Collaborative Commons, and the Eclipse of Capitalism.*' New York, NY: Palgrave Macmillan.

Ritter, Martin, and Heiner Schanz. 2019. 'The Sharing Economy: A Comprehensive Business Model Framework.' *Journal of Cleaner Production* 213: 320–331. https://doi.org/10.1016/j.jclepro.2018.12.154.

Schor, Juliet B., Connor Fitzmaurice, Lindsey B. Carfagna, Will Attwood-Charles, and Emilie Dubois Poteat. 2016. 'Paradoxes of Openness and Distinction in the Sharing Economy.' *Poetics* 54: 66–81. https://doi.org/10.1016/j.poetic.2015.11.001.

Sharing and Caring COST Action CA16121. 2021a. '*Official Website.*' Accessed April 15, 2021. http://sharingandcaring.eu.

Sharing and Caring COST Action CA16121. 2021b. '*Short Stories.*' Accessed April 15, 2021. http://sharingandcaring.eu/short-stories.

Stenmarck, Âsa, Carl Jensen, Tom Quested, Graham Moates, Michael Buksti, Balázs Cseh, Selina Juul, et al. 2016. '*Estimates of European food waste levels. IVL Swedish Environmental Research Institute.*' Accessed April 14, 2021. https://www.eu-fusions.org/phocadownload/Publications/Estimates%20of%20European%20food%20waste%20levels.pdf.

*Szatyorbolt, 'Bagshop.'* 2021. Accessed April 14, 2021. https://www.szatyorbolt.hu/.

Vivero-Pol, Jose L., Tomaso Ferrando, Olivier De Schutter, and Ugo Mattei. (Eds.). 2018. '*Routledge Handbook of Food as a Commons*.' Routledge. London.

*Youtyúk* (YourHen). 2021. Accessed April 14, 2021. https://www.youtyuk.hu/.

## Suggested Readings

Makov, Tamar, Alon Shepon, Jonathan Krones, Clare Gupta, and Marian Chertow. 2020. 'Social and Environmental Analysis of Food Waste Abatement via the Peer-to-Peer Sharing Economy.' *Nature Communications* 11 (1): 1–8.

Mont, Oksana, Yuliya Voytenko Palgan, Karin Bradley, and Lucie Zvolska. 2020. 'A Decade of the Sharing Economy: Concepts, Users, Business and Governance Perspectives.' *Journal of Cleaner Production* 269: 122215.

Rodrigues, Thomás Costa, Fabrício Oliveira Leitão, Karim Marini Thomé, and Giselle Cappellesso. 2021. 'Sharing Economy Practices in Agri-Food Settlements: Integration of Resources, Interdependence and Interdefinition.' *Journal of Cleaner Production* 294: 126357.

## Relevant Websites

SHAREABLE: People-powered solutions for the common good: https://www.shareable.net

SHARECITY: https://sharecity.ie.

ShareWaste: Give your waste a second chance!: https://sharewaste.com.

# 8

# Unpacking the Financial Services and Crowdfunding Evolution in the Sharing Economy

Agnieszka Lukasiewicz and Mijalche Santa

## Theoretical Background

As a start, it would be essential to have here some basics for contextualisation: why financial services are interesting areas for the sharing economy. Providing an alternative in the financial sector sharing economy presents many benefits—what are those? And why is it important? How does it disrupt the established systems of financial service provisions? Is there any sustainability ambitions in creating such alternative? How are sustainable finances redefined by those services? Do they integrate in some way or

A. Lukasiewicz (✉)
Management Systems and Telematics Division, Road and Bridge Research Institute, Warsaw, Poland
e-mail: alukas@ibdim.edu.pl

M. Santa
Faculty of Economics-Skopje, Ss. Cyril and Methodius University, Skopje, North Macedonia
e-mail: mijalche.santa@eccf.ukim.edu.mk


V. Česnuitytė et al. (eds.), *The Sharing Economy in Europe*,
https://doi.org/10.1007/978-3-030-86897-0_8

the other environmental, social, and governance (ESG) criteria? Which areas are the most penetrated by the new providers or look exciting for academic research with regard to financial service provisioning (such as leasing, hedging, insurance. banking)?

The financial crisis of 2008–2009 was a trigger for strengthening the proliferation of alternative forms of financing. At the same time, banks that hold more capital reduced lending, particularly in the small and medium enterprises sector, a need and gap in funding, especially those entities raised. Crowdfunding may be classified into four categories: social lending/donation crowdfunding, reward crowdfunding, peer-to-peer lending, and equity crowdfunding (Pierrakis and Collins 2013). Especially peer-to-peer lending and equity crowdfunding are growing rapidly and are easily accessible to both retail and sophisticated investors alike (Kirby and Worner 2014). Those crowdfunding forms have also drawn the attention of governments and the European Commission, who would wish to encourage the growth of SMEs. Crowdfunding is also referred to as sustainability by integrating with a triple bottom line approach, which embraces economic, environmental, and societal issues (Elkington 1999). It also indicates sustainable entrepreneurs regard a wide range of various stakeholder interests (Bocken 2015).

The most popular form of alternative financing—crowdfunding is expanding in different sectors filling the gap of funding, especially on the micro and small enterprises level. In the literature one finds different definitions of crowdfunding (Berns et al. 2020; Rossi and Vismara 2018; Short et al. 2017; Renwick and Mossialos 2017; Schwienbacher and Larralde 2012). Nevertheless, 'crowd' indicates the process needs contribution from many participants. The European Commission defines crowdfunding as an emerging source of financing involving open calls to the public, generally via the Internet, to finance projects through monetary contributions in exchange for a reward, product pre-ordering, lending, or investment (European Commission 2020a). For small businesses, access to this form of finance represents an alternative (or a complement) to more traditional sources of finance, such as debt finance. Crowdfunding platforms are websites where fundraisers such as small and medium enterprises can source financial pledges from a crowd (European Commission 2020a). Crowdfunding is also defined as an alternative channel for financing a project that uses an online platform to solicit generally small contributions from numerous participants (i.e. the crowd) (Renwick and Mossialos 2017). In a wide way, crowdfunding is defined as the financing of a project or a venture by a group of individuals instead of professional parties (e.g. banks, venture capitalists, or business angels), and the typical mode of communication is through the Internet (Schwienbacher and Larralde 2012). The phenomenon of crowdfunding brings out insight from micro-finance (Morduch 1999) and crowdsourcing (Poetz and Schreier 2012) concepts. However, it represents its own kind of fundraising, assisted by an increasing number of internet sites assigned to the issue. It is related mainly to small companies, micro-businesses, and individual entrepreneurs to find financial resources in an internet-dominated world. While entrepreneurs have an idea, it is not obligatory to prepare complex materials to apply for bank loans or government subsidies through complicated procedures (Zhao et al. 2017). What is needed to address funding using such platforms as Kickstarter and Indiegogo is to post general information, e.g. amount of requested capital, types of rewards, as well as make a presentation of a project.

According to (Belleflamme et al. 2014) there are three characteristics of crowdfunding:

- Crowdfunding initiatives rely on the advanced purchase of products that are not available on the market. Entrepreneurs who start crowdfunding projects describe what the final products are and offer a list of monetary or non-monetary rewards for sponsors who are willing to invest (cf. future markets).
- Consumers or sponsors pay more in the pre-ordering process than do traditional consumers, who wait to buy the finished products on the market (cf. spot markets).
- Crowdfunders identify themselves as members of the community. Such community can shape from receiving rewards up to being involved in the project. Entrepreneurs ensure the consumers value the community, benefits, as well as trust in the project.

Except for the social network theory, crowdfunding is often connected to a theory of 'warm-glow giving' (Andreoni 1990). The literature on altruism and the theory notes some individuals feel positive when helping others. Moreover, the theory could explain a backer's decision to participate in a crowdfunding campaign for a social impact project. The theory also leads to funders perceiving they are part of a civic project (Lagazio and Querci 2018). Furthermore, as stated by a resource-based theory, resources are the primary source of company performance and direct a firm's strategy (Grant 1991). In crowdfunding models and practices can be found the optimisation of both financial, as well as human resources. Furthermore, an entrepreneurial team is recognised as a positive one in those determinants of a firm's growth (Ensley et al. 2002; Ruef et al. 2003). It also can benefit from a wider network of contacts. Undoubtedly, internet technologies, social media, and various platforms have been a trigger to the development of networks. The networks which are becoming bigger, with no boundaries, are used in crowdfunding to the improvement in using financial and human sources. Also, the continuity of technology growth is followed by the FinTech (Financial Technology—the term refers to software and other new technologies used by businesses that provide automated and improve financial services) industry expansion. Thus, the power of crowd and technology is used in the funding/financing activity in the range of various creative initiatives.

## Financial Services Models in the Sharing Economy

There are two approaches to categorising the crowdfunding models. The most widespread is the one that is based on what the crowdfunders receive in exchange for their contributions. Based on it, we have donation-based, reward-based, equity-based, royalty-based, and lending-based financial services. Other taxonomies are based on the timing of the campaign. Money collection scheme and presence or absence of intermediary (Butticè et al. 2018). In this section, we will present an overview of the most dominant taxonomy.

## Donation-Based Platforms

The donation-based platforms request monetary and/or non-monetary resources without expecting to receive any material rewards (Salido-Andres et al. 2021). Donation-based crowdfunding is a niche crowd-funding focused on public goods (Guan 2016). They cover topics 'from rescuing homeless animals to overcoming medical crises, eliminating community problems to reallocating educational resources' (Wang et al. 2019, p. 1517). One example of this type of platform is GoFundMe. As online philanthropy innovation, this type of crowdfunding gains more and more popularity (Zhang et al. 2020). They provide an additional revenue stream for charitable organisations. The full potential of this type of crowdfunding is most evident during the COVID-19 pandemic, as we will present in the next sections.

## Reward-Based Funding

In reward-based crowdfunding, creators will provide tangible rewards to supporters (Guan 2016). The creators are typically individuals (Rossi and Vismara 2018) with an innovative idea for which they need financial support. To receive the financial support creators, explain their idea, the project through which they will instantiate their idea and the rewards they will provide to supporters if the funding goal is achieved (Herrero et al. 2020). Kickstarter is one of the largest rewards-based crowdfunding platforms. In some of the reward crowdfunding, supporters select to invest based on their interests to get certain perks such as advance versions of a funded product (Short et al. 2017). However, sometimes the reward can be merely symbolic, such as thank you note, and in these cases, the difference between donor and reward crowdfunding is not clear (Butticè et al. 2018). In reward-based funding, the goal is to try to raise as much as possible funds (Rossi and Vismara 2018). This is not the case for equity-based crowdfunding.

## Equity-Based Platforms

In equity-based crowdfunding, the proponent is a company that sells small ownership stakes in their firms (Mochkabadi and Volkmann 2020). The proponent offers a maximum number of shares that can be sold in order to not dilute equity ownership (Rossi and Vismara 2018). The benefit for the supporters is that through their investment, they will be eligible to receive a share of the profits in the form of a dividend to distribution (Wang et al. 2019). A representative example of this type of platform is the WeFunder platform. The benefit for the creators is that it can be an alternative financial investment instrument (Cai 2018) through which it can obtain not only funds in the early-stage projects (Martínez-Climent et al. 2018) but also receive feedback from the crowd on their entrepreneurial endeavour (Butticè et al. 2018). Thus, this is not only an innovative way to raise external capital for new ventures (Mochkabadi and Volkmann 2020) but also to engage in communication with potential customers. The platforms play a critical role in this communication 'in which they transition from active intermediaries that critically assess ventures to providers of lean business introduction services that assist ventures in reducing their information asymmetries with the crowd' (Löher 2017, p. 19). This is an important role because equity crowdfunding provides investment opportunities for small investors who lack the sense, knowledge, or capabilities of researching for investments (Martínez-Climent et al. 2018).

## Lending-Based Platforms

Peer-to-peer-lending crowdfunding involves investors making micro-loans to entrepreneurs (Short et al. 2017) by bypassing traditional banks (Belleflamme et al. 2015). The loans are returned over a pre-determined timeline (Wang et al. 2019) with interest, or only the principal is returned (Allison et al. 2013). The interest rate is flexible and can be determined by an algorithm (Butticè et al. 2018). Zopa in the UK is an example of this type of platform. Research demonstrates that the lenders in lending-based crowdfunding tend to follow strategic over altruistic motives (Berns et al. 2020).

In the next section, we present the value of all these different crowdfunding models.

## The Value Market of Alternative Financing

Depending on the source of information, as well as the scope of the definition of crowdfunding, the crowdfunding market in 2018 was valued at USD 10.2 billion reported by Valuates Reports (2019b), trough up to USD 357 billion reported by the Cambridge Centre for Alternative Finance (CCAF) (Ziegler and Shneor 2020). It is important that the phenomenon affects all continents and a very large number of countries. Crowdfunding platforms are developing both in Asia—with the Chinese market dominating and the largest in the world, and in Africa, although, in relation to the level of economic development, the value of crowdfunding on that continent is the lowest in terms of value.

Both in developed markets and developing, crowdfunding is a complement or alternative to the classical banking system. Still, even in the largest markets, it is only a fraction of the financial market, although the observed trend is a fast growth of the sector. For example, the Chinese market is estimated by the CCAF at 215 billion (a decrease from 358 billion in 2017, due to the introduction of detailed regulations on this market), which is negligible with Chinese banks' assets—only ISCB has assets of 4.3 trillion (Caplen 2020). Nevertheless, even if compared with banks, it is not a big amount. It needs to be remembered crowdfunding often is directed to a different group of users, filling the gap on the market.

The next largest is the market of the United States with 61 billion and the United Kingdom—10 billion. Countries with a crowd sharing market of more than 1 billion are also the Netherlands, Indonesia, Germany, Australia, and Japan. There are 26 countries with a market between more than 100 million and 1 billion, and there are both highly developed countries such as France, Canada, South Korea, Finland,

Sweden, and developing countries as Georgia, Armenia, Peru in this category. Furthermore, there are 38 countries in the USD 10–100 million category (Ziegler and Shneor 2020). The dominant form of crowdfunding is loans, while capital entries and other forms have a smaller share.

Of significance is that in many countries, there was a dynamic market growth in 2018, for which the latest data is available. In contrast, there are several countries where a notable reduction in the value of crowdfunding at that time has been. For example, in China, the decrease was from 358 billion in 2017 to 215 billion in 2018, as well as in South Korea from 1130 to 753 billion USD. At the same time, the market in Canada or New Zealand was stabilised (±10%). In most countries, the market growth between 2017 and 2018 was several dozen per cent. There were also countries where the market grew several times, e.g. the Netherlands (8x), Peru (5.4×), Argentina (4.3×), Japan (3×), and about twice: Israel (2.5×), Spain (2.3×), Poland (2.1×), Germany (1.9×). All sources report the rapid growth of this market. Valuates Reports (Valuates Reports 2019b) expects the Compound Average Rate of Growth (CAGR) will arise 16% by 2025, parallel it indicates the global Crowdfunding market size is projected to reach USD 23,200 Million by 2026, from USD 12,390 Million in 2019, at a CAGR of 11.2% during the forecast period 2021–2026 (Valuates Reports 2019a). Historical data collected by CCAF validate that growth rate. The Cambridge Centre for Alternative Finance identified 2322 companies globally in the research carried out in 2019, of which 1227 firms contributed to the study.

Statista estimates that transaction value is expected to show an annual growth rate (CAGR 2021–2025) of 3.33% resulting in a projected total amount of US$1,201.1 m by 2025 (Statista 2021, although such a low increase does not seem much credible. Looking regionally, Europe (including the UK) grew 52% in 2018, Asia Pacific (excluding China) 69%, Americas 44%, the Middle East 131%, and Africa 102%. Against this background, China stands out significantly (-39.8%), which is related to the introduction of new legal regulations related to crowdfunding loans (Ziegler and Shneor 2020).

Importantly, crowdfunding is widespread. The countries where that phenomenon exceeded USD 1 million per year. In most African countries, crowdfunding amounts are very small—for the entire continent, crowdfunding in 2018 was only $ 208 million, with only three countries accounting for half of the market: Zambia (40.7 million), Kenya (35 million), and South Africa (27.4 million USD) and the entire continent accounts for > 1% of the global crowdfunding market (Ziegler and Shneor 2020).

## Impact of the COVID-19 Pandemic

The COVID-19 pandemic presented unprecedented health, economic, political, and social situation. It challenged a large number of assumptions in all domains of our life. Thus, the question we ask regarding crowdsourcing is how crowdfunding adopted the challenges created by COVID-19? To provide an initial answer to this question on Google Scholar, we performed a general literature search of papers that researched 'crowdfunding' and 'COVID-19' and published in 2020 or 2021. We download the papers and read the abstracts to identify the papers that fit our criteria. In the next paragraphs, we demonstrate how crowdsourcing was impacted by COVID-19.

As the awareness of the impact of COVID-19 increased, there was a rapid increase in the number of active campaigns (Rajwa et al. 2020). The goal was, as the economic impacts multiplied, to use web-based crowdfunding to defray these costs (Saleh et al. 2021). In the beginning, in different parts of the world, the focus was on different needs. The USA was more focused on the economic relief issues, while the non-USA campaigns were more focused on the health workers or medical supplies, for example, in Italy (Rajwa et al. 2020). In the USA, from all the fundraising campaigns created between 1 January and 10 May 2020, 22.2% were identified as COVID-19–related. Through COVID-19 related campaigns, around the US $237 million were collectively raised by 10 May 2020 (Saleh et al. 2021).

What we can notice is that the emergence that COVID-19 imposed has triggered organisations that have not relied on crowdfunding to quickly adapt and launch crowdfunding campaigns. For example, the World Health Organisation (WHO) launched the COVID-19 Solidarity Response Fund and asked individuals and organisations to donate funds in support of their COVID-19 pandemic-related work. The result is that '10 days after its 13 March launch, it had raised US$71 million from 170 000 individuals and organisations, including Facebook, Google, and FIFA' (Usher 2020, p. 1024). The crowdfunding approach enabled the WHO to quickly respond and provide different revenue stream when their traditional donors failed to fund the response to this outbreak at the international level (Usher 2020). Another example is non-profit advocacy coalitions in Belgium that launched crowdfunding platform to secure funds for 'complementary material services and aid that was not provided in the regular food packages distributed by food banks and social groceries' (Raeymaeckers and Van Puyvelde 2021, p. 9). This response to immediate needs is also present in the research of Ahsen et al. (2020) that identified that the new crowdfunding campaigns responded to the immediate needs around digital learning infrastructure necessary for online education of pupils.

Based on the above, we can say that during the pandemic, the crowdsourcing platforms assisted in augmenting the traditional relief efforts. However, the flexibility of the crowdfunding platforms and the ability to provide space for the creation of campaigns for emergent needs can also serve as an indicator of several important issues in crises. First, in a time of public health emergencies, it can provide which communities are affected and second, a unique insight into the needs of those affected communities (Saleh et al. 2021). In this way, it can provide information to the governmental institutions where the available funds can be directed. Thus, the new role of crowdfunding platforms is to provide signals where assistance is most needed during emergency situations.

However, during the pandemic, it has been identified that crowdfunding campaigns were organised for dietary supplements and immune system boosters that purported COVID-19 treatments that are not validated. This could bring confusion with the effective preventative approaches. Thus, there is a need for crowdfunding platforms to take a more proactive role in restricting campaigns that are based on misinformation about COVID-19 (Snyder et al. 2021).

Finally, it is worth to be noted that as the COVID-19 pandemic persisted and progressed, the number of COVID-19 crowdfunding campaigns declined. In the USA, tenfold across all states (Saleh et al. 2021). However, 'COVID-19–related campaigns raised more money, had a long narrative description, and were more likely to be shared on Facebook than other campaigns in the study period' (Saleh et al. 2021). This decrease is due to rather successful campaigns that need to be explored further in order for a valid answer to be provided.

## Summary

There has been noticed the disruption of the role, structure, and competitive environment for financial institutions, the markets, and societies in which they operated. It offers a variety of new tools and services to customers to pursue to enlarge the sharing economy. That is because peer-to-peer financial services companies create new partnerships with the FinTech sector (PwC 2016).

Probably the most interesting market situation in crowdfunding is in Europe. On the one hand, we have intensive growth, in some European countries reaching several hundred % year-on-year. On the other hand, uncertainty related to undefined obstacles as a result of Brexit. The total alternative finance market volume in Europe (including the UK) reached $18 billion in 2018. The average growth rate between 2013 and 2018 was 69%. The UK's exit from the EEA will disconnect Europe's largest crowdfunding market worth over 10 billion from the rest of the European Economic Area. The UK accounts for more than half of the European market. That is due to both the UK's large domestic market and the fact that UK crowdfunding platforms have done well in the European market. In Crowdsourcing Week's 'Top 15 Crowdfunding Platforms in Europe' ranking, British platforms take first and second position, and the UK is only one country with three platforms in the ranking (Priti 2020). Crowdfunding in Europe has attained a significant level of growth, adoption, and maturity in recent years.

The development of the crowdfunding market in Europe is of interest to the European Commission. The first studies on crowdfunding date back to 2011 and culminated in Communication from the Commission to The European Parliament, The Council, The European Economic and Social Committee, and The Committee Of The Regions Unleashing the Potential of Crowdfunding in the European Union (European Commission 2014) clarifying the directions in which the regulation of legal crowdfunding framework across Europe head to.

Most crowdfunding markets in Europe have recorded significant growth rates of several tens of % per year in recent years. It is likely that such a pace will not be maintained. Three factors affecting that market are important in 2020 and 2021. The first is the COVID-19 epidemic, which is having a slowing effect on entire sectors of the economy, as confirmed by Eurostat statistics, such as falling household savings rates in 2020, rising unemployment (by one percentage point during the first six months of the pandemic), or a fall in GDP estimated at more than seven percentage points (European Commission 2020b). In a survey carried out by the European Crowdfunding Network, crowdfunding platform managers are most afraid of declines in the lending market. When looking at the perceived impact on incoming capital flows, there is a high negative impact found, especially on lending, with most respondents indicating a high decline in capital inflows of more than 50%. Equity platforms are also perceiving a high negative impact (European Crowdfunding Network 2020).

The second factor that could negatively impact the crowdfunding market is Brexit, which will remove UK-based crowdfunding platforms from outside the EEA market. Even if appropriate agreements are in place to allow such activity to continue to operate directly on the continent, trust in these platforms as coming from outside the single market is expected to decline.

A third factor that may, however, stimulate the market is the enactment of Regulation (EU) 2020/1503, which may significantly accelerate the development of the crowdfunding market, once it comes into force (Regulation (EU) 2020/1503 of the European Parliament and of the Council of 7 October 2020 on European Crowdfunding Service Providers for Business, and Amending Regulation (EU) 2017/1129 and Directive (EU) 2019/1937 (Text with EEA Relevance) 2020).

## References

Ahsen, Mehmet, Aravinda Garimella, Ramanath Subramanyam, and Anqi Angie Wu. 2020. '*Keeping Kids Learning: Online Crowdfunding Communities Respond to the COVID-19 Pandemic.*' Illinois Experts, Working Paper, *Available at SSRN 3779438*. Accessed December 15, 2020. https://doi.org/10.2139/ssrn.3779438.

Allison, Thomas H., Aaron F. McKenny, and Jeremy C. Short. 2013. 'The Effect of Entrepreneurial Rhetoric on Microlending Investment: An Examination of the Warm-Glow Effect.' *Journal of Business Venturing* 28 (6): 690–707. https://doi.org/10.1016/j.jbusvent.2013.01.003.

Andreoni, James. 1990. 'Impure Altruism and Donations to Public Goods: A Theory of Warm-Glow Giving.' *The Economic Journal* 100 (401): 464–477. https://doi.org/10.2307/2234133.

Belleflamme, Paul, Thomas Lambert, and Armin Schwienbacher. 2014. 'Crowdfunding: Tapping the Right Crowd'. *Journal of Business Venturing* 29 (5): 585–609. https://doi.org/10.1016/j.jbusvent.2013.07.003.

Belleflamme, Paul, Nessrine Omrani, and Martin Peitz. 2015. 'The Economics of Crowdfunding Platforms.' *Information Economics and Policy* 33 (4): 11–28. https://doi.org/10.1016/j.infoecopol.2015.08.003.

Berns, John P, Maria Figueroa-Armijos, Serge P da Motta Veiga, and Timothy C Dunne. 2020. 'Dynamics of Lending-Based Prosocial Crowdfunding: Using a Social Responsibility Lens.' *Journal of Business Ethics* 161 (1): 169–185. https://doi.org/10.1007/s10551-018-3932-0.

Bocken, Nancy M.P. 2015. 'Sustainable Venture Capital - Catalyst for Sustainable Start-up Success?' *Journal of Cleaner Production* 108 (December): 647–658. https://doi.org/10.1016/j.jclepro.2015.05.079.

Butticè, Vincenzo, Chiara Franzoni, Cristina Rossi-Lamastra, and Paola Rovelli. 2018. 'The Road to Crowdfunding Success: A Review of Extant Literature.' In *Creating and Capturing Value through Crowdsourcing*, edited by Christopher L. Tucci, Allan Afuah, and Gianluigi Viscusi, 97–115. New York, NY: Oxford University Press. https://doi.org/10.1093/oso/9780198816225.003.0005.

Cai, Cynthia Weiyi. 2018. 'Disruption of Financial Intermediation by FinTech: A Review on Crowdfunding and Blockchain.' *Accounting & Finance* 58 (4): 965–92.

Caplen, Brian. 2020. 'Top 1000 World Banks 2020 China Press Release.' *The Banker*, 2020. Accessed December 10, 2020. https://www.thebanker.com/

Top-1000-World-Banks/Top-1000-World-Banks-2020-China-Press-Release-English.

Elkington, John Brett. 1999. '*Cannibals with Forks: The Triple Bottom Line of Sustainability.*' *New Society Publishers.* Oxford: Capstone Publishing Ltd. https://doi.org/10.1002/tqem.3310080106.

Ensley, Michael D., Allison W. Pearson, and Allen C. Amason. 2002. 'Understanding the Dynamics of New Venture Top Management Teams: Cohesion, Conflict, and New Venture Performance.' *Journal of Business Venturing* 17 (4): 365–386.

European Commission. 2014. '*Communication from the Commission to The European Parliament, The Council, The European Economic And Social Committee And The Committee Of The Regions Unleashing the Potential of Crowdfunding in the European Union.*' Brussels: European Commission. Accessed December 5, 2020. https://eur-lex.europa.eu/legal-content/en/TXT/?uri=CELEX:52014DC0172.

European Commission. 2020a. '*Internal Market, Industry, Entrepreneurship and SMEs. Crowdfunding.*' Accessed November 15, 2020. https://ec.europa.eu/growth/access-to-finance/funding-policies/crowdfunding/.

European Commission. 2020b. '*Summer 2020 Economic Forecast: An Even Deeper Recession with Wider Divergences.*' Accessed April 20, 2021. https://ec.europa.eu/commission/presscorner/detail/%0Aen/ip_20_1269.

European Crowdfunding Network. 2020. '*The Impact of COVID-19 on the European Automotive Market.*' Brussels: European Crowdfunding Network AISBL. Accessed March 15, 2021. https://eurocrowd.org/wp-content/blogs.dir/sites/85/2020/04/ECN_COVID19_Survey_20200414.pdf.

Grant, Robert. M. 1991. 'The Resource-Based Theory of Competitive Advantage: Implications for Strategy Formulation.' *California Management Review* 33 (3): 114–135.

Guan, Lei. 2016. 'A Short Literature Review on Reward-Based Crowdfunding.' *Paper Presented at the 2016 13th International Conference on Service Systems and Service Management (ICSSSM),* 1–4. https://doi.org/10.1109/ICSSSM.2016.7538636.

Herrero, Ángel, Blanca Hernández-Ortega, and Héctor San Martín. 2020. 'Potential Funders' Motivations in Reward-Based Crowdfunding. The Influence of Project Attachment and Business Viability.' *Computers in Human Behavior* 106: 106240. https://doi.org/10.1016/j.chb.2019.106240.

Kirby, Eleanor, and Shane Worner. 2014. '*Crowdfunding : An Infant Industry Growing Fast*'. *International Organization of Securities Commissions,* 1–62. http://www.iosco.org/library/pubdocs/pdf/IOSCOPD459.pdf.

Lagazio, Corrado, and Francesca Querci. 2018. 'Exploring the Multi-Sided Nature of Crowdfunding Campaign Success.' *Journal of Business Research* 90: 318–324. https://doi.org/10.1016/j.jbusres.2018.05.031.

Löher, Jonas. 2017. 'The Interaction of Equity Crowdfunding Platforms and Ventures: An Analysis of the Preselection Process.' *Venture Capital* 19 (1–2): 51–74. https://doi.org/10.1080/13691066.2016.1252510.

Martínez-Climent, Carla, Ana Zorio-Grima, and Domingo Ribeiro-Soriano. 2018. 'Financial Return Crowdfunding: Literature Review and Bibliometric Analysis.' *International Entrepreneurship and Management Journal* 14 (3): 527–553.

Mochkabadi, Kazem, and Christine K Volkmann. 2020. 'Equity Crowdfunding: A Systematic Review of the Literature.' *Small Business Economics* 54 (1): 75–118.

Morduch, Jonathan. 1999. 'The Microfinance Promise.' *Journal of Economic Literature* 37 (4): 1569–1614. https://doi.org/10.1257/jel.37.4.1569.

Pierrakis, Yannis, and Liam Collins. 2013. *Banking on Each Other: Peer-to-Peer Lending to Business: Evidence from Funding Circle*. London: Nesta Operating Company. https://www.nesta.org.uk/documents/71/banking_on_each_other.pdf.

Poetz, Marion K., and Martin Schreier. 2012. 'The Value of Crowdsourcing: Can Users Really Compete with Professionals in Generating New Product Ideas?' *The Journal of Product Innovation Management* 29 (2): 245–256.

Priti, Ambani. 2020. '*Top 15 Crowdfunding Platforms in Europe*.' Crowd Sourcing Week. Accessed March 15, 2021. https://crowdsourcingweek.com/blog/top-15-crowdfunding-platforms-in-europe/.

PwC. 2016. 'Financial Services Technology 2020 and Beyond: Embracing Disruption.' New York. https://www.pwc.com/gx/en/financial-services/assets/pdf/technology2020-and-beyond.pdf.

Raeymaeckers, Peter, and Stijn Van Puyvelde. 2021. 'Non-profit Advocacy Coalitions in Times of COVID-19: Brokerage, Crowdfunding, and Advocacy Roles.' *Non-profit and Voluntary Sector Quarterly* (forthcoming). https://doi.org/10.1177/0899764021991675.

Rajwa, Pawel, Philip Hopen, Lin Mu, Andrzej Paradysz, Jakub Wojnarowicz, Cary P Gross, and Michael S Leapman. 2020. 'Online Crowdfunding Response to Coronavirus Disease 2019.' *Journal of General Internal Medicine* 35(8): 2482–2484. https://doi.org/10.1007/s11606-020-05896-x.

*Regulation (EU) 2020/1503 of the European Parliament and of the Council of 7 October 2020 on European Crowdfunding Service Providers for Business, and Amending Regulation (EU) 2017/1129 and Directive (EU) 2019/1937*

*(Text with EEA Relevance)*. 2020. Brussels: European Parliament and the Council. Accessed March 20, 2021 https://eur-lex.europa.eu/legal-content/EN/TXT/?uri=CELEX:32020R1503.

Renwick, Matthew J., and Elias Mossialos. 2017. 'Crowdfunding Our Health: Economic Risks and Benefits.' *Social Science and Medicine* 191: 48–56. https://doi.org/10.1016/j.socscimed.2017.08.035.

Rossi, Alice, and Silvio Vismara. 2018. 'What Do Crowdfunding Platforms Do? A Comparison between Investment-Based Platforms in Europe.' *Eurasian Business Review* 8 (1): 93–118. https://doi.org/10.1007/s40821-017-0092-6.

Ruef, Martin, Howard E. Aldrich, and Nancy M. Carter. 2003. 'The Structure of Founding Teams: Homophily, Strong Ties, and Isolation among US Entrepreneurs.' *American Sociological Review* 68 (2): 195–222.

Saleh, Sameh Nagui, Christoph U Lehmann, and Richard J Medford. 2021. 'Early Crowdfunding Response to the COVID-19 Pandemic: Cross-Sectional Study.' *Journal of Medical Internet Research* 23 (2): e25429.

Salido-Andres, Noelia, Marta Rey-Garcia, Luis Ignacio Alvarez-Gonzalez, and Rodolfo Vazquez-Casielles. 2021. 'Mapping the Field of Donation-Based Crowdfunding for Charitable Causes: Systematic Review and Conceptual Framework.' *VOLUNTAS: International Journal of Voluntary and Nonprofit Organizations* 32 (2): 288–302. https://doi.org/10.1007/s11266-020-002 13-w.

Schwienbacher, Armin, and Benjamin Larralde. 2012. 'Crowdfunding of Small Entrepreneurial Ventures.' In *The Oxford Handbook of Entrepreneurial Finance*, edited by Douglas Cumming, 23. Oxford: Oxford University Press. https://doi.org/10.1093/oxfordhb/9780195391244.013.0013.

Short, Jeremy C, David J Ketchen Jr, Aaron F McKenny, Thomas H Allison, and R Duane Ireland. 2017. 'Research on Crowdfunding: Reviewing the (Very Recent) Past and Celebrating the Present.' *Entrepreneurship Theory and Practice* 41 (2): 149–160.

Snyder, Jeremy, Marco Zenone, and Timothy Caulfield. 2021. 'Crowdfunding Campaigns and COVID-19 Misinformation.' *American Journal of Public Health* 111 (4): 739–742.

Statista. 2021. '*Crowdfunding*.' Accessed March 8, 2021. https://www.statista.com/outlook/dmo/fintech/alternative-financing/crowdfunding/worldwide.

Usher, Ann Danaiya. 2020. 'WHO Launches Crowdfund for COVID-19 Response.' *The Lancet* 395 (10229): 1024. https://doi.org/10.1016/S0140-6736(20)30719-4.

Valuates Reports. 2019a. '*Global Crowdfunding Market Size, Status and Forecast 2021–2027*.' tps://reports.valuates.com/market-reports/QYRE-Auto-1598/global-crowdfunding.

Valuates Reports. 2019b. '*The Global Crowdfunding Market Was Valued at 10.2 Billion US$ in 2018 and Is Expected to Reach 28.8 Billion US$ with a CAGR of 16% by 2025 - Valuates Reports*.' Accessed April 8, 2021. https://www.prnewswire.com/in/news-releases/the-global-crowdfunding-market-was-valued-at-10-2-billion-us-in-2018-and-is-expected-to-reach-28-8-billion-us-with-a-cagr-of-16-by-2025-valuates-reports-888819175.html.

Wang, Tao, Yalan Li, Minghui Kang, and Haichao Zheng. 2019. 'Exploring Individuals' Behavioral Intentions toward Donation Crowdfunding: Evidence from China.' *Industrial Management & Data Systems* 119 (7): 1515–1534. /https://doi.org/10.1108/IMDS-10-2018-0451.

Zhang, Yali, Chrissie Diane Tan, Jun Sun, and Zhaojun Yang. 2020. 'Why Do People Patronise Donation-Based Crowdfunding Platforms? An Activity Perspective of Critical Success Factors.' *Computers in Human Behavior* 112 (11): 1-9. https://doi.org/10.1016/j.chb.2020.106470.

Zhao, Qun, Chun Der Chen, Jin Long Wang, and Pin Chung Chen. 2017. 'Determinants of Backers' Funding Intention in Crowdfunding: Social Exchange Theory and Regulatory Focus.' *Telematics and Informatics* 34 (1): 370–84. https://doi.org/10.1016/j.tele.2016.06.006.

Ziegler, Tania, and Rotem Shneor, eds. 2020. 'The Global Alternative Finance Market Benchmarking Report.' Cambridge: University of Cambridge. Accessed March 30, 2021. https://www.jbs.cam.ac.uk/faculty-research/centres/alternative-finance/publications/the-global-alternative-finance-market-benchmarking-report/.

## Suggested Readings

Andreoni, Valeria. 2019. 'Sharing Economy: Risks and Opportunities in a Framework of SDGs.' In *Sustainable Cities and Communities*, edited by Walter Leal Filho, Anabela Marisa Azul, Luciana Brandli, Pinar Gökcin Özuyar, and Tony Wall, 1–9. Cham: Springer International Publishing. https://doi.org/10.1007/978-3-319-71061-7_60-1.

Munger, Michael C. 2018. *Tomorrow 3.0: Transaction Costs and the Sharing Economy*. New York: Cambridge University Press.

Parker, Geoffrey, Marshall Van Alstyne, and Sangeet Paul Choudary. 2017. *Platform Revolution: How Networked Markets Are Transforming the Economy - and How to Make Them Work for You. First published as a Norton paperback.* New York London: W. W. Norton & Company.

## Relevant Websites

Internal Market, Industry, Entrepreneurship and SMEs: https://ec.europa.eu/growth/single-market/services/collaborative-economy_en.
What do we share in a sharing economy?: https://www.un.org/development/desa/undesavoice/more-from-undesa/2020/03/48735.html.

# 9

# Education, Knowledge and Data in the Context of the Sharing Economy

Gabriela Avram and Eglantina Hysa

## Introduction

Many of the existing definitions of the collaborative economy refer to efficient access to underused goods and spaces making use of the internet and reputation systems (Sundarajan 2016). Schor (2014) speaks about recirculation of goods, increased utilisation of durable assets, exchange of services, sharing of productive assets and building of social connections. When attempting to apply such definitions to education, data and knowledge sharing, we are faced with difficulties. Benkler's (2004)

G. Avram (✉)
Computer Science and Information Systems Department,
University of Limerick, Limerick, Ireland
e-mail: gabriela.avram@ul.ie

E. Hysa
Department of Economics, Epoka University, Tirana, Albania
e-mail: ehysa@epoka.edu.al


V. Česnuitytė et al. (eds.), *The Sharing Economy in Europe*,
https://doi.org/10.1007/978-3-030-86897-0_9

approach that refers extensively to community building, social relationships, altruism, sustainable lifestyles and non-monetary exchanges as the main drivers of sharing or collaborative economies constituted for us a more appropriate context. In their discussion of the Sharing Economy, Schor et al. (2016, p. 75) refer to open learning as a practice 'that uses free or low-cost educational resources that are typically open access, peer-led, shareable, and digitally mediated'. The MOOCs (Massive Online Open Courses) discussed in this chapter, as well as a wide range of educational activities mediated by online platforms and open to large categories of the public, can be seen as open learning opportunities. Regarding both formal and nonformal education, there are a number of educational platforms widely used, such as Khan Academy, Udacity, Coursera, Skillshare, LinkedIn Learning, Udemy, Codecademy, and edX, that benefit students from all over the world. The attractivity of these platforms is enhanced by general accessibility and the quality of the user experience offered. Nevertheless, a problematic aspect is potential commercial, social, and political influences that could introduce a bias in educational content. Aspects related to incorporating case studies, data and other content belonging to former students in the new versions of a course raise questions regarding the intellectual ownership of this content. Also, data analytics are used to improve the sequence and automate further the delivery often without enough attention given to obtaining the students' consent to participate in research, and their privacy, identity, and anonymity (Marshall 2014). These other priorities need to be clearly communicated to prospective students.

In this chapter, we prioritise the group of initiatives focusing on social innovation and striving for more sustainable economic and environmental models based on sharing access to goods and services, which have been the focus of our Sharing and Caring COST Action (Sharing and Caring 2021), while looking at how open education and knowledge sharing can be seen as part of the collaborative economy. These domains are not among the frequently discussed examples of collaborative economy initiatives; however, learning objects, knowledge, and skills are particularly important intangible assets in today's digital economy and are at the basis of a whole range of evolving services. The following sections of this chapter are dedicated to collaborative developments in education, including examples of open education and shared resources in Europe, as well as knowledge and data sharing via open and inclusive approaches, providing examples of local European initiatives. We examined the Sharing and Caring COST Action collection of country reports (Klimczuk, Česnuitytė, and Avram 2021) and more than 130 short stories available on the Sharing and Caring website (Sharing and Caring 2021) and included a series of examples from the countries participating in the COST Action. Finally, the chapter offers a reflection on the particularities of these activities from the perspective of the sharing economy.

## Collaborative Developments in Education

The use of open educational resources (OER)—that are freely licensed and remixable learning resources, has increased in the last decade, mainly due to the abundance of user-generated content and new types of content licensing such as Creative Commons. Open Educational Practices (OEP) are also evolving, supporting the opening and sharing of educational processes, and new collaborations between students and lecturers emerge, with the goal of improving access and empowering learners (Cronin and MacLaren 2018). New formats, such as open, connected courses (enabling students to connect with students and educators in other institutions and countries) and co-creation of open textbooks with students (Stagg and Partridge 2019), are also evolving. The learning theory promoted by George Siemens (2005) and Stephen Downes (2010) titled 'connectivism' looks at learning that takes place online across peer networks. Technologies such as web browsers, email, wiki, blogs, online forums, social networks, education games, platforms such as YouTube and Vimeo enable users to learn together and from each other and to share information with peers. A key feature of connectivism is that much learning can happen across peer networks that connect online. In line with the knowledge and skills gained through online learning and education, social learning and interaction are seen as important components of the educational framework. As Downes (2014) stated, applications and environments in social learning include: collaborative (wiki-style document authoring); cooperative (social sharing of bookmarks and resources); and competitive (games and contests) learning. Siemens and Downes were the creators of the first MOOC—*Connectivism and Connected Knowledge*, that was offered at the University of Manitoba in 2008 (Hollands and Devayani 2014). This type of MOOC is 'based on the idea that learning happens within a network, where learners use digital platforms such as blogs, wikis, social media platforms to make connections with content, learning communities and other learners to create and construct knowledge' (Siemens 2012).

A couple of years later (2011), several famous universities such as Harvard, MIT and Stanford started online courses based on a traditional classroom structure, including pre-recorded video lectures and assessments (quizzes, tests, projects). These are usually centred around a teaching team rather than around an open community of learners. The Stanford-style MOOCs were designed to scale education originally offered face-to-face. Also, research undertaken in parallel with running these courses focused on structuring and sequencing efficiently the transmission of knowledge. The initial idea behind this offering was creating a global service by bringing in people that were until then excluded from higher education and turning them into online learners at some of the world's best universities (Reich and Ruipérez-Valiente 2019). But in the end, these courses attracted mainly learners from well-off countries and neighbourhoods, who were using these courses to complement their education. To help distinguish between the two educational approaches, the terms 'cMOOC' and 'xMOOC' were coined, 'c' denoting the focus on connectivism and 'x' denoting exponential, focusing on the massive enrolments, or extension (Hollands and Devayani 2014). The use of the term open in MOOC is often disputed, as the content of xMOOCs is seldom open reusable content licensed under Creative Commons. More often than not, the content is strictly copyrighted. Although in the beginning, participation in such courses was completely free, in time, platforms such as Coursera, edX, FutureLearn and Udemy have started charging for certificates. Another important set of aspects of xMOOCs that were addressed by researchers is related to ethical issues. Back in 2012, when Harvard first got involved in MOOCs by developing the MOOC platform edX, its president was quoted in a press release stating that the purpose for doing so was to extend its reach by conducting research into effective education (Marshall 2014). This way, he made clear that beyond the generous offer of elite university courses to anyone on the planet with good use of the English language and Internet access, the university's strategic goal was to build a better understanding of e-learning.

In Europe, Goldie (2016) examined the role of MOOCs, emphasising the role played by the European Commission in advocating open education through the use of MOOCs. Following this, a group of European Universities partnered and launched the Openup Ed initiative in 2013. Openup Ed focuses on online courses for large numbers of participants, courses that can be accessed by anyone anywhere via the Internet, open to everyone and offering a full course experience for free. Although based in Europe, Openup Ed has an international scope. The courses offered are hosted on various platforms.

Eshach (2007) created a taxonomy of education/learning types that can prove relevant when examining open education. Eshach distinguished the following three types: formal education, taking place mainly through the national education system, and including both academic studies and full-time specialised professional training; any organised educational activity happening outside the established education system, initiated for specific target groups, and having concrete learning objectives is categorised as nonformal education. Finally, the lifelong process of acquiring knowledge, skills, attitudes, and values in one's environment, without the express intention to learn, is termed as informal education. E-learning platforms offer both formal education (as in the cases of Coursera, edX, Udacity) and nonformal education/courses (the case of LinkedIn Learning, Instructables, Adobe, etc.). On the other side, informal learning happens daily and spontaneously when users check information on Wikipedia, consult YouTube or Vimeo user-generated content on a specific topic or ask questions on platforms such as Quora or Reddit. On the other hand, Reich (2020) considers three models of online learning: (1) MOOCs, where learning is guided by a human instructor (or team of instructors) following a set sequence; (2) Algorithm-led learning—where learners are assessed by software, and the sequence of lessons is reorganised automatically (Khan Academy) and (3)

Peer-guided learning, or networked environments learning, where the learners guide each other or learn from each other, like in the case of Do-It-Yourself (DIY) forums, crafts circles or sports group enthusiasts.

In today's world, the reach of e-learning platforms is going far beyond MOOCs. E-learning platforms are the mechanism that supports the sharing of diverse learning content with users, the gathering of learning analytics and the refinement of the content and sequence based on the users' response in a wide range of organisations, such as universities, specialised training companies, communities and large companies looking to train their staff or customers. During the COVID-19 pandemic, not only university education but also primary and secondary school activities, as well as numerous nonformal courses, were forced to shift online. Those institutions that already had an effective digital platform for either complementing face-to-face learning activities or for providing blended or fully online tuition were advantaged, as they were able to pivot online quickly and efficiently. Table 9.1 presents a selection of the most popular educational platforms in use worldwide.

Another concept based on sharing resources and large-scale collaboration is that of Open Science, seen as a movement seeking to 'leverage new practices and digital technologies to increase transparency and access in scholarly research' (van der Zee and Reich 2018, p. 2). Based on Open Science, van der Zee and Reich propose a framework for Open Education Science, including Open Access to publications, Open Design of educational resources and pedagogy, Open Data for collecting data on the outcomes, and Open Analysis for analysing the results. The idea of collaborative teaching and learning as peer learning and peer production also appears in the Peeragogy Project, initiated by Howard Rheingold in 2012 (Corneli et al. 2016). All these developments in education are supported by digital platforms and are based on sharing resources such as content, practices, and analytics, with or without financial incentives. Besides these educational platforms and initiatives, the Sharing and Caring COST Action also revealed a series of examples of networks and platforms from the participating countries in Europe and beyond that assist people to share knowledge and skills with each other, many using a digital platform and some also centred around a physical meeting place that is presented below in Table 9.2.

**Table 9.1** Educational Platforms

| Platform | For-profit/Non-profit | Origin | Starting year | Characteristics | Courses offer |
|---|---|---|---|---|---|
| Coursera | for-profit (start-up) | United States | 2012 | partnering with academic and governmental institutions—online courses, certifications, and degrees in a variety of subjects | Paid (7 days free taster)<br>Plus version |
| edX | non-profit | United States | 2012 | online university-level courses in a wide range of disciplines to a worldwide student body, including some courses at no charge; created open-source platform offered to other organisations | Free<br>Paid certification<br>edX for business |

(continued)

**Table 9.1** (continued)

| Platform | For-profit/Non-profit | Origin | Starting year | Characteristics | Courses offer |
|---|---|---|---|---|---|
| Khan Academy | non-profit | United States | 2008 | short lessons in the form of videos- initially maths but now expanded to include other domains | Free |
| Udacity | non-profit | United States | 2012 | academic, nanodegrees (upskilling) | Paid certification |
| Codecademy | non-profit | United States | 2011 | learning how to code | Free<br>Codecademy pro – subscription-based |
| LinkedIn Learning (was Lynda.com) | for-profit | United States | 1995 | courses in creative media, programming, business<br>In 2002, it started offering courses online<br>It was acquired by LinkedIn in 2015 and became part of Microsoft in 2016<br>Renamed LinkedIn Learning in 2017 | Paid |

| Platform | For-profit/Non-profit | Origin | Starting year | Characteristics | Courses offer |
|---|---|---|---|---|---|
| Skillshare | for-profit | United States | 2011 | courses based on educational videos in advertising, business, design, fashion and style, film and video, food and drink, music, photography, gaming, technology, and writing and publishing, often taught by industry leaders | Subscription-based<br>Not accredited |
| Google Digital Garage | For-profit | United States | 2015 | Digital marketing courses for training employees, partners, and customers | Free<br>Certification available |

*Source* Own elaboration

**Table 9.2** Examples of open education and shared resources in Europe

| Initiative | Description |
|---|---|
| CoderDojo (Ireland) https://coderdojo.com | Initiated in 2011 by a young person in Ireland to support other school children to acquire coding skills at a young age. The model proliferated to cities and villages in many countries around the world, where volunteers who know how to code offer to teach children and teenagers a couple of hours a month, usually at a specific location in the neighbourhood. During the COVID pandemic, all the activities moved online |
| Brainster (North Macedonia) https://brainster.co | Designed to fill the gap in formal education, the online platform is used for offering courses in subjects connected to the needs of the labour market and creating a significant economic and social impact |
| My Education Club (Bulgaria) www.myeducationclub.com | Initiative offering older people the opportunity of developing new skills in subjects such as mathematics, history, geography and Bulgarian language, but also in nonformal subjects such as cooking, playing a musical instrument, sewing, embroidery or chess |
| Klearlending (Bulgaria) https://www.klearlending.com | A combination of peer-to-peer lending and free financial education, created by an innovative FinTech company |
| BeeHome Coworking Subotica (Republic of Serbia) http://crnjakovic.com/beehome-coworking-subotica/ | Platform for supporting entrepreneurship and education |
| Seduo, Nostis (Czech Republic) https://www.seduo.cz https://www.nostis.org | Online platforms for education |

(continued)

**Table 9.2** (continued)

| Initiative | Description |
|---|---|
| Floqq, Cursopedia (Spain) https://www.floqq.com https://www.plataformasdecursos.gratis/cursopedia/ | Platforms allowing teachers to share knowledge on certain subjects by uploading video recordings made available for students for free or in exchange for a fee |
| BBOM (Baska bir okul mumkun) (Turkey) http://www.baskabirokulmumkun.org | An alternative school system that runs on a cooperative model. The BBOM coops integrate several ways of sharing and works with a lot of volunteer organisations to offer quality education |
| s:coop (Germany) https://www.scoop.vision | The platform was created to support commons-oriented innovation. It is the result of a collaboration between art students and educators. Its focus is on the creation of shared infrastructure and alternative innovation narratives to support the shift from start-up individualism to a collaborative agency |
| Speak (Portugal) https://www.speak.social/en | A platform that provides language lessons to non-local people, serving as a bridge towards social integration. Going beyond language teaching, the general goal is to familiarise newcomers with the local culture, support them in job search and integration in the local community. The classes are offered face-to-face |
| KIPOS3 (Garden in a Cube) (Greece) https://www.facebook.com/cityasaresource | This initiative aims to support the transformation of vacant urban sites into community gardens. Gardening is used as a tool to turn the neighbourhood into an active and engaged community. Another goal is increasing the city's resilience through food production and the reappropriation of common urban space. The initiative's Facebook page serves as a platform for co-creating not only gardening knowledge but also discussing wider environmental and social issues |

(continued)

Table 9.2 (continued)

| Initiative | Description |
|---|---|
| Kaptar (Hungary) https://kaptarbudapest.hu/en/ | This co-working space for freelancers, SMEs and digital nomads organise workshops for professional development for its members, as well as community events and a network of current and former members |

*Source* Own elaboration, based on (Klimczuk, Česnuitytė, and Avram 2021; Sharing and Caring 2021)

## Knowledge Sharing via Open and Inclusive Approaches

Besides education, there are other domains that benefitted heavily from the emergence of digital platforms and the opportunity of sharing information across the globe. Benkler (2004) introduced the term 'shareable goods' and illustrated his 'commons-based peer production' concept, seen as a large-scale cooperative effort in which what is shared among the participants is their creative effort, building on the example of Open-Source Software development communities. Benkler and Nissenbaum (2020, p. 70) stated that 'socio-technical systems of commons-based peer production offer not only a remarkable medium of production for various kinds of information goods, but also serve as a context for positive character formation'. Inspired by the Open-Source Software movement, the Wikipedia project started in 2001 and demonstrated the potential of global collaboration in creating a free and open encyclopaedia that could be delivered 'to every single person on the planet in their own language' (Cohen 2008). Several other projects followed, such as OpenStreetMap (an open maps collaboration space), Quora (a questions and answers platform), Instructables (a space for sharing step-by-step instructions for DIY projects), Open Plaques (a crowdsourced collection of information on historical commemorative plaques), and WikiVoyage (a crowdsourced travel guide for travel destinations written by volunteers), to name but a few.

One of the domains that received a strong boost from the open global collaboration is innovation. As digital platforms offer a suitable environment for value creation and sharing, new open and distributed models of innovation emerged (Nambisan et al. 2018). Collaborative innovation has become a global trend, involving multiple stakeholders who engage in non-copyrighted innovation and create new solutions and technologies using open, collaborative platforms (Biasin and Kamenjasevic 2019), open to companies and individuals, creating new business models.

The open design movement focuses on developing physical products, machines, and systems by making use of publicly shared design information. Within this movement, one trend sees volunteers coming together and donating their time and skills working on projects for the common good—either because funding is lacking, or because there is not sufficient commercial interest, or for helping developing countries, promoting environmentally friendly or cheaper technologies (Pearce et al. 2010). A second trend is bringing together people and resources from different companies and countries for developing advanced projects and technologies that would be beyond the resources of any single company. Another trend involves the use of high-tech open-source solutions developed globally that is further adapted to respond to solving local challenges in a sustainable manner, sometimes labelled as 'Design Globally, Manufacture Locally'. Schismenos et al. (2020) see this trend as being a new form of egalitarian and transnational collaborative networks (that they label as 'cosmo-localism'), which could challenge the core values of capitalism and invite to further reflection going beyond its effects on production and distribution. These digital platforms provide the necessary infrastructure for individuals and organisations to share ideas online, work on joint projects and co-create products working together, supporting collaborative innovation that happens online (Biasin and Kamenjasevic 2019).

In order to illustrate the variety of digital platforms supporting online collaboration and co-creation worldwide, we include here a series of examples. For instance, AguaClara is an engineering group at Cornell University publishing an open-source design tool and CAD designs for water treatment plants (AguaClara 2021), while Open Source Ecology (OSE) is a network comprising of farmers, engineers, architects, and supporters. The main goal of OSE is manufacturing a so-called Global Village Construction Set (GVCS), an open technological platform that will allow the fabrication of 50 types of industrial machines that would be necessary for 'building a small civilisation with modern comforts' (Open Source Ecology 2021). In a different vein, Wikispeed is an automotive manufacturer that produces modular design cars. The project participants apply scrum development techniques borrowed from the software world. They use open-source tools and lean management methods to improve productivity (Wikispeed 2021). In addition, focusing on 3D printing technology, some knowledge sharing projects such as e-NABLE and Thingiverse allow the dissemination of creativity outcomes online. e-NABLE is a global network of volunteers who are using their 3D printers, design skills, and personal time to create free 3D printed prosthetic hands for those in need—with the goal of providing them to underserved populations around the world (e-NABLE 2021). With a more general scope, Thingiverse is a platform dedicated to the sharing of user-created digital design files that provides mainly free, open-source hardware designs licensed under the GNU General Public License or Creative Commons licenses. Each contributor can select a user license type for the designs that they share. The digital blueprints shared can be used for creating physical objects using 3D printers, laser cutters, milling machines and other technologies. The platform is widely used by DIY enthusiasts and communities as a repository for shared innovation and dissemination of source materials to the public (Thingiverse 2021).

Knowledge sharing between various stakeholders, as Biasin and Kamenjasevic (2020) pointed out, is the common denominator across these kinds of platforms. Users and communities are enabled to collaborate online by using the advantages of new digital technologies. Open knowledge sharing contributes to the spread of designs and project ideas worldwide. However, some of the Open-Source projects, especially the ones related to open hardware, could face a few legal challenges. These are related mainly to privacy and data protection, as data are being widely shared and manipulated, and to intellectual property rights, which can be complicated when participants reside in various countries and work for different organisations. Another complex issue is a liability—who will be responsible for the malfunctioning of an open-source car, water installation, or prosthetic? Table 9.3 presents a selection of open and inclusive sharing initiatives identified by the participants in the Sharing and Caring COST Action.

In this type of community, knowledge is offered freely for mutual benefit. It is also difficult to quantify individual contributions, making knowledge sharing a different type of transaction. This category sees the production of so-called 'information goods' (Benkler 2004) that are going into the design of both physical and digital products. Value is created from collaboration and synergy. Learning and community building are side effects of the collaboration, mirroring the ethos of the early days of Open-Source Software projects. Such collaboration projects supported by online platforms are enhancing resilience all around the globe, providing a solution to a wide range of problems. In difficult times—such as natural disasters, pandemics, conflict—this kind of project take off rapidly based on existing experience. One example is the Coronavirus Tech Handbook, initiated in the early weeks of the pandemic at Newspeak House, a London hackerspace, that received rapid contributions from thousands of volunteers (Maddyness 2020). The handbook is a library of tools, services and resources relating to the COVID-19 response that was crowdsourced. The site, launched in March 2020, is hosted as an interlinked collection of user-editable online documents allowing frequent updates.

Open and inclusive knowledge sharing initiatives facilitated by online platforms are stimulating innovation and allow individuals and communities with similar interests to find each other and work together. The role and importance of these activities have become even more prominent during the COVID-19 pandemic. Information, skills and competencies are shared locally and globally with notable results.

**Table 9.3** Examples of open and inclusive sharing initiatives in Europe

| Initiative | Description |
|---|---|
| SmartWolf (Austria) https://smartcities.at/projects/smartwolf/ | SmartWolf is an Urban Lab established in 2016 in Vienna to encourage citizens' participation in the redesign of the public space in the city centre. Physical space was created in a vacant building as a meeting place for groups working on different ideas for revitalising the city centre. Several initiatives have emerged in the space, such as a Repair Café, a People's Kitchen, etc |
| Ekofil (Turkey) https://ekofilyayinlari.org | Ekofil is an initiative of a group of writers, illustrators, translators, editors, and readers who came together to design, implement, and develop a community-supported publishing model that takes into consideration the well-being of the planet and humanity |
| Fragnebenan (Austria) https://fragnebenan.com | The platform was founded in 2015 as a vehicle for neighbourly help in Austria. It supports the sharing of material goods, timesharing, and the sharing knowledge, experiences, and information. Its concept is based on geographical proximity: people register with their home address and receive an activation code by post. After activating their account, registered users can contact neighbours in a radius of 750 m. There are no fees for using the platform. Its impact is the promotion of communication among neighbours, the exchange of goods, support, and experience, as well as the re-use of unused products and idle resources |

(continued)

Table 9.3 (continued)

| Initiative | Description |
|---|---|
| K-space (Estonia) https://www.k-space.ee | A community-driven hackerspace founded in 2016. It is located on TalTech campus, IT College, in Tallinn, Estonia. Its facilities include a cybersecurity lab, a digital fabrication lab, a server room, a common kitchen, and co-working areas. It hosts several topic-related meetups, such as those of *Tallinn Sec*, a non-profit organisation of information security professionals, practitioners and enthusiasts, or *Hack the Box*, an online platform for penetration testing skills. Other events hosted include code clubs, crypto parties, or beer brewing |

*Source* Own elaboration based on (Klimczuk, Česnuitytė, and Avram 2021; Sharing and Caring 2021)

## Platforms Facilitating Collaborative Information Production and Consumption

The European Commission sees data-driven innovation as a 'key enabler of growth and jobs in Europe (European Commission 2018, p. 1). Data sharing is seen by the Commission as an economic activity. Richter and Slowinski (2019) point out the absence of a generally accepted definition when it comes to data sharing. The term 'sharing' involves a benign connotation and makes a connection to the 'sharing economy'. Based on defining the sharing economy as 'the more efficient use of resources – mostly products and services – as a consequence of a technically enabled reduction of transaction costs' (Richter and Slowinski 2019, p. 8) and on considering 'data sharing' as virtually all sorts of data flows between companies, with customers and even within companies—the perspective of the EU Commission (2018), the focus is put on sharing platforms as (third-party) enablers for sharing data. Access to information stored in digital datasets plays a major role in both societal development and the well-being of citizens. The possibilities of data-driven innovation based on machine learning and other technologies are based on the availability of extensive datasets for training the algorithms (Richter and Slowinski 2019). Lately, several citizen initiatives have started to explore how citizens could harness the value of their personal data themselves. We focus here on peer-to-peer data sharing and data sharing initiatives that rely on crowdsourcing. While in a lot of such data initiatives, there are no financial incentives, there are specific examples where individuals come together to form cooperatives and harness the economic value of data for the benefit of members.

Patients LikeMe, a private venture, started as an initiative persuading patients with rare conditions to donate their data for the use of professional medical researchers to help research progress faster. New European initiatives such as MiData (van Velthoven et al. 2019) raise awareness on the value of personal health data and encourage individuals to join forces in a cooperative so that they can be the ones who decide how their data is being used. Salus, is a citizen data cooperative based in Spain and focused on legitimising the right of citizens to maintain control over their own data while being able to facilitate data sharing to accelerate research and innovation in the health sector.

Citizen science projects invite the public to contribute the data they collect following specific guidelines to large-scale projects (Riesch and Potter 2014). While science should respond to citizens' concerns and needs, the citizens themselves must be able to produce reliable scientific knowledge. In this case, the peer-to-peer relationship is replaced with the centralisation of data for the general benefit of science. When the data collected is aggregated, analysed, and shared for the benefit of the public, a virtuous cycle is created, encouraging sustained participation. Reporting invasive species (Schade et al. 2019) is an activity that was made more attractive and accessible using smartphone applications that support both identification and geographic localisation of reports. An initiative that allowed citizens to map the noise levels data over a period in a specific area using a Smart Citizen kit was seen as useful for requesting a revision of legislation for bars and cafes (Balestrini et al. 2015). Another example of data crowdsourcing that benefits the wider community is citizen sensing and reporting projects that focus on air quality that complement the official sources of information (Wesseling et al. 2019). Many such projects are the result of grassroots initiatives, where contributors are sharing data with each other and also publicly. Table 9.4 presents a selection of data sharing initiatives revealed by participants in the Sharing and Caring COST Action.

Data sharing is by no means a new activity. However, examining data sharing from the perspective of the sharing economy has the advantage of revealing the importance of data as a resource in both peer-to-peer exchanges and transactions involving third parties.

**Table 9.4** Examples of data sharing initiatives in Europe

| Initiative | Description |
|---|---|
| Invasive Species (Ireland) https://invasivespecies.limerick.ie | Mobile phone application developed to address the issue of invasive plants spread, by educating citizens and facilitating easy reporting of this phenomenon. The local council collaborated with national organisations, farmers, community groups and local development companies to develop the concept. The resulting platform supports users to report invasive plants sightings by uploading a photograph with GPS coordinates of the location. After verifications, these reports appear on the map as open data and are added to a central national biodiversity database |
| GROW Observatory https://growobservatory.org | Platform for collecting and sharing information on soil, the land and on crops through growers' participation across Europe. Data collection was achieved via low-cost sensing technology kits communicating with citizens' own devices<br>The outcome is a hub of open knowledge and data created and maintained by growers, which supports both growers and other specialist communities |

*Source* Own elaboration based on (Sharing and Caring 2021)

## Summary

The activities included in this chapter: sharing education resources, knowledge and data, are seldom mentioned as being part of the sharing economy. Sharing intangible digital resources such as learning resources, domain knowledge and huge quantities of data—from personal data to analytics and sensor-generated data—have become the norm in today's world. According to the definition of the digital sharing economy elaborated by Pouri and Hilty (2021, pp. 129–130), the resources we discussed in this chapter qualify as durable immaterial goods, including 'durable information and competencies'—when examined from the shareable resources' perspective. With regard to the sharing practices, there are a variety of models employed. Initially, access to MOOCs was free, in principle 'without reciprocity or compensation' (Pouri and Hilty 2021, p. 131). However, both the content of students' assignments and learning analytics were used to improve successive versions of both the learning resources and pedagogic practices. In open knowledge sharing communities, participants contribute time, competencies and information without reciprocity or compensations. Where companies get involved in such communities, they usually support the digital infrastructure and offer premium access as a way to monetise content (as in the case of Instructables).

In all three domains presented in this chapter, open education, knowledge and data sharing, the role of online platforms is paramount. These types of sharing are made possible and facilitated by the platforms that set the terms of collaboration and support coordination in all these cases. Given the immaterial nature of the goods being shared, the inclusion of these exchanges in the sharing economy is disputed by many authors (see, for example, Frenken et al. 2015). Instead of dealing with idle capacity, these resources are highly shareable, and besides the direct creation of new services and products, they contribute to creating community, increasing social capital, and contributing to the common good. In all these cases, re-use, scaling, peer production, and consumption are made possible by the existence of digital platforms as a coordination mechanism.

## References

AguaClara. 2021. http://aguaclara.cornell.edu.

Balestrini, Mara, Tomas Diez, Paul Marshall, Alex Gluhak, and Yvonne Rogers. 2015. 'IoT Community Technologies: Leaving Users to Their Own Devices or Orchestration of Engagement?.' *EAI Endorsed Transactions on Internet of Things* 1 (1). https://doi.org/10.4108/eai.26-10-2015.150601.

Benkler, Yochai, and Helen Nissenbaum. 2020. 'Commons-Based Peer Production and Virtue' (reprint). In *The Handbook of Peer Production*, edited by O'Neil, Mathieu, Christian Pentzold, Sophie Toupin, John Wiley & Sons, 70–86, https://doi.org/10.1002/9781119537151.ch6.

Benkler, Yochai. 2004. 'Sharing Nicely: On Shareable Goods and the Emergence of Sharing as a Modality of Economic Production.' *Yale Law Journal* 114: 273–358. https://doi.org/10.2307/4135731.

Biasin, Elisabetta, and Erik Kamenjasevic. 2019. 'Made4You/Careables.org: D5. 3-White Paper on Legal Guidelines.' https://doi.org/10.5281/zenodo.408614.

Biasin, Elisabetta, and Erik Kamenjasevic. 2020. 'Open Source Hardware and Healthcare Collaborative Platforms: Common Legal Challenges.' *Journal of Open Hardware* 4 (1): 1–8. https://doi.org/10.5334/joh.31.

Cohen, Noam. 2008. 'Open-Source Troubles in Wiki World', *The New York Times*. https://www.nytimes.com/2008/03/17/technology/17wikipedia.html.

Corneli, Joseph, Charles Jeffrey Danoff, Charlotte Pierce, Paola Ricaurte, and Lisa Snow MacDonald. 2016. 'The Peeragogy Handbook.' https://peeragogy.org.

Cronin, Catherine, and Iain MacLaren. 2018. 'Conceptualising OEP: A Review of Theoretical and Empirical Literature in Open Educational Practices.' *Open Praxis* 10 (2): 127–143. https://doi.org/10.5944/openpraxis.10.2.825.

Downes, Stephen. 2010. 'New Technology Supporting Informal Learning.' *Journal of Emerging Technologies in Web Intelligence* 2 (1): 27–33.

Downes, Stephen. 2014. 'Vision 2030: Redesigning Education for the Future.' 28 October 2014. https://www.downes.ca/files/2018%2010%2028%20-%20Vision%202030.pdf.

e-NABLE. 2021. http://enablingthefuture.org/.

Eshach, Haim. 2007. Bridging In-school and Out-of-school Learning: Formal, Non-Formal, and Informal Education. *Journal of Science Education and Technology* 16: 171–190. https://doi.org/10.1007/s10956-006-9027-1.
European Commission. 2018. 'Commission Staff Working Document, Guidance on Sharing Private Sector Data in the European Data Economy, Accompanying the Document Communication from the Commission to the European Parliament, the Council, the European Economic and Social Committee and the Committee of the Regions '*Towards a Common European Data Space*' {COM (2018) 232 final} https://eur-lex.europa.eu/legal-content/EN/TXT/PDF/?uri=CELEX:52018SC0125&rid=2.
Frenken, Koen, Toon Meelen, Martijn Arets, and Pieter Van de Glind. 2015. 'Smarter Regulation for the Sharing Economy.' *The Guardian* 20: 5. https://www.theguardian.com/science/political-science/2015/may/20/smarter-regulation-for-the-sharing-economy.
Goldie, John Gerard Scott. 2016. 'Connectivism: A knowledge learning theory for the digital age?.' *Medical Teacher* 38 (10): 1064–1069.
Hollands, Fiona M., and Devayani Tirthali. 2014. 'MOOCs: Expectations and Reality.' Full Report, *Center for Benefit-Cost Studies of Education, Teachers College, Columbia University* 138. https://teachonline.ca/sites/default/files/moocs/moocs_expectations_and_reality.pdf.
Klimczuk, Andrzej, Vida Česnuitytė, and Gabriela Avram, eds. 2021. *The Collaborative Economy in Action: European Perspectives.* Limerick, Ireland: University of Limerick.
Maddyness. 2020. 'Coronavirus Tech Handbook', *Maddyness*, 26 March 2020, https://www.maddyness.com/uk/2020/03/26/coronavirus-tech-handbook/.
Marshall, Stephen. 2014. 'Exploring the ethical implications of MOOCs.' *Distance Education* 35 (2): 250–262, https://doi.org/10.1080/01587919.2014.917706.
Nambisan, Satish, Donald Siegel, and Martin Kenney. 2018. 'On Open Innovation, Platforms, and Entrepreneurship.' *Strategic Entrepreneurship Journal* 12 (3): 354–368. https://doi.org/10.1002/sej.1300.
*Open Source Ecology*. 2021. https://www.opensourceecology.org.
Pearce, Joshua, C. Blair, Kristen Laciak, Rob Andrews, Amir Nosrat, and Ivana Zelenika-Zovko. 2010. '3-D Printing of Open Source Appropriate Technologies for Self-Directed Sustainable Development.' *European Journal of Sustainable Development* 3 (4): 17–29. ⟨hal-02120493⟩.
Pouri, Maria J., and Lorenz M. Hilty. 2021. 'The Digital Sharing Economy: A Confluence of Technical and Social Sharing.' *Environmental Innovation*

*and Societal Transitions* 38: 127–139. https://doi.org/10.1016/j.eist.2020.12.003.

Reich, Justin, and José A. Ruipérez-Valiente. 2019. 'The MOOC Pivot.' *Science* 363 (6423): 130–131. https://doi.org/10.1126/science.aav7958.

Reich, Justin. 2020. *Failure to Disrupt: Why Technology Alone Can't Transform Education.* Harvard University Press. https://doi.org/10.4159/9780674249684.

Richter, Heiko, and Peter R. Slowinski. 2019. 'The Data Sharing Economy: On the Emergence of New Intermediaries.' *IIC-International Review of Intellectual Property and Competition Law* 50 (1): 4–29.

Riesch, Hauke, and Clive Potter. 2014. 'Citizen Science as Seen by Scientists: Methodological, Epistemological and Ethical Dimensions.' *Public understanding of science* 23 (1): 107–120, https://doi.org/10.1177/0963662513497324.

Schade, Sven, Alexander Kotsev, Ana Cristina Cardoso, Konstantinos Tsiamis, Eugenio Gervasini, Fabiano Spinelli, Irena Mitton, and Roberto Sgnaolin. 2019. 'Aliens in Europe. An Open Approach to Involve More People in Invasive Species Detection.' *Computers, Environment and Urban Systems* 78:1–14. https://doi.org/10.1016/j.compenvurbsys.2019.101384.

Schismenos, Alexandros, Vasilis Niaros, and Lucas Lemos. 2020. 'Cosmolocalism: Understanding the Transitional Dynamics towards Post-Capitalism.' *tripleC: Communication, Capitalism & Critique. Open Access Journal for a Global Sustainable Information Society* 18 (2): 670–684. https://doi.org/10.31269/triplec.v18i2.1188.

Schor, Juliet B. 2014, October. *Debating the Sharing Economy, Great Transition Initiative*. Available at http://greattransition.org/publication/debating-the-sharing-economy.

Schor, Juliet B., Connor Fitzmaurice, Lindsey B. Carfagna, Will Attwood-Charles, and Emilie Dubois Poteat. 2016. 'Paradoxes of Openness and Distinction in the Sharing Economy.' *Poetics* 54: 66–81.

Sharing and Caring COST Action CA16121. 2021. '*Short Stories*.' Accessed April 15, 2021. http://sharingandcaring.eu/short-stories.

Siemens, George. 2005. 'Elearnspace. Connectivism: A Learning Theory for the Digital Age.' https://jotamac.typepad.com/jotamacs_weblog/files/Connectivism.pdf.

Siemens, George. 2012. 'MOOCs are Really a Platform.' *Elearnspace: Learning, Networks, Knowledge, Technology, Community*. 25 July 2012. http://www.elearnspace.org/blog/2012/07/25/moocs-are-really-a-platform/.

Stagg, Adrian, and Helen Partridge. 2019. 'Facilitating Open Access to Information: A Community Approach to Open Education and Open Textbooks.' *Proceedings of the Association for Information Science and Technology* 56 (1): 477–480. https://doi.org/10.1002/pra2.76.

Sundararajan, Arun. 2016. *The Sharing Economy: The End of Employment and the Rise of Crowd-Based Capitalism.* Cambridge, MA: MIT Press. https://doi.org/10.1017/beq.2018.31.

Thingiverse. 2021. https://www.thingiverse.com.

van der Zee, Tim, and Justin Reich. 2018.'Open Education Science.' *AERA Open* 4 (3). 2332858418787466.

van Velthoven, Michelle Helena, Carlos Cordon, and Goutam Challagalla. 2019. 'Digitization of Healthcare Organizations: The Digital Health Landscape and Information Theory.' *International journal of medical informatics* 124: 49–57. https://doi.org/10.1016/j.ijmedinf.2019.01.007.

Wesseling, Joost, Henri de Ruiter, Christa Blokhuis, Derko Drukker, Ernie Weijers, Hester Volten, Jan Vonk, Lou Gast, Marita Voogt, Peter Zandveld, Sjoerd van Ratingen and Erik Tielemans. 2019. 'Development and Implementation of a Platform for Public Information on Air Quality, Sensor Measurements, and Citizen Science.' *Atmosphere* 10(8): 445–464. https://doi.org/10.3390/atmos10080445.

Wikispeed. 2021. https://wikispeed.com.

## Suggested Readings

Belk, Russell W., Giana M. Eckhardt, and Fleura Bardhi. 2019. 'Introduction to the Handbook of the Sharing Economy: The Paradox of the Sharing Economy.' In *Handbook of the Sharing Economy*, edited by Belk, Russell W., Giana M. Eckhardt, and Fleura Bardhi. Edward Elgar Publishing, 1–8, https://doi.org/10.4337/9781788110549.

John, Nicholas A. 2013. 'The Social Logics of Sharing.' *The Communication Review* 16 (3): 113–131.

Liew, Anthony. 2007. 'Understanding Data, Information, Knowledge and Their Inter-Relationships.' *Journal of knowledge management practice* 8 (2): 1–16.

Mejias, Ulises A. and Nick Couldry. 2018. 'Consumption as Production: Data and the Reproduction of Capitalist Relations.' In *The Oxford Handbook of Consumption*, edited by Frederick F. Wherry and Ian Woodward, 269–282, https://doi.org/10.1093/oxfordhb/9780190695583.013.14.

Zhang, Xi, Shan Jiang, Yuting Xiao, and Yihang Cheng. 2018. Global Challenges and Developmental Lessons in the Knowledge Sharing Economy'. *Journal of Global Information Technology Management* 21 (3): 167—171. https://doi.org/10.1080/1097198X.2018.1505071.

## Relevant Websites

Global Partnership for Sustainable Development, Data Initiatives: https://www.data4sdgs.org/initiative-listing.

Sharing and Caring COST Action CA16121 website: http://sharingandcaring.eu.

# 10

# Solidarity and Care Economy in Times of 'Crisis': A View from Greece and Hungary Between 2015 and 2020

Penny Travlou and Anikó Bernát

## Introduction

Solidarity economy is an umbrella term for a wide range of collective, collaborative practices that actuate the principle of solidarity through cooperation, mutual aid, co-creation, sharing, reciprocity, altruism, volunteerism, caring, and gifting. Defining solidarity economy as a specific, singular economic model is challenging. Definitions vary across the place, time, political perspectives, and happenstance; yet, there is an increasingly common, albeit broad, understanding of solidarity economy as an economic practice motivated by solidarity and characterised by non-monetised activities, such as care labour and community nurturing

P. Travlou (✉)
University of Edinburgh, Edinburgh, UK
e-mail: p.travlou@ed.ac.uk

A. Bernát
TÁRKI Social Research Institute, Budapest, Hungary
e-mail: bernat@tarki.hu


V. Česnuitytė et al. (eds.), *The Sharing Economy in Europe*,
https://doi.org/10.1007/978-3-030-86897-0_10

(e.g., from cooking, cleaning, child-rearing, and eldercare to community events, helping a neighbour, and volunteer work). Solidarity economy comprises activities that are 'the bedrock of reproduction and essential to participation in paid work' (Kawano 2016, p. 4). Care—nurturing and care labour—is thus integral to solidarity economy. A Solidarity economy is, in effect, an economy of care that recognises 'the multiple identities of individuals and groups and their interdependency and mutual bonds' (van Osch 2013, p. 4). This economic model aligns with the concept of the 'caring human being,' according to which interrelated people act on the basis of 'mutual trust and sensitivity' (van Osch 2013, p. 4) to repair the world they inhabit (Tronto 1993).

This chapter focuses on the emergence of practices and networks of solidarity economy in two countries of the European Union (EU), Greece and Hungary, in response to two recent events construed as 'crises': the 'refugee crisis' in 2015 and the COVID-19 pandemic in 2020. Each of these two countries, one in Southern and one in Eastern Europe, has a different socio-political past and present and distinct traditions of civic action. Here, we look at how solidarity economy emerged during crisis and how it was constituted not (only) through monetised value but also through care and nurture. Our observations are based on ethnographic fieldwork, interviews, and focus groups with grassroots solidarity collectives that assembled to respond to these two 'crises' in Greece and Hungary.

Since 2008, economies of sharing have proliferated in European societies affected by the financial crisis. The emergence of alternative economic networks in many European cities (Leontidou 2012a) illustrates the resurgence of sharing economy and exemplifies the potential of this economy to generate alternatives to the mainstream capitalist market in cities undergoing an economic recession. It is argued that the economic/financial/austerity crisis in economies of the European periphery (PIIGS: Portugal, Italy, Ireland, Greece, and Spain), which reinforced a North/South and centre/periphery divide within the Eurozone (Leontidou 2012b, 2015), benefited neoliberal economic regimes through the extensive privatisation of public wealth. In Hungary, the economic crisis of the late 2000s–early 2010s triggered predominantly individual responses, such as the acceleration of emigration, and state-level responses, such as an extensive public work programme. Sharing and collaborative economic initiatives also emerged, nonetheless, and, after some delay, became relatively widespread. In those European countries where solidarity economy became a major response to the austerity crisis, solidarity practices emerged in many different domains of economic and social life.

The sharing of resources, labour, ideas, and knowledge plays an increasingly more prominent role in emerging economies of solidarity. A culture of prosumption (where communities both produce and use/consume facilities, goods, and infrastructures) and an ethos of sharing may indeed be harbingers of systemic change. As the welfare state collapses and growing numbers of people become expelled from the formal economy, solidarity economy alternatives, informed by an ethos of caring, can release economic pressures while involving people in the co-development of hybrid participatory practices, tactics, and technologies of local communal control. The local success of solidarity economy networks may not bring about the elimination of capitalism; arguably, it may contribute to the ongoing re-organisation of capitalism under new, more flexible, informal, and blurred forms, influenced—and driven by—digitalisation. As the comprehensive and rapid socio-economic transformation produces its winners and losers, supporters and opponents, the principles and practices of sharing could gain a leading role in shaping this emerging world. The radical potential of solidarity in a post-capitalistic narrative, however, is not a given but something to be sought, constructed, and, inevitably, fought for.

One question is how the social and economic logics and networks of sharing could become something more than spontaneous attempts at local relief: how they could establish valid economic alternatives that operate across interconnected localities within and across European countries. Many of these economic solidarity networks begun as local efforts of collective survival through the austerity crisis (e.g., in Greece); yet, they drove radical change by establishing an economic culture of sharing that persisted even after the 'official' end of the economic recession, and out of which new initiatives of mutual aid and care emerged (e.g., migrant/refugee solidarity, support networks during the COVID-19 pandemic). Since crisis may be not a fleeting but a permanent condition, likely to intensify in the next decades of the twenty-first century (Margariti and Travlou 2018), the networking of solidarity economy initiatives may be crucial for both their success and sustainability in the long term.

As a political tactic that encourages political action at the local level and strengthens local communal control over resources, solidarity economy projects create opportunities for the democratisation of local institutions. The burgeoning of economic solidarity networks in conditions of economic, financial, and social crisis has formed the context of social and solidarity economy (SSE) across Europe over the last decade. According to the European Forum on Social and Solidarity Economy, organised by the European United Left/Nordic Confederation Group (GUE/NGL), the SSE represents over 14 million jobs (6.5% of the total employment in the EU) and has been 'extraordinarily resilient to the impacts of the crisis concerning unemployment.' The qualitative benefits generated by the SSE have the potential to improve the quality of democracy and help to shape a framework of production and reproduction that is more compatible with social justice and sustainability (Greek News Agenda 2016).

## From Refugee to Pandemic Crisis: Grassroots Initiatives and Their Evolution in Greece and Hungary

### Case Study 1: Athens, from Austerity to Lockdown

Greece, a country whose recent history is punctuated with multiple 'crises,' may be a paradigmatic locus of solidarity economy. When the economy of Greece collapsed in the early 2010s, the state became increasingly less able and/or unwilling to provide organised relief, while many people lost their employment, income, and homes and/or became excluded from the formal economy. In these conditions, many turned to each other for help. From the onset of the austerity crisis, local activists from different fractions of the left and the anarchist/anti-authoritarian movement mobilised to build self-organised networks that provided medical, housing, and other support to fellow citizens (Arampatzi 2017; Cabot 2016; Rakopoulos 2014). The emergence of numerous barter economy networks, time banks, ethical banks, community-supported agriculture, transition towns, degrowth initiatives, free bazaars, local market cooperatives, community currency networks, and other solidarity economy initiatives across Greece illustrates practices of solidarity and socio-economic alternatives based on non-monetary and/or non-capitalist economic models. By matching the use and exchange value of goods and balancing pressures of offer and demand, these projects strengthened community relations. Approximately 150 networks of economic solidarity emerged in the early 2010s, at the onset of the Greek austerity crisis, as alternatives to the dominant neoliberal economic paradigm and potential examples of economic resilience and restructuring at the local, grassroots level (Margariti and Travlou 2018). These networks thrived in several cities, towns, and villages of Greece; most of them, however, were located in the two largest cities, Athens and Thessaloniki (Margariti and Travlou 2018). It is important to note that these networks relied on bottom-up participation and open source ICTs to support further citizen engagement. Particularly, in Athens and Thessaloniki, ICTs facilitated urban economic networking as a means for enhancing local resilience, social inclusion, and community self-management (Margariti and Travlou 2018). Grassroots digital innovations also formed the nucleus of a number of events that attracted an international audience (Leontidou 2020). For example, CommonsFest, an annual event on 'the commons' that started in Crete in 2012 by a group of open-source hacktivists, local SSE initiatives and individuals, became so popular that it was also organised in Athens in 2014–2016.

This emerging solidarity economy also attracted the interest of mainstream political actors: In its electoral programme, SYRIZA, the radical left party elected in office in 2015, pledged to base the rebuilding of the Greek economy on a strategy for cooperative development that would draw its energy from Greece's solidarity movement (Greek News Agenda 2016). Although state support was at best sketchy and inconsistent after SYRIZA's election in office in 2015, solidarity economy initiatives continued to grow. According to a recent survey by Greece's Ministry of Labour and Social Affairs, in 2020, there were 320 social and solidarity economy-related businesses and initiatives across the country, with 40.9% of these being in Attica and the rest in other urban and rural regions (Ministry of Labour and Social Affairs 2020). Nonetheless, the important role of the SSE in Greece over the last decade is ignored by the current government of the conservative New Democracy party. For Koniotaki (2020), the lack of current governmental support for the SSE, particularly during the COVID-19 pandemic and the two strict lockdowns, is due to the SSE's lack of visibility.

The vibrant grassroots movement that emerged in austerity-ridden Greece in the early 2010s planted the seeds of the informal, solidarity economy infrastructures that would play a prominent role during the subsequent arrival of large numbers of migrants and refugees in the country. It is worth noting that, by early 2015, the grassroots solidarity movement was internationalised as activists from abroad came to Greece to experience first-hand the socio-political changes that the newly elected government, headed by the radical left SYRIZA party, had promised to foster. Lila Leontidou (2015) pointed out the crucial role of ICTs, social media, and digital platforms in facilitating this wave of 'cosmopolitan activism.' In the summer of 2015, the hope of a state-sanctioned radical shift evaporated with the concession of the SYRIZA-led government to yet another 'memorandum of understanding' with Greece's creditors, entailing further austerity. At the same time, the number of refugees arriving at the Greek islands from Syria and other conflict zones rose sharply. This acceleration of refugee arrivals since 2015 (what is construed as the 'refugee crisis') reshaped the geopolitical character of the European Union's borders.

Enacted in the territory of Greece, the austerity and refugee 'crises' gave rise to a solidarity network of local and foreign activists who came together to contribute to the building of infrastructures of care—especially for refugees (Dalakoglou and Agelopoulos 2018; Tziovas 2017). In the summer of 2015, most refugees were heading towards the Greek border with North Macedonia, on the route to Northern Europe. Athens was their main stopover (Evangelinidis 2016, p. 32). Local activist networks assembled to provide food and medical aid to the growing number of newcomers who were sleeping rough on the streets and parks (Cabot 2019). The first refugee housing squats, *City Plaza*, a hotel in central Athens abandoned for years due to bankruptcy, and a public office building, also abandoned, emerged soon after, in September 2015 (Agustín and Martin 2019; Raimondi 2019). A constellation of refugee housing squats and other solidarity initiatives—social clinics, collective kitchens, intercultural schools, training workshops, free shops, legal advice, and translation services, etc. (Travlou 2020; Zaman 2020)—was built through the redirection of the energy and infrastructures of the movement that had assembled during the preceding years of austerity crisis. In the following months, foreign volunteers and activists arrived in Athens and became involved in these networks. Refugee/migrant housing squats had a strong presence in the very centre of Athens, especially in and around the neighbourhood of Exarcheia, providing accommodation for around 2500–3000 persons (Georgiopoulou 2017). These initiatives did not have a legal status and were not formally recognised by the state and municipal authorities; neither did they relate to non-governmental organisations (NGOs). The latter was generally regarded with suspicion by members of the solidarity movement: many activists saw NGOs as proponents of humanitarianism and volunteerism, responsible for propagating a 'humanitarian neo-colonialism' (Bauer 2017) and for approaching refugees as a problem to be solved via legal and managerial solutions (Parsanoglou 2020).

Once again, the use of social media and digital platforms helped the solidarity networks to sustain their activities. Activists and volunteers from abroad used social networks (e.g., Facebook) to find their way in Greece, organise their accommodation and transport and explore and approach refugee solidarity initiatives. Refugees also made extensive use of social media to find information about legal matters, contact immigration authorities, communicate with friends and relatives, etc.

From the above discussion, it is evident that, in Greece, a solidarity economy emerged in response to multiple crises. The term 'crisis' was used systematically by national and international media to describe a moment of accelerated economic, social and demographic change in Greece (Douzinas 2013; Mitsopoulos and Theodore 2011; Mylonas 2014; Tsilimpounidi 2016). This crisis was usually portrayed as an impending—even accomplished—catastrophe. Yet, amidst the very real pressures generated by massive state debt, neoliberal austerity, extensive impoverishment, and the large numbers of newcomers in need (refugees, other migrants), there were agents and processes that facilitated the emergence of innovative ways of living, resource sharing, surviving, and resisting oppressive state policies. Many initiatives and projects of solidarity economy departed from the current mainstream representations of the 'crisis' ('financial'/'debt crisis;' 'refugee crisis') as (only) a catastrophe and exemplified opportunities for socio-political change. This change was clearly manifested in the novel forms of participatory citizenship that emerged from the collaboration, friendship, care, trust—in one word, comradeship—between people that this 'crisis' brought together. In the case of refugees, their participation in solidarity economy initiatives challenges their stereotypical representation as *homo sacer*: people refused the rights enjoyed by the citizens of nation-states (Agamben 1998); instead, it demonstrates that refugees can be political actors and catalysts of social and cultural change in the host society. Moreover, this theoretical shift challenges the tendency to view refugees/migrants as (merely) economic rather than socio-political actors—a tendency that often obscures the numerous ways by which refugees/migrants exercise political agency. Many of the actions undertaken by refugees and migrants are explicitly political acts, even though they may differ in form from the kinds of mobilisation and protest readily recognised as 'political' in the host society. Borrowing Papadopoulos' and Tsianos' words, what constructs active citizenship is 'the sharing of knowledge and infrastructures of connectivity, affective cooperation, mutual support and care among people on the move' (2013, p. 178).

In 2015–2016, one of chapter authors participated in a series of collective kitchen projects in Athens (Senait's Eritrean pop-up kitchen, the African Collective Kitchen: OneLoveKitchen, and Options FoodLab). The aim of these projects, run by refugees, migrants, and local and international activists, was to create safe, shared social spaces where migrants and locals would care for each other, cook together, share food, and organise events that would bring people together (Travlou 2017, 2020). Besides facilitating cultural exchange between all those involved in the kitchen projects and across the latter's wider social networks, this interaction challenged hegemonic notions of exchange value and the idea that value is produced only through paid labour (Wilson 2018). The kitchen projects confirmed that independent of their potential to produce goods and services for exchange, actions of solidarity constitute value-in-themselves. The value of these communal actions of solidarity was seen as determined by the potential of these actions to translate into, inform, and enrich meaning; to constitute 'meaningful [and, in our project, explicitly political] action' (Taylor 2007, p. 191).

The economic model of the Athenian collective kitchens was based on the principles of solidarity economy (participatory budgeting, heterarchy, horizontal decision-making, collective self-organisation, and peer learning), enriched with the experience in the informal economy contributed mainly by the projects' refugee and migrant members. These experiences were cross-pollinated with the experience from other solidarity economy projects in Greece and elsewhere other members had participated in. The economic principles and operational practices of the kitchens were explored, discussed, and reinforced in regular (usually weekly) assemblies. All four collective kitchens were self-funded through fees charged for catering services and individual donations. The budget was decided collectively through participatory decision-making practices inspired by citizen and neighbourhood assemblies in Latin American cities. In Athens, as in Latin America, participatory budgeting was deployed as a tool for economic democracy to involve those often excluded from conventional methods of public engagement (Travlou 2020).

Nevertheless, the heavy reliance on collective kitchen projects on affective infrastructures and voluntary labour jeopardised their sustainability. The kitchens lacked the means to continue and/or develop into projects that could support their members financially. This limitation proved especially challenging for migrant and refugee members who did not have any other financial means to survive in Athens. After some months or, in the case of the longer-lived *Options FoodLab* project, years, many project members could not anymore afford to work without earning an income. By early 2019, many of these projects had been discontinued.

In 2020, with the COVID-19 pandemic, the multiple crises in Athens intensified further—especially during the March–May 2020 lockdown

(Sideris 2020). Many people lost their employment and/or income and were unable to pay their rent or service their loans. The tourism economy paused, as international flights were reduced to a minimum, hotels had to close, and a great number of Airbnb flats remained empty during the lockdown, with a huge impact on the economy (Kordoni and Trakas 2020). A large number of Athenians, well beyond Exarcheia and the refugee squats, would be unable to access or afford food, medicine, and items of personal protection, such as face masks, disinfectants, and soap. At the same time, refugee housing squats and shelters continued to be targeted by the police. In a recent article (Christopoulos 2021 online), the conservative and anti-immigrant policies implemented by Greece's right-wing New Democracy government were explicitly compared to those of the Hungarian government. COVID-19 thus became, to borrow the term from human geographer Jess Ribot (2020 online), a 'revelatory crisis' that laid bare and accentuated the topography of the inequalities and crises that were already there.

When Greece went into strict lockdown, the government stressed that the people of Greece had to make the short-term sacrifice of staying at home in order to ensure that '*we can soon return to normality.*' As outlined above, even before the COVID-19 pandemic, it was already evident that this 'normality' was predicated on anti-immigration policies, oppressive policing, a crackdown on social movements, housing evictions, privatisation of public property, poorly paid and precarious labour. Against the odds, in Athens, the 2020 lockdown became an opportune moment for political action: the anarchist/anti-authoritarian movement that had gone through various ups and downs in the past five years reassembled its networks of solidarity almost immediately (Travlou 2021). In the months of the lockdown, mutual aid groups that focused on housing and refugee support proliferated in a demonstration of what Marina Sitrin (2020) '. Many of these initiatives emerged from the remarkably rapid mutation and merging of pre-existing social solidarity initiatives.

An example of this rapid mutation is Kropotkin-19, a mutual aid initiative in Athens during the first COVID-19 lockdown in March 2020. The initiative was organised by members of the anti-authoritarian movement in Athens who were actively involved in housing squats, collective kitchens (including the African *OneLoveKitchen*), social clinics, self-organised schools, and other refugee solidarity collectives. Kropotkin-19 focused its actions on the provision of food and other essentials, medicine, legal and psychological support to refugees, migrants, and the unemployed. The initiative operated both online and offline. Due to the lockdown and social distancing measures, most of the communication and organisation of the group's actions were conducted online using various communication platforms—mostly open source and encrypted, such as Telegram, Jitsi, Discord, WhatsApp, and, for internal communication and the collection and delivery of food, Facebook Messenger (Travlou 2021).

One explanation for the swift emergence of Kropotkin-19 and similar solidarity economy groups is the previous collective experience with multiple crises: in Athens, tried and proven practices of mobilising, group assembling, and networking were already in place. Interlinked mutual aid groups had already formed networks of care based on 'affective infrastructures' (Berlant 2016)—the relations, associations, and practices of resistance that enable people to be with each other and to enact politics of care and solidarity.

## Case Study 2: Hungary: Solidarity Economy Between the 'Long Summer of Migration' and the COVID-19 Pandemic

The evolution of a post-millennial, grassroots-driven solidarity economy in Hungary bears only a few parallels with the developments in Greece. In Hungary, solidarity economy initiatives were embedded in the rich history of civic solidarity to vulnerable groups (people of low income, Roma, homeless, and others) that emerged during the political transition of 1989 and flourished in the 1990s–early 2000s. Despite this remarkable and extensive tradition, in the years of the financial crisis and right before the refugee crisis, the Hungarian context of solidarity economy was generally characterised by a low level of civic activity and general trust (Boda and Medve-Báint 2012; Tóth 2009), and a relatively high level of trust in NGOs and formal associations for civic engagement and participatory democracy (Eurobarometer 2013). From the 2000s to the 2010s, however, the NGO sector weakened as the Hungarian society became increasingly more polarised politically. In the highly polarised political landscape of these years, cleavages emerged across political lines, with tribalist divisions between a pro-government 'tribe' and a diverse opposition bonded by their deep anti-government frustration.

In Hungary, the financial/economic/austerity crisis begun in 2008. Like in Greece, this crisis was unexpectedly deep and protracted. Unlike in Greece, however, civic, non-state-level responses to the crisis did not assemble into a large and vigorous solidarity movement at that time. Moreover, by 2015, when the 'migration crisis' begun in Hungary, the austerity crisis was declared as settled. The effects of the 2015 immigration in Hungary differed, in both their manifestation and extent, from those in Greece. Hungary's 'crises' were neither as multiple nor as overlapping as the Greek ones. During the so-called 'long summer of migration' in 2015, grassroots-level civic action in Hungary was predominantly taken up by volunteer initiatives. These refugee solidarity initiatives emerged in a markedly hostile political and somewhat hostile social context (Bernát et al. 2015; Hunyadi et al. 2015). The political polarisation that, by that time, had become integral to the country's social reality and public life was instantly reflected in the public reception of the 'migration crisis.' This reception was dominated—and framed by—an increasingly xenophobic, right-wing populist governmental stance (Bernáth and Messing 2016), to which the weak opposition and its supporters did not manage to articulate an effective response. Frustrated pro-migrant, liberal/leftist civic activists who were politically aligned with the opposition, and a significant number of non-partisan, humanitarian civic activists, met with the unexpectedly large number of worn-out asylum-seekers, refugees, and migrants who were crossing Hungary, yet another transit country, on their journey to their ultimate destination.

Faced with the vulnerability of migrants lost around the travel hubs and cities of Hungary's migration routes, these volunteers—at the beginning, often 'ordinary locals' with little to no previous experience in civic activism—immediately found each other or joined rudimentary initiatives that often stemmed from very small groups of friends and acquaintances, and formed effective Facebook groups that co-ordinated solidarity actions (Bernát et al. 2016). These 'ordinary local citizens' were independent and often lived far apart from each other but shared extraordinarily similar experiences of encounter with migrants and, also, the ethical imperative for a humanitarian, solidarity-informed response to the apparent lack of official aid. The state and municipal authorities abstained from migrant relief, obviously in compliance with the government's anti-migration policy. This government policy may have also been partly the reason for the reluctance of professional NGOs and charities to contribute to migrant relief. Hungary's large, institutional charities had the capacity and expertise to make a substantial contribution to humanitarian relief (their core activity field); nevertheless, their activity was limited to a bare minimum, especially initially. Some professional NGOs and charities with a previous record in refugee aid attributed their inactivity during the 'long summer of migration' in 2015 to capacity, resource, infrastructural, and organisational limitations. According to the political opposition and grassroots volunteers, however, the reasons for this inactivity were political (Bernát 2016).

By contrast, a more political motivation than they themselves were prepared to acknowledge was often attributed to the grassroots volunteers. Refugee solidarity in Hungary was borne in the strong political headwind of a wider political movement against the government's anti-immigration policy (Kallius et al. 2016). At first sight, therefore, refugee support looked like a fundamentally political, oppositional act. This image was propagated intentionally by the pro-government media and also, for different reasons, by the oppositional media. This thesis, however, was only partially true. Based on the interviews and focus groups with refugee support volunteers conducted by one of the chapter authors, political motivation was only one of the reasons for joining this solidarity endeavour. The volunteers' motivation comprised three principal sets of motives: Dominant among these was not a political, but rather an altruistic motivation, stemming from solidarity and empathy that urged to be articulated in a real, personal contribution of care for, and support to, those in need. The political motivation, stemming from outrage and the intention to express oppositional views, was less prominent. Typically, a third motivation was also present: one linked to affectedness and driven by emotions such as duty or sadness. This motivation was often based on some common ground between the volunteers and the recipients of support, such as the volunteers' immigrant or Arab background or family relations, or a personal experience of exile (Bernát et al. 2016). These three principal motivations often overlapped and were realised in a complex manner dominated by altruistic, humanitarian motives. The simplistic explanation of the motivation for refuge support activity as politically oppositional cannot, therefore, provide an adequate understanding of how the solidarity movement emerged, operated, and was represented in Hungary.

The reluctance of official, professional aid providers to mobilise in a humanitarian and migration crisis larger than anything Hungary had experienced since WWII created a 'solidarity void.' This void was filled by initially independent but very quickly networked volunteers: online networks of refugee solidarity (mainly Facebook groups) rapidly grew to include tens of thousands of members. These citizens' initiatives introduced a new kind of solidarity economy in Hungary.

In Hungary, like in Greece, grassroots initiatives operated without any legal status or formal registration and were not related to any established NGOs. The lack of legal status was a condition of both freedom and constant anxiety. Freedom was experienced mostly at an emotional level, while anxiety characterised the operational level: activities such as the collection and distribution of donations by organisations that lacked official recognition and whose actors were merely private persons as actors, or issues related to taxation, bookkeeping, and the compliance with hygiene regulations in community kitchens and food distribution venues. The anxiety generated by the irregular legal status of the refugee solidarity initiatives was further exacerbated by the increasingly hostile tone of governmental communications that directly targeted the new grassroots initiatives and the civic sector in general. This anxiety was also reinforced by the extreme right-wing threats expressed occasionally in more or less explicit terms by xenophobic actors.

Hungary's refugee solidarity economy required few specific skills, which were contributed by a few medical and legal professionals, translators, and logistics/IT experts. Most of the tasks fulfilled by the volunteers required little or no special expertise but skilful organising. The basic platform for organisation, as well as the gate to on-site solidarity work, was Facebook groups and websites. It was the setting up and operation of these websites that made the joining or recruitment of volunteers, organisation of the offline activity, fundraising and collection of donations, and the internal and external communication of, and awareness-raising by, these refugee solidarity groups highly effective. 'Going online to act offline' speeded up and eased both the online and offline activities and provided a low entry threshold for anyone willing to contribute with donations or voluntary work.

Refugee solidary groups in Hungary developed a hybrid, online-offline operational setting that was unique among similar groups across Europe. The intensity of the presence of solidarity grassroots groups in the social media, as well as the efficiency of Facebook groups in offline activity, provided several lessons to both the activists and outsiders (Bernát 2021). Activists faced the migrants' demand for support—a demand that grew rapidly and unexpectedly. At the same time, there was a similarly burgeoning supply of volunteers eager to join the movement, both online, as Facebook group members, and offline, as on-site volunteers helping with donations and organisational tasks. The acceleration of the demand for and supply of support forced the grassroots groups to continue improving their internal communication and operational methods to fulfil on-site demand for aid and donations and also to continue developing their external communications. As a new grassroots phenomenon, Hungary's refugee solidarity movement attracted media attention and generated public awareness to a remarkable extent.

The refugee solidarity movement remained active only for the relatively short time that refugees and migrants were present in the country. The Hungarian chapter of the 'migration crisis' lasted for only five months (June–October 2015) before severe legal measures and the physical closure of Hungary's southern borders blocked the entry of migrants. As migration routes shifted around the now practically sealed country, the migrant solidarity movement withered away. The short lifetime of Hungary's refugee solidarity movement may seem to suggest that this type of solidarity economy is viable only during crises but cannot make a sustainable contribution to 'regular' support activities such as those addressed to local poor, homeless, and other vulnerable people, in the country, at least to a large extent and on the long run.

A similar solidarity movement emerged in Hungary in response to the next crisis, the COVID-19 pandemic (since March 2020). Due to the distinct nature of the COVID-19 crisis, this movement differed in aims, actions, and forms from that of migrant/refugee support were actuated by various volunteers and brought together a more diverse activist circle. In a broad sense, during the COVID-19 pandemic, almost anyone could be either a victim or an aid provider. For this reason, the pandemic affected a much broader and heterogeneous segment of the Hungarian society than the refugee crisis. The direct, public health-related threat combined with the pandemic's indirect social impacts. The lockdown measures, unlike anything ever experienced by most people in Hungary, came suddenly and affected almost everyone, but to very different degrees. Both the health and the social impacts were the most severe for people belonging to 'high-risk groups'—mainly older people and the chronically ill; active wage earners mostly suffered from the threat of the loss of income; families with children, whose homes turned to be offices, schools and private spaces at the same time, frontline workers, such as medical staff or those basic operating infrastructure such as public transport and retail, were also exposed to the risk of infection, and also to overworking and exhaustion.

The COVID-19 pandemic emerged in most European countries almost simultaneously. Like the refugee crisis, it unfolded in several countries almost instantaneously; therefore, the grassroots responses to this crisis, including the emergence of a solidarity movement in Hungary and Greece, present several parallels. In both countries, in addition to the health risks caused by the virus, various forms of confinement and lockdown affected almost all spheres of daily life (economy, work, study, and leisure). The lockdown measures not only limited or significantly transformed working, schooling, and private life, thus causing daily frustration and angst many found difficult to cope with but also increased the number of people who were affected very acutely: people who were older, chronically ill, or otherwise at a higher risk of severe infection and thus having to self-isolate; families with children; frontline workers (e.g., medical professionals, shop assistants, bus drivers), workers in hospitality, catering, tourism, and the cultural industry and gig economy, who were suddenly left without an income.

The broad range of those hit hard by the pandemic, directly and indirectly, induced compassion and revived and transformed the solidarity economy in Hungary (and in most European countries) almost immediately, just like the 'refugee crisis.' The solidarity economy initiatives that emerged in response to the COVID-19 crisis included a wide range of actors from the state and the civic sectors, from established (health and social) care institutions to private companies and volunteer grassroots groups and individuals. A relief movement driven by civic solidarity tried to respond to the wide range of health-related, economic, and emotional needs of their fellow citizens. Support was provided by a wide variety of citizens—practically by anyone who was willing to help by shopping for older neighbours, donating food to others in need, establishing a Facebook page to broadcast evening storytelling to children or free yoga classes. The variety of the initiatives triggered by the pandemic and stemming from an ethos of solidarity was endless.

Due to the very nature of the COVID-19 pandemic and the requirement to avoid face-to-face contacts, these civic actors who responded to the pandemic organised solely online. The online activity was, therefore, even more, pronounced during the pandemic than during the 'long summer of migration' in 2015. The aims, target groups, activists, activities, and time span of the COVID-19-related initiatives in Hungary were much more diverse than those during the 'long summer of migration.' Although some activities, such as the provision of food and other in-kind donations (e.g., sanitary products, medicine) to older people, unemployed, people of low income, or other persons at risk, were similar to those undertaken in 2015, new target groups, with new needs, were also identified: frontline workers (mainly medical staff) received quality hot meals or other food prepared by workers in the catering industry, at restaurants that were anyway closed to business due to the pandemic; medical staff were invited to stay free of charge, or for a low price, in unused Airbnb properties, etc.

The COVID-19 pandemic in Hungary added a new layer of meaning to solidarity and care provision—a layer that, arguably, may constitute an extension of solidarity economy: activities that catered for stereotypically middle-class preferences, such as yoga and workout sessions, online cultural events (e.g., theatrical and other performances), or other forms of entertainment (films, live discussions on art or cultural products, etc.), and which were limited or discontinued due to the pandemic, were provided partly through solidarity economy networks. While maintaining the core aim of providing relief in a difficult situation, nevertheless, this new kind of 'care' stretched the original definition of solidarity economy, as well as the meaning of 'donation,' 'donor,' 'recipient,' and 'non-monetised activity.' In the case of online cultural events, such as theatre plays, for instance, the cultural product itself can be construed as 'relief': a donation to recipients in (non-monetary) need. The donor (the theatre, actors, or company), however, was also in (both monetary and non-monetary) need. The provision of such a donation to the audience (also) served as a promotion of future performances that may be paid events, which, in turn, may be perceived by the paying audience as a form of support for artists left without income. This transformation, and the complex interrelation between solidarity/care economy and the wider context of the traditional market relations within which the latter operates, generate new questions for research and practice.

## Solidarity and Care Across Crises and Borders: Lessons from Greece and Hungary

The initiatives of refugee/migrant solidarity in Greece and Hungary were similar in both their grassroots character and their range of activity: in both countries, the primary objective of these initiatives was to support migrants with their basic needs, such as food, clothing, medical care, and physical and legal safety (including legal counselling), while actively involving them in grassroots political action and the processes of active citizenship. Beyond these similarities, however, solidarity economy initiatives differed between these two countries, owning to the distinct conditions of solidarity infrastructures, the different relative strength of supportive political movements, and wider reception of refugees/migrants by the host society in Greece and Hungary.

As the first EU member country on the Eastern Mediterranean migration route, Greece had been receiving migrants/refugees for much longer before 2015, and at much higher numbers than Hungary, and had also attracted many more foreign volunteers/activists. The accommodation of these activists was another need to be addressed within the framework of solidarity economy, which had already developed, matured, and diversified in response to the austerity crisis. In Greece, the solidarity economy movement was called and had the infrastructural capacity to produce sustainable solutions on a relatively large scale. Athens' collective kitchens, with their comprehensive remit of provision and their location within a constellation of other interacting initiatives of solidarity economy (Travlou 2020), exemplify an attempt to fulfil this call. The remit of solidarity economy initiatives in Hungary, however, was limited to addressing the basic needs of exhausted people who had travelled for a long time and wanted to keep going until they reached their destination(s). For them, Hungary was only a transit country, typically a few-days-long section of the journey. Solidarity actions and donations were in line with this: distribution of basic, take-away food, durable clothes appropriate for travelling and physical activity, medical and legal assistance, and practical guidance on how to continue the journey. The accommodation was only offered on limited occasions and only for a few nights; legal assistance and practical guidance were only about matters of immediate relevance in the transit country, and no foreign activists were present.

For over a decade, both Greece and Hungary have been affected by the local deployment of global crises. Notwithstanding their different social and political context, pace, and, to a lesser extent, particular focus, in both countries, local grassroots responses to these crises charted the evolution of solidarity economy. The emergence of the solidarity economy in Greece was, quite clearly, a response to the austerity crisis that begun in 2008 and, over a decade later, is still ongoing. This crisis overlapped with the acceleration of migrant arrivals to Greece since 2015 and, since 2020, the COVID-19 pandemic. These overlapping crises set the context for a solidarity economy that continues to develop and mutate as its targets, and participant actors are shifting, and its practices are transforming; yet remains driven by a coherent set of principles.

This continuity is evident, despite the differences between the drivers and nature of, and damage caused by, each of the multiple facets of crisis. The uninterrupted evolution of the solidarity economy in Greece is also related to an effect common across the three pulses of the long, multiple crises that continues to affect the country: material deprivation—poverty, loss of income, housing, etc. Material deprivation has conditioned the constant leitmotif of goals and interventions across the various practices of solidarity over the last ten years. Community kitchens, housing squats, and volunteer activists and grassroots organisations that have persisted across these years exemplify this continuity (Travlou 2021).

A similar continuity has not been manifested in Hungary, where the solidarity and care economy initiatives during the country's financial crisis were rarer, shorter-term, sometimes delayed, and often not closely interlinked. Although the challenges facing the Hungarian society were similar to those in Greece, organised grassroots responses of economic solidarity and care were sporadic. In Hungary, the financial crisis was instead addressed either through state-level measures with a strong focus on employment rather than welfare or through individual initiatives, such as the escalation of the emigration of Hungarians to the UK, Germany, and other Western European countries. The solidarity movement that emerged in Hungary during the 'long summer of migration' in 2015 was not, therefore, built on the foundations laid by an earlier movement. In Hungary, the birth of a grassroots-based, solely voluntary, often (but not exclusively) politically radical solidarity economy came later, with the spontaneous solidarity to migrants and refugees crossing the country in 2015. The 'long summer of migration' was the childhood of this civic movement, with all its inspiring revelations and childhood diseases. As migration through Hungary effectively ceased in late 2015 due to the legal and physical barriers erected by the state, the migrant solidarity groups also ceased their activity and soon faded away.

This pattern of discontinuity and interruption of solidarity economy was repeated in the next crisis in Hungary, the COVID-19 pandemic (March 2020). At that time, although the underpinning principles and motivations of the solidarity economy activists were similar, no continuity, in either actors or practices, with earlier solidarity economy initiatives could be detected. The differences, in scope and actions, between the solidarity-motivated responses to migration and the COVID-19 pandemic could perhaps be explained—but only in part—by the different nature of these two crises. The migration in 2015 was part of a global movement of people from particular places of origin: sites of armed conflict and/or deprivation that left them without a home and livelihood and propelled them to a perilous journey to an uncertain future. The global pandemic, on the other hand, affected most countries in the world almost simultaneously: directly, as an epidemic threat, and indirectly, through its economic and social impacts that were surprisingly similar in most countries of Europe.

In both Greece and Hungary, solidarity economy initiatives transformed and proliferated in the COVID-19 pandemic in terms of scale, participants, the interconnection between projects, and range of activities. This expansion stemmed from several factors: the duration (in Hungary, longer than the 2015 migration crisis) and risks of the pandemic, the number of people that could potentially support solidarity economy initiatives, and, also, the ways with and extent at, these people could interact. The pandemic condition also increased the range and scale of goods and services that flowed through solidarity economy networks: there were more volunteers and a higher contribution of labour and donations. During the peak of migration, in both Greece and Hungary, solidarity was mainly (although by no means exclusively) directed to people outside the personal network of participating activists. During the COVID-19 pandemic, however, this circle of solidarity expanded to also include people from the close personal network (family, friends, neighbours, etc.) of solidarity actors. It could perhaps be argued that the COVID-19 pandemic encouraged solidarity economy networks to assume a more horizontal topology.

In addition, in both Hungary and Greece, the social impact of the pandemic was much stronger than that of migration. Firstly, it was the risk of infection, which concerned everyone, but was particularly high for older people and the chronically ill. The latter was in dire need of support, both in order to avoid infection and to cope with the consequences of confinement and the drastic restriction of their everyday activity. Due to the lockdown measures, new vulnerabilities also emerged among healthy adults and children: students struggling with online education; adults struggling with working from home; families juggling the challenges and tensions of confinement at home; workers on compulsory leave from work, faced with the prospect of income loss or unemployment; overworked medical staff struggling with burn-out, the trauma of mass morbidity and mortality, and the fear of infecting family members; the multitude of (the often overlooked) frontline workers (shop assistants, bus drivers, pharmacists, hospital cleaners, supermarket and public transportation staff, etc.). The cross-sectional character of the COVID-19 pandemic posed new challenges that reshaped the networks of solidarity and care.

The COVID-19 pandemic did not unfold in a vacuum: in both Greece and Hungary, it ravaged societies that were already impacted by long-term austerity and accentuated and laid bare the multiple oppressions and vulnerabilities experienced by the poor, the unemployed, the ill, and older people—those who, historically, had been the key focus of grassroots solidarity economy initiatives. At the same time, the pandemic demonstrated the precariousness and vulnerability of many of those hitherto considered to be on the safe side of the capitalist economy: middle-class families, employees in formerly thriving businesses, successful artists and other cultural workers, entrepreneurs in tourism and the gig economy, etc. Whole industries that were portrayed as the 'winners' of the last austerity crisis, such as tourism, hospitality, and other sectors of the gig economy, were decimated and became potential recipients of state or charitable aid, while workers were thought to be lucky if they could weather the lockdown without substantial impacts on their health, wellbeing, and/or livelihood. These people, and the challenges of confinement that traditionally had not been key concerns of the solidarity economy, gained relevance.

Mutual aid proliferated in these conditions, as various groups that were heavily impacted by the COVID-19 pandemic took it upon themselves to help each other as 'victims' and aid providers of the pandemic at the same time. In Hungary, tourism entrepreneurs (from a one-property Airbnb business to large hotels) offered their unused properties free of charge or at a reduced price to medical staff and other frontline workers who needed an alternative accommodation to protect the family from potential infection or to reduce commuting to work during the crisis. Similarly, restaurants temporarily closed to business prepared and donated meals to the medical staff at their own expense, despite the food providers themselves also being victims of the pandemic. This mutual solidarity was often framed as a gesture of gratitude to those who took the highest risk to sustain the community.

Another novel characteristic of the solidarity economy during the COVID-19 pandemic was that most of its transactions took place online. This may have generated further inequalities by disadvantaging those who did not use or had no access to the Internet. People with a solely offline life—many of them already vulnerable pre-lockdown—received less solidarity and care and may have had fewer opportunities for social interaction.

Finally, another distinctive aspect of the solidarity economy during the COVID-19 pandemic was that this was less explicitly political as compared with, for instance, migrant/refugee solidarity. In Hungary, both migration and the pandemic, and the responses of solidarity and care triggered by these events, were (and remain) embedded in a context of political contestation, polarised across pro- *vs* anti-government fault lines. Nevertheless, during the COVID-19 pandemic, these fault lines were often less evident in the political underpinnings of solidarity initiatives. This was partly due to the much wider, cross-sectional effects of the pandemic: unlike the migrants of 2015, those affected by the COVID-19 pandemic were not strangers coming from faraway countries, escaping vaguely understood armed conflicts, and carrying with them different cultures and religions, but relatives, friends, neighbours, and other fellow Hungarians.

## Summary

Since 2010, Greece and Hungary have been affected by different socio-political and economic issues, i.e., austerity, the arrival of large numbers of refugees/migrants, and the COVID-19 pandemic, events often construed as 'crises.' In both countries, local grassroots responses to these 'crises,' notwithstanding their different social and political underpinnings, pace, and, to a lesser extent, particular focus, chart the emergence and evolution of an economy of solidarity and care. In Athens, a solidarity economy emerged in response to the austerity crisis that begun in 2008 and, over a decade later, is ongoing. This crisis overlapped with the acceleration of migrant arrivals to Greece since 2015 and, since 2020, the COVID-19 pandemic. These overlapping crises set the context for a solidarity economy that continues to develop and mutate as its targets and participant actors are shifting, and its practices are transforming while remaining driven by a coherent set of principles. The uninterrupted course of solidarity economy in Athens is also related to a common facet of all three pulses of the long, multiple crisis: material deprivation—poverty, loss of income, housing, etc. Material deprivation has set a constant leitmotif of goals and interventions across the various practices of solidarity over the last ten years. Community kitchens, housing squats, and the volunteer activists and grassroots organisations that have persisted across these years exemplify this continuity. A similar continuity was not manifested in Hungary, where the solidarity movement that emerged during the 'long summer of migration' in 2015 was not built on the foundations laid by the rare and often not interlinked solidarity and care economy initiatives during the country's earlier financial crisis. As migration through Hungary effectively ceased in late 2015 due to the legal and physical barriers erected by the state, the migrant solidarity groups also ceased their activity and soon faded away.

In both Greece and Hungary, solidarity economy initiatives transformed and proliferated in the COVID-19 pandemic in terms of scale, participants, the interconnection between projects, and range of activities. This expansion stemmed from several factors: the long duration of, and novel risks generated by, the pandemic, the number of people solidarity economy initiatives could potentially include, and, also, the ways with, and levels at, these people could interact. During the peak of migration, in both countries, solidarity was mainly directed to people outside the personal network of participating activists. During the COVID-19 pandemic, however, this circle of solidarity expanded to also include people from the close personal network (family, friends, neighbours, etc.) of solidarity actors. The COVID-19 pandemic thus encouraged solidarity economy networks to assume a more horizontal topology.

This notion of a 'common risk' that lies at the heart of solidarity economy initiatives during the COVID-19 pandemic in both Greece and Hungary obfuscates some very real inequalities in the social distribution of risk, vulnerability, and suffering and, at the same time, shapes a different political context for solidarity activity. The challenges of the pandemic, unlike those posed by migration, cannot be easily framed as a division between 'us' and 'them,' 'patriots,' and 'renegades.' The fact that the pandemic results in tragic loss and suffering among people who had rarely been on the 'losing' side before creates new challenges to, and responses by, the networks of solidarity economy in both Greece and Hungary. The way(s) the solidarity movement will address these challenges without losing sight of the stark inequalities in risk and suffering, the structural causes of these inequalities, and the explicitly (bio)political nature—and often oppressive character—of the responses to the pandemic by the state and capital are crucial for the forms, relevance, and efficacy of solidarity and care economy in a future likely to be replete with the multifaceted ecological, epidemic, economic, and humanitarian crises.

## References

Agamben, Georgio. 1998. *Homo Sacer: Sovereign Power and Bare Life*. Stanford, CA: Stanford University Press.

Agustín, Óscar García, and Bak Jørgensen Martin. 2019. 'Autonomous Solidarity: Hotel City Plaza.' In *Solidarity and the 'Refugee Crisis' in Europe*, 49–72. London: Palgrave Pivot. https://doi.org/10.1007/978-3-319-91848-8_3.

Arampatzi, Athina. 2017. 'The Spatiality of Counter-Austerity Politics in Athens, Greece: Emergent "Urban Solidarity Spaces".' *Urban Studies* 54 (9): 2155–2171. https://doi.org/10.1177/0042098016629311.

Bauer, Irmgard. 2017. 'More Harm Than Good? The Questionable Ethics of Medical Volunteering and International Student Placements.' *Tropical Diseases Travel Medicine and Vaccines* 3: 5. https://doi.org/10.1186/s40794-017-0048.

https://doi.org/10.1177/0263775816645989.

Bernát, Anikó. 2016. 'Hosts in Hostility: The New Forms of Solidarity and the Role of Volunteer and Civilian Organizations in the Migration Crisis in Hungary.' In *The Social Aspects of the 2015 Migration Crisis in Hungary*, edited by Bori Simonovits and Anikó Bernát. Budapest: TÁRKI Social Research Institute. pp. 72–100.

Bernát, Anikó. 2021. 'The Online-Offline Hybrid Model of a Collaborative Solidarity Action: Migrant Solidarity Grassroots Groups in Hungary.' In *Ethnographies of Collaborative Economies across Europe: Understanding Sharing and Caring*, edited by Penny Travlou and Luigina Ciolfi. London: Ubiquity Press.

Bernát, Anikó, Anna Kertész, Fruzsina Márta Tóth. 2016. 'Solidarity Reloaded: Volunteer and Civilian Organizations During the Migration Crisis in Hungary.' *Review of Sociology of the Hungarian Sociological Association* 26 (4): 29–52.

Bernát, Anikó, Endre Sik, Bori Simonovits, and Blanka Szeitl. 2015. *Attitudes Towards Refugees, Asylum Seekers and Migrants*. Budapest: TARKI Social Research Institute. http://www.tarki.hu/hu/news/2015/kitekint/20151203_refugee.pdf.

Bernáth, Gábor, and Vera Messing. 2016. 'Bedarálva. A menekültekkel kapcsolatos kormányzati kampány és a tőle független megszólalás terepei.' [The Bulldozer: The Government's Anti-Immigration Campaign and Platforms for Independent Voices].' *Médiakutató* [Media Research] 16 (4): 7–17.

Boda, Zsolt, and Gergő Medve-Bálint. 2012. 'Intézményi bizalom a régi és az új demokráciákban (Institutional trust in old and new democracies).' *Politikatudományi Szemle* [Hungarian Political Science Review] 21 (2): 27–54. http://www.poltudszemle.hu/szamok/2012_2szam/boda.pdf.

Cabot, Heath. 2016. '"Contagious" Solidarity: Reconfiguring Care and Citizenship in Greece's Social clinics.' *Social Anthropology* 24 (2): 152–166. https://doi.org/10.1111/1469-8676.12297.

Christopoulos, Dimitris. 2021. 'Could Greece Turn into Another Hungary?' *Open Democracy*. https://www.opendemocracy.net/en/can-europe-make-it/could-greece-turn-another-hungary/?fbclid=IwAR0WNt9YAs5C-G4r989s9cqkuMp8O8CG220b3fhK9PF9HOIJbtJaHtKSlK8. Accessed May 7, 2021.

Dalakoglou, Dimitris, and Georgios Agelopoulos. Eds. 2018. *Critical Times in Greece: Anthropological Engagements with the Crisis*. Oxford: Routledge.

Douzinas, Costas. 2013. *Philosophy and Resistance in the Crisis: Greece and the Future of Europe*. Cambridge: Polity.

Eurobarometer. 2013. *Flash Eurobarometer 373: Europeans' Engagement in Participatory Democracy*. European Commission Directorate-General for Communication. https://www.eesc.europa.eu/sites/default/files/resources/docs/fl373---report-final-en.pdf.

Evangelinidis, Angelos. 2016. 'The Greek State's Response to the Refugee Crisis and the Solidarity Movement.' *Contemporary Southeastern Europe* 3(1): 32–36.

Georgiopoulou, Tania. 2017. 'More Than 2,500 Refugees Live in Athens Squats.' *Ekathimerini*, 10 May. https://www.ekathimerini.com/218260/article/ekathimerini/community/more-than-2500-refugees-live-in-athens-squats.

Greek News Agenda. 2016. *Promoting Social and Solidarity Economy in Greece*. https://www.greeknewsagenda.gr/topics/politics-polity/6213-promoting-social-and-solidarity-economy-in-greece. Accessed November 23, 2016.

Hunyadi, Balázs, Attila Juhász, and Edit Zgut. 2015. *Focus on Hungary: Refugees, Asylum and Migration*. Prague: Heinrich Böll Stiftung. https://www.boell.de/sites/default/files/2015-focus-on-hungary_refugees_asylum_migration.pdf.

Kallius, Annastina, Daniel Monterescu, and Prem Kumar Rajaram. 2016. 'Immobilizing Mobility: Border Ethnography, Illiberal Democracy, and the Politics of the "Refugee Crisis" in Hungary.' *American Ethnologist* 43: 1–12. https://www.academia.edu/20386757/Immobilizing_Mobility_Border_Ethnography_Illiberal_Democracy_and_the_Politics_of_the_Refugee_Crisis_in_Hungary_American_Ethnologist_43_1_1-12_.

Kawano, Emily. 2016. 'Solidarity Economy: Building an Economy for People & Planet.' *US Solidarity Economy Network*. https://cooperationhumboldt.com/wp-content/uploads/2018/02/Kawano.pdf. Accessed January 8, 2016.

Koniotaki, Anna. 2020. *Social and Solidarity Economy in Greece During COVID-19*. Thessaloniki: Heinrich Böll Stiftung. https://gr.boell.org/el/2020/06/02/don-kihotes-kihotes-i-apla-romantikoi-i-koinoniki-kai-allilenggya-oikonomia-stin-ellada.

Kordoni, Gelina, and Trakas Themis. 2020. 'Impact of COVID-19 on Greek Tourism: Industry Experts' Opinion.' *HVS*, 22 May. https://www.hvs.com/article/8792-impact-of-covid-19-on-greek-tourism-industry-experts-opinion.

Leontidou, Lila. 2012a. 'Athens in the Mediterranean "Movement of the Piazzas" Spontaneity in Material and Virtual Public Spaces.' *City* 3: 299–312. https://doi.org/10.1080/13604813.2012.687870.

Leontidou, Lila. 2012b. 'The Reconstruction of the "European South" in Post-Colonial Europe: from Class Conflict to Cultural Identities.' In *Inequality in the Period of the Crisis: Theoretical and Empirical Investigations*, edited by A. Afouxenidis, 25–42. Athens: Propobos.

Leontidou, Lila. 2015. 'Smart Cities' of the Debt Crisis: Grassroots Creativity in Mediterranean Europe.' *The Greek Review of Social Research* 144: 69–101. https://doi.org/10.12681/grsr.8626.

Leontidou, Lila. 2020. 'Mediterranean Cities of Hope.' *City* 24 (1–2): 263–275. https://doi.org/10.1080/13604813.2020.1739906.

Margariti, Eleni, and Penny Travlou. 2018. 'Sharing Within a City in Crisis: Two ICTs-Supported P2P Economic Networks In Thessaloniki, Northern Greece.' *International Journal of Electronic Governance* 10 (2): 196–217.

Ministry of Labour and Social Affairs. 2020. *Social and Solidarity Economy: Report 2019–2020*. https://kalo.gov.gr/wp-content/uploads/2020/11/%CE%95%CE%A4%CE%97%CE%A3%CE%99%CE%91-%CE%95%CE%9A%CE%98%CE%95%CE%A3%CE%97-%CE%9A%CE%91%CE%9B%CE%9F-2019-2020-TELIKO-docx.pdf.

Mitsopoulos, Michael, and Pelagidis Theodore. 2011. *Understanding the Crisis in Greece: From Boom to Bust*. London: Palgrave Macmillan.

Mylonas, Yiannis. 2014. 'Crisis, Austerity and Opposition in Mainstream Media Discourses of Greece.' *Critical Discourse Studies* 11 (3): 305–321. https://doi.org/10.1080/17405904.2014.915862.

Papadopoulos, Dimitris, and Vassilis Tsianos. 2013. 'After Citizenship: Autonomy of Migration, Organisational Ontology And Mobile Commons.' *Citizenship Studies* 17 (2): 178–196. https://doi.org/10.1080/13621025.2013.780736.

Parsanoglou, Dimitris, 2020. 'Volunteering for Refugees and the Repositioning of State Sovereignty and Civil Society: The Case of Greece.' *Citizenship Studies* 24 (4): 457–473. https://doi.org/10.1080/13621025.2020.1755158.

Raimondi, Valeria. 2019. 'For "Common Struggles of Migrants and Locals." Migrant Activism and Squatting in Athens.' *Citizenship Studies* 23 (3): 559–576. https://doi.org/10.1080/13621025.2019.1634373.

Rakopoulos, Theodoros. 2014. 'Resonance of Solidarity: Meanings of a Local Concept in Anti-Austerity Greece.' *Journal of Modern Greek Studies* 32: 95–119. https://doi.org/10.1353/mgs.2014.0040.

Ribot, Jesse. 2020. 'Africa, COVID-19, and the Commons.' *Panel presentation at the African Commons IASC 2020 Web Conference*, 13 July. https://africa.iasc-commons.org/recorded-webinars/.

Sideris, Sotiris. 2020. 'COVID-19 Is Exposing Inequalities of the Past.' *Athens Live*. https://medium.com/athenslivegr/covid-19-is-exposing-inequalities-of-the-past-fa9e0ade224f. Accessed May 1, 2020.

Sitrin, Marina, and Sembrar Colectiva. 2020. *Pandemic Solidarity: Mutual Aid During the Covid-19 Crisis*. London: Pluto Press.

Taylor, Timothy. 2007. 'The Commodification of Music at the Dawn of the Era of "Mechanical Music".' *Ethnomusicology* 51 (2): 281–305.

Tóth, István György. 2009. 'Bizalomhiány, normazavarok, igazságtalanságérzet és paternalizmus a magyar társadalom értékszerkezetében.' *A gazdasági felemelkedés társadalmi felemelkedés társadalmi-kulturális feltételei című kutatás zárójelentése*. [Lack of Trust, Norm Disorders, Injustice, and Paternalism in the Value Structure of Hungarian Society: Final report of the research entitled Socio-Cultural Conditions of Economic Ascension and Social Ascension] Budapest: TÁRKI Social Research Institute.

Travlou, Penny. 2017. 'The Making of *OneLoveKitchen:* Commoning the Assembly. In *Organizing from Below/HOW Assemblies Matter?*, edited by Marketou Jenny and Bailey Stephanie, 6–7. New York: Naked Punch Publications.

Travlou, Penny. 2020. 'From Cooking to Commoning: The Making of Intangible Cultural Heritage in *OneLoveKitchen, Athens*.' In *Cultural Heritage in the Realm of the Commons*, edited by Lekakis Stelios, 159–182. Berkeley, CA: Ubiquity Press.

Travlou, Penny. 2021. 'Kropotkin-19: A Mutual Aid Response to COVID-19 in Athens.' *Design and Culture* 13(1): 65–78. https://doi.org/10.1080/17547075.2020.1864119.

Tronto, Joan. 1993. *Moral Boundaries: A Political Argument for an Ethic of Care*. New York, London: Routledge.

Tsilimpounidi, Myrto. 2016. *Sociology of Crisis: Visualising Urban Austerity*. London: Routledge.

Tziovas, Dimitris. Ed. 2017. *Greece in Crisis: The Cultural Politics of Austerity*. London: Bloomsbury Publishing.

Van Osch, Thera. 2013. *Towards a Caring Economic Approach*, May 2013. https://oqconsulting.eu/wp-content/uploads/2020/04/The-Economy-of-Care.pdf.

Wilson, Dave. 2018. 'Commoning in Sonic Ethnography (or, the Sound of Ethnography to Come).' *Commoning Ethnography* 1(1): 125–136. https://doi.org/10.26686/ce.v1i1.4134.

Zaman, Tahir. 2020. 'Neighbourliness, Conviviality, and the Sacred in Athens' Refugee Squats.' *Transactions of the Institute of British Geographers* 45 (3): 529–541. https://doi.org/10.1111/tran.12360.

## Suggested Readings

Amin, Ash. 2013 *The Social Economy: International Perspectives on Economic Solidarity*London: ZED Books.

Cabot, Cabot. 2019. 'The European Refugee Crisis and Humanitarian Citizenship in Greece.' *Ethnos* 8 4(5): 747–771. https://doi.org/10.1080/00141844.2018.1529693.

della Porta, Donatella. Ed. 2018. *Solidarity Mobilizations in the 'Refugee Crisis.'* London: Palgrave Macmillan.

Feischmidt, Margit, Ludger Pries, and Celine Cantat. Eds. 2019. *Refugee Protection and Civil Society in Europe.* London: Palgrave Macmillan.

Kawano, Emily, Thomas Neal Masterson, and Jonathan Teller-Elsberg. Eds. 2009. *Solidarity Economy I: Building Alternatives for People and Planet Papers and Reports from the 2009 US Forum on the Solidarity Economy.* Amherst, MA: Center for Popular Economics.

Yeats, Nicola. 2005. 'A Global Political Economy of Care.' *Social Policy and Society* 4 (2): 227–234. https://doi.org/10.1017/S1474746404002350.

## Relevant Websites

Avaros Mindenkie Blog. https://avarosmindenkie.blog.hu/2009/01/01/english_107?fbclid=IwAR2cLsnHEPsou6JTGZ0GzDrwRwnbtS30W_QLKz0f5PuDII-81_NFdPp3gB0.

Bagázs—A Comprehensive Integration Program In A Segregated Village in Hungary: https://bagazs.org/about-bagazs/?lang=en.

British Council: Greece Social and Solidarity Economy Report. https://www.britishcouncil.org/society/social-enterprise/greece-social-and-solidarity-economy-report.

InDaHouse. https://indahousehungary.hu/.

Kropotkin-19 Mutual Aid Initiative. https://www.facebook.com/kropotkin19/.

RIPESS: International Network for the Promotion of Social Solidarity Economy. http://www.ripess.org/?lang=en.

Rosa Parks Foundation (Budapest). https://www.rosaparks.hu/about-us/?fbclid=IwAR00LXTs7EVGF0SCzLkEjfKjcPbq8CakuPqeB2Bcx24tUtlgJFYPd37aWiM.

# Part IV

## Country-Specific Case Studies

# 11

# From a Sharing Economy to a Platform Economy: Public Values in Shared Mobility and Gig Work in the Netherlands

Martijn de Waal and Martijn Arets

## Introduction

Initiatives in the sharing economy started to emerge in the Netherlands at the beginning of the 2010s, making the country one of the world's pioneers. At the beginning of the 2010s, many local initiatives such as Peerby (borrow tools and other things from your neighbours), SnappCar (peer-to-peer car sharing), and Thuisafgehaald (cook for your neighbours) launched that enabled consumers to share underused resources or provide services to each other. This was accompanied by a wide interest

M. de Waal (✉)
Civic Interaction Design Research Group, Amsterdam
University of Applied Sciences, Amsterdam, the Netherlands
e-mail: B.g.m.de.waal@hva.nl

M. Arets
Independent Platform Expert, Houten, the Netherlands
e-mail: martijn@collaborative-economy.com



V. Česnuitytė et al. (eds.), *The Sharing Economy in Europe*,
https://doi.org/10.1007/978-3-030-86897-0_11

from the Dutch media, zooming in on the perceived social and environmental benefits of these platforms. International commercial platforms such as Uber, UberPop, and Airbnb followed soon after. There have been various attempts to map the sharing economy platforms in the Netherlands. In 2018, the research project Deeleconomie in Nederland (The Sharing Economy in the Netherlands) found 250 different platforms. More than 200 of these have been documented in an online spreadsheet (Data aangemelde initiatieven, 2015). In terms of use, various studies have produced various results, depending on the exact definitions used of the sharing or platform economy. According to the Rathenau Institute (Frenken et al. 2017), 23% of the Dutch population took part in the sharing economy in 2016, growing from 6% in 2013. In 2019 Statistics Netherlands (CBS 2020) investigated the use of online platforms for ordering and exchanging goods or services and found that 58% of all Dutch citizens older than 12 had done so. This rose to the uptake of 80% in the age group 25–44.

For the population at large, food delivery (used by 35% of the population above 12 years in 2019) was the most popular, followed by second-hand goods (32%) and accommodation (20%). Transport was less in demand, with 8% of the population using a platform to order car sharing, taxi services, or other transportation platforms (CBS 2020). According to the Deeleconomie Monitor 2018 (Hoekstra 2018), the largest growth is taking place in the use of commercial platforms providing services. Idealistic motives to take part in the sharing economy only play a limited role. Especially in the use of mobility platforms, ease of use and attractive pricing are the main drivers for usage (Hoekstra 2018). At the same time, there are still numerous more ideological-driven attempts to reorganise resource production and usage. For instance, in the Netherlands, in the past few years, many citizens have started to form energy cooperatives. Their number rose from 248 in 1015 to 582 in 2019, now servicing close to a quarter-million households (Schwenke 2019).

After their entrance to the market, the societal debate about the impact of these platforms also started to include the negative consequences. Early on, universities and national research and policy institutes took part in these discussions by providing definitions, frameworks, and analysis from a perspective of public values (Straathof et al. 2017; Frenken et al. 2017; Van Dijck et al. 2018; Van Eijk et al. 2015). In the last few years, the attention has shifted from the sharing economy to the much broader defined platform economy and its societal impact. In this chapter, this shift in the sharing economy and its societal repercussions will be illustrated by focussing on two discussions that have recently been waged around the sharing and platform economies in the Netherlands: shared mobility and gig work. Before we zoom in on these two domains, first, an overview will be given of the definitions of the sharing economy in the Netherlands and the most important issues brought up in the debate.

## Definitions and Debates of the Sharing Economy in the Netherlands

In the Netherlands, the term 'deeleconomie' is a literal translation of the concept of the sharing economy (to share = delen). It started to gain popularity in 2013 when mainstream media such as newspapers and magazines started to report on the phenomenon highlighting Dutch start-ups in this field, such as Peerby and SnappCar. Originally, the term was used to refer to platforms that allow citizens to make use of each other's goods as well as to platforms that offer various kinds of services.

Another term used early on in the debate is that of the *collaborative economy*, amongst others, by ShareNL—a Dutch organisation that explores and consults on the sharing economy. They define this as referring to 'economic systems of decentralised networks and marketplaces that unlock the value of underused assets by matching needs and haves, in ways that bypass traditional institutions' (ShareNL 2016).

Early on, the sharing economy was often discussed as part of the debate on smart cities as well as related to the discussion on the emergence of a 'participation' or 'energetic society' (de Waal and De Lange 2019; Hajer 2011) in which citizen collectives are empowered to self-organise around various issues of communal concern. In these interpretations, the term sharing referred to alternative forms of political and economic bottom-up organisation. More formal definitions started to appear around 2015 when the success of various platform services started to lead to questions with regard to regulation. In order to help policymakers discern between informal citizen initiatives and commercial services belonging to the formal economy, Koen Frenken, Toon Meelen, Martijn Arets, and Pieter van de Glind narrowed down the definition of the sharing economy as 'consumers granting each other temporary access to under-utilised physical assets ('idle capacity'), possibly for money' (Frenken et al. 2017). This definition has three elements. Primarily, the sharing economy concerns transactions between consumers ('consumer-to-consumer' also referred to as 'peer-to-peer'). Secondly, the transactions involve 'temporary accesses to an asset'. Thirdly, it involves assets and not services. Later on, in the debate, the term gig economy or 'kluseconomie' has been introduced to refer to platforms that provide access to services. In the gig economy, consumers provide services for one another rather than providing access to goods (Frenken et al. 2017).

Initially, the sharing economy was hailed as a positive force in society, as it was thought to contribute to both social and economic capital. It was also seen as a positive force for the environment. Sharing resources, it was hoped, would lead to a smaller ecological footprint, and the peer-to-peer relations enabled by the platforms were hoped to contribute to improving social relations at the neighbourhood level. In that vein, the sharing economy was also embraced as an opportunity to brand a city and stimulate local innovation. The city of Amsterdam, for instance, started to promote itself as a European capital of innovation that is based on the 'Amsterdam-approach.' This means an approach to smart cities that is not based on technology per se but rather seeks alliances with civil society and is organised around societal challenges. In this framework, the city has adopted an action plan for the sharing economy that consists of five main actions: Stimulating the sharing economy; Leading by example; A sharing economy for all Amsterdam citizens; Rules and regulations; and Putting Amsterdam on the map as a Sharing City (ShareNL 2016). In Amsterdam, this programme so far has led to a small number of experiments.

Yet already in 2017, the more critical views started to appear in the debate, as epitomised by the newspaper headline 'de deeleconomie heeft zijn onschuld verloren' (the sharing economy has lost its innocence) (Hermanides 2017). The emergence of UberPop and Uber led to discussions about the regulation of labour. Platforms such as Airbnb started to have an effect on the livability in cities such as Amsterdam, tying debates about the sharing economy to broader debates about the negative consequences of tourism. Especially Amsterdam has joined the ranks of cities such as Barcelona and Venice, in which local residents feel overwhelmed by masses of tourists who – in the views of these locals – are taking over their city. In Amsterdam, the city council has decided that residents can only rent out their houses and apartments for a maximum of 30 days a year. So far, enforcement of this rule has been problematic as Airbnb does not want to provide data about rentals to the local government.

In the past few years, discussions on the sharing or collaborative economy have become part of broader discussions about the platform economy. Platforms are now seen as possibly new institutional forms becoming part of the economy, possibly undermining traditional regulation and social arrangements. In a report to the Dutch government, TNO (Nederlandse Organisatie voor Toegepast Natuurwetenschappelijk Onderzoek; Netherlands Organisation for Applied Scientific Research) defined the term 'platform' as 'a (technological) basis for delivering or aggregating services/content from service/content providers to end-users' (Van Eijk et al. 2015). Their examples include not only sharing economy platforms but also entertainment and e-commerce platforms such as Netflix, Bol.com, and Facebook. In a recent study from the Social and Economic Council of the Netherlands (SER 2020, p. 16), platforms are defined as intermediaries that 'organise the coordination of supply and demand for services and commodities.' In addition, Van Dijck et al. (2018, p. 4) defined a platform as 'a programmable digital architecture designed to organise interactions between users—not just end-users but also corporate entities and public bodies.' What many of these definitions have in common is that they focus on the role of (sharing) platforms as intermediaries and that through their particular design (interface, algorithms, business models, etc.) govern the interactions between third parties such as users and service providers. Whereas originally, the public debate was mostly focussed on the functions of these platforms (they allow sharing and collaborating in new ways), more recently, the exact mechanisms of their intermediation and their governmentalities have come into full scrutiny, especially in relation to regulation by governments.

Various academic studies, as well as advisory councils of the Dutch government, started to research platforms from a framework of institutions, arguing that platforms could be understood as a new institutional form of organising economic, social, and cultural activities with its own logic. Increasingly, platforms are seen as de facto private regulators, disrupting the balance between the institutional logics of the market, corporation, and the regulatory powers of the state. Platforms provide opportunities for individuals to trade services but may also entail risks for these individuals as well as their customers and violate their rights or endanger other public values. Preventing these risks through public regulation and enforcement poses huge challenges to public regulatory authorities, as existing legal powers and instruments fall short in this new context (Frenken and Van Slageren 2018; Frenken et al. 2017; Ranchordas 2015). Public values and public interests were introduced as a lens to analyse and regulate the platform economy in studies such as *The Platform Society* and *A Fair Share: Safeguarding Public Interests in the Sharing and Gig Economy* (Frenken et al. 2017; Van Dijck et al. 2018). Debates have centred amongst others on transparency and accountability of platforms, data ownership and data portability, and issues related to algorithmic governance in platforms and the need for algorithmic transparency. Two instantiations of the sharing economy are particularly insightful to highlight discussions about the sharing economy in the Netherlands: shared mobility and the gig economy.

## Shared Mobility: Contributing to a More Sustainable City, or Usurping Public Space and Undermining Worker's Rights?

Discussions on shared mobility in the Netherlands are tightly connected to the broader debates about the sharing economy. On the one hand, shared mobility and especially car sharing is seen as a possible contribution to a greener and more sustainable economy. On the other hand, negative consequences have been discussed with regard to public values such as consumer and worker protections as well as qualities of public space. Three forms of shared mobilities have been debated widely in the Netherlands: bike-sharing, car sharing, and ride-hailing.

## Bike-Sharing and Electric Scooters

Bike ownership in the Netherlands has been one of the highest in the world. Its 17 million inhabitants own 23 million bikes. Already 25% of daily mobility takes place by bike (Harms and Kansen 2018). Since 2003, the OV-fiets (Public Transport Bike), a bike rental scheme at Dutch public transit stations, has grown increasingly popular. With their public transport chip card, users of public transport can pick up and return a bike at a train station or bus terminal for a small fee (currently 3.85 euro for 24 h). Usage has grown from around 100,000 rides in 2004 to more than five million in 2019 (OVPro 2019). Private lease constructions for bike usage have also become more popular in the last few years. The Dutch start-up Swapfiets is now active in four countries and has reported 200,000 customers leasing their bikes (De Ondernemer 2020).

Combined, these developments have left less room for the docked and dockless public bike-sharing schemes that have been set up in some other countries. Still, a number of providers have started experiments in the Netherlands. For instance, Mobike has distributed its dockless bikes in Rotterdam and Delft. Flickbike introduced between 4000 and 6500 bikes in Amsterdam. Especially in Amsterdam, this led to lots of discussions about the negative impact of the parked and abandoned bikes in public spaces, and hence the desirability of commercial companies usurping public space for their services. In 2017 the City of Amsterdam, after an injunction against Flickbike, the city removed all the bikes on the ground of a regulation prohibiting commercial service provisions in public space. In 2020 the City allowed four new small-scale experiments for a total of 1400 (partly electric) bikes (Fietsberaad Crow 2020).

So far in the Netherlands, electric scooters such as those offered by Lime and Bird have been deemed illegal. A number of cities have started to experiment with electric motor scooters through companies such as

Go Mobility and Felyx. The national government has taken an interest in bike-sharing systems as part of a larger mobility policy, in which bike-sharing can play a role for first and last-mile solutions in broader Mobility as a Service provision. Although there are yet no figures available that show the long-term impact of bike-sharing, it is expected that each new shared bike could contribute to 0.1–0.6 people avoiding rush hour (car) traffic per day, and as such contribute to $CO_2$ reduction, which is calculated at around 0.37–2.22 kg (Ministerie van Verkeer en Waterstaat 2020).

## Car Sharing

Similar hopes have been expressed around the development of car sharing systems. In 2017, various parties signed a so-called 'Green Deal' (a covenant between various parties, including (local) governments in the Netherlands) about car sharing. Parties involved included car sharing providers, insurers, municipalities, environmental organisations, and the ministries of Economic Affairs and Infrastructure and Environment. The goal of this programme was to stimulate car sharing and contribute to a better environment. In the first Green Deal, the parties committed to developing a total of 100,000 shared cars by 2018. Although this number was not realised, there was enough interest to renew the commitment in 2018, now aiming for 100,000 shared cars and 700,000 users by 2021. Parties involved have projected that participants who exchange their regular car for a shared one contribute to a reduction of between eight and 13% of their $CO_2$ emissions. In addition, the goal is to free up parking places in cities and make these spaces available for green spaces and recreation (RVO 2018). By the end of 2020, the ambition with regard to the number of users had already been met, whereas the number of available cars had grown to 64,000. Part of the new interest has been ascribed to the COVID-19 crisis. As a result of the crisis, citizens wanting to avoid public transport turned to car sharing, whereas commuters no longer needing their car to travel to work could more easily offer these through platforms (Kennisplatform Crow 2020).

The interest in car sharing is accompanied by the emergence of experiments around 'Mobility as a Service' that include various modalities of transport in a single platform. In the Netherlands, seven national pilots have been set up in different cities across the country. International initiatives such as Whim have announced plans to enter the market in the Netherlands, but so far have not implemented these. Looking at developments in car sharing, a wide variety of options are now available (Münzel et al. 2017). Most cars are available through peer-to-peer services, with the Dutch start-up SnappCar being one of the pioneers in this field worldwide. However, in the last few years, more offerings have appeared in the product-service economy, with various companies offering subscription services or private lease constructions for consumers to make use of their fleets. In line with this development, Snapcar itself has also started offering private lease constructions to customers, who then make their cars available for sharing through the SnappCar platform. In addition, there is a rise in community car sharing, in which local groups of residents manage small fleets of cars (Arets 2019).

Experts expect that commercial services will grow in popularity due to their ease of use, yet they still see a future for peer-to-peer models of sharing. These will especially have a future in renting out 'specials' such as old-timers, convertibles, or campers (Arets 2020). In general, it can be said that the sharing economy in the Netherlands has become more commercial and professional in character, where peer-to-peer sharing between consumers is increasingly meeting alternatives offered by commercial services.

## Ride-Hailing

This commercial perspective is especially prominent in the third domain of shared mobility: ride-hailing. Whereas in car sharing, consumers use a car offered by a peer or a company, ride-hailing concerns mobility services in which the consumer is a passenger, either sharing a ride with another consumer or making use of a commercial mobility service platform such as Uber. The latter has tried to disrupt the Dutch market for taxi services by introducing the peer-to-peer service Uberpop in the

Netherlands in 2014. At the time, the company claimed it did not need to comply with taxi regulations, as the drivers were private individuals offering a peer-to-peer service. After it was fined several times, the company shut down the service in 2015 and, in the end, received a 2.3 million euro fine for its illegal activities in 2019 (Van de Weijer 2019).

The rise of commercial ride-hailing platforms has led to numerous debates about the safeguarding of public values, such as protecting consumer safety and worker's rights. Uber made headlines in late 2018 and early 2019 after a number of deadly accidents were caused by Uber drivers (e.g. Van Bergeijk 2018). Now the debate focussed on the responsibility of organising shared mobility. Does the platform itself have a responsibility, or does it lie with the individual service providers who operate through the platform? Critics of the company claimed that Uber's business model stimulates drivers to make long hours on the road, cruising around the city looking for a fare and thus compromising safety (e.g. Kruyswijk 2018). In reaction, the city of Amsterdam and Uber started discussions in the Uber Taskforce, leading to a social charter in which Uber pledges to improve safety, amongst others, by introducing in the future facial recognition technologies to make sure drivers do not mislead systems that check on maximum driving times. Uber will also start sharing data with the city of Amsterdam to make the practises of its drivers more transparent. With these discussions, another aspect of the sharing economy has come into play: that of labour relations and the gig economy. The next session will further elaborate on the debates around the organisation of labour and the safeguarding of public values that have arisen in the Netherlands in the past few years.

## The Gig Economy in the Netherlands: New Economic Opportunities, or Deterioration of Workers' Rights?

As shown in the previous paragraph, discussions about Uber do not only address the organisation of shared mobility but have started to include discussions about the organisation of labour in the platform economy.

These are part of a broader debate about the gig economy and the organisation of platformised work. Since the sharing economy in the Netherlands was quickly delineated with a narrow definition referring to consumers making use of each other underused resource, it was clear from the start that (paid) labour could not be placed under the umbrella of the sharing economy. With the gig economy, a separate definition was minted for the supply of paid labour services through platforms. It was defined as follows: 'The gig economy consists of freelancers who perform one-off physical tasks (jobs), where the assignment is paid for and is created via an online platform (a website or an app)'. Although there is consensus about the definition, in practise, providers do not have the status of a freelancer in all cases. For example, providers on platforms that mediate between the supply and demand of services in and around the home (babysitting, home cleaning, and homework supervision) often work under the Dutch 'Regulations for Services at Home.' A scheme that indemnifies the consumer as an employer against certain responsibilities, but in principle, has little impact on the position of the provider.

## Size and Shape of the Gig Economy: Mostly Facilitating Low-Skilled Labour

Various studies have made an effort to map the gig economy in the Netherlands. For example, in an online survey of 2125 Dutch adults, a representative for all Dutch citizens aged 16–70 years, conducted by the University of Hertfordshire and Ipsos MORI, in 2016, 18% indicated that they had at some point tried to find work through gig economy platforms. About one in eight (12%) of the respondents indicated that they made money this way at some point (Dhondt et al. 2020). SEO Economic Research conducted a sample of more than 5440 people in 2019 and concluded that a total of 1.7% of the working population has been or has ever been active as a gig worker. A large part (1.2% of the working population) indicated that they have been active as a gig worker in the past year (Ter Weel et al. 2020).

In 2020 independent research organisation TNO made an overview of the gig economy landscape in the Netherlands. For this, they used, amongst other things, a dataset set up by Martijn Arets as input for the Dutch website Platformwerk (2020). As of December 2020, this website listed 82 platforms in the Netherlands for various forms of work, from cleaning and construction to creative and legal jobs. TNO analysed the platforms based on skills level for the execution of the work (Pesole et al. 2018). They use the International Standard Classification of Occupations ISCO 2008 classification 2 according to a professional level. They concluded that 23 out of 66 platforms offered opportunities to low-skilled workers. Examples are food delivery, cleaning, freight transport, and walking dogs. Eighteen platforms offered jobs that require medium-level skills such as construction, tourism, and health care. Only five platforms provided opportunities for high-skilled work such as IT, business services, education, the legal profession (Verbiest et al. 2020).

## Impact on Labour Conditions: Enabling Easier Access to Paid Work at the Risk of Increasing Precarity

The potential of the gig economy can be significant, according to a survey by the ING (Internationale Nederlanden Groep; International Netherlands Group) Economic Agency. In this survey, the authors predict that platforms will take over between 20% and 70% of the temporary employment sector in 10 years' time. This depends on the further development of technology and the complexity of regulations (Blom 2018). The fact that this prediction has yet to come true is endorsed in 2020 by the SER (Social and Economic Council), an institute that advises the Dutch Government and Parliament on social and economic policy. SER President Mariëtte Hamer, on the basis of an exploration of 'Platform Economy and Work.' states that 'the insane tension that the platform economy would create on the labour market' has not yet materialised (Sociaal Economische Raad 2020). The SER report underlines the advantages of gig economy platforms that bring together supply and demand for work. The platforms enable access to paid work, even if that is normally difficult due to a lack of formal education. They offer opportunities for entrepreneurs to generate profit and increase choice and convenience for consumers (Sociaal Economische

Raad 2020). At the same time, the SER warns against the risks of dependence on the platform, the lack of certainty and perspective and the risk of low rates and long hours.

These opportunities and uncertainties are also endorsed by researcher Niels van Doorn of the University of Amsterdam. He has researched meal deliverers and home cleaners in the cities of New York, Amsterdam, and Berlin (Platform Labor 2021). One of his conclusions is that a lot of the work organised through these platforms was taken up by immigrants. Without a residence permit, they often end up in jobs in construction, cleaning, food delivery, or restaurants. Platforms are an easy entry into these work fields, as usually, a few questions are asked. Interviewed in the book *Platform Revolution* (Arets 2020, p. 126), he states: 'Platform work is usually the best option, as they can get started quickly, and quickly paid, and generally few questions are asked, so they need little to worry about their lack of language skills being higher than what they would earn elsewhere—especially at the outset, due to the fact that platform companies use venture capital keep wages artificially high in markets with very thin margins.' Van Doorn concludes that platform work initially seems to be a great opportunity for many migrants. However, in due time they find that there are many risks involved and that their position is precarious. They get paid less, lose their income when involved in an accident or when they become ill. Sometimes they are thrown off the platform, or they get problems with the tax authorities when they do not have their tax affairs in order. Without alternatives, they have little choice and tend to absorb these risks for as long as possible (Arets 2020).

This precarity came once more to the light during the recent COVID-19 crisis. At Helpling, a platform broker for home cleaning services, already 40% of the jobs were cancelled during the first week of the lockdown in the Netherlands (Hueck 2020). This figure was expected to rise quickly to 50–60%. Also, Uber drivers complained about a huge decline in work and hardly covered their costs. Uber reported a fall in demand of 70 to 80% during that first period. A similar setback was noticed by drivers not working through an app. Research shows that 71% of the cab drivers in Amsterdam expect to quit within a year; amongst Uber drivers, this rate is as high as 76% (de Ruiter 2020).

Special attention in many of the debates of the platform economy has been paid to the role of platform organisers as private regulators (Boudreau and Hagiu 2009). They have become de facto private regulators and market superintendents who are able to unilaterally set the rules for interaction and mediation on their platforms. This is all the more problematic as platforms continuously change their terms of engagement and mechanisms. Platforms continuously monitor their internal mechanisms and output and adjust many of their features on an ongoing basis. They are able to quickly change the rules and conditions of their intermediation, adding or deleting features or new aspects to their interfaces.

Another issue at stake is data portability. As reputation scores are an important aspect in the matchmaking between service providers and potential customers, it is hard for service workers to shift their business to a new platform as they would have to start all over again building up their reputation. This means they have a weak position negotiating terms with platforms and makes it difficult to leave once; for instance, platforms change their terms or their fee. To investigate how experience gained via a gig economy platform can contribute to better job opportunities, Martijn Arets started an exploration and pilot with six platforms, supported by various partners such as the Dutch and Swedish Employment Services, a large trade union and the Ministry of Economic Affairs and Climate (Kluspaspoort 2021). One of the issues explored is how experienced and reputation profiles can be converted into digital CV that can be shared across platforms.

These discussions show that the development of the gig economy in the Netherlands is still in full swing. In the beginning, the focus was mainly on platforms that serviced individual consumers as their end customers. More recently, the debate has shifted to platforms that cater to businesses and have started to compete directly with temping agencies. More and more government departments have started to research the gig economy. For example, the Ministry of Finance initiated a study into tax collection via platforms in 2020 (Rijksoverheid 2020). This indicates that more and more stakeholders believe that platforms will continue to play an important role in bringing together supply and demand for labour in the future. The aim now is to enhance positive effects and prevent risks.

## Summary

The Netherlands was an early adopter of the sharing economy. Whereas initially, the sharing economy was framed from a perspective of social relations and its potential positive impact on society, increasingly, it is now seen from an economic perspective. Services themselves have commercialised with commercial companies offering, for instance, mobility in a product-service economy through platforms, although there are also some interesting counter developments. In car sharing, community car sharing between groups of local residents has grown increasingly popular, and energy communities consisting of citizens who collaboratively produce and consume their own energy, both pointing to the emergence of citizen organised resource communities.

In general, though, the debate has turned from a sharing and collaborative economy to a platform economy. With that shift, platforms are now seen as new factors in the organisation of the economy at large as well as the provision work, acting as private regulators that set the conditions for interaction and mediation in many markets. Debates are now focussing on the effects of this on public values. Platforms may still positively contribute to these, for instance, by greening mobility or by making it easier for people to find paid work. Yet, at the same time, it is feared that the commercialisation and extractive nature of some of the main platforms could lead to precarious working conditions. The fact that many of these commercial platform operators position themselves merely as mediators and as having no responsibility themselves for the sector they operate in adds to fears that they are offloading responsibility for issues such as consumer safety or workers' rights to society at large. Meanwhile, governments at various levels are trying to get a grip on these developments, as in many cases, they have not yet found the right answer to regulate these platforms as, for instance, platforms such as Airbnb have refused to cooperate with local regulation. This struggle for the provision of public values and the regulation of and within platforms is likely to remain an important theme in the years to come.

## References

Arets, Martijn. 2019. 'Het Einde van de deeleconomie (The End of the sharing Economy).' *Platformrevolutie* (*Platform Revolution*), 19 January 2019. http://rev.vu/7PDV36.

Arets, Martijn. 2020. *Platformrevolutie Hoe platformen als Amazon en Apple de maatschappij en economie veranderen* (*Platform Revolution. How Platforms Such as Amazon and Apple Change Society and the Economy*). Amsterdam: Boom.

Blom, Marieke. 2018. *Platformen kunnen arbeidsmarkt drastisch veranderen* (*Platforms Could Drastically Change the Labor Market*). Amsterdam: ING Economisch Bureau.

Boudreau, Kevin, and Andrei Hagiu. 2009. 'Platform Rules: Regulation of an Ecosystem by a Private Actor.' In *Platforms, Markets and Innovation* (pp. 163–191), edited by Annabelle Gawer. Cheltenham, Northampton, MA: Edward Elgar.

CBS (Statistics Netherlands). 2020. 'Bijna 3 op de 5 Nederlanders maakte in 2019 gebruik van online platforms (Nearly 3 in 5 Dutch People Used Online Platforms in 2019).' *CBS.nl*. https://www.cbs.nl/en-gb/news/2020/14/nearly-3-in-5-dutch-people-used-online-platforms-in-2019. Accessed April 3, 2020.

De Ondernemer. 2020. 'Verdubbeling cijfers Swapfiets mede dankzij internationale expansie (Swapfiets Grows 100%, Partly Due to Its International Expansion).' *De ondernemer.nl*. https://www.deondernemer.nl/mobiliteit/verdubbeling-groeicijfers-swapfiets~2295356. Accessed June 22, 2020.

de Ruiter, Marieke. 2020. 'Crisis toont kwetsbare positie platformwerker: 'Hoofdpijn, veel hoofdpijn' (Crisis Shows Preciarious Position Gig Worker: "Headaches, Lots of Headaches").' *de Volkskrant*. https://www.volkskrant.nl/economie/crisis-toont-kwetsbare-positie-platformwerker-hoofdpijn-veel-hoofdpijn~bccd205c/?utm_campaign=Platform%20Talks&utm_medium=email&utm_source=Revue%20newsletter. Accessed June 4, 2020.

de Waal, Martijn, and Michiel De Lange. 2019. 'Introduction—The Hacker, the City and Their Institutions: From Grassroots Urbanism to Systemic

Change.' In *1 BT-The Hackable City*, edited by Michiel De Lange and Martijn de Waal. Singapore: Springer. https://doi.org/10.1007/978-981-13-2694-3.

Dhondt, Steven, Ursula Huws, E. Zander, and Catalin Dragonimerescu-Gaina. 2020. *Nieuwe schatting van de omvang van de Nederlandse Gig Economie* (*New Estimation of Size of Dutch Gig Economy*). Leiden: TNO. https://repository.tno.nl//islandora/object/uuid:68d7f02f-d24b-458b-bb3e-6d69cd6a5da2.

Fietsberaad Crow (National Knowledge Center Biking Policy for Dutch Governments). 2020. '*Amsterdam kiest vier aanbieders van deelfietsen (Amsterdam Chooses Four Providers for Bikesharing).*' https://www.fietsberaad.nl/Kennisbank/Amsterdam-kiest-vier-aanbieiders-van-deelfietsen. Accessed August 26, 2020.

Frenken, Koen, and Jaap Van Slageren. 2018. 'Kluseconomie is meer dan Uber en Deliveroo (The Gig Economy Is More than Uber and Deliveroo).' *Economisch Statistische Berichten.* https://esb.nu/esb/20047499/kluseconomie-is-meer-dan-uber-en-deliveroo. Accessed 20 December 20, 2018.

Frenken, Koen, Arnoud Van Waes, Magda Smink, and Rinie Van Est. 2017. *A Fair Share: Safeguarding Public Interests in the Sharing and Gig Economy.* The Hague: Rathenau Instituut. Available at: https://www.rathenau.nl/en/publication/fair-share%C2%A0%E2%80%93-safeguarding-public-interests-sharing-and-gig-economy.

Hajer, Maarten. 2011. *De Energieke Samenleving. Op Zoek Naar Een Sturingsfilosofie Voor Een Schone Economie.* Den Haag: Planbureau voor de Leefomgeving.

Harms, Lucas, and Maarten Kansen. 2018. *Fietsfeiten (Biking facts*). Den Haag: Kennisinstituut voor Mobiliteitsbeleid (Knowledge Institute for Mobility Policy).

Hermanides, Elisa. 2017. 'De deeleconomie heeft zijn onschuld verloren (The Sharing Economy Lost Its Innocence).' *Trouw.* https://www.trouw.nl/nieuws/de-deeleconomie-heeft-zijn-onschuld-verloren~be430509/. Accessed September 2, 2017.

Hoekstra, Hans. 2018. 'taat van de Deeleconomie in Nederland (State of the Sharing Economy in the Netherlands).' *Newcom Research & Consultancy.* https://www.newcom.nl/2018-deeleconomie. Accessed March 27, 2018.

Hueck, Hella. 2020. 'De werkster is ineens niet meer nodig (The Cleaner Is No Longer Needful).' *Het Financiele Dagblad.* https://fd.nl/ondernemen/1338913/de-werkster-is-ineens-niet-meer-nodig?utm_campaign=Pla tform%20Talks&utm_medium=email&utm_source=Revue%20newsletter. Accessed March 23, 2020.

Kennisplatform Crow. 2020. 'Met 730.000 deelautogebruikers is het doel overtroffen (With 730.000 Users of Car-Sharing Systems, the Goal Has Been Exceeded).' *CROW (Technology Platform for Transport Infrastructure and Public Space).* https://www.crow.nl/over-crow/nieuws/2020/oktober/met-730-000-deelautogebruikers-is-het-doel-overtro. Accessed October 29, 2020.

Kluspaspoort. 2021. www.kluspaspoort.nl. Accessed June 14, 2021.

Kruyswijk, Marc. 2018. 'Uber opnieuw in opspraak: "Het is wachten op de volgende dode".' *Het Parool.* https://www.parool.nl/nieuws/uber-opnieuw-in-opspraak-het-is-wachten-op-de-volgende-dode~b942d937/. Accessed December 5, 2018.

Ministerie van Verkeer en Waterstaat. (Ministry of Transport and Public Works). 2020. '*Factsheet Deelfietssystemen (Fact Sheet Bike Sharing Systems).*' https://rwsduurzamemobiliteit.nl/kennis-instrumenten/toolbox-slimme-mobiliteit/fiets/factsheet-deelfietssystemen/. Accessed December 10, 2020 and June 14, 2021.

Münzel, Karla, Wouter Boon, Koen Frenken, and Taneli Vaskelainen. 2017. 'Carsharing Business Models in Germany: Characteristics, Success and Future Prospects.' *Information Systems and e-Business Management* 16: 271–291.

OVPRO. 2019. 'Eén miljoen extra OV-fietsritten afgelegd in 2019 (One Million Extra Rides on Public Transport Bikes in 2019).' *OVPro.nl.* https://www.ovpro.nl/innovatie-2/2019/12/18/een-miljoen-extra-ov-fietsritten-afgelegd-in-2019/?gdpr=accept&gdpr=accept. Accessed December 12, 2019.

Pesole, Annarosa, Maria Cesira Urzí Brancati, Enrique Fernández-Macías, Federico Biagi, and Ignacio González Vázquez. 2018. *Platform Workers in Europe.* Luxembourg: Publications Office of the European Union.

Platformwerk. 2020. 'Alle Kluseconomie Platformen (All Gig Economy Platforms).' www.platformwerk.nl. Accessed December 10, 2020.

Platform Labor. 2021. www.platformlabor.net. Accessed June 14, 2021.

Ranchordas, Sofia. 2015. 'Innovation Experimentalism in the Age of the Sharing Economy.' *Lewis & Clark Law Review* 871–924. https://doi.org/10.1525/sp.2007.54.1.23.

Rijksoverheid. 2020. 'Bouwstenen voor toekomstig belastingstelsel gepresenteerd. (Building Blocks for New Tax System Presented).' *Rijksoverheid.nl.* https://www.rijksoverheid.nl/actueel/nieuws/2020/05/18/bouwstenen-voor-toekomstig-belastingstelsel-gepresenteerd. Accessed May 18, 2020.

RVO Rijksdienst voor Ondernemend Nederland (Netherlands Enterprise Agency). 2018. '*Green Deal Autodelen II (Green Deal Car Sharing II).*' https://www.greendeals.nl/green-deals/green-deal-autodelen-ii. Accessed December 10, 2020.

Schwenke, Anne Marieke. 2019. *De Lokale Energie Monitor (The Local Energy Monitor).* HIER opgewekt and RVO. https://www.hieropgewekt.nl/uploads/inline/Lokale%20Energie%20Monitor%202019_DEF_28-11-2019_1.pdf

ShareNL. 2016. '*Welcome to the Collaborative Economy Ecosystem.*' https://www.sharenl.nl/welcome-to-the-collaborative-economy-ecosystem. Accessed December 10, 2020.

SER Sociaal Economische Raad. 2020. *Hoe werkt de platformeconomie (How Does the Platform Economy Work?).* Den Haag: Sociaal Economische Raad (The Social and Economic council of the Netherlands).

Straathof, Bas, Sander van Veldhuizen, and Michiel Bijlsma. 2017. *Platforms Veranderen de Wereld.* Den Haag: CBS.

Ter Weel, Bas, Justus van Kesteren, and Siemen van der Werff. 2020. *Meting kluseconomie (Measuring the Gig Economy).* Amsterdam: SEO Economisch Onderzoek.

Van Bergeijk, Jeroen. 2018. 'Uber-chauffeur voor rechter na dodelijk ongeval: 'Een zaak met alleen maar verliezers' (Uber-Driver Appears in Court After Deadly Accident: "A Case With Only Losers."' *De Volkskrant.* https://www.volkskrant.nl/nieuws-achtergrond/uber-chauffeur-voor-rechter-na-dodelijk-ongeval-een-zaak-met-alleen-maar-verliezers~bfc00ea9/. Accessed Oktober 31, 2018.

Van Dijck, José, Thomas Poell, and Martijn de Waal. 2018. *The Platform Society: Public Values in a Connected World.* New York, NY: Oxford University Press.

Van Eijk, Nico, Ronan Fahy, Harry Van Til, Pieter Nooren, Hans Stokking, and Hugo Gelevert. 2015. *Digital Platforms: An Analytical Framework for Identifying and Evaluating Policy Options.* The Hague: TNO. http://www.ivir.nl/publicaties/download/1703.

Verbiest, Sarieke, Hardy Van de Ven, and R. E. C. Van Den Bergh. 2020. *Platformarbeid in kaart brengen (Mapping gig work).* Leiden: TNO.

Van de Weijer, Bard. 2019. 'Boete van 2,3 miljoen euro wegens UberPop; Uber zegt leven te hebben gebeterd. *de Volkskrant.* https://www.volkskrant.nl/nieuws-achtergrond/boete-van-2-3-miljoen-euro-wegens-uberpop-uber-zegt-leven-te-hebben-gebeterd~b0a7ff5c/#:~:text=Taxidienst%20Uber%20moet%202%2C3,taxi%2C%20zonder%20de%20benodigde%20v ergunningen.&text=Het%20bedrijf%20heeft%20hiermee%20de%20wet%20overtreden. Accessed March 8, 2019.

## Suggested Readings

Arets, Martijn. 2020. *Platformrevolutie Hoe platformen als Amazon en Apple de maatschappij en economie veranderen (Platform Revolution. How Platforms Such as Amazon and Apple Change Society and the Economy)*. Amsterdam: Boom.

Dhondt, Steven, Ursula Huws, E. Zander, and Catalin Dragonimerescu-Gaina. 2020. *Nieuwe schatting van de omvang van de Nederlandse Gig Economie (New Estimation of Size of Dutch Gig Economy)*. Leiden: TNO. https://repository.tno.nl//islandora/object/uuid:68d7f02f-d24b-458b-bb3e-6d69cd6a5da2.

Hajer, Maarten. 2011. *De Energieke Samenleving. Op Zoek Naar Een Sturingsfilosofie Voor Een Schone Economie*. Den Haag: Planbureau voor de Leefomgeving.

Pesole, Annarosa, Maria Cesira Urzí Brancati, Enrique Fernández-Macías, Federico Biagi, and Ignacio González Vázquez. 2018. *Platform Workers in Europe*. Luxembourg: Publications Office of the European Union.

## Relevant Websites

Deeleconomie in Nederland. http://www.deeleconomieinnederland.nl.
Platformwerk. http://www.platformwerk.nl.
Platform Labor. http://www.platformlabor.net.
ShareNL. http://www.sharenl.nl.

# 12

# The Sharing Economy in France: A Favourable Ecosystem for Alternative Platforms Models

Myriam Lewkowicz and Jean-Pierre Cahier

## Introduction

Throughout the last decade in France, the forefront of news and debates concerning the collaborative economy has been occupied by the development of commercial platforms, by their destabilising economic and social consequences, and by the measures taken or to be taken to regulate them (with, for the moment, effects which remain very insufficient). But in the background, less spectacularly, the cooperative platform sector has also sparked public action and has grown successfully, until it now occupies a significant space in this country.

M. Lewkowicz (✉) · J.-P. Cahier
LIST3N/Tech-CICO, Université de Technologie de Troyes, Troyes, France
e-mail: myriam.lewkowicz@utt.fr

J.-P. Cahier
e-mail: jean_pierre.cahier@utt.fr


V. Česnuitytė et al. (eds.), *The Sharing Economy in Europe*,
https://doi.org/10.1007/978-3-030-86897-0_12

This chapter starts by giving an overview of the French ecosystem, highlighting why and how a number of platform cooperatives could emerge successfully in France. The focus is first put on actors such as think tanks and associations and then facilitating measures that were undertaken by the state, which help businesses, public sector institutions, and local communities to anticipate changes inspired by technology and its uses and to open up their innovation processes. The French cooperative movement is one of the most important in the world. At the end of 2019, the Scop (Société cooperative et participative; Participative and Cooperative Society) movement counted 3439 cooperatives active throughout the territory and 63,000 cooperative jobs. The aggregate turnover of cooperative enterprises was 5.6 billion euros (Scop 2020). The second part of this chapter focuses on three examples of cooperatives that were raised as alternatives of capitalistic or monopolistic models and that significantly developed during this decade. Indeed, these cooperatives took advantage of the intellectual and legal French ecosystem described previously—the examples concern three domains: meal delivery service, carpooling, and energy. The way original business models and social or organisational forms used by these collectives contributed to their economic development is then described. Finally, this chapter ends by discussing how some factors could be considered as characteristics of a 'French touch' in terms of platform cooperativism.

## A Favourable Private and Public Ecosystem

The French economy is still traditionally characterised by strong intervention from a centralised state, driving public policies from the national level. However, this path is now moderated by strong compensatory trends, with several movements towards openness occurring over the last few decades: regional decentralisation, European integration, and progressive deregulation of sectors such as transportation or energy—deregulation that is still ongoing and came later than in other European countries. Another characteristic is that the state has long been encouraging a strong trend of social and solidarity economy enterprises (community-based associations, mutual insurance companies, etc.), contributing to a certain 'French distinctiveness' of the collaborative economy sector while also supporting the growth of dozens of start-ups or 'unicorns' with international critical mass, such as DoctoLib or BlaBlaCar.

## The Ecosystem of Actors

In France, there are actually many interactions in all directions between public, semi-public, or private actors, supported to varying degrees at the national, regional, or sectoral level by the public authorities. Drawing on various research and discussion forums, this ecosystem helps to support exchanges and the development of public strategies, with numerous effects in terms of pilot operations, calls for projects, recommendations, and standardisation. In particular, it includes government agencies with specific roadmaps for their mission, think tanks (such as FING, Fondation Internet Nouvelle Génération; New Generation Internet Foundation), associative and citizen networks (e.g. Coop des Communs, OuiShare, La Fabrique des communs), scholarly societies, the French government, and the social and solidarity economy (SSE) sector.

One can, in particular, quote two government agencies: ADEME (Agence de la Transition Écologique; Agency for Ecological Transition) (2020 budget: €721 million), which supports the objectives of environmental public policies, and CNIL (Commission Nationale de l'Informatique et des Libertés; National Commission of Informatics and Freedom), in charge of guaranteeing freedoms in a digital context. In place for several decades, these agencies, which have been able to serve as a model internationally, are supporting digital economy projects in the background. Think tanks, associations, and scholarly societies are also experienced and active in the sector. They maintain numerous relationships with each other, but also with the companies and the state that support them, and draw extensively on their discussions, constituting a melting pot of expertise favourable to innovations. The involvement of the French government can be seen specifically through the work of several ministries (Ministère de l'économie, Secrétariat national au Numérique, Ministère du travail) carrying out studies such as the PIPAME (Pôle Interministériel de Prospective et d'Anticipation des Mutations Economiques; Interdepartmental Unit for Foresight and Anticipation of Economic Changes) one (Baecher et al. 2015) and driving initiatives in a coordinated manner. Finally, the social and solidarity economy (SSE) sector has demonstrated a strong commitment to a collaborative economy. Supported by a Secretary of State, the SSE is particularly important in France with several cooperative or financial institutions (CAMIF, La Poste, Banque des Territoires, etc.), mutual insurance companies (MGEN, MAIF, etc.), or cooperative banks (Crédit Coopératif, LaNef, etc.). Its scope and role have been specified (LOI N° 2014–856) in a way that allows it to embrace all business sectors. This law has strengthened the SSE in its objectives 'to create an ecosystem that is favourable to socially responsible businesses and to promote new entrepreneurial methods that reconcile economic development with employee protection and in cooperation with the territories' (LOI N° 2014–856). The associated groups often function as learning communities rich in internal and external debates, with strong connections to the agencies and think tanks mentioned above. All these actors are interested in experimenting with new common spaces, at the crossroads of the challenges of commodification and environmental and social issues, in a country with a long tradition of social innovation. The confrontation between actors with different statuses and points of view encourages new projects and interdisciplinarity.

## Facilitating Measures

Upstream reflection projects throughout the ecosystem have led to an important series of measures that have defined the last decade. Public policies in France have tried to better regulate the sector of platform capitalism through all kinds of regulatory or fiscal means while supporting the search for alternative routes for 'French-style public services,' which are valued by the citizens. In particular, the ESS sector has contributed to the dynamism of certain cooperative or non-market digital platforms.

At the same time, an array of legal, regulatory, or practical measures had encouraged entrepreneurial and cooperative experiments and their scaling up when public interest was at stake, as in the case of priority environmental issues. These measures outline a medium-term policy, ramped up since 2015, which has strengthened the above-mentioned ecosystem of actors. In this way, a whole regulatory and practical infrastructure has been put in place, now enabling players with innovative social and economic models to develop and achieve success faster.

First, statutes or case laws have been introduced to provide a better framework for the status of platform companies and their fiscal and social environment and better protection for employees and other stakeholders in collaborative economy organisations. More than half of the collectives in France which are involved in the community or cooperative economy platforms have developed sustainably because of the SCIC (Société Coopérative d'Intérêt Collectif; collective interest cooperative company) status, in fields as varied as education, health, energy, territorial development via third place networks, etc. A SCIC can bring together without any limitation the whole variety of possible actors, individuals, or legal entities, whether they are employees, users, producers, communities, volunteers, etc. SCICs can represent society in all its diversity, thus encouraging new avenues for citizen services: 'the SCIC form can be an effective tool for transitioning from public services to citizen services' (Liénard 2016, p. 65). Some SCICs can offer services that are necessary for the everyday and social life of all, and their cooperative form facilitates or even requires an egalitarian treatment, equitable treatment, and one that emphasises general interest related to the notion of public service. Already in 1984, facing the crisis in the welfare state, Pierre Rosanvallon (2000) thought of experimenting with self-managed collective services working together with public services or replacing them.

Rather than creating their own organisation, a new entrepreneur can also join a CAE (Coopérative d'Activités et d'Emplois; business and employment cooperative). This form of collective entrepreneurship is an economic grouping that allows several entrepreneurs gathered within the same organisation to enrich their expertise and share their feedback. This collectivity thus creates development opportunities (innovation, business opportunities, etc.). This status, introduced in 2014, has helped solve some of the problems encountered by platforms, for example, in the mobility sector, as can be seen in the case studies below. In order to launch their business, the project owner has a legal framework, the status of a salaried entrepreneur with a permanent contract and social protection. Any administrative, tax, and accounting management is shared. This framework allows them to concentrate on their business with greater security.

France also offers the ESA (Entrepreneur Salarié Associé; salaried partner-entrepreneur) status, which joins the solution of wage portage, which appeared in France in the late 1980s as a solution to modernise the labour market. Wage portage allows self-employed workers to be paid as if they were employees of a company. It is a tripartite relationship between the portage company, the employee, and the client company. The portage company collects the fees paid by the client and then pays a salary to the freelancer after deduction of management fees and all the social taxes. Wage portage remained marginal for a long time before experiencing significant growth after its entry into the French Labour Code by Act No. 2008–596 of 25 June 2008 on the modernisation of the labour market. Order No. 2015–380 of 2 April 2015 then revised its conditions of exercise.

Modernisation, in terms of management and accounting tools, was also a favourable factor. The innovation of new types of businesses can, in fact, be greatly stimulated by new accounting approaches extended to environmental and societal assessment reports. France was the first EU country to introduce extra-financial reporting through the NRE (Nouvelle Régulation Economique; New Economic Regulation) law in 2001, supplemented by the Grenelle 1 and Grenelle 2 laws in 2012. Innovations from research in Management Science in France tend to give rise to in-depth debates and to spread to companies in the cooperative digital economy. For example, work on accounting standards (Rambaud et Richard 2016; Charolles 2019) aimed in particular at connecting the treatment reserved for work and the environment with the type of company and the economic process they represent.

Finally, the labour laws, amended recently in particular because of reports from the general inspection of social affairs (Amar and Viossat 2016) and from the Ministry of Employment, Labour and Social Cohesion (Montel 2017), have changed social law and are also a favourable factor. The measures that have already been taken or are planned aim in particular to offset the imbalances (dumping, unprofessionalisation, etc.) linked to the platform company sector. Other aspects target the status of work on platforms in a non-market or hybrid context.

In addition to these legal, regulatory, or accounting developments, other types of more operational actions also contribute to a favourable context. First, the state creates or encourages standards or support organisations to unite the actors, create or support the creation of intermediate tools, remove regulatory barriers using the law, stimulate start-ups, and create a talent pool (beta.gouv.fr infrastructure). These actions may concern intersecting problems or priority public policy areas. For example, on the theme of new mobility, 'La fabrique des mobilités' (the mobility factory) network and the regulatory clearing for ride-sharing registers have enabled pilot experiments and the removal of barriers blocking the transition to a new generation of platforms.

The state or other actors in the ecosystem have also created standards, supporting organisations, and shareable methodological building blocks, which have encouraged an explosion and multiplication of uses at the level of local platforms bolstered by local authorities. For example, FING has developed detailed recommendations of principles and methods to guide the design of ethical and sustainable alternative platforms (FING 2020), in particular as part of its Transition2 program ('Transitions2 Relier transition écologique et transition numérique'). In terms of digital identity, the state has created a unique identifier infrastructure, which is now operational and used by both public and private platforms, thereby saving money and facilitating service for users. Another example is the open data distribution platform: data.gouv.fr, created in 2011 on the initiative of Etalab, a mission under the authority of the Prime Minister.

This rich ecosystem constantly supports an exchange of ideas, bringing together the state, companies and both reformist and activist circles in the world of associations. This diversity is having a positive impact on discussions related to the digital economy in a country that traditionally sees a lot of tension between different schools of thought which fuels lively discussions. It fosters plurality around a broad range of approaches ranging from pure commons sharing platforms to platform cooperativism solutions generating more value and jobs. For example, the platform ‘C’est qui le patron?!’ (Who’s the Boss?!) (Gueutin and Zimmer 2020), under the brand founded in 2018 by Nicolas Chabanne, proposes that consumers pay a fair price to properly compensate dairy farmers. This initiative has continued to expand to products other than milk and to other countries. ‘C’est qui le patron?!’ is not limited to a win–win model (between producers and eco-responsible consumers, thus imposing pressure on distribution intermediaries and thereby creating fair trade in local food products) but also explores additional avenues with a focus on general cooperation. For example, during the COVID-19 crisis in the spring of 2020, this brand created a fund to help the struggling self-employed and small merchants. The French ecosystem, therefore, appears to be an open crossroads where social and cooperative initiatives taking advantage of a favourable context intersect with those of actors committed to models of stronger profitability, who are sometimes their partners or their competitors.

## Examples of Alternative Cooperatives in France

Taking advantage of the ecosystem described in the previous section, a number of cooperatives related to the sharing economy have emerged in France. The objective here is not to provide an exhaustive description, but rather to focus on three sectors that are interesting because they illustrate different themes; what is happening in the meal delivery service portrays a new way of working that is no longer salaried, carpooling—a domain in which France illustrated itself by creating Blablacar—allows to discuss resources (cars) that are no longer individual, and finally, the energy domain is very particular because infrastructure needs to exist to produce the resource that will be shared.

## Coopcycle: A New Model for Food Delivery

Delivery is a rapidly growing sector in France for more than five years: 3900 jobs were created in this sector in 2015 compared to 900 in 2014, and more than 8000 were created in the last three months of 2019 (INSEE). Food delivery is a particular form of delivery that does not wait. This activity existed in France before the platform economy (AlloResto was created in France in 1998), but some big platforms have deployed this activity since 2000. Instant meal delivery platforms organise the relationships between meal producers, consumers, and delivery people. The costs of the platform are mainly related to the development of the technological side of the platform and marketing, to which are added insignificant salary costs: the ratio between the number of employees and the number of delivery people is from one to ten for Deliveroo in France: 1000 employees for nearly 10,000 delivery men (Aguilera et al. 2018). It is then obvious that the only variable of the economic model on which the platform can really act is the remuneration of the delivery person.

The workers of these platforms are most of the time self-employed, which allows the platforms to ignore the regulation of salaried work and to make considerable savings in terms of social benefits. In addition, the platforms declare that they do not fall under transport regulations. However, the work of delivery people or drivers corresponds to a relationship of subordination constituting a salaried relationship, as the platform fixes the prices and the nature of the services. A redefinition of the relationship into an employment contract would make the platforms non-viable in the current market context. The low level of remuneration that results from this situation is denounced for many years (Block and Hennessy 2017). Facing that, demonstrations by Deliveroo couriers took place in 2017 and 2018 against brutal price changes in France (shift from hourly remuneration to payment per trip). A call for a strike by deliverers was launched in France during the last FIFA World Cup (2018). Activist groups of couriers have been the main drivers of resistance in France, mainly around Paris and Nantes. Couriers have also been represented by traditional unions, in particular SUD (Solidaires Unitaires

Démocratiques) and CGT (Confédération Générale du Travail), especially in Bordeaux, Dijon, and Lyon, other French big cities (Vandaele 2020).

In this context, Coopcycle was developed in France to offer platform software to any local cooperative who would like to benefit from a platform. Forty-one cooperatives, two in Canada, and 39 in Europe (nineteen in France), currently use the software (CoopCycle). Everything started after the bankruptcy of Take Eat Easy in 2016, led by a developer and a former courier for Take Eat Easy and Deliveroo, who created CLAP (Collectifs des Livreurs Autonomes de Paris; Collective of Autonomous Couriers from Paris). It developed as an association that brings together riders and restaurants who want to engage in ecological and socially responsible delivery service, and it ensures the development and the mutualisation of the software platform. The platform is made of a website that allows the cooperative to manage the logistics and the orders and a smartphone application that is used by the clients to put orders. The association also supports the different cooperatives for their back-office activities (e.g. administrative and legal issues and insurance). Coopcycle became a member of 'Plateformes en Commun.' An initiative launched in 2017 by the French association 'Coop des Communs' (*Plateformes En Communs* 2020) to federate cooperative platform projects that bring social and solidarity economy and the 'commons' together. The source code of CoopCycle is available on GitHub, but its commercial use is reserved for cooperative companies. The license of the software (Coopyleft) is available only to structures that adopt a cooperative model, employ their riders with a traditional contract or through a wage portage company, and that meet the definition of social and security economy as stipulated by the national law of the country in which the platform operates (Chagny 2019).

In the Coopcycle organisation, different statuses are possible, as the state of salaried employees is not possible to apply in all countries, neither desired by all riders. In France, the status of an employee can be obtained through wage portage or by leaning on a CAE (Coopérative d'Activité et d'Emploi; activity and employment cooperatives) (Chagny 2019). CAE offers independent workers to become 'contracted-entrepreneurs'

(entrepreneurs-salariés in French), which means being bound to a cooperative by an employment contract. The cooperative collects the business sales revenue and gives it back to the project owner in the form of a salary once societal charges and management fees have been deducted. In most of the employment and activity cooperatives in France, the payment is approximately 50–60% of the sales revenue. This work status is close to the wage portage but goes further by offering individual support. As of three years from the date they joined, entrepreneurs become associates of the employment and activity cooperative. As an associate, they participate in the daily life and decisions of the cooperative. The legal status of employment and activity cooperatives in France was specified in a law on Social and Solidarity Economy that passed on 31 July 2014 (LOI N° 2014–856). This system offers an alternative to the creation of a company or to working freelance.

The objective for Coopcycle is to make it possible for drivers and employees of the associations to work on a full-time basis, paid approximately 25% above the legal minimum wage (€1229 net monthly as of 1 January 2020). Another important decision is that the remuneration is set on an hourly basis, not by shift and that a minimum number of working hours per week is guaranteed, as well as predictability on working hours. Working conditions (bicycle load, climatic conditions, and length of tours) are integrated into the cooperatives' internal regulations in the form of charters. The collective provides the equipment (bicycles worth about €4000). The cooperatives also provide all other materials (headphones, etc.). Coopcycle is also negotiating insurance contracts with MAIF, a mutual insurance company highly committed to supporting the so-called 'collaborative' economy (Chagny 2019).

The first budget for the Coopcycle association was approved in spring 2019, with a grant obtained from the City of Paris. The grant is planned to cover travel and infrastructure costs (server, hosting, and some necessary services). Most of the costs of developing the tools were based on free work. It raises the question of financial means allocated to initiatives based on 'Commons.' One possible approach is to recognise the positive externalities for cities of this type of platform and to provide them with public subsidies. Examples of subsidies granted by municipalities exist in France, particularly in Paris, with an integration platform 'Les lulu dans ma rue.' Today, approximately 12% of the revenue of the Coopcycle association comes from public funding ('coopcycle, nous socialisons la livraison à vélo').

## Mobicoop: Carpooling as Common Good

In France, the driver is alone on board in seven vehicles out of ten (Raballand and Laharotte 2019), and even nine out of ten during rush hour. The potential for carpooling is then significant, but practices remain marginal: around 3% of trips between home and work are made by carpooling in France (ADEME 2015). More precisely, carpooling practised from the centre of Paris is almost exclusively limited to occasional long-distance journeys via digital platforms (BlaBlaCar). On the contrary, in sparsely populated areas, carpooling is more likely to be used for everyday trips, where car-poolers organise themselves mainly with people they know. Where carpooling makes sense, for example, for a 20-km journey to an employment area in the inner suburbs, the carpooling market share can reach 10–20% and still has room for improvement (Pigalle et al. 2020).

In France, carpooling is regulated by the French Transport Code, which specifies that the public use of a vehicle is conducted 'free of charge, except for the sharing of costs.' The legislative framework makes it possible to distinguish carpooling from individual passenger transport offered by professional taxis or transport car services with a driver (such as Uber, Kapten, Marcel, Lecab, or even Snapcar) (Pigalle et al. 2020). Some cities are starting to integrate carpooling into their transport policy with ambitious projects; in Grenoble, three complementary services coexist: organised hitchhiking, spontaneous carpooling lines, and planned carpooling with an appointment. These services are combined with a lane that is reserved for carpooling on the A48 motorway and a 'Mobility Pass,' allowing residents to use these diverse types of mobility with a single account (Pigalle et al. 2020).

Mobicoop was developed in this context. The association Covoiturage-libre.fr was born in 2011 when Blablacar changed its business model and imposed a commission on all journeys. A number of users felt that this was against the core values of carpooling. One of them developed a small website to offer routes. Very quickly, the site attracted many users, publishing more than 100,000 trips per year (Mobicoop 2020b), and a tight-knit community has developed on Facebook around the values of the association. From 2013 to 2015, the association had a difficult time because it lacked a management team truly dedicated to the project. Nonetheless, the site continued to operate, demonstrating the resilience of its user community. At the end of 2015, a new team took over the management of the association, positioned the website as a common good, and developed actions in this direction, such as relaunching volunteer activities and developing partnerships with social economy actors.

In 2017, after six years, the association noted that carpooling can and must be a common good, that is to say, a transport service serving all, which benefits should remain in the hands of its users, but also that carpooling must improve, both in terms of quantity (number of trips) and quality (user experience). The associative status did not allow improvement nor the right to decision-making to the donors. The association then decided to transform itself into a cooperative (SCIC), in which everyone (a user, an employee, a private company, or a public body) can take a share by becoming a member. Mobicoop, under its new name, can also recruit people to improve services and offer a real alternative to existing carpooling sites (Mobicoop 2020a). Indeed, the cooperative aims at preserving carpooling as a 'common good.' unlike other platforms such as BlaBlaCar that push individuals to monetise services that were formerly free of charge (Compain et al. 2019).

The Mobicoop cooperative now comprises 20,000 active members (for 420,000 users involved in 800,000 rides per year) (Mobicoop 2020a) organised in four categories: volunteers, beneficiaries, and any other natural or legal person with no weighting among them: each member has one vote, and the general assembly has the right to choose the board members. Some 'participatory circles' are also established: some contributors are not cooperative members but have a seat on the board of directors (Compain et al. 2019).

## Enercoop: 100% Renewable

Until the 2000s, the energy sector in France was a stable sector. A monopolistic national company (EDF) took charge of the production, transportation, and distribution of electricity. The development of the energy sector has been regulated by strategic plans, such as the development of nuclear energy in France after World War II. Four characteristics of this sector in France make the emergence of sharing unlikely (Vernay and Gauthier 2017). First, the characteristics of the production of electricity favour a centralised organisation. Second, as mentioned above, the sector is dominated by a few large multinationals, which do not have any interest in promoting the emergence of sharing. Third, new actors who are inspired by social movements advocate the sharing economy rather than companies in a dominant position, which do not have any interest in sharing their market. Finally, consumers only participate in sharing activities if they benefit from them, which is difficult to meet in this sector. Indeed, one of the reasons why few consumers change their supplier is that they have a limited perception of the associated benefits. In addition, electricity is an abstract product: invisible, intangible, and in which consumers pay little interest except when they have to pay their bill. What is then the interest of consumers to share such a product? However, even with all these obstacles, sharing is indeed taking place.

In France, European ambitions related to energy transition were first addressed in the Energy Transition Law for Green Growth (LTECV), adopted in 2015. Indeed, France was the first EU Member State to introduce incentives (called 'participatory bonuses') to promote the financial participation of local actors in renewable projects (article 111 of the law). This law resulted from lobbying efforts of the Collective for Citizen Energy (le 'Collectif pour l' 'energie citoyenne'). In particular, the law simplified the juridical conditions for setting up citizen renewable energy production projects by paving the way for joint-stock companies and cooperative companies to develop renewable energy production projects capitalised or financed in part by local citizens or municipalities (Sebi and Vernay 2020). In November 2019, within the framework of the Energy and Climate Law, the French government first mentioned community renewable energy projects (CREP). A CREP involves a group of citizens, social entrepreneurs, public authorities, and community organisations who participate directly in the energy transition by jointly investing in, producing, selling, and distributing renewable energy (Interreg 2018). In France, CREPs are emerging but evolving quickly as their number multiplied fourfold between 2014 and 2019, at the end of which there were 240 CREPs in the country (Vernay and Sebi 2020).

Enercoop was created for managing the energy produced from renewable energy sources and for providing energy services aiming at reducing energy consumption and increasing the share of renewable energies in the national energy balance (Soulias 2018). Enercoop was born in 2005 from the reflection of several Greenpeace activists wishing to supply 100% 'green' electricity. It started with commercial partners such as Biocoop stores, WWF, and Greenpeace France. Enercoop is also thought of as a lobbying tool for changing energy management practices, ensuring a counterpoint of view to EDF (Becuwe and Cateura 2010). In addition to promoting renewable energies and the desire to offer a different industrial model, Enercoop directly involves the end consumer by having adopted the SCIC model. The governance is then ensured by a variety of stakeholders (producers, employees, and consumers) who may have divergent interests. However, the discussion around the purposes necessary to ensure the sustainability of the company can lead to an awareness of their interdependence. Enercoop has also added legal entities to the governance (partners, communities, and funders), which can help in sustaining the project (Liénard 2016).

Enercoop supports their members to lower electricity consumption through diverse interventions: (a) 'TupperWatt' meetings arranged and led by a member of Enercoop where they introduce Enercoop's values and topics revolving around the energy transition; (b) 'Dr. Watt' a training course to help consumers make a self-diagnosis of their electricity consumption, using a software platform. By 2016, 'Dr. Watt' had been tested successfully in three local cooperatives, with a reported energy-saving potential of 40% (Hoppe et al. 2019); the 'Energie Partagée' citizen investment fund to support projects. By 2016, the investment fund had 4312 subscribers and raised over 11 million euros (Hoppe et al. 2019). Enercoop also issues newsletters and provides personal advice to users. Although Enercoop started as one single cooperative, it has become a network of ten cooperatives and 300 producers ('Les coopératives' 2020) that allow citizens to reconnect with the challenges of the energy transition on the regional level. These figures remain modest compared to those of other European countries, but in view of the French context and history described above, they reflect a certain evolution.

## Discussion and Summary

The three cases described above depict three successful cooperatives in France that started as a confrontation with powerful capitalistic competitors that are not sufficiently regulated, although some progress has been made. In these cases, actors were actively searching for new ways to implement the sharing economy, receiving public support through the SSE (social and solidarity economy) while keeping a realistic eye on the market. These circumstances have acted as opportunities for actors to mobilise other actors and even more motivated stakeholders to join alternative platforms in the roles they offer (clients, members, donors, and partners). However, for these opportunities to be taken to allow a rapid response, on a larger scale, to an amplifying social demand, the economic models, the legal conditions, as well as the appropriate social and organisational forms had to be present.

The actors of the three cooperatives mentioned succeeded because these conditions were met. First, because these cooperatives have been able to quickly handle the managerial dimension sometimes by innovating strongly in the forms of coordination and governance. The resulting organisations imply more democracy, helping to create communities that are more united and to involve all the actors in the management and the sharing of created value. Thus, increasing importance has been placed on the remuneration of contributors at a fair price (differentiating from the models of pure free access to commons that had prevailed in previous periods). The underlying software components of these initiatives were also discussed, with the launch of adapted free licenses. All these decisions have fostered open modes that create jobs and confidence and that are economically sustainable in the long term. Finally, these projects were successful because they benefited from a favourable ecosystem of actors and facilitating conditions that were set up upstream with public support, as was underlined before.

All in all, one can see from the examples presented, and following other authors (Forestier et al. 2020; Giusti and Thévenoud 2020), that a favourable dynamic has started in France for cooperative platforms, promoting them both as a type of collective and as a support for new social statuses. Indeed, cooperatives appear increasingly as alternative forms of collectives to a deleterious capitalist approach in the debate on the opportunities and risks of platform economies within the general digital transition of territories. In particular, legal forms such as the new SCIC, open to all types of stakeholders, including local communities, guaranteeing more egalitarian governance, are now recognised as significant progress and are popular with stakeholders. Cooperative platforms thus appear as viable solutions in locally anchored arrangements where local public authorities can gather to face territorial problems (transportation, logistics, and data access). In terms of new statuses, the actors of the French movement of cooperative platforms have indeed appropriated the important opportunities given by the creation of new staff statuses that particularly fit the activity of platform workers, such as the CAE (Cooperative of activity and employment, since 2014) and ESA (salaried partner-entrepreneur, since 2016) for the cooperation between freelancers. In addition to these statuses, some measures were also taken, allowing platform workers to come together or unite within organisations that can represent their collectives.

To conclude, our work goes in the same direction as the one from (Compain et al. 2019), who, after studying several French cooperative platforms, claim that they have some common goals: 'ensuring the welfare of the platform workers and contributors (mainly by including them in the governance), encouraging reciprocal exchange, or paying attention to the impact on the nature of platform-mediated activities' (Compain et al. 2019, p. 19). These authors envision in these characteristics, which can also be noticed in the three cases presented above, a dynamic of 're-embedding' (Polanyi and Pearson 1977) the transactions that take place on these platforms so that transactions serve a general interest. Therefore, the engagement of such shared initiatives with multi-stakeholder governance presents a connection and a natural synergy with public action. Accordingly, public policies may look for promoting platforms that offer new frameworks for partnerships with civil society. Although a more in-depth study would be necessary to support this hypothesis, such a synergy seems to characterise the dynamic observed in France, where the public authorities appear to seek to seize this opportunity through a supportive framework.

## References

ADEME (Agence de la transition écologique - Agency for Ecological Transition). 2015. 'Leviers d'actions pour favoriser le covoiturage de courte distance, évaluation de l'impact sur les polluants atmosphériques et le CO2 – Enquête auprès des utilisateurs des aires de covoiturage' 1362C0009. *ADEME*. Accessed Octobre 28, 2020. https://www.ademe.fr/sites/default/files/assets/documents/etude_nationale_covoiturage_courte_distance-aires_de_covoiturage.pdf.

Aguilera, Anne, Laetitia Dablanc, and Alain Rallet. 2018. 'L'envers et l'endroit des plateformes de livraison instantanée: Enquête sur les livreurs micro-entrepreneurs à Paris.' *Réseaux* 212 (6): 23–49. https://doi.org/10.3917/res.212.0023.

Amar, Nicolas, and Louis-Charles Viossat. 2016. 'Les Plateformes Collaboratives, l'emploi et La Protection Sociale.' 2015–121R. *IGAS*. Accessed November 1, 2020. https://www.igas.gouv.fr/IMG/pdf/2015-121R.pdf.

Baecher, Cedric, Fanny Frécon, Pauline Renard, Laure Salvaing, and Quentin Llewellyn. 2015. 'PROSPECTIVE – Enjeux et perspectives de la consommation collaborative.' Etudes économiques. PIPAME – Pôle Interministériel de prospective et d'anticipation des mutations économiques. Paris: Ministère de l'économie de l'industrie et du numérique.

Becuwe, Audrey, and Olivier Cateura. 2010. 'Le transfert d'une opportunité d'affaire d'une association militante à une équipe entrepreneuriale.' In *10ème Congrès International Francophone en Entrepreneuriat et PME – CIFEPME*, Octobre 27–29, Bordeaux. 19pages. Accessed October 14, 2020. http://www.airepme.org/images/File/2010/BECUWE-CIFEPME2010x.pdf.

Block, Sheila, and Trish Hennessy. 2017. '"*Sharing Economy" or on-Demand Service Economy? A Survey of Workers and Consumers in the Greater Toronto Area.*' Canadian Centre for Policy Alternatives, ON. Accessed October 22, 2020. https://www.policyalternatives.ca/sites/default/files/uploads/publications/Ontario%20Office/2017/04/CCPA-ON%20sharing%20economy%20in%20the%20GTA.pdf.

Chagny, Odile. 2019. '*Casestudy_FR.Pdf*.' Accessed October 22, 2020. http://www.dontgigup.eu/wp-content/uploads/2019/11/Casestudy_FR.pdf.

Charolles, Valérie. 2019. 'Faire Du Travail Une Valeur Comptable : Une Approche à Partir de Ludwig Wittgenstein et Adam Smith'. Hal-02429097. Post-Print. Post-Print. HAL. https://ideas.repec.org/p/hal/journl/hal-02429097.html.

Compain, Guillaume, Philippe Eynaud, Lionel Morel, and Corinne Vercher-Chaptal. 2019. *Alternative Platforms and Societal Horizon: Characterisation and Strategies for Development.* Accessed August 20, 2020. https://halshs.archives-ouvertes.fr/halshs-02140104.

*CoopCycle, La fédération.* Accessed September 15, 2020. https://coopcycle.org/fr/federation/.

*Coopcycle, nous socialisons la livraison à vélo.* Accessed February 18, 2021. https://coopcycle.org/fr/.

FING (Fondation Internet Nouvelle Génération; New Generation Internet Foundation). 2020. '#RESET Quel numérique voulons-nous pour demain?' *Questions Numériques - cahiers d'enjeux et de prospective.* Accessed October 30, 2020. https://fing.org/wp-content/uploads/2020/02/cahier-d-enjeux-fing-questions-numeriques-reset.pdf.

Forestier, Florian, Odile Chagny, Mathias Dufour, and Franck Bonot. 2020. *Désubériser, reprendre le contrôle.* Collection Les nouveaux possibles. Editions du faubourg, Paris.

Giusti, Jérôme, and Thomas Thévenoud. 2020. 'Pour travailler à l'âge du numérique, défendons la coopérative!' *Fondation Jean-Jaurès.* Accessed October 29, 2020. https://jean-jaures.org/nos-productions/pour-travailler-a-l-age-du-numerique-defendons-la-cooperative.

Gueutin, Claire-Agnès, and Benjamin Zimmer. 2020. *Une entreprise responsable et rentable, c'est possible - avec 18 entretiens de dirigeants d'entreprise - Claire-Agnès Gueutin, Benjamin Zimmer - Books On Demand - Grand format - Place des Libraires.* ContentA. Accessed October 29, 2020. https://www.placedeslibraires.fr/livre/9782956969730-une-entreprise-responsable-et-rentable-c-est-possible-avec-18-entretiens-de-dirigeants-d-entrepri-gueutin-zimmer/.

Hoppe, Thomas, Frans H. J. M. Coenen, and Maria T. Bekendam. 2019. 'Renewable Energy Cooperatives as a Stimulating Factor in Household Energy Savings.' *Energies* 12 (7): article 1188. https://doi.org/10.3390/en12071188.

INSEE (Institut National de la Statistique et des Etudes Economiques – National Institute of Statistics and Economy Studies). 'Augmentation des créations d'entreprises en Juillet 2020.' Accessed September 10, 2020. https://www.insee.fr/fr/statistiques/4644216.

Interreg. 2018: '2018–08–30_Policy_brief_Renewable_Energy_Communities_PB_TO4_final.Pdf.' Accessed October 28, 2020. https://www.interregeurope.eu/fileadmin/user_upload/plp_uploads/policy_briefs/2018-08-30_Policy_brief_Renewable_Energy_Communities_PB_TO4_final.pdf.

'Les coopératives.' 2020. *Enercoop*. https://www.enercoop.fr/les-cooperatives.

Liénard, Yves-Alain. 2016. 'Du service public au service citoyen.' *RECMA* 340 (2): 65–76. https://www.cairn.info/revue-recma-2016-2-page-65.htm.

LOI N° 2014–856 Du 31 Juillet 2014 Relative à l'économie Sociale et Solidaire. 2014. *2014–856*. https://www.legifrance.gouv.fr/loda/id/JORFTEXT000029313296.

Mobicoop. 2020a. Mobicoop. Accessed October 14, 2020. https://www.mobicoop.fr/article/fonctionnement.

Mobicoop. 2020b. '*Mobicoop History*.' Accessed October 14, 2020. Mobicoop. https://www.mobicoop.fr/article/histoire.

Montel, Olivia. 2017. 'L'économie Des Plateformes: Enjeux Pour La Croissance, Le Travail, l'emploi et Les Politiques Publiques.' 213. *Document d'études. DARES* (Direction de l'Animation de la Recherche, des Etudes et des Statistiques). Accessed November 1, 2020. https://dares.travail-emploi.gouv.fr/IMG/pdf/de_2013_economie_collaborative.pdf.

Pigalle, Éléonore, Jean-Baptiste Ray, and Sylvanie Godillon. 2020. 'Entretien. Quelles perspectives pour le covoiturage en France?' *Flux* 119–120 (1): 192–196. https://www.cairn.info/revue-flux-2020-1-page-192.htm.

*Plateformes En Communs*. 2020. Accessed August 25, 2020. https://coopdescommuns.org/fr/plateformes-en-communs/.

Polanyi, Karl, and Harry W. Pearson. 1977. *The Livelihood of Man*. Studies in Social Discontinuity. New York: Academic Press.

Raballand, Wilfried, and Pierre-Antoine Laharotte. 2019. *Estimation du potentiel de covoiturage par la modélisation des déplacements*. Accessed October 28, 2020. https://hal.archives-ouvertes.fr/hal-02284065.

Rambaud, Alexandre, and Jacques Richard. 2016. 'The "Triple Depreciation Line" Accounting Model and Its Application to the Human Capital'.

In *Finance and Economy for Society: Integrating Sustainability*, 11: 225–252. Emerald Group Publishing Limited. https://doi.org/10.1108/S2043-905920160000011010.

Rosanvallon, Pierre. 2000. *The New Social Question: Rethinking the Welfare State. New French Thought*. Princeton, NJ: Princeton University Press.

Scop. 2020. *Les Chiffres Clés Des Scop En France*. Accessed November 19, 2020. https://www.les-scop.coop/chiffres-cles.

Sebi, Carine, and Anne-Lorène Vernay. 2020. 'Community Renewable Energy in France: The State of Development and the Way Forward.' *Energy Policy* 147: 111874. https://doi.org/10.1016/j.enpol.2020.111874.

Soulias, Emmanuel. 2018. *Statuts Enercoop SCIC-SA à Capital Variable*. Accessed October 28, 2020. https://www.enercoop.fr/sites/default/files/statuts_enercoop_18-06-16.pdf.

*Transitions2 Relier transition écologique et transition numérique*. Accessed October 30, 2020. http://www.transitions2.net.

Vandaele, Kurt. 2020. 'Collective Resistance and Organizational Creativity Amongst Europe's Platform Workers: A New Power in the Labour Movement?' *SSRN Scholarly Paper ID 3672260*. https://doi.org/10.2139/ssrn.3672260.

Vernay, A.-L., and C. Sebi. 2020. 'Energy Communities and Their Ecosystems: A Comparison of France and the Netherlands.' *Technological Forecasting and Social Change* 158 (September): article 120123, 10 pages. https://doi.org/10.1016/j.techfore.2020.120123.

Vernay, Anne-Lorène, and Caroline Gauthier. 2017. 'Tempête dans le secteur de l'électricité: l'émergence de l'économie du partage aux Pays-Bas.' *Entreprises et histoire* 86 (1): 105–124. https://www.cairn.info/revue-entreprises-et-histoire-2017-1-page-105.html.

## Suggested Readings

Giraudet, Louis-Gaëtan, Bénédicte Apouey, Hazem Arab, Simon Baeckelandt, Philippe Begout, Nicolas Berghmans, Nathalie Blanc, et al. 2021. '*Deliberating on Climate Action: Insights from the French Citizens' Convention for Climate*.' Hal-03119539. https://hal-enpc.archives-ouvertes.fr/hal-03119539/document.

Marty, Frédéric. 2020. 'Accès aux données, coopétition intra-plateforme et concurrence inter-plateformes numériques.' *Revue d'economie industrielle*

169 (1): 221–246. https://www.cairn.info/revue-d-economie-industrielle-2020-1-page-221.htm.

## Relevant Websites

Association “coop des communs.’ https://coopdescommuns.org.
FING, Fondation Internet Nouvelle Génération; New Generation Internet Foundation. https://fing.org/.
La fabrique des mobilités’ (the Mobility Factory) Network. https://lafabriquedesmobilites.fr.
La marque du consommateur, a Brand Created by the Consumers to Support the Producers. https://lamarqueduconsommateur.com/.
Ouishare Citizen Network. https://www.ouishare.net/.
The Shift Project, the Carbon Transition Think Tank. https://theshiftproject.org/.

# 13

# A Critical Perspective on the Sharing Economy in Tourism Using Examples of the Accommodation Sector in Austria

Malte Höfner and Rainer Rosegger

## Introduction

This chapter focuses on the area of tourism in Austria, specifically in the short-term accommodation sector. In Austria, tourism has an important status. With 89.3 million overnight stays by non-residents in 2018, Austria ranks fifth compared to other European countries in terms of absolute overnight stays (Eurostat 2020). In recent years, digital platforms have gained increasing importance in the rental accommodation sector and have changed consumption patterns in other realms of daily life too (e.g., food delivery services). Today platforms serve as providers or

M. Höfner (✉)
Department of Geography and Regional Science, University of Graz, Graz, Styria, Austria
e-mail: malte.hoefner@uni-graz.at

R. Rosegger
SCAN, Agency for Market and Social Analysis, Graz, Styria, Austria
e-mail: rainer.rosegger@scan.co.at



V. Česnuitytė et al. (eds.), *The Sharing Economy in Europe*,
https://doi.org/10.1007/978-3-030-86897-0_13

mediators for sharing different sets of (in)tangible resources. As a result of digitalisation, the rise of the platform economy has changed modes of economic production and consumption in society (Kenney and Zysman 2016; van Dijck et al. 2018). And as in many other countries, there have been debates on how to regulate this upcoming sector (Kirchner and Schüßler 2020). Especially in cities, so-called 'platform urbanism' has significantly altered the production of space since platform activities have changed the relationship between people and their urban spatial environment (Graham 2020). Despite numerous efforts in Austria, attempts to counteract the changes associated with the sharing economy regulatorily have so far been unsuccessful.

In addition to structural changes, the tourism sector has been hit heavily by COVID-19, the consequences of which are not yet foreseeable. However, it is obvious that there will be fundamental changes because a decline in the total number of overnight stays can already be observed. Overall, the number of overnight stays in Austria fell by 36% in 2020 compared to the previous year. This corresponds to a decline of 98 million in overnight stays. Compared to other provinces, the federal capital Vienna was hit hardest by this decrease, overnight stays dropping by 74%. In December 2020, there was a 94% drop in overnight stays in Austria. The country's well-known winter tourism has thus been severely affected by the pandemic in the 2020/2021 season (Statistik Austria 2021).

Starting with a description of various business and governance models within the sharing economy and a characterisation of the tourism market in Austria, this chapter will focus on alternatives within the sharing economy and describe possibilities for individual and (mainstream) state-regulatory action. In this chapter, references to terms or reports on the so-called collaborative economy are to be understood as part of the sharing economy since uniform terminologies have not been established (Botsman and Rogers 2010; Krok 2019), and conceptual explorations are not part of this chapter. It takes a closer look at the consequences and opportunities of the development of market-based sharing platforms by juxtaposing two cases in terms of their business models within peer-to-peer accommodation as an economic mode between platform capitalism and platform cooperatives. By presenting examples of 'non-economic fields', which fulfil basic structures of (commons-based) sharing, the chapter introduces various forms of collaborative consumption within the sharing economy, including platforms as facilitators and mediators for enabling civic participation.

## Sharing Economy Business Models: Between Market-Based Services and Platform Cooperatives

Within the sharing economy, there are different business and usage models. Petropoulos (2017) structures the models into the following three groups: (1) P2P/C2C peer-to-peer/customer-to-customer: a platform (online/offline) through which a private person trades with another person or creates services for the latter (e.g., Airbnb, Blablacar); (2) B2C business-to-customer: trading activities or service provision between companies and customers (private individuals); and (3) B2B business-to-business: used to trade between companies or create services. Most authors developed these models in relation to digital technologies—unlike, for example, analogue exchange or 'swapping' circles (Hamari et al. 2016). The success of these models lies in the platform being perceived as an engine of trust. With the help of reputation and evaluation systems, platforms disguise the fact that things are being 'shared' among 'strangers' (Schor 2014). What is primarily shared on platforms is rarely an actual resource or good, but instead access to the platform, which mediates the services being shared. The good (e.g., housing space, cars, or food) is mediated by means of commission fees and thus further commodified as immaterial value for the operator (e.g., Airbnb). Regardless of whether platforms are for-profit or not-for-profit, Pentzien (2019) names three principles of operation. Firstly, they generate value by coordinating interactions and transactions between two or more actors. Secondly, they integrate supply and demand and shape the relationships between these actors. This gives them the power to exclusively determine rules and governance mechanisms. And thirdly, they generate data by acting as information brokers between the actors. This data is analysed and sold as a commodity itself. This creates competition between the platforms in the data market (Pentzien 2019).

Today's sharing economy operates within the contested field between the commodification and the commoning of social capital 'such as "trust" in the form of peer ratings and reviews' (Thompson 2015, cited in Dobusch 2019, p. 114), which is situated in networks mediated through platforms. Dobusch (2019) distinguishes between digital platforms that are commons-based and market-based. The essential difference is the respective resource pool and exchange process. While commons-based platforms generally make material resources available without imposing remunerated conditions of reciprocal exchange on their users, market-based platforms, on the other hand, make use of a data-driven pool of resources linked to reciprocal monetary exchange.

In the case of market-based platforms, the business model relies on the extraction of data. These platforms integrate supply and demand. Unlike data mining on social media platforms, where micro-targeting is used for advertising, short-term rental (STR) platforms such as Airbnb, recommendation algorithms wield power over providers on the platforms (Dobusch 2019). In terms of neoliberal logics of the generation of capital, the model is therefore based on the constant collection of data (Srnicek 2017; Pentzien 2019; Grabher and König 2020). With the collection of data and its processing (datafication), competitive advantages in new areas are opened up. Revenue is generated by outsourcing personnel and infrastructure costs, workers' rights, and the costs of the operational business. Markets are monopolised and made inaccessible for other players, as is best exemplified by the business models of Uber and Airbnb (Heiland 2018; Srnicek 2017). These developments have led to sharing (economies) with commons-based platforms to pursue different strategies. Often summarised under the buzzword of 'platform cooperativism' (Scholz 2016), these models differ from the classical market-based sharing economy in their governance structure and the participation possibilities for their users. These platforms aim to counteract 'extractive capitalism' by returning surpluses to local economic cycles and local communities, as opposed to the business models of Airbnb and Uber, which exploit local resources as a global competitive advantage (Foramitti et al. 2020).

In summary, the platform acts as a mediator. A resource is made available, owned by one party but shared with others. Thus, the platform generates a higher value for the provided resource. The advent of digital technologies has led to an increase in exchange practices, so platforms today also need to establish a 'set of formal and informal rules' to ensure that collaborative usage can indeed be guaranteed (Dobusch 2019, p. 110). For the sharing economy and its actors, these areas are legal grey zones. Political actors often lack the means for regulatory intervention.

## The Austrian Sharing Economy

Austria generated about €536 million in revenue from sharing economy activities in 2016 (Naumanen et al. 2018). This corresponds to about 0.15% of the national gross domestic product (GDP). Austria's economic performance in the sharing economy is thus slightly below the average EU GDP of 0.17%. The largest revenues are generated in the financial sector (€248 million) and the accommodation sector (€236 million), followed by the sector of online skills (€27 million) and transport (€24 million) (Naumanen et al. 2018). Looking at the respective sectors according to their underlying business models, the accommodation sector is characterised by international platforms offering services for short-term rentals (STRs)—usually, fully furnished apartments or rooms, rented on a daily/weekly basis. Especially in popular tourist destinations, the emergence of Airbnb has increased rents on the local housing market (Naumanen et al. 2018).

Within the EU, the internationalisation of platforms is most evident in Austria. In total, 221 platforms identified in the study by Naumanen et al. (2018), 39 are active in Austria, about half of which (19) are international (calculations by the chapters' authors based on data provided in aforesaid study). With the exception of the financial sector, international platforms predominate. To illustrate this, in 2016, there were no domestic platforms, and the accommodation sector was instead dominated by six international players, such as Airbnb and Booking.com, to name the two largest (Naumanen et al. 2018). In terms of the total number of people (19%) who have ever made use of service via an online platform, Austria is below the EU average of 23%. However, in relation to total platform activity (EU average = 57%, EC 2018: 1; online fact-sheet Austria), almost two-thirds of Austrian users have availed of accommodation service. As for persons who have provided service via a platform, Austria is among the EU average of 6% (EC 2018, pp. 8, 63).

## Austrian Tourism Sector and the Rise of Airbnb

The tourism sector in Austria is of great significance, both economically and culturally. In 2018 the tourism sector generated 6.5% of the Austrian GDP. In the Organisation for Economic Co-operation and Development comparison, this is above average (OECD 2021). In terms of turnover, the accommodation sector generated the highest financial share of 48% (Fritz et al. 2020, p. 18). In the 2018 winter season, 1.13 million beds were available as accommodation in Austria. Since the year 2000, this number has increased by 3.1%. Significantly above-average growth was recorded in this period for beds in private accommodations (+574%) and commercial vacation apartments (+2730%). Experts believe that this increase, especially in the capital city of Vienna, can be traced back to the global trend of collaborative consumption, driven by C2C-platforms such as Airbnb (Fritz et al. 2020, p. 1). In 2018, Airbnb reported that 1.1 million guests booked accommodation in Austria via their service. It is estimated that in Austria, 30,000 hosts are providing private short-term accommodation via digital platforms (Kurier 2019).

In the accommodation sector, which relies on tourism, Airbnb has taken on the role of a digital frontrunner for services mediated via platforms. In 2017 alone, Airbnb made a profit of $93 million out of $2.56 billion in revenues, reaching $4.81 billion by 2019, only to drop by 50% in 2020. Travel restrictions due to the pandemic resulted in just 150 million bookings worldwide (Airbnb 2020). In Vienna, about half of the offers (49.8%) in 2019 were made by hosts with multiple listings, which indicates commercially organised STRs (Inside Airbnb 2019). An empirical study for Salzburg (Smigiel et al. 2019, p. 161) indicates that accommodation offered via Airbnb is to a large degree facilitated by professionalised providers (e.g., commercial hosts with multiple listings approximately 55%). Furthermore, very few people actually 'share' their own apartment. According to a quick search on the market minder platform AirDNA the type of accommodation that is actually 'shared' (shared room) is higher in the capital, with a quarter of all listed offers than in the much smaller cities of Salzburg (15%), Graz (17%), Innsbruck (18%), and Linz (19%). One possible explanation could be the higher demand for housing in larger cities. According to conservative estimates by Smigiel et al. (2019, p. 163), Airbnb is depriving Salzburg's housing market of around 50% of its overall stock in the long term. In Vienna, Seidl et al. (2017), who used the same methodology as Smigiel et al. (2019), found an effective deprivation of 38% through the same type of accommodation. Both studies used a mixed-methods approach in which all Airbnb offers were quantitatively surveyed and analysed on two cut-off dates in June 2017 and June 2018. Subsequently, guided in-depth interviews were conducted with 10% (Salzburg) of the Airbnb providers according to provider structure (Smigiel et al. 2019, p. 156). The method proved successful and was later also used in a similar fashion for the Thessaloniki case study in Greece (Katsinas 2021).

The commercialisation of platforms will become more widespread in the future and move away from the former practice of 'sharing' by expanding the original offer with complementary services. Such developments can already be observed with Airbnb integrating city tours, photo tours, food tours in hip restaurants, and the like in their offers (O'Regan and Choe 2017). The world market leader Airbnb is expanding into new business areas in order to become an all-around travel provider on a global scale (Behrendt et al. 2017). However, Airbnb also struggled with the effects of the COVID-19 pandemic. Expecting revenues of only $2.4 billion in 2020 (half of the previous year's sales of $4.8 billion), the company announced that it would lay off 1900 employees. This represents a quarter of the total workforce at Airbnb (Grieß 2020). Contrary to expectations, Airbnb joined the public stock market in December 2020. Two months later, in February 2021, Airbnb presented its quarterly figures from the previous year with the surprising result that instead of a 50% drop in revenue, it only made a 30% loss (FAZ 2021).

This is explained by the pandemic-related geographical reorientation of customers towards more remote regions. Media research (Glusac 2020; Grieß 2020; Twickel 2020) on tourism during the pandemic and official numbers on overnight stays in 2020 (Statistik Austria 2021) reveal how vulnerable supposedly stable industries such as Austrian tourism can be, especially when they have been impacted by neoliberal exploitation mechanisms, where players like Airbnb are very quick to adapt to unstable markets in times of crisis.

In the year 2020, overnight stays in Vienna were 74% down from 2019. This equals a decline of around 13 million in absolute numbers. The year before the COVID-19 crisis, overnight stays and sales in Austria reached all-time highs (Statistik Austria 2021). At the time of writing, COVID-19 infection rates in Austria and Europe are still high. Therefore, it is hardly realistic to expect a return to an 'old normal' in tourism. It can be assumed that the crisis will lead to bankruptcies and a restructuring of the tourism industry, which in Austria is strongly characterised by the winter season and ski tourism. These are both areas of tourism where adaptation to climate change will be necessary and global warming poses major long-term challenges. In 2020 the Austrian Federal Government established financial support funds to deal with the COVID-19 crisis, with companies in the tourism sector receiving financial support (Martins et al. 2020).

Overall, and despite previous regulatory efforts by the authorities, it is not foreseeable at this time how the crisis will affect the STR market industry. It can be assumed, however, that STRs could benefit from the situation, and already prevailing platforms could further expand their market dominance. Recent media reports indicate that Airbnb and similar platforms could emerge as winners from the current crisis: especially in times of physical distancing where people tend to look for remote locations, independent units, and are more flexible by working remotely. Despite temporary setbacks and city tourism dwindling, Airbnb will adapt its business model to include close to home destinations ('staycations') and enable holidays outside the major city regions (Glusac 2020; Twickel 2020).

The case of STRs in general and Airbnb, in particular, has so far involved many regulators and caused municipalities to react in various ways without resulting in any standardised regulation on a national or international level. For this reason, Austria introduced the recording obligation for platforms in 2020. Since the beginning of the year 2021, information must be made available by the platforms to the responsible tax authorities (BMLRT 2019a).

In 2018 the development of a new strategy for Austria as a tourism destination was started but had not been completed. In interim reports, it is emphasised that digitalisation poses an enormous challenge for the industry. Blockchain, artificial intelligence, and similar technologies are seen as ground-breaking for future developments (BMLRT 2019b). As demonstrated above, it can be assumed that the Austrian tourism industry will face changes, which bear challenges but also opportunities. At present, the state-run Corona Aid Fund is intervening strongly in markets, attempting to mitigate the negative consequences of the pandemic. It would therefore be the right time to support local, regional, or fair alternatives in the field of digital STRs and to support the development of commons-based platform cooperatives. The *Commons Manifesto* by Michel Bauwens et al. (2019) can serve as a guideline on how to better initiate such development processes and as a good working basis for practice at the local level. It is necessary to draw attention to new and more sustainable concepts in tourism. The following section draws attention to two different platform models providing alternative structures of peer-to-peer accommodation.

## Interest in Hybrid Sharing Models in the Austrian Accommodation Sector

Due to restrictions on travel and contact, traditional accommodation services are available to a limited extent. Demand has fallen sharply as a result of the pandemic. The situation illustrates that platform-based services require reorganisation in order to remain viable even in times of crisis. The following two examples show how local actors in the field of platform economy are contributing to a critical discourse on alternative futures alongside global players of techno-capitalist platformisation such as Airbnb (Graham 2020). The two Austrian examples from the accommodation sector given below illustrate alternative possibilities for entering a niche market alongside players such as Airbnb and Booking.com. Although both examples can be summarised as for-profit models, their offers are different from those of players such as Airbnb. Reposée and Schau auf's Land illustrate how current challenges can be tackled by innovation in the segments of slow tourism, rural regions, and food consumption in combination with touristic accommodation.

## Reposée

The Viennese start-up Reposée has created a niche market for 'seasonal sharing,' says Felix Woldt, its co-founder (Tourismuspresse 2018). The platform allows users to book holiday flats as well as weekend homes that are easy to reach and can be rented regularly over a long period of time. The Austrian platform was established in 2017, received financial support from the federal government and rents out properties that are empty over a long period of time during the year. On their website, accommodation is provided to users within a radius of maximum 300 km from their permanent residence, so they can travel there regularly over the weekend or even during the week (Sharing Economy Wien 2021). Proprietors remain flexible and save high initial investments in their own (second) homes. One of the aims of the project is to counteract the seasonal vacancy in tourism communities. In contrast to STRs, long-term rental and swapping models make it easier to book an apartment even in difficult times, as their business models do not require frequent rentals. In addition, individual usage and exchange models can (informally) be agreed upon between the hosts and the guests. Assuming that the business model is intended to work on a long-term basis and is not based primarily on algorithm-driven rating systems, stronger bonds between consumers and providers can also be expected, making the latter less dependent on short-term guests.

## Schau auf's Land

This platform is aimed at a specific target group (e.g., 'Eco Camping' labelled) within the agri-tourism and eco-tourism sector (Röser 2020). The main objective is to bring together caravan and motorhome travellers with agricultural businesses in rural regions, such as farms and wineries that market directly. The concept is not new—the idea comes from French wineries and is now present in many European countries with similar platforms. At present, about 150 farms are listed on the Austrian platform. Travellers can stay 'free of charge' (paying an annual fee of €35) on one of the farms, providing agriculturalists with the opportunity to extend their sources of income through direct marketing (Derbrutkasten 2020). Even though traditional segments of the accommodation sector, such as the hotel industry, suffered financial losses due to drastically falling numbers of overnight stays (Statistik Austria 2021) caused by the COVID-19 restrictions (Martins et al. 2020), it remains unclear whether a concept such as Schau auf's Land is viable because no jobs are attached to it. Furthermore, it remains unclear whether a tourism levy in the form of a visitor's tax is paid to the respective municipality for each overnight stay. During a pandemic, an overnight stay with Schau auf's Land is a good alternative and further empirical research on the example Schau auf's Land is currently in planning.

What can be observed is the necessity but also an opportunity for a change in tourism. Austria has the potential to focus more on factors such as regionality, authenticity, and deceleration, which can be subsumed as 'slow tourism' to advocate rural regeneration, as Alison Caffyn (2012) puts it. In this chapter, the examples of Reposée and Schau auf's Land illustrated how hybrid platform models could become established alternatives in the field of touristic accommodation. Another alternative to fill gaps in hospitality infrastructure is creating networks of peer-to-peer accommodations in order to balance 'substantial growth in tourism demand while having serious shortages in tourism accommodation' (Kneževič Cvelbar and Dolnicar 2017, p. 98). Even if they currently play a minor role in terms of competitiveness and overall market performance, they can nevertheless take on a pioneering role of alternative approaches within platform economies and peer-to-peer network relations. Enterprises like Reposée and Schau auf's Land should continue to be supported by the public sector in terms of funding schemes in their start-up periods. The two examples illustrate opportunities within the regimes of market-based sharing and may be able to occupy niches in places with less competition than in large city regions such as Vienna.

Also, in urban contexts, more and more initiatives (e.g., Fairbnb) have appeared alongside the global players in the STR industry and counteract well-known upshots such as the gradual subtraction of residential housing and gentrification (Foramitti et al. 2020; Katsinas 2021). At the local level, there are now a number of initiatives as alternatives to market-based sharing. The goal of these initiatives is to provide paths for urban commoning via city-owned platform cooperatives and 'produser'-owned platforms (neologism composed of the term producer and user), which are engaged in collaborative cycles and circular economies (Scholz 2016). In the accommodation sector, no such examples exist in Austria.

## Summary

In the past, areas such as the sharing economy and other dynamic economic sectors created by digitalisation have often initiated processes of change in a pioneering way in society—with both positive and negative consequences. Terms such as sharing or collaboration must be brought into a new discourse since they have long been undermined by the capitalist logic of extraction by the majority of (market-based) platforms, differing from the initial idea of non-commodified sharing. The promise of a post-capitalist alternative to neoliberalism, originally attributed to the new sharing economy, dissipated when the business logic of the majority of digital platforms surfaced, and the expected revival of community and network effects did not lead to a transformation in the current economic growth paradigm (Grabher and König 2020).

Concluding, it can be said that STRs play an important role in the Austrian tourism sector. Looking at the number of domestic STR platforms, it should be emphasised that a main source of revenue in Austria is increasingly at risk of being undermined by global players such as Airbnb. In order to prevent the popular Austrian hospitality sector from slowly (and literally) being 'rented' out to international companies and no longer being 'shared' with its global tourists, the national authorities should—especially in times of crisis—provide additional support to cooperative platforms and models similar to Resposée and Schau auf's Land within market-based economies. Such efforts must be coordinated within the EU. Stefan Kirchner and Elke Schüßler (2020) emphasise the importance of understanding the underlying organisational structures for a functioning regulation of the field. Regarding possible regulatory interventions, they emphasise the role of various actors from the public sector, private actors, civil society associations, and unions (Kirchner and Schüßler 2020). Only then can a transition to a new, more sustainable tourism based on supply structures of digital platforms be gradually put on a more resilient path.

## References

Airbnb. 2020. *Revenue of Airbnb Worldwide from 2017 to 2020 (in Billion U.S. Dollars)*. Chart. Last modified 16 November 2020. Statista. Accessed March 2, 2021. https://www.statista.com/statistics/1193134/airbnb-revenue-worldwide/.

Bauwens, Michel, Vasilis Kostakis, and Alex Pazaitis. 2019. *Peer to Peer: The Commons Manifesto*. London: University of Westminster Press. https://doi.org/10.16997/book33.

Behrendt, Siegfried, Christine Henseling, Christian Flick, Sabrina Ludmann, and Gerd Scholl. 2017. 'Zukünfte des Peer-to-Peer Sharing. Diskurse, Schlüsselfaktoren und Szenarien.' *Institut für ökologische Wirtschaftsforschung (IÖW)*, PeerSharing Arbeitsbericht 5. Berlin. Accessed November 15, 2020. https://www.peer-sharing.de/data/peersharing/user_upload/Dateien/PeerSharing_AP_5.pdf.

BMLRT (Bundesministerium für Landwirtschaft, Regionen und Tourismus). 2019a. *Tourismus in Österreich*. Wien: Bundesministerium für Nachhaltigkeit und Tourismus. Accessed March 12, 2021. https://www.bmlrt.

gv.at/dam/jcr:124f45aa-dc53-4ab0-b7d5-7f5950b43cf8/TOURISMUSBERICHT%202019_final_barrierefrei.pdf.

BMLRT (Bundesministerium für Landwirtschaft, Regionen und Tourismus). 2019b. *Plan-T. Masterplan für Tourismus.* Wien: Bundesministerium für Nachhaltigkeit und Tourismus. Accessed March 5, 2021. https://www.bmlrt.gv.at/dam/jcr:e94d2ad3-caa9-4ef0-b67d-f79dbfdc72dd/PLAN%20T%20-%20MASTERPLAN%20FÜR%20TOURISMUS_FINAL_barrierefrei.pdf.

Botsman, Rachel, and Roo Rogers. 2010. *What's Mine Is Yours How Collaborative Consumption Is Changing the Way We Live*. London: Collins.

Caffyn, Alison. 2012. 'Advocating and Implementing Slow Tourism.' *Tourism Recreation Research* 37 (1): 77–80. https://doi.org/10.1080/02508281.2012.11081690.

Derbrutkasten. 2020. 'Grazer Startup „Schau aufs Land" matcht Camper mit Landwirten.' *derbrutkasten*, July 7. Accessed March 6, 2021. https://www.derbrutkasten.com/schau-aufs-land-camping/?ref=share.

Dobusch, Leonhard. 2019. 'Dynamics of the Sharing Economy between Commons and Commodification.' *Momentum Quarterly: Zeitschrift für sozialen Fortschritt* 8 (2): 109–115. https://doi.org/10.15203/momentumquarterly.vol8.no2.p109-115.

EC (European Commission). 2018. 'Flash Eurobarometer 467.' *The Use of the Collaborative Economy*. European Commission. Brussels: DG COMM. https://doi.org/10.2873/312120.

Eurostat. 2020. *Tourism Destinations: Nights Spent at Tourist Accommodation Establishments, 2018*. Last modified 23 February 2021. Accessed March 1, 2021. https://ec.europa.eu/eurostat/statistics-explained/index.php?title=Tourism_statistics.

FAZ (Frankfurter Allgemeine Zeitung). 2021. 'Airbnb trotzt der Corona-Krise. Zimmervermittler schlägt sich besser als erwartet.' *FAZ (Frankfurter Allgemeine Zeitung)*, February 27. *Printausgabe* 49: 25.

Foramitti, Joël, Angelos Varvarousis, and Giorgos Kallis. 2020. 'Transition within a Transition: How Cooperative Platforms Want to Change the Sharing Economy.' *Sustainability Science* 15 (4): 1185–1197. https://doi.org/10.1007/s11625-020-00804-y.

Fritz, Oliver, Sabine Ehn-Fragner, Peter Laimer, Johanna Ostertag-Sydler, and Jürgen Weiß. 2020. *Bericht über die Bedeutung, Entwicklung und Struktur der österreichischen Tourismuswirtschaft im Jahr 2019. Wien: Österreichisches Institut für Wirtschaftsforschung*. Accessed March 12, 2021. https://www.

wifo.ac.at/jart/prj3/wifo/resources/person_dokument/person_dokument.jart?publikationsid=66095&mime_type=application/pdf.

Glusac, Elaine. 2020. 'The Future of Airbnb.' *New York Times*, September 24. Accessed November 15, 2020. https://www.nytimes.com/2020/09/24/travel/airbnb-pandemic.html.

Grabher, Gernot, and Jonas König. 2020. 'Disruption, Embedded: A Polanyian Framing of the Platform Economy.' *Sociologica* 14 (1): 95–118. https://doi.org/10.6092/issn.1971-8853/10443.

Graham, Mark. 2020. 'Regulate, Replicate, and Resist: The Conjunctural Geographies of Platform Urbanism.' *Urban Geography* 41 (3): 453–457. https://doi.org/10.1080/02723638.2020.1717028.

Grieß, Andreas. 2020. 'Airbnb entlässt ein Viertel seiner Mitarbeiter.' *Turi2*, May 5. Accessed November 15, 2020. https://www.turi2.de/aktuell/airbnb-entlaesst-ein-viertel-seiner-mitarbeiter/.

Hamari, Juho, Mimmi Sjöklint, and Antti Ukkonen. 2016. 'The Sharing Economy: Why People Participate in Collaborative Consumption.' *Journal of the Association for Information Science and Technology* 67 (9): 2047–2059. https://doi.org/10.1002/asi.23552.

Heiland, Heiner. 2018. 'Review-Artikel: Zum Aktuellen Stand des Plattformkapitalismus.' *Industrielle Beziehungen/The German Journal of Industrial Relations* 25 (1): 128–139. https://doi.org/10.3224/indbez.v25i1.06.

Inside Airbnb. 2019. *Adding Data to the Debate, Vienna.* Last modified 15 December 2019. Accessed March 1, 2021. http://insideairbnb.com/vienna/.

Katsinas, Philipp. 2021. 'Professionalisation of Short-Term Rentals and Emergent Tourism Gentrification in Post-Crisis Thessaloniki.' *Environment and Planning A: Economy and Space*, January, 0308518X21988940. https://doi.org/10.1177/0308518X21988940.

Kenney, Martin, and John Zysman. 2016. The Rise of the Platform Economy. *Issues in Science and Technology* 32 (3): 61–69.

Kirchner, Stefan, and Elke Schüßler. 2020. 'Regulating the Sharing Economy: A Field Perspective.' In *Theorizing the Sharing Economy: Variety and Trajectories of New Forms of Organizing*, edited by Indre Maurer, Johanna Mair, and Achim Oberg, 66: 215–236. Research in the Sociology of Organizations. Bingley, Emerald Publishing Limited. https://doi.org/10.1108/S0733-558X20200000066010.

Kneževič Cvelbar, Ljubica, and Sara Dolnicar. 2017. 'Chapter 9—Filling Infrastructure Gaps.' In *Peer-to-Peer Accommodation Networks: Pushing the Boundaries*, edited by Sara Dolnicar, 98–108. Oxford: Goodfellow Publishers. https://doi.org/10.23912/9781911396512-3607.

Krok, Ewa. 2019. 'Collaborative Consumption in a Sharing Economy.' *Zeszyty Naukowe. Organizacja i Zarządzanie / Politechnika Śląska*. No. 135: 99–108. https://doi.org/10.29119/1641-3466.2019.135.8.

Kurier. 2019. 'Wieso und wem Airbnb und Co. Probleme machen.' *Kurier*, December 6. Accessed November 15, 2020. https://kurier.at/chronik/oesterreich/wieso-und-wem-airbnb-und-co-probleme-machen/400695596.

Martins, Antje, Tyler Riordan, and Sara Dolnicar. 2020. 'A Post-Covid-19 Model of Tourism and Hospitality Workforce Resilience.' *SocArXiv*. https://doi.org/10.31235/osf.io/4quga.

Naumanen, Mika, Lison Rabuel, Kristina Karanikolova, Ricardas Juskevicius, and Lucas Porsch. 2018. 'Study to Monitor the Business and Regulatory Environment Affecting the Collaborative Economy in the EU.' *Final Report*, February. Luxembourg: Publications Office of the European Union. https://doi.org/10.2873/97234410.2873/83555.

O'Regan, Michael, and Jaeyeon Choe. 2017. 'Airbnb and Cultural Capitalism: Enclosure and Control Within the Sharing Economy.' *Anatolia* 28 (2): 163–172. https://doi.org/10.1080/13032917.2017.1283634.

OECD (Organisation for Economic Co-operation and Development). 2021. '*Tourism GDP (Indicator)*.' Total, % of GDP, 2008–2019. Accessed March 1, 2021. https://doi.org/10.1787/b472589a-en. https://data.oecd.org/industry/tourism-gdp.htm.

Pentzien, Jonas. 2019. 'Conceptualising the Role of the State in the Digital Platform Economy.' In *Perspectives on the Sharing Economy*, edited by Dominika Wruk, Achim Oberg, and Indre Maurer, 166–172. Newcastle: Cambridge Scholars Publishing.

Petropoulos, Georgios. 2017. 'An Economic Review of the Collaborative Economy.' *Bruegel Policy Contribution* Issue Nr. 5: 1–17. http://hdl.handle.net/10419/173101.

Röser, Leonard. 2020. 'Nachhaltige Campingplätze in Österreich.' *Schau auf's Land*, July 3. Accessed March 6, 2021. https://www.schauaufsland.at/nachhaltige-campingplaetze-in-oesterreich/.

Scholz, Trebor. 2016. 'Platform Cooperativism: Challenging the Corporate Sharing Economy.' In *Building a Digital Economy We Own*, edited by Stefanie Ehmsen and Albert Scharenberg, 1–26. New York: Rosa Luxemburg Stiftung.

Schor, Juliet B. 2014. 'Debating the Sharing Economy.' *Great Transition Initiative*. Last modified October 2014. Accessed March 15, 2021. https://greattransition.org/publication/debating-the-sharing-economy.

Seidl, Roman, Leonhard Plank, and Justin Kadi. 2017. A*irbnb in Wien: eine Analyse. Interaktiver Forschungsbericht*. Last modified 19 October 2017. Accessed March 15, 2021. http://wherebnb.in/wien.

Sharing Economy Wien. 2021. '*Reposée - Freizeitimmos mieten, tauschen, teilen*.' Accessed May 17, 2021. https://www.sharing-economy.at/atlas/reposee-freizeitimmos-mieten-tauschen-teilen.

Smigiel, Christian, Angela Hof, Karolin Kautzschmann, and Roman Seidl. 2019. 'No Sharing! Ein Mixed-Methods-Ansatz zur Analyse von Kurzzeitvermietungen und ihren sozialräumlichen Auswirkungen am Beispiel der Stadt Salzburg.' *Raumforschung und Raumordnung/Spatial Research and Planning* 78 (2): 153–170. https://doi.org/10.2478/rara-2019-0054.

Srnicek, Nick. 2017. 'The Challenges of Platform Capitalism: Understanding the Logic of a New Business Model.' *Juncture* 23 (4): 254–257. https://doi.org/10.1111/newe.12023.

Statistik Austria. 2021. *Nächtigungen im Jahr 2020 unter die 100-Millionen-Marke gefallen; Zahl der Gäste nahezu halbiert*. Last modified 27 January 2021. Wien: Statistik Austria. Accessed March 5, 2021. https://www.statistik.at/web_de/statistiken/wirtschaft/tourismus/beherbergung/125241.html.

Tourismuspresse. 2018. 'Neu - saisonales Sharing von Wochenendhäusern.' *TPT0003*, April 13. Accessed March 6, 2021. https://www.tourismuspresse.at/presseaussendung/TPT_20180413_TPT0003/neu-saisonales-sharing-von-wochenendhaeusern-anhaenge.

Twickel, Christoph. 2020. 'Mehr als Luftmatratze mit Frühstück.' *ZEIT Online*, November 30. Accessed March 1, 2021. https://www.zeit.de/wirtschaft/unternehmen/2020-11/airbnb-corona-wirtschaftskrise-boersengang-erfolg-unternehmen.

van Dijck, José, Thomas Poell, and Martijn de Waal. 2018. *The Platform Society*. New York: Oxford University Press.

## Suggested Readings

Gyódi, Kristóf. 2019. 'Airbnb in European Cities: Business as Usual or True Sharing Economy?' *Journal of Cleaner Production* 221 (June): 536–551. https://doi.org/10.1016/j.jclepro.2019.02.221.

Mair, Johanna, and Georg Reischauer. 2017. 'Capturing the Dynamics of the Sharing Economy: Institutional Research on the Plural Forms and Practices of Sharing Economy Organizations.' *Technological Forecasting and Social*

*Change* 125 (December): 11–20. https://doi.org/10.1016/j.techfore.2017.05.023.

Peuckert, Jan, and Maike Gossen. 2019. 'Herausforderungen der gesellschaftlichen Verankerung von Peer-to-Peer Sharing.' In *Digitale Kultur des Teilens: Mit Sharing nachhaltiger Wirtschaften*, edited by Siegfried Behrendt, Christine Henseling, and Gerd Scholl, 119–147. Wiesbaden: Springer Fachmedien. https://doi.org/10.1007/978-3-658-21435-7_8.

Richardson, Lizzie. 2018. 'Sharing Economy.' In *Digital Geographies*, edited by James Ash, Rob Kitchin, and Agnieszka Leszczynski, 200–209. London: Sage.

Vith, Sebastian, Achim Oberg, Markus A. Höllerer, and Renate E. Meyer. 2019. 'Envisioning the "Sharing City": Governance Strategies for the Sharing Economy.' *Journal of Business Ethics* 159 (4): 1023–1046. https://doi.org/10.1007/s10551-019-04242-4.

## Relevant Websites

Arbeit & Wirtschaft Magazin. Bundesarbeitskammer, Österreichischer Gewerkschaftsbund. https://awblog.at/?s=Sharing+Economy.

EURACTIV Media Network BV. https://www.euractiv.com/sections/sharing-economy/.

European Commission—Internal Market, Industry, Entrepreneurship and SMEs. Collaborative Economy. https://ec.europa.eu/growth/single-market/services/collaborative-economy.

IÖW, IZT, IFEU. https://www.peer-sharing.de.

i-share Vienna. https://www.sharing-economy.at.

i-share. https://www.i-share-economy.org/de.

SMASH. https://cityofcollaboration.org/smash/.

# 14

# Unsettled State of Regulation: Italy's Hard Path Towards Effective Rules for the Sharing Economy

Giulia Priora, Monica Postiglione, Stefano Valerio, Venere Stefania Sanna, and Chiara Bassetti

## Introduction: The State of the Art of the Italian Sharing Economy

In recent years, a variety of terms have been used to describe the shift towards new forms of economic activities and business models occurring online and fundamentally characterised by the rising culture of sharing

G. Priora (✉)
NOVA School of Law, NOVA University, Lisbon, Portugal
e-mail: Giulia.priora@novalaw.unl.pt

M. Postiglione
Istituto di Ricerche Economico Sociali del Piemonte (IRES Piemonte), Turin, Italy

S. Valerio
Turin School of Regulation, Fondazione Per L'Ambiente Teobaldo Fenoglio Onlus, Turin, Italy
e-mail: Stefano.valerio@fondazioneambiente.org



V. Česnuitytė et al. (eds.), *The Sharing Economy in Europe*,
https://doi.org/10.1007/978-3-030-86897-0_14

underused resources. The idea of sharing economy in Italy is generally associated with a vast array of practices related to the swapping, exchanging, borrowing, lending, or renting, crowdsourcing, collective purchasing, shared owning, or shared managing of resources. As it has been often emphasised, 'businesses in the sharing economy range from the small, grassroots-funded variety (…) to the big and venture-backed, many of which are online platforms' (Balaram 2016, p. 11). In full awareness of the unsettled and volatile definition that the term may acquire, the chapter focuses on and tries to identify the most distinctive traits of the Italian sharing economy reality, embracing a cross-disciplinary perspective on the phenomenon.

The sharing economy in Italy has experienced rapid growth in the last decade. Both the number of companies and start-ups operating on the national territory offering a wide-ranging and diverse array of activities and services and the bases of users and consumers relying on such new market offerings have steadily increased (Ciuffini et al. 2020). In broad brush, one can identify two main clusters of active sharing economy realities: on the one side, consolidated services of shared mobility and shared accommodation and, on the other, a set of miscellaneous business realities, ranging from food sharing and social eating experiences to financial services and co-working spaces. Both these macro-categories of Italian sharing economy activities will be taken into consideration in the following sections of the chapter.

In one way or the other, all the operating sharing economy sectors have been profoundly affected by the outbreak of the COVID-19 pandemic.

---

V. S. Sanna
Centre for Politics and International Studies (CeSPI), and MEMOTEF, Department of Sapienza University, Sapienza University of Rome, Rome, Italy

C. Bassetti
Department of Sociology and Social Research, University of Trento, Trento, Italy
e-mail: chiara.bassetti@unitn.it

Institute of Cognitive Sciences and Technologies, Italian National Research Council, Rome, Italy

Italy was the first European country to declare a state of emergency in March 2020, suddenly facing lockdown restrictions without the possibility to draw assessments or replicate any reactive regulatory development in other countries in the continent. The emergency response of the Italian government resulted in a rapid expansion of online interactions among its population both in social and economic terms. Among others, the Italian sharing economy sectors had to operate unprecedented moves of re-organisation and re-purposing of their offered services and activities. A series of interviews conducted by the Turin School of Regulation between June and September 2020 showcases that, while the traditional economy was struggling, the sharing economy proved particularly dynamic during the initial phase of emergency measures, thanks to considerably malleable business structures and a consolidated ability to adapt the business models to fluctuating demands on the digital markets (Turin School of Regulation 2020). Several sharing economies experiences have arisen as new means through which it was possible to continue to relate to the local dimension of everyday life. Numerous examples can be found across the sectors mentioned above, from shared accommodation services to neighbourhood networks created and used by local communities to the re-shaping of small local platform-based businesses to meet the changing needs of the Italian society during the lockdown (Turin School of Regulation 2020).

The presence of sharing economy services across the entire Italian peninsula proves to be highly meaningful not only vis-à-vis the recent impact of the COVID-19 pandemic but, more generally, in terms of transactions volumes, organisational models, and growth expectations. Giving account to the overall landscape and its most recent developments, the following sections will provide an overview of the Italian sharing economy reality, focusing on its most advanced experiences in the mobility and accommodation sectors as well as on its most innovative facet, looking at food and other services on the rise. The analysis fundamentally retraces the main legislative responses that have been put forward until now to govern the challenges posed by the sharing economy in Italy, highlighting critical aspects thereof. In this light, the chapter serves a threefold purpose: it offers a snapshot of the most active sharing economy sectors in Italy, with special attention paid to those activities which are platform-mediated and recently affected by the COVID-19 pandemic, it outlines the legal measures that aim to govern sharing economy activities in the country, and lastly, it draws considerations on the policy directions that most urgently call for attention.

## The Italian Take on Shared Mobility and Shared Accommodation

Looking at the Italian sharing mobility scenario, two ambivalent and apparently clashing elements emerge. On the one side, commercial ride-for-hire services (e.g., UberPop, Lyft), which match passengers with non-professional drivers of vehicles for hire, are either banned or subject to significant legal restrictions (see Italian Constitutional Court 2016). On the other side, shared mobility platforms are flourishing, often coupled with a growing sensitivity towards environmental protection and awareness of climate change. Most of these services are demand-driven, meaning that travellers share a vehicle either simultaneously as a group (ride-sharing) or over time (vehicle-sharing) as a short-term rental. When opting for the former (see Blablacar; JoJob; Scooterino), passengers share the cost of the journey with the driver, who provides the vehicle and fuel. Similarly, car-pooling platforms (see Autostrade per l'Italia) facilitate arrangements among automobile owners whereby each of them takes turns in driving the others to and from a designated place. On the other hand, sharing platforms of vehicles (see ShareNow; Enjoy), motor scooters (see Cooltra; ZigZag), and bikes (see Mobike; Tobike) differ from ride-sharing services, as individuals locate, hire, and drive means of transportation they do not own, typically paying by the minute or hour. Several of these platforms offer collateral services, such as short-term parking on public or private property (see Sparkyclub; Parkopedia). Inevitably, the impact of the pandemic on the mobility sector has been dramatic: mobility towards workplaces is estimated to have decreased by 60% during the first months of lockdown, while mobility towards public transport nodes and retail activities reduced by 76% and 80% respectively (Celata et al. 2020). However, part of the shared mobility scenario underwent a swift transformation, showing a remarkable resilience. For instance, some platforms offered health sector workers the possibility to use their services for free (see Bicinicittà; E-vai; Popmove). After a first collapse, the number of average daily rentals showed some signs of recovery, especially in the case of bike sharing and e-scooter sharing services, whereas car sharing services seem far from rebounding to the pre-COVID baseline (Ciuffini 2020). Numerous Italian cities witnessed a sharp rise in the presence and use of on-street e-scooters (see among others Bird, Dott, Helbiz, Keriscooters, Lime), which can be presumably related to the market opportunities created by people's reluctance to use public transport during the pandemic.

The tourism and accommodation sectors are vital to the Italian economy, with tourism, directly and indirectly, accounting for over 15% of employment and 13% of the gross domestic product in 2017, which, according to the World Travel and Tourism Council, is higher than the average of EU countries and of the global economy as a whole (Barone et al. 2019). Sharing economy platforms offering private accommodation solutions seem to have steadily increased their relevance in the sector over the last decade. Among the most prominent players is Airbnb, a service that was originally conceived as a platform for individuals to share and exploit underused space in their homes. Alongside Airbnb's popularity, several other short-term rental international platforms operate on Italian soil, such as Booking.com and VRBO, as well as home exchange platforms which enable the swapping of residential or summer houses (see Scambiocasa; LoveHomeSwap). In addition to accommodation platforms, there is a minority of tourism-oriented sharing economy players that offer support services, such as management intermediaries, cleaning crews, deposit holders, and facilitate the organisation of sightseeing tours, holiday equipment, and experiences (see Guidemeright; Playaya). The short-term rental market sector was strongly affected by the travel restrictions imposed in the spring of 2020, not only in an economically detrimental way (Watson 2020). Several market actors opted for offering alternative products: Airbnb started offering online experiences and activities—such as meditation, virtual visits, and cooking classes—and providing financial support to its own hosts (see Airbnb 2020a). Airbnb put aside a 250-million-dollar fund to support hosts who were required to fully refund guests between 14 March and 31 May 2020, with reimbursement up to 25% (Biondi 2020). Italy was also the first country where the platform launched the initiative 'Airbnb for doctors and nurses,' soon extended to other countries, with the aim to offer health and community workers free or low-priced accommodation near their workplace or homes to self-isolate (Airbnb 2020b). At the urban level, the decrease in touristic demand exacerbated the perception of silence and emptiness, especially in the historic centres of those Italian cities with a huge artistic and cultural heritage, thereby making more visible the processes of depopulation induced in those areas by the rise of short-term rentals mediated by sharing economy platforms (Picascia et al. 2017; Celata and Romano 2020). This led some to argue that the tourism-led economy is too fragile and unable to guarantee sustainable paths of growth (Bozzato 2020; Giossi 2020) and, in turn, to advocate for a more decentralised regulation of, among others, short-term rentals and other sharing economy sectors (Bonciani 2020). Meanwhile, according to data gathered by AirDNA, there are five Italian cities among the top ten European cities with the highest growth in new Airbnb bookings during the month of May 2020, compared to the continent's negative peak at the end of March 2020 (DuBois 2020), showing the ability of the Italian tourism and accommodation sectors to rapidly recover and potentially return to pre-pandemic activity levels. In this light, it is reasonable to expect that the debate about how to regulate the tourism-led growth model will acquire increasing importance in the near future.

## Sharing Economy Innovation in the Italian Food Sector

The sector of food sharing is well-developed in Italy, with a considerable number of active online services. In recent years, there has been a boom in so-called social eating platforms, also known as home restaurants or social cooking services, that offer users the possibility to organise meals, cooking courses, or other culinary events in their homes or other private locations. Le Cesarine, a nationwide community of local home cooks founded in 2004, is a glaring example, aiming to safeguard Italy's food culture through home cooking, and recognised in 2019 as an official Slow Food community (see Le Cesarine). The Italian start-up Gnammo has become one of the most prominent players on an international scale, with more than 200,000 users and around 13,000 events organised as of 2020 (see Gnammo). Taking this idea to a socially driven model, Peoplecooks has combined an online cooking experience with elements of mutual support, building a platform explicitly aimed at students or off-site workers, tourists, and those who are seeking or can only afford low-cost meals (see Peoplecooks, platform currently inactive). The initiative aims to be a practical solution for social assistance and solidarity. Pursuing a similar aim, Scambiocibo is one of the main services supporting the fight against food waste by facilitating the exchange of food products and leftovers, a practice that has been consolidating and has attracted the attention of the Italian legislator (Act Nr. 166 of 19 August 2016; see also Scambiocibo). Since the outbreak of the pandemic, with restaurants closed or limited in their activities, only businesses that proved capable of quickly adapting to lockdown restrictions have been able to thrive (Farrer 2020). Many social eating platforms were forced to change their business models, opting for re-purposing their services towards virtual online cooking classes with hosts from all around the world (see Travelingspoon; Eatwith). The perception of the economic and social innovation in the food sector in Italy sees the sharing economy scenario dovetailing with the digital platformisation of food delivery. Numerous platforms are exponentially growing their market power, steadily increasing the value of the food sector in the Italian digital economy. Even though falling beyond the scope of this analysis, the role of food delivery players is highly relevant to grasp the perception by the Italian population of the changing digital economic landscape and the general propensity to support new business models. Online services in the food sector have recently experienced a steep increase in their market share, reaching 18% of the total, and experiencing growth at levels significant enough to influence consumer behaviours (Oncini et al. 2020). Stemming from this trend, important questions and a strong social sensitivity have arisen concerning the employment status and legal protection of delivery riders, animating a vibrant debate that directly or indirectly also affects workers in sharing economy activities (Quarta 2020; Tassinari et al. 2020).

## Miscellaneous: Sharing Economy Innovation in Other Market Sectors in Italy

Along with the mobility, accommodation, and food sectors, the Italian sharing economy landscape boasts a wide-ranging corollary of activities and services on the rise. Finance is a good example of a growing area worth considering. Numerous crowdfunding platforms are flourishing, providing services that are based on reward—where donors receive a reward with a value that is much lower than the money raised (see Be Crowdy), donation—for ethical and social purposes to benefit not-for-profit organisations and charities (see Let's Donation; Rete del Dono; Universitiamo), lending—to help low-income population obtain mainly micro-credit schemes without specialised intermediaries (see Prestiamoci; Borsa del Credito; Smartika), or equity—where investors can mainly finance innovative start-ups, often linked to sustainability and green issues (see CrowdFundMe; Buonacausa; Produzione dal basso; see also Mainieri and Pais 2016). Sharing economy platforms are also active in the supply of consumer goods and services, with growing attention being paid to platforms that facilitate exchanges, rentals, sales, and donations of various items (see Coseinutili; Zerorelativo; Te lo regalo se vieni a prenderlo), among which books (see Comprovendolibri; Biblioshare) and train tickets (see Scambiotreno). Several social and family-related platforms offer selected household services, such as babysitting and caregiving (see Le Cicogne; Oltretata; Sitterlandia) or, pet-sitting (see Animaliallapari; Holidog; Petme). Some platforms facilitate relationships between neighbours, enabling users to barter food or handiwork support with other members of their neighbourhood (e.g., Nextdoor; BarattoB&B). Most of the professional services offered on sharing economy platforms rely on skilled workers, who receive monetary payments or credits as a reward (see Fiverr; Solvercity; Tabbid; Timerepublik). Lastly, in contrast to many other EU Member States, Italy's market of shared spaces for professionals and co-working activities and events (see What a Space) is rather limited, with more than half of these services being concentrated in the metropolitan areas of Milan, Rome, Turin, and Florence (Akhavan et al. 2019).

## A Fragmented Legal Response

If the most evident feature characterising the Italian sharing economy scenario is the variety of consolidated activities and business models involved, the second-most glaring aspect is the lack of a consistent regulatory response to the manifold disruptions caused by the rapid growth of the digital sharing culture. The situation has remained unaltered and de facto worsened with the crisis induced by the outbreak of the COVID-19 pandemic, with some sharing economy sectors thriving and others suffering dramatic economic losses. Challenged by the heterogenous variety of sharing economy practices active across the national territory, the Italian legislator has, to date, failed to formulate a comprehensive and forward-looking regulatory response to the challenges posed by the phenomenon. To start with, in the national legal system, there is no binding definition of sharing economy. At EU level, in the first steps undertaken by the European Commission, the focus has been set on the notion of collaborative economy, addressing all 'business models where activities are facilitated by collaborative platforms that create an open marketplace for the temporary usage of goods and services often provided by private individuals' (European Commission 2016, p. 3). Following the same direction, the Italian legislator has embraced a wide-spectrum approach towards the regulation of platform-based, gig, collaborative, and sharing economy realities, focusing on the common key role of digital intermediaries and platforms (Fabozzi and Bini 2019; Smorto 2015a), and mostly ignoring the specific differences between the various business models. In this light, three draft laws have been proposed, specifically tackling the role and obligations of digital platforms in the evolving Italian economy (i.e., Draft Law Nr. 3564 of 27 January 2016; Draft Law Nr. 2268 of 3 March 2016; Draft Law Nr. 1497 of 15 January 2019). Despite lively doctrinal and public debates surrounding them (Delronge et al. 2018; d'Ippolito 2018), none of these bills has been adopted. The inclusive take on the sharing—and not only sharing—economy, the Italian legal landscape has developed a peculiar focus on the relationship between digital platforms and workers. Questioning the status and qualification of 'workers' in evolving economic sectors (see Quarta 2020), the national case law as well as regional and local legislative proposals have primarily looked at the protection of the rights of delivery riders in the food sector (e.g., Lazio Regional Law Nr. 4 of 12 April 2019; Emilia Romagna Resolution Nr. 206 of 26 June 2019; Campania Draft Regional Law Nr. 794 of 13 May 2020). These efforts culminated in the adoption of ad hoc national provisions ensuring minimum standards of protection for both permanent and occasional workers in the platform-based economy (Act Nr. 128 of 2 November 2019).

Looking at the sharing economy strictly intended—the sole direct supply of products and services from peer to peer (Smorto 2015b)—the relevant Italian legal scenario is characterised by a deep uncertainty concerning the applicability of the same rules tailored for the platform-based economy. Presumably due to the presence of big international players and a tendency towards the concentration of market power in the hands of few sharing economy actors in sectors that are key to the Italian economy, such as mobility, tourism, and accommodation, taxation has been one of the first and main legal tools that Italian governments have relied on. Such a reaction is not a typical within the Italian legislative environment, where according to some 'the need to regulate a phenomenon often instinctively translates into mere taxing of that phenomenon' (Picascia et al. 2017, p. 17). A new taxable category of income named 'income deriving from non-professional sharing economy activities' was envisioned, and further, more sectorial interventions have been promoted, such as the introduction of a 21% flat-rate tax on all short-term rentals (recently limited to a maximum of four property units, Act Nr. 178 of 30 December 2020) and the obligation for sharing economy intermediaries operating in the country to elect a fiscal representative on Italian territory (Act Nr. 96 of 21 June 2017). Surprisingly, the Italian legislator's approach towards the needs and changes generated by the sharing economy proves more mature and sensitive towards taxation issues than towards problems of unfair competition between old and new market players. The judicial saga involving Uber is a good example. In light of the missing liberalisation of the mobility sector in Italy, the UberPop service has been declared an unfair competitor and, hence, unauthorised to operate on national territory (Tribunal of Rome 2017). Nevertheless, Uber showed resilience in the country, trying to become a platform accessible only to traditional taxi drivers and aiming to overcome policy resistance by establishing relationships with municipalities and local economic actors.

A few attempts to regulate the growing Italian sharing economy more effectively have been moved forward, yet without passing into law. It is the case of Draft Law Nr. 4059 of 27 September 2016, which intended to promote and incentivize car sharing practices, and of Draft Law Nr. 3528 of 28 July 2015, attempting to introduce specific rules on home restaurant activities. A fragmented and rather involuted regulatory background can be noticed also with regards to the short-term accommodation sector. Due to its consolidated and relevant role in the Italian economy, the sector is quite emblematic of the main features of the national legal response to the sharing economy, that is to say (i) its substantial regulatory fragmentation, (ii) the emphasis on taxation, and (iii) the hard path towards building a more cohesive legal framework to tackle emerging social issues. The relevant legislation has evolved from a first phase of regional norms (commonly labelled as 'Airbnb rules,' e.g., Toscana Regional Law Nr. 86/2016; Lazio Regional Regulation Nr. 8/2015; Veneto Regional Law Nr. 11/2013), which showed considerable divergences, some tightening, some losing the grip on innovative accommodations options for tourists within private homes.

A subsequent push towards a national regulation has stemmed from the need to enhance clarity on the taxation schemes applying and provide the Italian Tax Authority with the necessary data (Act Nr. 96/2017). Only then the legislator's intention has moved towards a full-fledged consistent response defining how many house units could have been made available by private citizens, for how many days a year, establishing the obligation to notify the public authority about the guests (Act Nr. 132/2018), and setting up a registration database for tax, public security, and liability purposes (Act Nr. 58/2019). A comprehensive legislative reform of the short-term accoommodation sector was at the horizon, promising sensitive adjustments regarding historical city centres and an organic system of licenses to house owners (Draft Law Nr. 2079/2019). Yet, not only the outbreak of the pandemic but also heated discussions in the Italian Parliament and the lack of political consensus over the same definition of professional activity and new bureaucratic burdens hold the bill hostage, leaving most legal uncertainties still standing.

## Summary

In light of the outlined reality of sharing economy experiences that are consolidating and arising in Italy, overcoming significant difficulties from the recent pandemic emergency, the legal framework that applies to these specific market services proves fragmented and most likely ineffective to sustain the sector. Regulatory gaps and grey zones of uncertain legal interpretation jeopardise the development and smooth operation of most of the activities forming the Italian sharing economy landscape. The present and future of the Italian sharing economy landscape seem to require sound and targeted policy intervention, with particular respect to three core aspects.

First and foremost, the most pressing need emerging is for a clear-cut definition of sharing economy, which reflects state of the art: while it is undisputed that the role of digital intermediaries is key to the business models relating to this notion, it is also true that sharing practices and experiences flourishing in Italy are not merely characterised by the 'platformisation' component. Second, the regulatory path should pursue and value regulatory consistency. The legislative interventions required to regulate the sector are potentially numerous, and only a coordinated effort of policymaking and cohesive legal principles can achieve the objective of enhancing legal certainty among the sharing economy stakeholders. In particular, defining the role and obligations of platforms and service providers, the principles to prevent and fight discrimination practices across the involved economic sectors, a common taxation system, and principles of social sustainability, environmental protection, and community welfare seem to be top priorities in the prospective and inevitable process of structured legislative intervention on the sharing economy. Lastly, there are numerous open issues related to the COVID-19 pandemic and its social impact, with restrictions and changes that will potentially affect the sharing economy (the tourism and mobility sectors *in primis*) in Italy and beyond, both in the medium and long run. Despite the resilience demonstrated to date, it is likely that some sectors will continue to experience important transformations and limitations, thus making the pandemic not only a disruption of everyday life and urban spaces but also a 'forced opportunity' to rethink the growth and economic model at play in Italy, and its related systems of rules and incentives.

**Acknowledgements** The authors would like to thank Dr. Cary Yungmee Hendrickson for the insightful comments and generous feedback on prior drafts of this chapter.

## References

Act Nr. 58 of 28 June 2019, Official Gazette Nr. 151 of 29 June 2019.

Act Nr. 96 of 21 June 2017, Official Gazette Nr. 144 of 23 June 2017.

Act Nr. 128 of 2 November 2019, Official Gazette Nr. 257 of 2 November 2019.

Act Nr. 132 of 1 December 2018, Official Gazette Nr. 281 of 3 December 2018.

Act Nr. 166 of 19 August 2016, Official Gazette Nr. 202 of 30 August 2016.

Act Nr. 178 of 30 December 2020, Official Gazette Nr. 322 of 30 December 2020.

Airbnb. 2020a. '*Introduzione alle Esperienze Airbnb.*' Accessed 15 May 2021. https://www.airbnb.it/help/article/1581/introduzione-alle-esperienze-airbnb.

Airbnb. 2020b. '*Una casa per medici e infermieri durante l'emergenza.*' Accessed March 12, 2021. https://www.airbnb.it/d/medicieinfermieri.

Akhavan, Mina, Ilaria Mariotti, Lisa Astolfi, and Annapaola Canevari. 2019. 'Co-working Spaces and New Social Relations: A Focus on the Social Streets in Italy.' *Urban Science* 3 (1): 2–11 https://doi.org/10.3390/urbansci3010002.

Animaliallapari. '*Animali alla pari pet community.*' Accessed May 15, 2012. http://www.animaliallapari.net/.

Autostrade per l'Italia. '*Consulta per la Sicurezza e la Qualità del Servizio.*' Accessed May 15, 2021. http://www.autostrade.it/it/tecnologia-sicurezza/sicurezza/consulta-per-la-sicurezza.

Balaram, Brhmie. 2016. '*Fair Share: Reclaiming Power in the Sharing Economy.*' Accessed March 12, 2021. https://medium.com/rsa-reports/fair-share-reclaiming-power-in-the-sharing-economy-499b46bd4b00.

BarattoB&B. '*Baratta un soggiorno in B&B tutto l'anno.*' Accessed May 15, 2021. http://www.barattobb.it/.

Barone, Guglielmo, Emanuela Breda, Alberto Felettigh, Andrea Petrella, Fabio Quintiliani, Giacomo Roma, and Roberto Torrini. 2019. '*Turismo in Italia: numeri e potenziale di sviluppo.*' Accessed March 12, 2021. https://www.bancaditalia.it/pubblicazioni/qef/2019-0505/QEF_505_19.pdf.

Be Crowdy. '*BeCrowdy Crowdfunding culturale italiano.*' Accessed May 15, 2021. https://www.becrowdy.com/.

Biblioshare. '*La biblioteca socializzante.*' Accessed May 15, 2021. http://www.biblioshare.it/.

Bicinicittà. '*Il Bike Sharing in Italia.*' Accessed May 15, 2021. http://www.bicincitta.com/default.aspx.

Biondi, Andrea. 2020. 'Airbnb raccoglie 1 miliardo di dollari per il post-coronavirus.' *Il Sole 24 Ore*, April 7, 2020.

Bird. '*Bird Scooters Launch in Florence as Italy Grows Its Micromobility Service.*' Accessed May 15, 2021. https://www.bird.co/blog/bird-scooters-launch-florence-italy-grows-micromobility-service/.

Blablacar. '*Blablacar Viaggia in Carpooling o in Autobus.*' Accessed May 15, 2021. https://www.blablacar.it/.

Bonciani, Mauro. 2020. 'Un limite agli affitti turistici. Il governo promette la legge.' *Corriere fiorentino*, July 16, 2020.

Borsa del Credito. '*Peer to Peer Lending per Aziende – Borsadelcredito.it.*' Accessed May 15, 2021. https://www.borsadelcredito.it/.

Bozzato, Fabio. 2020. '*Venezia è in apnea, per ripensare il turismo serve una nuova residenzialità.*' Accessed March 12, 2021. https://www.che-fare.com/bozzato-venezia-turismo-residenzialita/.

Buonacausa. '*Buonacausa.org – raccolte fondi, fundraising, crowdfunding.*' Accessed May 15, 2021. https://buonacausa.org/home.

Campania Draft Regional Law Nr. 794 of 13 May 2020.

Celata, Filippo, and Antonello Romano. 2020. 'Overtourism and Online Short-Term Rental Platforms in Italian Cities.' Ahead of print in *Journal of Sustainable Tourism*. https://doi.org/10.1080/09669582.2020.1788568.

Celata, Filippo, Cristina Capineri, and Antonello Romano. 2020. '*Spazi chiusi, dati aperti: come viene misurata la nostra immobilità.*' Accessed March 12, 2021. https://www.che-fare.com/spazi-dati-mobilita-lockdown/.

Ciuffini, Massimo. 2020. '*Come cambia la sharing mobility durante e dopo il lockdown.*' Accessed March 12, 2021. https://rienergia.staffettaonline.com/articolo/34574/Come+cambia+la+sharing+mobility+durante+e+dopo+il+lockdown/Ciuffini.

Ciuffini, Massimo, Sofia Asperti, Valeria Gentili, Raimondo Orsini, and Luca Refrigeri. 2020. '*Quarto Rapporto Nazionale sulla sharing economy 2020.*' Accessed March 12, 2021. http://osservatoriosharingmobility.it/cover-galleries/.

Comprovendolibri. '*Libri usati: Compro Vendo Libri – il mercatino dell'usato.*' Accessed May 15, 2021. https://www.comprovendolibri.it/home.asp.

Constitutional Court, Judgement Nr. 265 of 15 December 2016, docket nr. 83/2015.

Cooltra. '*Cooltra: Noleggio scooter per minuti, giorni e mesi.*' Accessed May 15, 2021. https://www.cooltra.com/it/.

Coseinutili. '*Il sito di baratto online asincrono per lo scambio, il riuso e il riutilizzo di oggetti usati, nonchè la banca del tempo.*' Accessed May 15, 2021. https://www.coseinutili.it/.

CrowdFundMe. '*Crowdfundme, il portale italiano di crowdinvesting ed equity.*' Accessed May 15, 2021. https://www.crowdfundme.it/.

Delronge, Cynthia, Rossana Ducato, Anne-Grace Kleczewski, Enguerrand Marique, Alain Strowel, and Céline Wattecamps. 2018. '*Protection of Users in the Platform Economy: A European Perspective.*' Accessed March 12, 2021. https://www-itforchange.net.

d'Ippolito, Guido. 2018. 'Sharing economy: l'esperienza italiana della XVII legislature alla luce degli orientamenti europei.' *MediaLaws Rivista di Diritto dei Media* (2): 298–317.

Dott. '*Small Ride Big Change. Corse ecosostenibili.*' Accessed May 15, 2021. https://ridedott.com/it.

DuBois, Dillon. 2020. '*Global Vacation Rental Bookings Skyrocket by 127% After Surge in Domestic Tourism.*' Accessed March 12, 2021. https://www.airdna.co/blog/global-vacation-rental-bookings-skyrocket-by-127-after-surge-in-domestic-tourism.

Eatwith. '*Esperienze culinarie con incredibili host online e in giro per il mondo.*' Accessed May 15, 2021. https://it.eatwith.com/online.

Emilia Romagna Resolution Nr. 206 of 26 June 2019.

Enjoy. '*Enjoy benvenuto.*' Accessed May 15, 2021. https://enjoy.eni.com/it.

European Commission. 2016. 'A European Agenda for the Collaborative Economy' (Communication) COM(2016)356 final.

E-vai. '*E-vai. Il tuo car-sharing elettrico regionale.*' Accessed May 15, 2021. https://www.e-vai.com/.

Fabozzi, Raffaele, and Stefano Bini. 2019. 'Algoritmi, piattaformedigitali e diritto del lavoro.' *Analisi Giuridica dell'Economia* 1: 357–371.

Farrer, James. 2020. 'A Tokyo Restaurant Community Faces *COVID*-19.' *Etnografia e ricerca qualitativa* 13 (2): 245–254. https://doi.org/10.3240/97809.

Fiverr. '*Fiverr – Marketplace di service freelance per le aziende.*' Accessed May 15, 2021. https://it.fiverr.com/.

Giossi, Giacomo. 2020. '*L'economia turistica di Venezia tra sfruttamento e resistenza: intervista a Giacomo Maria Salerno.*' Accessed October 16, 2020. https://www.che-fare.com/giossi-critica-turistica-venezia-resistenza/.

Gnammo. '*Cucina condividi incontra.*' Accessed May 15, 2021. https://gnammo.com/.

Guidemeright. '*Travel with a Local Friend: Activities and Things to Do in Italy.*' Accessed May 15, 2021. https://www.guidemeright.com/it/.

Helbiz. '*Cities.*' Accessed May 15, 2021. https://helbiz.com/it/cities.

Holidog. '*Holidog: Dog sitter e cat sitter in Italia.*' Accessed May 15, 2021. https://it.holidog.com/.

JoJob. '*JoJob Carpooling Aziendale.*' Accessed May 15, 2021. https://www.jojob.it/.

Keriscooters. '*Keriscooters Ride for Fun.*' Accessed May 15, 2021. https://keriscooters.com/.

Lazio Regional Law Nr. 4 of 12 April 2019.

Lazio Regional Regulation Nr. 8 of 7 August 2015.

Le Cesarine. '*Cesarine: Lezioni di cucina e food experience.*' Accessed May 15, 2021. https://cesarine.com/.

Le Cicogne. '*Le Cicogne. Trova la tua babysitter in modo facile e veloce.*' Accessed May 15, 2021. https://www.lecicogne.net/.

Let's Donation. '*Let's Donation. Il Profit sostiene il Non-profit.*' Accessed May 15, 2021. https://www.letsdonation.com/.

Lime. '*Locations.*' Accessed May 15, 2021. https://www.li.me/locations.

LoveHomeSwap. '*Home Exchange in Italy.*' Accessed May 15, 2021. https://www.lovehomeswap.com/homes/Italy.

Mainieri, Marta, and Ivana Pais. 2016. '*Il crowdfunding in Italia. Report 2016.*' Accessed November 6, 2016. https://collaboriamo.org/pubblicazioni-email/.

Mobike. '*Mobike Launches in Florence.*' Accessed May 15, 2021. https://mobike.com/global/blog/post/mobike-italy.

Nextdoor. '*Nextdoor.*' Accessed May 15, 2021. https://it.nextdoor.com/.

Oltretata. '*Oltretata.*' Accessed May 15, 2021. https://www.oltretata.it/.

Oncini, Filippo, Emanuela Bozzini, Francesca Forno, and Natalia Magnani. 2020. 'Towards Food Platforms? An Analysis of Online Food Provisioning Services in Italy.' *Geoforum* 114 (1): 172–180.

Parkopedia. '*Parkopedia.*' Accessed May 15, 2021. https://www.parkopedia.it/.

Peoplecooks. '*Peoplecooks Page Account.*' Accessed May 15, 2021. https://www.facebook.com/peoplecooks/.

Petme. '*PetMe – Il più grande motore di ricerca per dog sitter, car sitter.*' Accessed May 15, 2021. https://www.petme.it/.

Picascia, Stefano, Antonello Romano, and Michela Teobaldi. 2017. 'The Airification of Cities: Making Sense of the Impact of Peer-to-Peer Short Term Letting on Urban Functions and Economy.' *Proceedings of the Annual Congress of the Association of the European Schools of Planning*. Aesop (Lisbon): 2212–2223.

Playaya. '*Playaya.*' Accessed May 15, 2021. https://www.playaya.it/.

Popmove. '*popmove: Noleggio Flessibile.*' Accessed May 15, 2021. https://www.popmove.com/.

Prestiamoci. '*Prestiamoci: Prestiti tra Privati – Prestiti Online – Peer to Peer.*' Accessed May 15, 2021. https://www.prestiamoci.it/.

Produzione dal basso. '*Produzioni dal basso – Idee e storie da finanziare.*' Accessed May 15, 2021. https://www.produzionidalbasso.com/.

Quarta, Alessandra. 2020. 'Narratives of the Digital Economy: How Platforms Are Challenging Consumer Law and Hierarchical Organization.' *Global Jurist* 20 (2): 1–21.

Rete del Dono. '*Rete del Dono. Fundraising, crowdfunding e raccolta fondi.*' Accessed May 15, 2021. https://www.retedeldono.it/.

Scambiocasa. '*Scambiocasa.com il leader mondiale nello scambio di casa.*' Accessed May 15, 2021. https://www.scambiocasa.com/it/.
Scambiocibo. '*Scambiocibo. Innovazione e Alimentazione.*' Accessed May 15, 2021. https://www.scambiacibo.it/.
Scambiotreno. '*Scambiotreno.it - Treni low cost.*' Accessed May 15, 2021. http://www.scambiatreno.it/.
Scooterino. '*Scooterino. Il passaggio ogni volta che ti serve.*' Accessed May 15, 2021. http://scooterino.it/.
ShareNow. '*La nuova era del car sharing ShareNow Italia.*' Accessed May 15, 2021. https://www.share-now.com/it/it/.
Sitterlandia. '*Sitterlandia.it. Il portale del mondo sitter.*' Accessed May 15, 2021. https://www.sitterlandia.it/.
Smartika. '*Smartika: Prestito tra Privati.*' Accessed May 15, 2021. https://www.smartika.it/.
Smorto, Guido. 2015a. 'I contratti della sharing economy.' *Il Foro Italiano* 5 (1): 221–242.
Smorto, Guido. 2015b. 'Verso la disciplina giuridica della sharing economy.' *Mercato, Concorrenza e Regole* 2 (1): 245–277.
Solvercity. '*Solvercity.*' Accessed May 15, 2021. http://solvercity.com/.
Sparkyclub. '*Sparky.club Parcheggia ovunque.*' Accessed May 15, 2021. http://www.sparky.club/.
Tabbid. '*Cerco Lavoretto Diventa Tuttofare.*' Accessed May 15, 2021. https://tabbid.com/.
Tassinari, Arianna, Riccardo Emilio Chesta, and Lorenzo Cini. 2020. 'Labour Conflicts Over Health and Safety in the Italian COVID-19 Crisis.' *Interface* 12 (1): 128–138.
Timerepublik. '*Timerepublik.*' Accessed May 15, 2021. https://timerepublik.com/.
Tobike. '*ToBike.it.*' Accessed May 15, 2021. http://www.tobike.it/default.aspx.
Toscana Regional Law Nr. 86/2016.
Travelingspoon. '*Italy – Travelingspoon.*' Accessed May 15, 2021. https://www.travelingspoon.com/countries/italy.
Tribunal of Rome, Section IX, Order, 4 April 2017, docket Nr. 76465/2016.
Turin School of Regulation. 2020. '*Videos.*' Accessed March 12, 2021. https://turinschool.eu/videos?page=1.
Universitiamo. '*Universitiamo: Home.*' Accessed May 15, 2021. https://universitiamo.eu/.
Veneto Regional Law Nr. 11/2013.

Vrbo. '*Italia: case vacanze, ville in affitto, etc – Vrbo.*' Accessed May 15, 2021. https://www.vrbo.com/it-it/case-vacanze/italia.

Watson, Meg. 2020. 'Disrupting the Disruptors: How COVID-19 Will Shake Up Airbnb.' *The Guardian*, April 5.

What a Space. '*Cos'è What a Space.*' Accessed May 15, 2021. https://www.whataspace.it/about.

Zerorelativo. '*ZeroRelativo – La prima community di scambio riuso e baratto.*' Accessed May 15, 2021. https://www.zerorelativo.it/.

ZigZag. '*ZigZag sharing*.' Accessed May 15, 2021. https://www.zigzagsharing.com/it/.

## Suggested Readings

Arcidiacono, Davide. 2017. 'Economia collaborativa e startup: forme alternative di scambio economico o mito della disintermediazione?' *Quaderni di sociologia* 73 (1): 29–47. https://doi.org/10.4000/qds.1656.

Ghisellini, Patrizia, and Sergio Ulgiati. 2020. 'Circular Economy Transition in Italy: Achievements, Perspectives and Constraints.' *Journal of Cleaner Production* 2020 (1): 243–293. https://doi.org/10.1016/j.jclepro.2019.118360.

Noto La Diega, Guido. 2016. 'Uber Law and Awareness by Design. An Empirical Study on Online Platforms and Dehumanised Negotiations.' *European Journal of Consumer Law* 2 (1): 383–426.

Quarta, Alessandra, and Guido Smorto. 2020. *Diritto Privato dei Mercati Digitali.* Firenze: Le Monnier.

Ramella, Francesco, and Cecilia Manzo. 2019. *L'economia della collaborazione. Le nuove piattaforme digitali della produzione e del consumo.* Bologna: Il Mulino, 2016.

## Relevant Websites

Collaboriamo! http://collaboriamo.org.

Osservatorio Nazionale sulla Sharing Mobility. http://osservatoriosharingmobility.it.

Turin School of Regulation. https://turinschool.eu.

# 15

# Time Banks in the United Kingdom: An Examination of the Evolution

Rodrigo Perez-Vega and Cristina Miguel

## Introduction

Sharing economy platforms provide access to other peoples' skills or their time, while others grant access to resources or assets (Wosskow 2014). Sharing initiatives include peer-to-peer lodging and transportation services, time banks, goods exchanges, and other forms of collaboration (Schor et al. 2016). Time banks were created to overcome the dynamics of the commodification of time resources via an alternative system based on reciprocity (Arcidiacono and Podda 2017). The premise of the system is that no one charges for help, 'instead, individuals voluntarily help each other' (Felländer et al. 2015, p. 27). According to

R. Perez-Vega
Kent Business School, University of Kent, Chatham, UK
e-mail: r.perez-vega@kent.ac.uk

C. Miguel (✉)
Applied IT, University of Gothenburg, Gothenburg, Sweden
e-mail: cristina.miguel@ait.gu.se



V. Česnuitytė et al. (eds.), *The Sharing Economy in Europe*,
https://doi.org/10.1007/978-3-030-86897-0_15

Whitham and Clarke (2016), a time bank is 'a unique type of generalised exchange that formalises the process of repayment, thus reducing the risk of giving without receiving any benefits in return and the potential for free-riding to occur' (p. 87). There are different models of time banks with diverse aims, and they are implemented in different settings, such as prisons, homeless shelters, schools, and health centres. As observed by Perez-Vega et al. (2021), time banks can be hyperlocal (e.g., Rushey Green Time bank), aimed at serving a particular neighbourhood or community, while others, such as the Economy of Hours, are at the national level. Most time banks include a broad range of services, such as child and older care, car rides, legal services, and gardening (Felländer et al. 2015; Han et al. 2019; Schor et al. 2016). The coordination is done by a central figure called a time bank coordinator or time broker. The time broker minimises the risks of members who directly exchange services (Simon 2004). The Time Online is a time bank software that was created for the brokers to manage the daily exchanges of their time banks (TBUK 2020b).

Teruko Mizushima is widely believed to be the creator of time banking, as he developed and practised it in Japan immediately after the war in 1973. Her time banking revolved around housewives across Japan, and it was called Volunteer Labour Bank (VLB) (Weaver et al. 2016). In the West, time banking originated in the United States in 1955 (Cahn and Grey 2015). Today the United Kingdom (UK) has built a diverse ecosystem around times and skills sharing of both generic (e.g., Time Banking UK, Communities Together) and specialist skills (e.g., Frontline19). For instance, Time Bank is a charity that works across five key themes: social isolation; community cohesion and integration; health and well-being; education and employment; and environmental and regeneration (Time Bank 2020). On the other hand, Frontline19 connects frontline healthcare providers with counsellors and psychotherapists that will provide mental health support for free.

Confusion can be noticed in the spelling of time banking among different parties with the ultimate goal of making their models unique from others. The different spelling formats of time bank include the use of space, a hyphen, and two upper case letters on the two words (Weaver et al. 2016). This chapter will mainly use the term 'time bank' since it is the most popular term used in the literature (e.g., North 2003; Seyfang 2004, 2006; Gould 2009; Collom 2012; Válek and Jašíková 2013; Dubois et al. 2014; Arcidiacono and Podda 2017). This chapter aims to define the main characteristics and benefits of time banks. The chapter also provides a typology of platforms that can be found in the UK based on the types of transactions and the types of assets being exchanged (Gerwe and Silva 2020). Later, there is an extensive account of the evolution of time banks in the UK and how the COVID-19 pandemic has fostered the development of new initiatives. Finally, the chapter also provides a discussion of the economic and social impact of time banks as conclusions.

## Definitions and Characteristics of Time Banks

Time banks, according to Schor et al. (2016), are 'multilateral barter service economies that aim to be an alternative to conventional market procurement' (p. 69) where different services can be exchanged at an equal value per hour expended, independently of their market value. For example, an accountant may exchange the time with a cleaner, who may earn a lower hourly rate. Time banks can be defined as rule-based exchange services within a network of community, where the value of services provided is measured in terms of time (hours) as the unit of currency (Weaver et al. 2016). The community network in question could either be a group of individuals, an organisation, or both, where exchange services could either be rendered or received. However, time banks are guided by the egalitarian principle, which supports that the value of time is the same, without minding its actual market value (Seyfang 2001). For instance, one hour of painting is the same as that of babysitting in time banks. Through time banks, those within the community with no financial capacity can also earn similar goods and services by earning the trust of others.

It is noteworthy to state that time banking cannot be regarded as barter; because in barter, there is prior negotiation between the concerned parties, and services may be more valuable than others due to scarcity (Weaver et al. 2016). Unlike time banking, in bartering, there is an exchange of services between the parties. Time banks can also not be likened to voluntary work, as the latter is unidirectional, in terms of giving with no intention of receiving, while the former involves elements of reciprocity in its approach, and its members earn credits for all the services rendered. Furthermore, the reflection of the 'bank' in time bank is relative in some countries; for instance, in the US, there is no legal correlation between the two currencies ('time' and money); and in Japan, since 1998, no service exchange can be registered under the name 'time bank', as the term 'bank' is exclusive to financial institutions (Weaver et al. 2016).

Time banks allow people to exchange and trade their skills, an hour for an hour (Wosskow 2014). Indeed, the premise that any type of skill is valuable and the idea that anyone can join is part of the inclusive ideology of time banks. In their study, Schor et al. (2016) found the fact that all contributions are considered equal (the bank is seen as a utopian space of fairness) is one of the main attractions for members. Within time banks, the network of reciprocity is nurtured, thereby creating values for the once untapped resources, skills and making people who had been marginalised to be valuable in the conventional economy (Han et al. 2019). Cahn (2004) affirmed that those who are under-valued and economically irrelevant in society are among those who will likely join time banks because they would have more time available to them. Examples include out of work, carers, the retired, and many others. Interestingly, in their comparative study about different sharing economy platforms, Schor et al. (2016) found that time banks members are overwhelmingly female.

From the economic crisis of 2008, according to Arcidiacono and Podda (2017), time banks are now redefining themselves 'following the logic of the sharing economy' (p. 42), becoming digital time banks. One of the main transformations of time banks because of the digitisation relates to the scalability of the participation from local communities (neighbourhoods and small towns) to global space. In their digital transformation, as observed by Arcidiacono and Podda (2017), time banks have opened up to an unprecedented set of users, 'increasingly highly educated young people who exchange expertise that is typically more highly skilled and qualified' (p. 43). Nevertheless, these high-skilled time bank users often reject time-swap with other members whom they considered lower skilled. In their study, Schor et al. (2016) found that high-skilled members refused to offer certain services such as coding or legal services, 'preferring to exercise a class privilege of confidence and entitlement by trying their hand at manual or creative services' (p. 79). In addition, Schor et al. (2016) observed that some time bank members with high expertise used the time bank just as a place to give charity, 'which allows one-sided trades but does not operate according to the underlying values of the institution' (p. 67). This mismatching ultimately can reduce time exchanges as far as it generates unbalanced accounts. Furthermore, it creates more issues in terms of accessibility and discrimination (Arcidiacono and Podda 2017).

## Models of Time Banks

Over the years, quite a number of rule-based service exchange models have emerged, however not following the egalitarian principle through the exchange of service for goods, money, or other incentives, thus compounding the confusion of the 'original' time bank (Weaver et al. 2016). For instance, the Local Exchange and Trading Systems (LETS) comprises local organisations where people exchange skills through a local currency to equate the actual market value of the exchanged service (Seyfang 2001). According to the New Economics Foundation, the models of time banks can be classified into three: (i) person-to-person, (ii) person-to-agency, and (iii) organisation-to-organisation (Ryan-Collins et al. 2008).

### Person-to-Person Time Banks

This is the most common model of time banking where the time broker enquires from the community members of their service needs and the kind of service they can render to other members. The responses of the members are logged into the computer using Time Online to match services offered to those in need. Person-to-person time banking is also considered as a low-cost model of volunteering as part of the social care efforts conducted by an organisation, as members can support other community members but also, they can 'buy' support for themselves (Naughton-Doe et al. 2020). It is noteworthy to state that there are two different types of person-to-person time banks, which are community-based and organisation-based (Ryan-Collins et al. 2008).

The organisation-based or service credit model of person-to-person was developed by Edgar Cahn in the US around the 1980s (Cahn and Barr 1986). With this type of model, the organisation, such as a voluntary agency or public service, was responsible for its hosting, funding, and implementation. A typical example of this model is the Elderplan time bank, which was created in the US by a healthcare provider, with the ultimate goal of providing a reciprocal support network for the aged to live an independent life (Lasker et al. 2011). In the UK, Rushey Green Time bank was established in a General Practitioner (GP) surgery to promote mutual support and improved well-being among patients (Gould 2009). Since the number of time-swappers grown continuously, there is now a distributed model which includes five hubs (Perez-Vega et al. 2021). The ultimate goal of the community-based time banks is to encourage and develop social capital in the community, and its membership is open to anyone interested (Ryan-Collin et al. 2008). A classic example of a non-monetary person-to-person time bank is the time bank Zumbara, launched in Turkey in 2011. According to Subasi and Kirkulak-Uludag (2021), Zumbara is a platform that allows people to earn time in exchange for their service, where people use their know-how, experiences, and talents to support each other.

## Person-to-Agency Time Banks

This model was developed in Wales in 2006, whereby individuals earn credits for volunteering or participating in public services, local agencies, and community groups (Ryan-Collins et al. 2008). In compensation for the service rendered, members of the community could stand the chance of receiving a reward, 'thank you' note, or the opportunity to attend leisure activities. Again, this model can either be community-based or organisation-based. The community-based person-to-agency time banks sought after the development of the community by building a bridge between individuals and local organisation. A typical example is Blaengarw time bank, located in South Wales, where working in the community is rewarded with time currency through the local development agency (NEF 2008). The organisation-based person-to-agency time banks encourage their members to be actively engaged in activities that suit their goals. For instance, residents of the housing association could earn credits for attending residents' meetings (Naughton-Doe 2011).

### Organisation-to-Organisation Time Banks

The organisation-to-organisation model of time bank was launched in London in 2013, and it involves the direct exchange of services, skills, and resources between two organisations (NEF 2008). The ultimate goal of this time bank is to facilitate the exchange of resources among businesses and to build a local network (Ryan-Collins et al. 2008). Services such as room space, marketing, software support, and many others are exchanged.

## Benefits and Limitations of Time Banks

One intended benefit of time banks relates to the co-production of output or services, which can offer additional resources for social care and is perceived as being of higher value than traditional volunteering activities (Evans et al. 2012; Boyle and Bird 2014). Nevertheless, time banks are mainly posited to champion the course of social capital development (North 2003). Social capital can be described as the productive social relationship that occurs between individuals, organisations, and communities (Putnam 2000). Hawkins and Maurer (2012) affirmed that the collaboration between the social network and social support pathway for opportunities, resources, and outcomes for communities, organisations, and individuals. Strong ties could be developed as a result of the frequent exchange between members, and there could be possibilities of weak ties among members who are infrequent acquaintances. In addition, time banks can contribute to the development of well-being. Huppert (2009) argued that an individual is said to experience well-being if such a person is contented, resilient and with high esteem. Huppert (2009) identified the five ways to well-being, which include: connect, give, keep active, take notice, and keep learning. Relationships could be built through time banks, where exchanges could further enhance social capital; thus, well-being becomes improved.

Despite the potential for the development of personal relationships and sociability to be established via time banks, many time bankers end up engaging in an instrumental and pragmatic use of time banks, which does not develop into a deeper sociality. As Arcidiacono and Podda (2017) observed, for-profit time bank platforms may prefer this limited sociability because 'when relationships become too recurrent, the users tend to bypass platform brokering, substituting or competing with it' (p. 56). Therefore, this instrumental use (with minimum sociality involved) of time banks seems to question the sharing economy ethos and the ability of time banks to 're-socialise' economic exchange as it seems more similar to the traditional market trade. Indeed, this is in line with other studies (Dubois et al. 2014; Valor and Papaoikonomou 2019), which also found a significant level of homophily within sharing economy transactions (Dubois et al. 2014; Valor and Papaoikonomou 2019). Likewise, Valor and Papaoikonomou (2019), in their study about time banks in Spain and Greece, found that the reason why time banks are often not successful is that they fail to institutionalise the principles of social and market exchange.

One of the potential uses of time banks is community development, as it is believed that communities with strong interaction and relationships often have fewer challenges of poor health, social crimes, unemployment, and many others (Simon 2004). With the help of time banks, communities provide social care for each other through the development of a reciprocal support network of volunteers, and this, in turn, reduces the government's cost of social care. However, some of the intended benefits do not always materialise. For instance, Naughton-Doe et al. (2020) have found that the aim of delivering support to communities did not materialise, in particular for low-level activities such as cooking or helping with shopping. Naughton-Doe et al. (2020), in their study of time banks in England, also pointed out that often these aims were not achieved as vulnerable members needed additional protection or support, which led to lower or non-existent levels of co-production. In addition, despite the ethos of time banks as member-led activities, evidence has found that often times, the brokers were the ones with the sole responsibility of facilitating the exchange and defining the rules from which exchanges were implemented (Naughton-Doe et al. 2020). Finally, the level of resources needed to organise these activities was generally high, and usually, there were low levels of engagement from community members, which led to many requests unfulfilled (Dentzer 2001).

## A Historical Overview of Time Banks in the UK

The introduction and emergence of time banks in the UK were in 1998, through the effort of Martin Simon and David Boyle (Simon 2004). It is noteworthy to state that the duo had different interests. For instance, Martin is a community organiser who sees the time bank as an innovative tool for community development (Simon 2004). Simon (2004) went ahead to the first-time bank called Stonehouse Fairshares. David, on the other hand, sees the time bank as an avenue to expand the frontier in the co-production of public services (Simon 2004). Indeed, there are two models of time banking in the UK due to the different perspectives of the two originators—community time bank and time bank that is premised on existing services. Although the motives of the originators of the time bank in the UK might be different, ultimately, the beneficiaries of these initiatives are those who are socially excluded and those who use public services (DHSC 2019).

Thereafter, time banks adopted the organisational structure of formal settings in an attempt to comply with the legislation binding working with vulnerable people in the UK. In the Rushey Green Time bank, based in London, time is banked and swapped (i.e., there is no voucher system). This bank's funding model is based on support from the local authorities and other grants (Perez-Vega et al. 2021). This type of time bank is usually funded by councils, community regeneration projects, or charity grants. On the recommendation of Cahn (2004), who posited that for the sustainability of time banking, it must be integrated into councils or services to make it eligible for funding from the public sector. Another typical example of a community-based time bank located in Glasgow is Gorballs Time bank, which promotes social inclusiveness in a diverse community (Seyfang 2004). On the other hand, there are time banks about arts and creativity, such as Leeds Creative Time bank, which was established in 2010 with Arts Council England funding to research informal exchange cultures (Leeds Creative Time bank 2020a). Leeds Creative Time bank employs a non-monetary form of exchange (time credits) and fosters creative activity, from creative writing to sound art and visual arts (Leeds Creative Time bank 2020b), thus providing a rich model for community building (Briggs et al. 2015).

In 2002, Time banking UK (TBUK) was founded by Martin to function as a national umbrella that would coordinate time banking activities. TBUK is not a new time bank, but it welcomes the public sector and individual time banks to join, and it offers both training and operational support for them. In addition, TBUK promotes the activities of time banks to potential funders, and it lobbies on behalf of time banks among the policy community (TBUK 2020a). Time banking UK is an organisation that coordinates many of the time banking activities happening in the country. According to their own statistics, at the time of writing, the organisation had coordinated 278 time banks and facilitated the exchange of 5.6 million hours (Time banking UK 2020).

Some of the time banking organisations in the UK have made attempts to measure the social return on investment on some of their time banking activities. A common measurement used among time banks to assess the impact of their activities is the HACT Social Value methodology (HACT 2018). The methodology provides an assessment of social impact, providing evidence of value for money, and compare the impact of different programmes (Fujiwara 2014). A few time banks have adopted this measurement to assess the impact of their activity. For example, a study conducted by the Barnet time bank found that outcomes related to volunteering and civic engagement, community and neighbourhood, health and well-being, and employment and access to services could be identified from the operations of this time bank. The study found that the outcomes measurement using the HACT Social Value methodology showed that the initiative generated £518,251 through the outcomes being measured over a period of three years (Time banking UK 2017). Since the initiative required an investment of only £55,479, the report concludes that the initiative generated a social return of investment for every £1 spent of £9.34 of social value.

The COVID-19 pandemic impacted several initiatives as face-to-face interaction was significantly reduced as part of the efforts to reduce the spread of the virus (Cabinet Office 2020). However, as self-isolation also had an impact on the well-being and mental health of vulnerable people, initiatives started to appear in the country. For example, Time banking UK, in partnership with Made Open, launched a free national emergency platform called *Communities Together.* The platform aimed to facilitate the exchange of offers and requests between people in communities to help people who were self-isolating access support and stay connected during this time of crisis (Communities Together 2020). The platform allowed people to exchange general tasks such as walking dogs, helping vulnerable people do their shopping, and organising other forms of assistance. There were also other more specialist initiatives that were involved in the exchange of time, such as Frontline19. Frontline19 is an independent UK nationwide service delivering psychological support where counsellors and other mental health professionals could offer therapy hours free of charge to those who are or have been on the frontline of COVID-19 which many of them were also volunteering their time to support others during the pandemic (Fronline19 2020).

## Summary

Time banks have emerged as a manifestation of the sharing economy where participants can exchange skills and time with one another. In the UK, the time banks began as community-led initiatives, and the country is now a host of over 200-time banks (Time banking UK 2020). The UK Government has been involved in promoting and supporting time banks across the country, as the government perceives time banks as being vehicles of social care and inclusion of marginalised communities. However, there is still contesting evidence whether the aims of time banks are, in fact, achieved. Some effort to assess the social impact of time banks in the communities where they operate has led to new methodological approaches, such as the HACT scale, and early evidence seems to suggest that they can benefit the communities where they operate and the participants of time banks (Time banking UK 2017). The COVID-19 pandemic has also forced time banks to rethink their delivery model. Initially, time banks were restricted in their operation as face-to-face interaction was reduced during the lockdown and the subsequent tiered system implemented by the UK Government (DHSC 2020). However, as the pandemic highlighted the need to support the most vulnerable, time banks adapted to their new environment and with the help of technology, they were able to resume their supporting role and organise the exchange of skills and time to serve as support during these unprecedented times.

Future research directions involve both methodological and theoretical developments in the implementation of time banks. From a methodological perspective, simplified scales that can assess the (social) impact and return of investment of time banks initiatives would make their assessment more accessible to smaller time banks. Currently, the HACT scale involves over 122 items, which makes the measurement both time consuming for the respondent, and resource-consuming for the time bank organisers. From a theoretical perspective, a typology of time banks has been developed, but there is a gap on how to overcome the engagement hinderers identified in the current literature (Collom 2007). Research on what mechanisms could drive participant engagement, in particular from the segments that the government is trying to benefit the most, would provide not only theoretical advancements in this manifestation of the sharing economy but would also have a wider impact on improving the quality of life of those participating in this activity.

## References


Arcidiacono, Davide, and Antonello Podda. 2017. 'Sharing Time: New Forms of Reciprocity in the Digital Economy.' *Work Organisation, Labour and Globalisation* 11 (2): 39–58. https://doi.org/10.13169/workorgalaboglob.11.2.0039.

Bird, Sarah, and David Boyle. 2014. *Give and Take: How Timebanking Is Transforming Healthcare*. Timebanking, UK.

Briggs, Jo, Celia Lury, and Sarah Teasley. 2015. *Creative Temporal Costings: A Proto-Publics Research Project with Leeds Creative Timebank*. Accessed March 3, 2021. https://researchonline.rca.ac.uk/2220/1/Teasley%20Creative%20Temporal%20Costings%202015.pdf.

Cabinet Office. 2020. *Guidance: New National Restrictions from 5 November (2020)*. Accessed November 30, 2020. https://www.gov.uk/guidance/new-national-restrictions-from-5-november?priority-taxon=774cee22-d896-44c1-a611-e3109cce8eae.

Cahn, Edgar S. 2004. *No More Throw-Away People: The Co-production Imperative*. Washington, DC: Essential Books.

Cahn, Edgar, and Christine Gray. 2015. *The Time Bank Solution*. Accessed March 15, 2021. https://ssir.org/articles/entry/the_time_bank_solution.

Cahn, Edgar S., and Nicholas Barr. 1986. *Service Credits: A New Currency for the Welfare State*. Welfare State Programme Discussion Papers (WSP 008). Centre for Analysis of Social Exclusion, The London School of Economics and Political Science, London, UK.

Collom, Ed. 2007. 'The Motivations, Engagement, Satisfaction, Outcomes, and Demographics of Time Bank Participants: Survey Findings from a US System.' *International Journal of Community Currency Research* 11 (1): 36–83. https://doi.org/10.15133/j.ijccr.2007.004.

Collom, Ed. 2012. 'Key Indicators of Time Bank Participation: Using Transaction Data for Evaluation.' *International Journal of Community Currency Research* 16 (A): 18–29. https://doi.org/10.15133/j.ijccr.2012.002.

Communities Together. 2020. *About*. Accessed November 24, 2020. https://together.madeopen.co.uk/about.

Dentzer, Susan. 2001. 'Service Credit Banking.' In *To Improve Health and Health Care*, edited by S. Isaacs and J. Knickman, 1–23. Washington, DC: Robert Wood Johnson Foundation, San Francisco: Jossey-Bass.

DHSC (Department of Health and Social Care). 2019. 'The NHS Long Term Plan.' *The British Medical Journal* 364 (January): 1–2. https://doi.org/10.1136/bmj.l84.

DHSC (Department of Health and Social Care). 2020. *Local Restriction Tiers: What You Need to Know*. Accessed December 3, 2020. https://www.gov.uk/guidance/local-restriction-tiers-what-you-need-to-know.

Dubois, Emilie A., Juliet B. Schor, and Lindsey B. Carfagna. 2014. 'New Cultures of Connection in a Boston Time Bank.' In *Sustainable Lifestyles and the Quest for Plenitude: Case Studies of the New Economy*, edited by J. B. Schor and C. J. Thompson, 95–124. New Haven, CT: Yale University Press.

Evans, Simon, Sarah Hills, and Judy Orme. 2012. 'Doing More for Less? Developing Sustainable Systems of Social Care in the Context of Climate Change and Public Spending Cuts.' *British Journal of Social Work* 42 (4): 744–764. https://doi.org/10.1093/bjsw/bcr108.

Felländer, Anna, Claire Ingram, and Robin Teigland. 2015. 'Sharing Economy.' In Embracing Change with Caution. *Näringspolitiskt Forum Rapport*, no. 11. 2015. Accessed May 27, 2021. https://www.academia.edu/download/37923227/Sharing-Economy_webb.pdf.

Fronline19. 2020. *About*. Accessed November 11, 2020. https://www.frontline19.com/therapists/.

Fujiwara, Daniel. 2014. *Measuring the Social Impact of Community Investment: The Methodology Paper*. HACT Ideas and Innovation in Housing. Accessed March 15, 2021. https://hact.org.uk/sites/default/files/uploads/Archives/2014/3/HACT%20Methodology%20Paper%20FINAL.pdf.

Gerwe, Oksana, and Rosario Silva. 2020. 'Clarifying the Sharing Economy: Conceptualization, Typology, Antecedents, and Effects.' *Academy of Management Perspectives* 34 (1): 65–96. https://doi.org/10.5465/amp.2017.0010.

Gould, Vanessa. 2009. *Lewisham Time Bank Development Strategy 2009–2012*. London: NHS Lewisham.

Han, Kyungsik, Patrick Shih, Victoria Bellotti, and John Carroll. 2019. 'It's Time There Was an App for 30 That Too: A Usability Study of Mobile Timebanking.' *International Journal of Mobile Human Computer Interaction* 7 (2): 1–22. https://doi.org/10.4018/ijmhci.2015040101.

Hawkins, Robert L., and Katherine Maurer. 2012. 'Unravelling Social Capital: Disentangling a Concept for Social Work.' *British Journal of Social Work* 42 (2): 353–370. https://doi.org/10.1093/bjsw/bcr056.

Housing Associations' Charitable Trust (HACT). 2018. *Value Calculator*. Accessed November 24, 2020. https://www.hact.org.uk/value-calculator.

Huppert, Felicia A. 2009. 'Psychological Well-Being: Evidence Regarding Its Causes and Consequences.' *Applied Psychology: Health and Well-Being* 1 (2): 137–164. https://doi.org/10.1111/j.1758-0854.2009.01008.x.

Lasker, Judith, Ed Collom, Tara Bealer, Erin Niclaus, Jessica Young Keefe, Zane Kratzer, Lauren Baldasari et al. 2011. 'Time Banking and Health: The Role of a Community Currency Organization in Enhancing Well-Being.' *Health Promotion Practice* 12 (1): 102–115. https://doi.org/10.1177/1524839909353022.

Leeds Creative Timebank. 2020a. *About Leeds Creative Timebank*. Accessed March 15, 2021. https://leedscreativetimebank.org.uk/about/.

Leeds Creative Timebank. 2020b. *Skills List*. Accessed March 15, 2021. https://leedscreativetimebank.org.uk/people-skills/skills-list/.

Naughton-Doe, Ruth. 2011. 'Time Banking in Social Housing: A Toolkit for Co-production in Public Services.' *International Journal of Community Currency Research* 15: 71–68. https://doi.org/10.15133/j.ijccr.2011.025.

Naughton-Doe, Ruth, Ailsa Cameron, and John Carpenter. 2020. 'Time-banking and the Co-production of Preventive Social Care with Adults; What Can We Learn from the Challenges of Implementing Person-to-Person Timebanks in England?' *Health & Social Care in the Community* 1 (9): 1–11. https://doi.org/10.1111/hsc.13166.

New Economics Foundation (NEF). 2008. *The New Wealth of Time: How Timebanking Helps People Build Better Public Services*. Accessed October 3, 2020. https://nwi.pdx.edu/webinars/Webinar13-materials1.pdf.

North, Peter. 2003 'Time Banks—Learning the Lessons from LETS?' *Local Economy* 18 (3): 267–270. https://doi.org/10.1080/0269094032000111048.

Perez-Vega, Rodrigo, Brian Jones, Penny Travlou, and Cristina Miguel. 2021. 'United Kingdom: An Examination of the Configuration of the Sharing Economy, Pressing Issues, and Research Directions.' In *The Collaborative Economy in Action: European Perspectives*, edited by Andrzej Klimczuk, Vida Česnuitytė, and Gabriela Avram. Limerick, Ireland: University of Limerick.

Putnam, Robert D. 2000. 'Bowling Alone: America's Declining Social Capital.' In *Culture and politics*, 223–234. New York: Palgrave Macmillan.

Ryan-Collins, Josh, Lucie Stephens, and Anna Coote. 2008. *The New Wealth of Time: How Timebanking Helps People Build Better Public Services*. London: New Economics Foundation.

Schor, Juliet B., Connor Fitzmaurice, Lindsey B. Carfagna, Will Attwood-Charles, and Emilie Dubois Poteat. 2016. 'Paradoxes of Openness and

Distinction in the Sharing Economy.' *Poetics* 54: 66–81. https://doi.org/10.1016/j.poetic.2015.11.001.

Seyfang, Gill. 2001. 'Working for the Fenland Dollar: An Evaluation of Local Exchange Trading Schemes as an Informal Employment Strategy to Tackle Social Exclusion.' *Work, Employment and Society* 15 (3): 581–593. https://doi.org/10.1177/09500170122119165.

Seyfang, Gill. 2004. 'Time Banks: Rewarding Community Self-Help in the Inner City?' *Community Development Journal* 39 (1): 62–71. https://doi.org/10.1093/cdj/39.1.62.

Seyfang, Gill. 2006. 'Harnessing the Potential of the Social Economy? Time Banks and UK Public Policy.' *International Journal of Sociology and Social Policy*. https://doi.org/10.1108/01443330610690569.

Simon, Martin. 2004. *On Becoming a Time Broker*. Gloucester: Fairshares.

Subasi, Ozge, and Berna Kirkulak-Uludag. 2021. 'A Socially Engaged Model of Sharing Platforms in Turkey: Design as a Blueprint of Practices and Local Cooperations.' In *The Collaborative Economy in Action: European Perspectives*, edited by Andrzej Klimczuk, Vida Česnuitytė, and Gabriela Avram. Limerick, Ireland: University of Limerick.

Time Banking United Kingdom (TBUK). 2020a. *About TBUK*. Accessed October 3, 2020. https://www.timebanking.org/about-tbuk/.

Time Banking United Kingdom (TBUK). 2020b. *Time Online 2 Unleashed*. Accessed October 3, 2020. https://www.timebanking.org/time-online-2-unleashed/.

Timebanking United Kingdom (TBUK). 2017. *Calculating the Social Value of Person to Person Timebanking*. Accessed November 24, 2020. https://www.timebanking.org/wordpress/wp-content/uploads/2011/09/Barnet-SROI-impact-report-2017.pdf.

TimeBank. 2020. *Who We Are*. Accessed October 3, 2020. https://timebank.org.uk/about/who-we-are/.

Válek, Lukáš, and Veronika Jašíková. 2013. 'Time Bank and Sustainability: The Permaculture Approach.' *Procedia-Social and Behavioral Sciences* 92: 986–991. https://doi.org/10.1016/j.sbspro.2013.08.788.

Valor, Carmen, and Eleni Papaoikonomou. 2019. Sharing Economy to the Rescue? The Case of Timebanking. In *Handbook of the Sharing Economy*, edited by R. Belk, G. Eckhardt, and F. Bardhi, 136–152. Cheltenham, UK: Edward Elgar Publishing.

Weaver, Paul, Adina Dumitru, Ricardo García-Mira, Isabel Lema, Loes Muijsers, and Veronique Vasseur. 2016. *Transformative Social Innovation Report: Timebanking*. TRANSIT: EU SSH.2013.3.2-1 Grant agreement no: 613169. Accessed March 15, 2021. http://www.transitsocialinnovation.eu/content/original/Book%20covers/Local%20PDFs/253%20Time%20Banks%20-%20Case%20study%20report%20Time%20Banks-2017.pdf.

Whitham, Monica M., and Hannah Clarke. 2016. 'Getting Is Giving: Time Banking as Formalized Generalized Exchange.' *Sociology Compass* 10 (1): 87–97. https://doi.org/10.1111/soc4.12343.

Wosskow, Debie. 2014. *Unlocking the Sharing Economy: An Independent Review. Department for Business, Innovation and Skills.* Accessed May 27, 2021. Available at: https://assets.publishing.service.gov.uk/government/uploads/system/uploads/attachment_data/file/378291/bis-14-1227-unlocking-the-sharing-economy-an-independent-review.pdf.

## Suggested Readings

Ottlewski, Lydia. 2021. *Platforms for Social Innovation.* Thesis. University of St Gallen. Accessed March 15, 2021. https://www.alexandria.unisg.ch/262414/.

Pill, Madeleine. 2021. 'Neighbourhood Collaboration in Co-production: State-Resourced Responsiveness or State-Retrenched Responsibilisation?' *Policy Studies*: In press ahead of publication. https://doi.org/10.1080/01442872.2021.1892052.

## Relevant Websites

MadeOpen: https://madeopen.co.uk/timebank.
Timebanking UK: https://timebanking.org.

# 16

# The Sharing Economy Business Models in Poland: Aspects of Trust, Law, and Initiatives Facing the COVID-19 Pandemic

Agnieszka Lukasiewicz and Aleksandra Nadolska

## Introduction

The collaborative economy is a social and economic phenomenon covering both the direct provision of services by people, as well as sharing, co-creating, co-buying, co-financing, and co-deciding. The appearance can be regarded as based on people's willingness to cooperate, help others, and share different kinds of resources, including time, money that is reciprocated in different ways (both material and non-material). In some way, it is related to the theory of 'warm-glow giving' (Andreoni 1990). The literature on altruism and the theory

A. Lukasiewicz (✉)
Transport Systems and Telematics Division, Road and Bridge Research Institute, Warsaw, Poland
e-mail: alukas@ibdim.edu.pl

A. Nadolska
Gdańsk University, Gdańsk, Poland



V. Česnuitytė et al. (eds.), *The Sharing Economy in Europe*,
https://doi.org/10.1007/978-3-030-86897-0_16

notes that some individuals feel positive when helping others. Nevertheless, some models of sharing economies, such as well-known Uber or Airbnb, are often perceived as pure business, sometimes with the element of inequality repeatedly leading to conflicts. The boundary between individuals and enterprises is not clear. Obviously, the economy is developing largely thanks to the Internet and mobile technologies that facilitate access to products and services. Moreover, the sharing likewise, the sharing economy is firmly based on trust. There are various types of collaborative economy initiatives in Poland—both non-profit and commercial. The country has both large international players (Uber, Airbnb, and BlaBlaCar) as well as thriving domestic players, including some going to international markets. For several years there can be noticed a kind of flourish of local initiatives, especially in the food sector. Nevertheless, where the shortage of resources appears, and many various stakeholders are involved. Also, a probability of conflict arises. Hence, such a situation was noticed in Poland in the case of Uber and taxi drivers until the new law Republic of Poland (2019) was enforced from the beginning of 2021.

Undoubtedly, since the World Health Organization (WHO) officially declared the outbreak of coronavirus disease 2019 (COVID-19) in March 2020, the financial situation in sharing economy gets worsen. As the basic need during COVID-19 time is to significantly reduce movements and keep social distance, there has been a drop in accommodation or transportation services. However, the crisis caused by the coronavirus triggers a reaction from the side of consumers, entrepreneur leading to the emergence of new initiatives within the collaborative economy. Efforts are being made to protect local entrepreneurs and to build customer engagement through social campaigns or applications (e.g., Knajp.pl that helps restaurants in the COVID-19 time gain more customers and orders).

## Regulations Related to the Sharing Economy

The sharing economy business models often are under a significant challenge to the regulators since the law is reactive and just follows the development of such new models generally, firmly based on technology. Those initiatives can be a profitable or unforeseen risk to society, contest the validity of outdated regulations or force them to change their policy. In turn, the law can support the development of collaborative economy ventures or undermine their economic meaning in submitting to regulatory pressure from traditional companies operating in a given sector. The development of innovative technologies also creates new types of uncertainty and risk that often require a different approach to legal regulations (Nadolska and Nadolski 2019).

It is worth remembering that the law is an element of culture, as well as the market, and in that sense, it must remain in constant feedback with them. That does not have to mean the sharing economy requires completely new legal solutions, as it is possible to properly qualify modern business models, at least in certain specific areas. It should be borne in mind; however, the over-activity of the Polish legislator in that area may pose a sui generis threat to the progress in the sharing economy, which is not desirable from the point of view of the country's economic development. The proposals concern, for example, the introduction of an obligation registration of flats for short-term rent. The changes made include, among others, an amendment to the Act on Road Transport (Republic of Poland 2019), which requires Uber or Bolt drivers to hold a taxi licence and changes in the vehicle (marking the body). The European Parliament's motion for the resolution of 11 May 2017 proposes that the Member States ensure legal clarity and calls for the sharing economy not to be seen as a threat to the traditional economy. It stresses the importance of regulating the economy of sharing in such a way as to facilitate and create opportunities, rather than restricting. The rationale behind that is the collaborative economy creates new and interesting business opportunities, generates jobs and growth, and often plays an important role not only in improving the efficiency of the economic system but also makes it more socially and environmentally sustainable. It also enables a better allocation of resources and assets that would otherwise be underutilised, thus contributing to the transition to the circular economy. Furthermore, the economy of sharing can have a profound impact on long-established business models in many strategic sectors, such as transport, accommodation, food, health, and finance. On the basis of the above, it must be assumed that, in the implementation of the sharing economy, it becomes necessary to ensure a high level of consumer protection and respect for workers' rights, as well as to spread the tax burden properly. The regulation of those issues is primarily attributable to the European Union's (EU) Member States, as they are in the area of local economies. It is, therefore, up to the Member States to adapt their legislation to the challenges posed to them by the sharing economy in the first place, but this may lead to the stratification of the single market in that area.

## Issue of Trust in the Sharing Economy Evolution

In the framework of the sharing economy, trust is regarded as playing a key role along with referring it to currency (Botsman and Rogers 2011). Analysing sharing economy, those are seen not only as business models and markets but also meet the fundamental human need to be part of a community, build relationships, share with others, and entrust things to other people. Basically, people trust each other enough to share (Roland Berger Strategy Consultants 2014). From the perspective of the sharing economy, the stakeholders/users are of much significance, and they (Osztovits et al. 2015) share with each other their ideas, capacities, and resources (e.g., fixed assets, services, money) on an on-demand basis (as and when the consumer need arises), usually via an IT platform, on the basis of trust, ascribing particular importance to personal interaction and the community experience, and with an eye on sustainability.

An increasing amount of people are demanding a form of consumption that entails a high degree of personal interaction, and a community experience, with products offered by individuals rather than 'faceless' companies. In this way, business services go from being transaction-based to experience-driven, and the basis for this is trust (Osztovits et al. 2015). According to Hawlitschek et al. (2016), trust is one of 24 drivers and obstacles for participation in a peer-to-peer rental. Thus, platform operators have created devices to establish and maintain trust among their users, including mutual review and rating schemes, verification mechanisms, or meaningful user profiles (Teubner 2014). Hawlitschek et al. (2016) developed a research model for the role of trust in C2C sharing economy platforms that are based on the 3P of trust, for example, towards peer, platform, or product—represented by the dimensions of ability, integrity, and benevolence. It incorporates both the consumers' and suppliers' intentions to consume or supply a resource, as both are represented by private, for example, non-professional and persons. They come to the conclusion trust is without any doubt a highly complex construct—especially within the context of the sharing economy.

Notwithstanding, the sharing economy is still regarded as strongly connected to ICT (information and communication technologies). The report *Information Society in Poland: Results of Statistical Surveys in the Years 2015–2019* (GUS 2019) includes the results of the survey about using the Internet for sharing economy. Thus, in 2019, respondents were asked about the use of websites or applications that operate in the framework of the sharing economy. The survey was focussed on private providers of accommodation or transport services and those wishing to use these services. The questions were restricted to the demand side; for example, they concerned the use (paid or free of charge) or application to arrange (rent) accommodation or transport from another private person.

According to the survey, it is more common in the economy of sharing to organise accommodation than transport (20.1 and 7.0% of people respectively). The websites or applications in the sharing economy were more often used by younger age groups than older people. Taking into account the level of education, accommodation services, and transport within the framework of the sharing economy were mostly used by people with higher education (44.3 and 14.2%, respectively). Regarding the professional activity, the most common use was made by the self-employed (38.6%) in the case of accommodation and pupils and students in the case of transport (13.8%) (Table 16.1).

**Table 16.1** Usage of websites or apps for the sharing economy in 2018 and 2019

| Specification | Arranging accommodation | | | | | | Arranging transport services | | | | | |
|---|---|---|---|---|---|---|---|---|---|---|---|---|
| | Total | | via | | | | Total | | via | | | |
| | | | Dedicates websites or applications | | Other websites or applications | | | | Dedicates websites or applications | | Other websites or applications | |
| | In % of total individuals in a group | | | | | | | | | | | |
| *Year* | '18 | '19 | '18 | '19 | '18 | '19 | '18 | '19 | '18 | '19 | '18 | '19 |
| **TOTAL** | **17.1** | **20.1** | **13.4** | **15.7** | **6.5** | **8.0** | **7.2** | **7.0** | **5.7** | **5.6** | **2.4** | **2.4** |
| Sex | | | | | | | | | | | | |
| Men | 17.3 | 20.1 | 13.4 | 16.0 | 6.8 | 7.6 | 7.9 | 7.8 | 6.4 | 6.5 | 2.4 | 2.6 |
| Women | 16.9 | 20.2 | 13.3 | 15.4 | 6.2 | 8.4 | 6.5 | 6.1 | 5.0 | 4.8 | 2.3 | 2.2 |
| Age | | | | | | | | | | | | |
| 16–24 years | 16.3 | 20.8 | 11.5 | 15.3 | 7.0 | 9.6 | 12.5 | 12.9 | 8.9 | 10.1 | 5.3 | 5.7 |
| 25–34 | 26.2 | 30.0 | 20.5 | 23.1 | 10.6 | 13.1 | 11.9 | 10.9 | 9.9 | 9.2 | 3.7 | 3.5 |
| 35–44 | 25.3 | 30.2 | 20.3 | 24.7 | 9.2 | 10.7 | 8.8 | 8.2 | 7.2 | 6.7 | 2.4 | 2.6 |
| 35–54 | 16.5 | 16.5 | 13.4 | 13.3 | 5.6 | 6.1 | 5.6 | 6.1 | 4.5 | 5.1 | 1.8 | 1.8 |
| 55–64 | 8.4 | 12.0 | 6.3 | 8.5 | 3.3 | 4.8 | 2.8 | 2.7 | 2.1 | 1.7 | – | 1.1 |
| 65–74 years | 3.9 | 5.3 | 2.9 | 4.0 | 1.3 | 1.7 | – | 1.0 | – | – | – | – |
| Educational level | | | | | | | | | | | | |
| Primary or lower secondary | 4.5 | 4.5 | 3.0 | 3.4 | 2.0 | 2.2 | 4.0 | 3.6 | 2.7 | 2.6 | 1.6 | 1.8 |
| Upper secondary | 11.3 | 13.2 | 8.4 | 9.7 | 4.4 | 5.4 | 4.9 | 4.6 | 3.8 | 3.7 | 1.6 | 1.6 |
| Tertiary | 38.2 | 44.3 | 31.2 | 35.9 | 14.2 | 17.0 | 14.6 | 14.2 | 12.0 | 11.7 | 4.8 | 4.8 |
| Employment situation | | | | | | | | | | | | |

| Specification | Arranging accommodation | | | | | | Arranging transport services | | | | | |
|---|---|---|---|---|---|---|---|---|---|---|---|---|
| | Total | | via | | | | Total | | via | | | |
| | | | Dedicates websites or applications | | Other websites or applications | | | | Dedicates websites or applications | | Other websites or applications | |
| | In % of total individuals in a group | | | | | | | | | | | |
| Students | 14.4 | 16.4 | 9.9 | 12.7 | 6.4 | 7.9 | 12.8 | 13.8 | 9.1 | 11.0 | 5.4 | 6.3 |
| Persons employed | 23.7 | 27.5 | 18.8 | 21.5 | 8.8 | 10.9 | 9.4 | 8.8 | 7.5 | 7.2 | 3.0 | 2.9 |
| Employees | 24.5 | 28.3 | 19.4 | 22.4 | 9.2 | 11.0 | 9.7 | 9.1 | 7.8 | 7.5 | 3.0 | 2.8 |
| Self-employed | 34.6 | 38.6 | 27.8 | 30.1 | 12.3 | 16.7 | 14.3 | 12.9 | 11.6 | 9.8 | 4.9 | 5.3 |
| Farmers | 2.9 | 3.7 | 2.3 | 1.6 | 1.1 | – | – | – | – | – | – | – |
| Unemployed | 6.9 | 7.5 | 4.5 | 5.0 | 3.2 | 3.7 | 3.3 | 4.3 | 2.8 | 3.1 | – | – |
| Retired or other not in the labour force | 5.1 | 7.2 | 3.8 | 5.5 | 2.0 | 2.3 | 1.4 | 1.4 | 1.1 | 1.1 | – | – |
| Domicile | | | | | | | | | | | | |
| Large cities | 27.6 | 30.6 | 23.2 | 24.7 | 9.2 | 12.0 | 12.7 | 13.4 | 10.4 | 11.1 | 4.0 | 4.4 |
| Small cities | 17.3 | 21.1 | 12.6 | 15.7 | 7.5 | 9.0 | 6.5 | 5.7 | 4.9 | 4.5 | 2.3 | 2.1 |
| Rural areas | 9.3 | 11.9 | 6.9 | 9.1 | 3.8 | 4.3 | 3.8 | 3.3 | 2.9 | 2.5 | 1.3 | 1.3 |
| Degree of urbanisation | | | | | | | | | | | | |

(continued)

**Table 16.1** (continued)

| Specification | Arranging accommodation | | | | | | Arranging transport services | | | | | |
|---|---|---|---|---|---|---|---|---|---|---|---|---|
| | Total | | via | | | | Total | | via | | | |
| | | | Dedicates websites or applications | | Other websites or applications | | | | Dedicates websites or applications | | Other websites or applications | |
| | In % of total individuals in a group | | | | | | | | | | | |
| Thinly populated | 8.7 | 12.2 | 6.4 | 8.9 | 3.6 | 5.2 | 3.6 | 3.4 | 2.7 | 2.6 | 1.4 | 1.4 |
| Intermediate | 17.8 | 19.3 | 12.9 | 15.0 | 7.7 | 7.6 | 6.5 | 5.2 | 5.1 | 4.0 | 1.9 | 2.0 |
| Densely populated | 25.4 | 29.3 | 21.0 | 23.5 | 8.6 | 11.3 | 11.6 | 12.2 | 9.3 | 10.2 | 3.8 | 3.9 |
| Regions | | | | | | | | | | | | |
| Eastern Poland | 11.8 | 9.0 | 9.0 | 9.0 | 4.3 | 5.3 | 6.0 | 4.7 | 4.7 | 4.0 | 2.0 | 1.3 |
| Central Poland | 19.9 | 17.1 | 15.6 | 17.1 | 7.4 | 9.8 | 8.2 | 8.3 | 6.5 | 6.6 | 2.7 | 2.9 |
| Western Poland | 16.3 | 18.7 | 12.7 | 18.7 | 6.8 | 6.7 | 6.3 | 6.0 | 4.9 | 5.0 | 2.1 | 2.3 |

*Source* Own elaboration based on GUS (2018, 2019)

Wide disparities in the shares of persons using websites or applications under the sharing economy have been noted between the different professions. Unquestionably, more percentage of users of websites or applications has been observed among occupations with white-collar employees rather than among those with blue-collar employees. People associated with the IT and telecommunications industry (ICT-related) are much more likely to use websites or applications as part of the sharing economy compared to persons not involved in the ICT industry (Fig. 16.1).

According to the Eurobarometer (European Commission 2018), in all but one country, less than a quarter of non-users mention a lack of trust in services offered via collaborative platforms as a reason for not using them. The exception is Spain (27%), where just over a quarter mention this reason. In the majority of the remaining countries, the proportions of non-users giving this answer ranges from one in ten to around a quarter. However, in Estonia (8%), Italy (7%), Lithuania (6%), and Malta (5%), just less than one in ten non-users mention the lack of trust in the services offered as a reason for not using collaborative platforms.

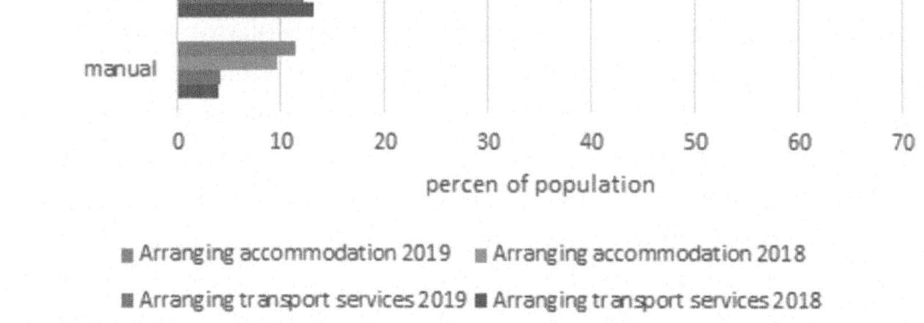


**Fig. 16.1** Individuals using websites or apps for the sharing economy by occupation, comparison of 2018 and 2019 (*Source* Own elaboration based on GUS [2018, 2019])

It is the second most frequently mentioned reason in Denmark (18%) and Cyprus (13%). It is also the third most frequently mentioned reason in 12 other countries, including Poland. Furthermore, Polish people still prefer using services offered via traditional channels. That they pointed as a reason not to use services offered via collaborative platforms. However, there is a significant variation, in 11 EU countries the most frequently mentioned such reason for not using the platform, less than half of non-users give this answer, ranging from well over four in ten in Poland (45%) to just over one in ten in Cyprus (11%) and Romania (12%). Nevertheless, Poland is among the countries that 60% answers point to recommend these services to some extent, ranging from six in ten or more in Latvia (66%) and Poland (60%) to less than one third in Malta (29%) and Croatia (31%).

## COVID-19 Impact on the Sharing Economy Initiatives' Development

As the world economy, also the sharing economy, was strongly affected by the coronavirus crisis, the especially negative impact was noticed in the short-term rental and transportation. Because of lockdown and quarantine, as well as general assumption not to move much during the pandemic 2020, in many touristic countries, reservations on Airbnb, Expedia, and Booking.com declined significantly. During the summertime, the situation was better, however still lower than in 2019.

In Poland, the number of offers on the Airbnb platform has continuously increased, mainly in touristic cities such as Cracow, Gdansk, and Warsaw (Śledziewska et al. 2019). To solve the impact of COVID-19, a large part of short-term rental advertisements appeared on such platforms as Otodom or Gumtree, offering medium-term and long-term rentals with promotions ending on a specific date. It indicates the owners hope to wait out the difficult period and return to Airbnb after the situation calms down (Szostak 2020). Expecting short-term rental gains, investors are willing to pay more to buy the property. In this sense, the use of platforms such as Airbnb or Booking.com by developers increased the bubble on the real estate market in Poland. Thus, that affected the housing market and the quality of life of the residents. Nowadays, the price of flats can be expected to fall down. The approach to the market has changed. Previously, there was a belief that prices would only go up. At the moment, there is a high expectation that they will start to decline, for what many citizens have been waiting for.

Another sector that has been severely influenced by COVID-19 is transportation. Before the COVID-19s time, shared mobility, bikes, scooters, motorbikes together with car sharing, as well as trip sharing, gained popularity. Nevertheless, the general idea during COVID-19 time is to significantly reduce movements as well as keep a social distance. Those do not match the assumptions of sharing mobility, especially in the case of car sharing, trip sharing ideas. That is why a significant drop in using shared modes of transportation has been observed. Real-time ridesharing and the industry have very quickly lost both passengers and profits (Andersson et al. 2020). Hence, the high-level risk of sharing vehicles with other people pushed many companies to stop their services. Uber stopped pooling rides in some markets, and Lyft did it in all of its operational areas. Facing the collapse, Lyft offered its drivers to work for Amazon as shoppers, warehouse workers, or as drivers (Lozzi et al. 2020). Moreover, the virus has had an impact on micro-mobility (e.g., bike sharing, scooter sharing) too: Lime stopped its services in 23 out of the previously served 30 countries, and Uber (Jump) and Bird (Circ) stopped their operations in almost all European countries. Contrary to such, Budapest introduced temporary nearly-free fares for their MOL Bubi bike-sharing service, limited to the first harder phase of lockdown.

Nevertheless, in Poland has been observed increasing movements of goods, particularly food, medications, fast-moving consumer goods (FMCG), to people confined in their homes and those who prefer to stay home not to take the risk to be infected. Due to COVID-19, 4% of the population made their first online purchases, 6.5% ordered services for the first time, and 20% had their first e-vision (Orange Polska 2020b). That is why the need, e.g., food delivery services, increased. Furthermore, online working and learning have contributed to the increased use of computers, cameras, desks, and online shopping. In Poland, as in other European countries, people restricted movements, especially by sharing mobility. On the contrary, the trust has been put to a private mode of transport, especially private car. Moreover, in April 2020, Veturilo bikes disappeared from Warsaw. It came back in May after a month-long break caused by the government driving ban. It provoked widespread criticism because, in many countries, it was even encouraged to ride on two wheels, particularly that in April, the number of confirmed coronavirus infections in Poland reached around 250–520 per day. Unfortunately, the pandemic contributed to the bankruptcy of the Polish branch of Nextbike, the operator of Veturilo, since 2012.

A different situation is in the crowdfunding sector in Poland. The coronaviral downturn has not closed investors' portfolios for equity crowdfunding. On the contrary, the industry boasts further records and great interest on the part of both issuers and cash holders. In general, although the economic meltdown usually entails strong restrictions on household spending and reduces the willingness of households to invest, capital markets are experiencing a renaissance during the coronavirus era in Poland (Torchała 2020). However, it is difficult to determine unequivocally whether the increased interest of issuers should be linked to the crisis or the natural development of the idea of equity crowdfunding. Besides, there are increasingly public collections on the Internet for health reasons. The money collected in this form is intended to help hospitals to combat the coronavirus epidemic. It is about purchasing protective measures and medical equipment. One of the actions is run by the Siepomaga Foundation (Koślicki 2020). On the other hand, this year was dominated by the lowest transfers—up to 50 złotych (around 10 €). Such small support constitutes more than three-quarters of all payments (in 2019, it was less than 70%). The limited generosity of Poles might be caused by the negative effects of the COVID-19 crisis, which affected the condition of the economy and household finances. However, that could also be influenced by a significant increase in the share of two age groups in crowdfunding collections, for example, the youngest and oldest internet users. Nearly 200% growth among the youngest and over 150% among the oldest internet users (Duszczyk 2020).

In Poland, similarly to other countries, the sector of the online course has recorded a big growth, as well as dynamic development. The coronavirus has forced many people to organise their lives anew, both privately and professionally. Many areas of activities have moved to the Internet—from work and learning to shopping and entertainment. In addition, all the universities have gone to remote studies. Some private universities have managed to transfer their educational activities to online platforms such as Microsoft Teams within two working days. Some people also use their time at home to develop their qualifications. Thus, platforms such as Khan Academy, Coursera, Skillshare, and Akademia PARP—programming, finance, marketing, law, management, and personal skills have been gaining popularity.

Moreover, the co-working sector has been negatively affected by the COVID-19 crisis. The possibility of having an office in a co-working space definitely allows for greater comfort of work. It is a great alternative to an office in a situation of money shortage to rent separate premises and gives the opportunity to collaborate with other entrepreneurs. Besides, it is conducive to establishing new business relations. An additional advantage is low costs of space rental, assured access to utilities, and often even other benefits—such as coffee machine, kitchen, and bathroom. The co-working industry has met with great interest from micro-entrepreneurs. Unfortunately, the coronavirus pandemic has slowed down the development of that sector.

During the COVID-19 pandemic, nearly 60% of Poles got involved in helping people in need of support. The survey conducted by Orange Polska (2020a) shows that people most often donated material resources, including financial ones, and almost 41% of citizens actively participated in aid actions, offering time and skills to others, for example, by sewing masks, doing shopping and cooking meals for seniors. More than half of the respondents realised that only by helping each other can they live more easily among the specific forms of involvement, the sewing of masks for foundations and hospitals, shopping, and the preparation of meals for seniors, as well as learning how to use messengers. Poles also have paid a lot of attention to children, helping them with homework or giving them online tutoring. Furthermore, also Polish artists in the range of #hot16challenge2, have organised a collection of money to support healthcare workers in the fight against the coronavirus, as well as to equip medical staff. The collection has been an effect of collaboration between artist and crowdfunding platform Siepomaga.pl.

## Initiatives Operating Under the Sharing Economy in Poland

Accommodation and transport are the services regarded as the most commonly related to the sharing economy. However, the catalogue of sectors and included services is a lot much bigger. Beyond, there are some examples of initiatives under sharing economy operating in Poland:

- Car and scooter sharing in cities, such as Panek (car-sharing), jedenslad (scooters). Unfortunately, one of the main electric car-sharing platforms, Vozilla, ended its operation in April 2020.
- Sharing bicycles (e.g., NextBike, Mevo), sharing bicycles and electric scooters operate in every central city, e.g., NextBike, Mevo, as well as international big scooter platforms are active: Lime, Bolt.
- Mobility services, BlaBlaCar—hitchhiking, Yanosik—exchange of information about incidents on the road (accidents, road works, radars, road checks, traffic jams, navigation—little similar to Waze) and hitchhiking, jadezabiore.pl—a unique form of parcel delivery. There are also international platforms such as Uber or Bolt in this area.
- Sharing a flat or room, e.g., Otodom, gratka.pl, gumtree.pl and international: Airbnb, Couchsurfing, Booking.com.
- Online courses: Akademia PARP—finance, marketing, law, management, personal skills, strefakorsow.pl—informatics/programming. According to the pandemic situation, almost all form of education is currently moved to the online method. Exceptions are practical classes in technical or medical studies, which require students to participate in laboratories.
- Provision of services by private persons, e.g., pozamiatane.pl (housekeeping), niania.pl (nursery). Such services are also available on generic classified portals. They have been particularly popular during the COVID-19 lockdown, while many people helped to organise free daily shopping for older people.
- Shared office—co-working: spacing.pl—a platform presenting the local offer of many co-working places (currently 280) in all major cities

of the country, allowing for localisation maps, specific services, forms of lease.

- Crowdfunding platforms: in Poland, there are platforms with a general profile (there are no fundamental restrictions as to the subject of the collection)—zrzutka.pl (PLN 115 m /28 m €, 4.5 × growth since 2017), PolakPotrafi.pl (PLN 24.3 m/5.6 m €, 11 × growth since 2017), support.to (PLN 23.9 million, 3 × growth). There are also specialist platforms, e.g., providing financing for start-ups, co-financing of projects/equity—beesfund.pl (PLN 57 million), findfunds.pl (PLN 10 million), foundedbyme.com. Popular are platforms supporting donation/charity, e.g., Siepomaga (typical collections for the needy), or similar activities, e.g., aukcje.wosp.org.pl (operated by the allegro.pl auction portal), where people put items up for sale and payment is transferred to the largest charity buying in Poland—the Great Orchestra of Christmas Charity. Moreover, there are specialist platforms for the patronage of the arts and artists: patronite.pl and wspieramkulture.pl.
- Sale of food products directly from farmers (e.g., Local-Rolnik.pl, food cooperatives—not applicable to markets).
- Sharing resources—lost keys or other objects equipped with a Bluetooth geolocative—over a million mobile phone users in Poland (mainly car drivers) use the Yanosik application, whose main function is to inform about the situation on the road. If any of the phones with the Yanosik application is similar to a lost object equipped with a low-voltage Bluetooth geolocative (range up to several dozen or several dozen metres), it sends information about the approximate location of that object to the owner of the lost object via the platform. An interesting solution is a platform for exchanging opinions about doctors and medical facilities with the possibility of making an appointment: znanylekarz.pl (and its foreign branches in Turkey, Spain, Italy, Czech Republic, Mexico, Colombia, Brazil, Argentina, Peru and Chile; e.g., Doctoralia, MioDottore, DoctorTakvimi, ZnamyLekar) or ktomalek.pl—a platform allowing you to check the availability of medicine in pharmacies, which is particularly important when you urgently need medicine, and it is not a commonly available one.

- Second hand/second use—gratka.pl, Vinted, tablica.pl—bought by Naspers NPN (JSE) and rebranded to olx.pl (abbreviation from the 'online exchange').
- Local initiatives—platforms for participatory budgets in cities, local groups, and societies.

A lot of confusion arose around the sharing economy, largely due to the lack of one coherent definition. Inevitably the development of initiatives goes into a significant polarity between bottom-up projects based on sharing economy, such as item exchange groups, food farms, different types of cooperatives, and often huge corporations using that trend for business purposes. Observing the presence, everything points that there will be a further increase in a variety of initiatives in the future, from equity crowdfunding to local initiatives concerned with the needs of locally active groups and societies. Actually, in Poland, the fastest developing sector is crowdfunding.

## Summary

Over the past decade, many companies using sharing economy business model have started and conducted global expansion. From promising start-ups, they have become global companies. The sharing economy is the phenomenon that dynamically develops in many sectors of the economy, on different levels: global, international, national, local. In many aspects, it is a challenge for law regulators as it is related to various regulations, such as tax, labour, and consumer law. However, countries with a higher level of economic freedom have a larger sharing economy (Bergh et al. 2018). Thus, on the one side, that means economic freedom is important for the development of a collaborative economy, and on the other side, it shows that it is worth opposing excessive state regulation. The rationale behind that is the collaborative economy creates new and interesting business opportunities, generates jobs and growth, and often plays an important role in creating business more socially and environmentally sustainable. It also enables a better allocation of resources and hence contributing to the transition to the circular economy. Furthermore, the economy of sharing can have a profound impact on long-established business models in many strategic sectors, such as transport, accommodation, food, health, and finance. Nevertheless, in the implementation of the sharing economy, it becomes necessary to ensure a high level of consumer protection and respect for workers' rights, as well as to spread the tax burden properly.

As the global economy, also sharing economy, was strongly affected by the coronavirus crisis, the especially negative impact was noticed in the short-term rental, transportation, as well as co-working. The social distance, restrictions in movement, along quarantine have caused those sectors needed to adjust their activity to the new, adverse situation. For example, in the case of Uber, a new branch of it has developed, namely Uber Eats, in case of a short-term rental, owners offering such services, using platforms such as Airbnb and Booking.com decided to make mid-term or long-term rental for the time of coronavirus pandemic. Besides, among residents, there is an expectation of decreasing the prices of apartments as before COVID-19, the use of platforms such as Airbnb or Boo king.com by developers increased the bubble on the real estate market in Poland.

Except for sectors such as crowdfunding, transportation, short-time rental, can be observed rapidly growing development of local cooperatives, especially in the food sector. Those cooperatives are entirely based on trust between consumers and suppliers. They want to buy food directly from farmers, without intermediaries. Besides, they want it to be organic, but it does not always have to be certified. Throughout the years of activity, they believe that their suppliers do not cheat. Such cooperatives are a way to shorten supply chains. A cooperative, such as Future Farms, is a way not to transport food from a distance and to decentralise crops. Monocultures are not good for the environment. Bringing food closer to consumers affects not only the quality of food but also the level of food waste. A lot of food goes to the basket already at the transport stage (Skiba 2019).

# References


Andreoni, James. 1990. 'Impure Altruism and Donations to Public Goods: A Theory of Warm-Glow Giving.' *The Economic Journal* 100 (401): 464–77.

Andersson, Lennart, Andreas Gläfke, Timo Möller, and Tobias Schneiderbauer. 2020. *Why Shared Mobility Is Poised to Make a Comeback After the Crisis*. Atlanta: McKinsey & Co. Accessed November 15, 2020. https://www.mckinsey.com/~/media/McKinsey/Industries/AutomotiveandAssembly/OurInsights/Why-shared-mobility-is-poised-to-make-a-comeback-after-the-crisis-vF.pdf?shouldIndex=false.

Bergh, Andreas, Alexander Funcke, and Joakim Wernberg. 2018. *Timbro Sharing Economy Index*. https://timbro.se/ekonomi/timbro-sharing-economy-index/.

Botsman, Rachel, and Roo Rogers. 2011. *What's Mine Is Yours: How Collaborative Consumption Is Changing the Way We Live*. New York: Harper Collins Publishers.

Duszczyk, Michał. 2020. 'Crowdfunding bez hojnego wsparcia Polaków.' *Rzeczpospolita*, October 1. Accessed November 20, 2020. https://www.rp.pl/Finanse/310019890-Crowdfunding-bez-hojnego-wsparcia-Polakow.html.

European Commission. 2018. *Flash Eurobarometer 467 Report: The Use of the Collaborative Economy April 2018 October 2018 Survey Requested by the European Commission*. Flash Eurobarometer 467 Report. Brussels: European Commission, Directorate-General for Communication. Accessed December 18, 2020. https://data.europa.eu/data/datasets/s2184_467_eng?locale=en.

GUS (Główny Urząd Statystyczny). 2018. *Information Society in Poland Results of Statistical Surveys in the Years 2014–2018*. Warszawa, Szczecin: Główny Urząd Statystyczny. Accessed February 15, 2021. http://stat.gov.pl/en/topics/science-and-technology/science-and-technology/.

GUS (Główny Urząd Statystyczny). 2019. *Information Society in Poland Results of Statistical Surveys in the Years 2015–2019*. Warszawa: Główny Urząd Statystyczny. Accessed February 24, 2021. http://stat.gov.pl/en/topics/science-and-technology/science-and-technology/.

Hawlitschek, Florian, Timm Teubner, and Christof Weinhardt. 2016. 'Trust in the Sharing Economy.' *Die Unternehmung* 70 (1): 26–44. Accessed March 15, 2021. https://doi.org/10.5771/0042-059x-2016-1-26.

Koślicki, Krzysztof. 2020. '*Zbiórki publiczne na walkę z epidemią koronawirusa mają skutki podatkowe*.' Accessed October 23, 2020. https://www.prawo.

pl/podatki/zbiorki-publiczne-na-walke-z-epidemia-koronawirusa-jakie-skutki,498849.html.

Lozzi, Giacomo, Maria Rodrigues, Eduardo Marcucci, Tharsis Teoh, Valerio Gatta, and Valerio Pacelli. 2020. *Research for TRAN Committee: COVID-19 and Urban Mobility: Impacts and Perspectives*. Brussels: European Parliament, Policy Department for Structural and Cohesion Policies. Accessed February 19, 2021 https://www.europarl.europa.eu/thinktank/en/document.html?reference=IPOL_IDA(2020)652213.

Nadolska, Aleksandra, and Wojciech Nadolski. 2019. 'Ramy prawne aspektów sharing economy w Polsce (Legal Framework of Sharing Economy in Poland).' *Zeszyty Prawnicze Biura Analiz Sejmowych Kancelarii Sejmu* 2 (62): 9–42.

Orange Polska. 2020a. '*Co o pomaganiu pokazał nam COVID-19, a co zostanie z nami po pandemii? (What Has COVID-19 Shown Us About Helping, and What Remains of the Pandemic?).*' Accessed February 10, 2021. https://biuroprasowe.orange.pl/informacje-prasowe/co-o-pomaganiu-pokazal-nam-covid-19-a-co-zostanie-z-nami-po-pandemii/.

Orange Polska. 2020b. '*Jak zmieniła nas pandemia (How Did the Pandemic Change Us)?*' Accessed January 15, 2021. https://biuroprasowe.orange.pl/blog/jak-zmienila-nas-pandemia/.

Osztovits, Ádám, Árpád Kőszegi, Bence Nagy, and Bence Damjanovics. 2015. *Sharing or Paring? Growth of the Sharing Economy*. Budapest: PriceWaterhouseCoopers Magyarország.

Republic of Poland. 2019. Parliament. *O zmianie Ustawy o transporcie drogowym towarów oraz niektórych innych ustaw.* Law no. Dz.U. 2019 poz. 1180. Enacted May 16, 2019. http://isap.sejm.gov.pl/isap.nsf/download.xsp/WDU20190001180/U/D20191180Lj.pdf.

Roland Berger Strategy Consultants. 2014. 'Shared Mobility.' *Think Act*, no. July: 1–18. Accessed January 11, 2021. https://www.rolandberger.com/publications/publication_pdf/roland_berger_tab_shared_mobility_1.pdf.

Skiba, Paulina. 2019. '*Future Farms: Lekarstwo na problemy żywieniowe świata? Wywiad z Dr Anną Urbańską, biologiem molekularnym, współzałożycielką Projektu Future Farms [Future Farms – a Cure for the World's Nutritional Problems? Interview with Dr. Anna Urbańska].*' Accessed November 5, 2020. Biotechnologia.pl. 2019. https://biotechnologia.pl/biotechnologia/future-farms-lekarstwo-na-problemy-zywieniowe-swiata-wywiad-z-dr-anna-urbanska-biologiem-molekularnym-wspolzalozycielka-projektu-future-farms,19211.

Śledziewska, Katarzyna, Kristóf Gyódi, Wojciech Hardy, and Joanna Mazur. 2019. '*Airbnb w Warszawie. Charakterystyka rynku i wyzwania dla miasta.*' Accessed April 5, 2021. https://www.delab.uw.edu.pl/en/publikacje/airbnb-w-warszawie-charakterystyka-rynku-i-wyzwania-dla-miasta/.

Szostak, Piotr. 2020. 'Pandemia koronawirusa zmieni miasta? Setki mieszkań z Airbnb wracają na rynek najmu długoterminowego.' *Gazeta Wyborcza*, March 31.

Teubner, Timm. 2014. 'Thoughts on the Sharing Economy.' *Proceedings of the International Conferences on ICT, Society and Human Beings 2014, Web Based Communities and Social Media 2014, e-Commerce 2014, Information Systems Post-Implementation and Change Management 2014 and e-Health 2014: Part of the Multi Conf*, no. July 2014: 322–326.

Torchała, Adam. 2020. 'Equity crowdfunding z rekordami mimo pandemii.' *Bankier.pl*, May 14. Accessed November 17, 2020. https://www.bankier.pl/wiadomosc/Equity-crowdfunding-z-rekordami-mimo-pandemii-7882816.html.

## Suggested Readings

Bucher, Eliane, Christian Fieseler, Matthes Fleck, and Christoph Lutz. 2018. 'Authenticity and the Sharing Economy.' *Academy of Management Discoveries* 4 (3): 294–313. https://doi.org/10.5465/amd.2016.0161.

Ertz, Myriam, and Sébastien Leblanc-Proulx. 2018. 'Sustainability in the Collaborative Economy: A Bibliometric Analysis Reveals Emerging Interest.' *Journal of Cleaner Production* 196: 1073–1085. https://doi.org/10.1016/j.jclepro.2018.06.095.

Kostakis, Vasilis, and Michael Bauwens. 2014. *Network Society and Future Scenarios for a Collaborative Economy*. London: Palgrave Macmillan. https://doi.org/10.1057/9781137406897.

Zgiep, Łukasz. 2019. '*Polish Collaborative Economy Honeycomb 3.0.*' Accessed November 13, 2020. https://zgiep.com/wp-content/uploads/2019/06/Honeycomb-PL-3.0-.jpg.

## Relevant Websites

Jadęzabiorę: https://www.jadezabiore.pl.
Polakpotrafi: https://polakpotrafi.pl.

Siepomaga: https://www.siepomaga.pl.
Wymiennik: http://wymiennik.org.
Zrzutka: https://zrzutka.pl.

# 17

# Advances of Sharing Economy in Agriculture and Tourism Sectors of Albania

Eglantina Hysa and Alba Demneri Kruja

## Introduction

This chapter is looking at the agricultural and tourism sectors in Albania to show how sharing/collaborative economy is gaining ground and what are the potentialities. Additionally, this study aims to look at how stakeholders from the quadruple helix can meaningfully contribute to sharing economy and its' expansion throughout these sectors.

The definition of Wosskow (2014) describing the 'sharing economy' as 'online platforms that help people share access to assets, resources, time and skills' (p. 7), is found to fit with the sharing economy practices in Albania and at the same time how the sharing concept is being

E. Hysa (✉)
Department of Economics, Epoka University, Tirana, Albania
e-mail: ehysa@epoka.edu.al

A. D. Kruja
Department of Business Administration, Epoka University, Tirana, Albania
e-mail: akruja@epoka.edu.al



V. Česnuitytė et al. (eds.), *The Sharing Economy in Europe*,
https://doi.org/10.1007/978-3-030-86897-0_17

perceived in this country. Meanwhile, in order to have people that actively use digital platforms, it is important to screen the digitalisation capacities in this country. As such, although a middle-income country, the digitisation process has progressed relatively on similar criteria as with developed countries. Nearly 97.5% of enterprises have made usage of computers during 2019 for job-related issues (Institute of Statistics 2020a). Meanwhile, 97.8% of them have internet access, while in the European Union (EU) countries, this ratio is, on average, around 97%. Albania government has done some concrete steps towards digitalisation and convergence with the EU countries. As such, being in full compliance with the EU Acquis Communautaire, Albania adopted the legal framework of digitalisation. In this line, Albania is having a full understanding and compliance with the Digital Single Market too (Ministry of Innovation and Public Administration 2014). Even though there are many adoptions in this area, still the concept of the term 'collaborative economy' and 'sharing economy' is not well-perceived from the business side, and this awareness is being modest in Albania (Economy Co-Responsibility Learning 2016). There are evidenced implementations of collaborative platforms in sectors such as tourism, agriculture, health, food delivery, and transportation, but still there cannot be found a collaborative economy definition of the country.

Referring to the Timbro Sharing Economy Index (TSEI), Albania is listed 79th out of 213 countries, wherein 2018 scored 3.3 points, considering the highest value of this index to be 100 (TIMBRO 2018). Even though Albania is found in the 2nd quarter of the list, the sharing index of this country is still below the other Western Balkan Countries (WBC). Montenegro is being at the top of WBC, ranked 4th in the overall list and having the sharing index equal to 58 points. Based on the TIMBRO (2018) database, the rest of the countries are found to be listed as follows: Bosnia and Herzegovina are placed in 64th place (5.7 sharing index), Macedonia is placed in 67th place (4.7 sharing index), and Serbia is placed in the 71st place (4.2 sharing index).

Kemp (2020) measures internet penetration in Albania for 2020 as 72%, which is much higher than the worldwide penetration of 59%. A high level of Internet's dissemination and usage is an indication of a high potential of social networks users, as well as a potential for the sharing economy further developments as its main infrastructure condition. Yet, the information and communication technology (ICT) industry's contribution is recognised as a policy framework aiming to strengthen the economy and central to the medium- and long-term vision of Albania's development (International Telecommunication Union 2016). A synergic collaboration among the ecosystem stakeholders is crucial for the industries' as well as the economic development of the country (Kruja 2020a). The emergence of collaborative clusters composed of purposive stakeholders from diverse industry areas such as agriculture, tourism, public sector, and others are decisive in sitting side by side the main actors of these industries (International Telecommunication Union 2016). Moreover, the role and support of ICT is determinant, as it is in the centre of interaction with different ICT cluster ecosystems such as agriculture ecosystem, tourism cluster ecosystem, public sector cluster ecosystem, and another cluster ecosystem (International Telecommunication Union 2016).

However, not to be underestimated, these sectors need to have incentives and ongoing processes of entrepreneurial actions. For instance, as one of the essential sectors in Albania, the agriculture sector needs to be pushed by the entrepreneurial spirit to be boosted (Hysa and Mansi 2020). In addition, there are many multi-dimensional contributions of the sharing economy to a country's development, but at the same time, its implementation is combined with many multi-dimensional challenges. Researchers argue that through these collaborative platforms, it is achieved an increase in employment as well as resource usage efficiency (Stahel 2010; Hysa et al. 2020). Another main contribution is the transparency of all the processes, as they are performed online, by reducing corruption and building trust among partners.

Meanwhile, there are some developments in sharing and collaborative economy, Albania as many other countries, still lack legislative regulations on performing necessary sharing economy-related activities and transactions. In terms of specific policies, there were concerns about taxation on ICT firms and start-ups, the role procurement plays in supporting the ecosystem, support for key actors and projects in the ecosystem, and the enforcement of intellectual property rights (ITU

2016). So legislative regulations are needed for taxation, social security, and health insurance (Hysa et al. 2021). Besides these concerns, Corradini and Re (2016) point out the financial support required for digital investments, which is mostly facilitated by public–private partnerships, along with ICT skilled personnel appropriate for maintaining this continuous development.

To exploit the digitalisation potentiality, bottlenecks need to be removed, and an adequate environment has to be created (Corradini and Re 2016). Hysa et al. (2020) propose the quadruple helix, as a collaboration framework of sustainable innovation, by also integrating the society helix as the main component of consumer awareness. Meanwhile, Tukiainen et al. (2015) introduce the city as an orchestrator for innovation by arguing that 'cities should establish an active dialogue with their citizens, and private and public sectors actors to co-create, develop, test, and offer service innovations that utilise diverse sets of platforms such as living labs' (p. 16). In this study, taking into consideration that Albania is a developing country in need of government policymaking and infrastructure support of sustainable innovation, it is proposed the quadruple helix collaboration framework, in-between and among academia-industry-government-society to achieve an effective and efficient collaborative economy.

## Sharing Economy Developments in Albania

Even though the concept of sharing is relatively new to the Albanian market, Albania succeeded to make significant progress in the sharing economy. In this last decade, the usage of sharing platforms was widely used by both public, private, and not for profit entities. Digitalisation, technology advancement and innovation should be the fundamental tools to develop the sharing economy. As such, the Government of Albania developed two strategies supporting innovation and platforms needed for the sharing economy. The first strategy, the National Strategy for Science, Technology, and Innovation (STI) 2009–2015, provisioned the capacity building of public and private entities with special emphasis on STI. The National Strategy for STI is the first strategy of this kind, settling a long-term platform of research and innovation development in Albania (Council of Ministers 2009). This strategy was followed by the 'Digital Agenda for Albania 2015–2020,' which presents a cross-cutting strategy and serves to strengthen the process of innovation. Concretely, different from the first one, this second strategy aimed to digitalise as much as possible all public institutions. Through this strategy, Albania lined up the embracement of the digital revolution, supporting the creation of new opportunities for citizens and business to benefit (Ministry of Innovation and Public Administration 2014).

In this regard, and in compliance with the first and second strategy, in 2014, the government of Albania launched the governmental platform, a central one, e-Albania. E-Albania offers an extensive list of services that help each and every individual, citizens of Albania or foreigners to download instant official documents. This portal is an important support structure for businesses and public institutions too. The COVID-19 lockdown increased the visibility and usage of this portal. Due to some constraints, citizens were obliged to use the portal, increasing both awareness and usage. At the same time, it is seen that the portal has multiplied its' functions and services, increasing this support to its' users. Apart from governmental incentives to become an 'e-service government,' another important factor in the sharing economy is the municipality of Tirana. Starting with the example of the Chinese bike-sharing giant Mobile in 2018, the municipality of Tirana intends to become a smart city.

With regard to private entities, the sharing economy is introduced by some globally operating firms. At the same time, the Albanian companies have been substantial influencers in adopting the international markets and trends and becoming crucial drivers to innovation in the domestic market. As aforementioned, two main sectors for Albania, agriculture, and tourism, have also been mostly influenced by the collaborative economy. Table 17.1 presents the examples of domestic and global scaled division of sectoral analysis division industries having some examples of sharing (collaborating) economy for the case of Albania.

**Table 17.1** Industry-based examples of the sharing economy in Albania

| Analysed sectors | Selected collaborative examples |
|---|---|
| Agriculture | Agroquality (domestic)<br>MIA (domestic) |
| Tourism | |
| | IntoAlbania (Innovative Tourism in Albania) (domestic)<br>Innovation Map Albania (domestic)<br>Team Albanians (domestic)<br>Softmogul (domestic) |

*Source* Own elaboration

# Sectorial Developments and Complementary Strengths, Weaknesses, Opportunities, and Threats Analysis

This session is focussed at the sectorial analysis of agriculture and tourism. These sectors are found to be key sectors for Albania, given its' natural resource endowment and geographic position. Moreover, it can be noticed that the sharing economy is mainly evident in these sectors. This might be because of their swift development and their success in the developments of the same sectors abroad.

## Agriculture Sector Endowments

Agriculture is one of the main critical economic sectors of Albania as it contributes to approximately one-fifth of the country's GDP (Gecaj et al. 2019). The country's geographic positioning, 1/3 of which is wet by the Adriatic and Ionian Seas, enables cultivating agricultural products in a fertile land of coastal areas where is concentrated most of the production of vegetables as well as the cultivation of fruit trees, while in the northern part, chestnut cultivation occupies significant weight, and in mountainous areas, a wide range of medicinal plants and aromatic plants are grown (Kruja 2020b). According to the Institute of Statistics (2020b), for the year 2019, around 40% of the Albanian population is registered as a labour force working in the agriculture sector. Sustainability is critical in this sector as 'for local food producers requires a balance of supply (from producers) with demand (from consumers) in the face of volatile wealthier and prices' (Flora and Bregendahl 2012, p. 329). This makes the sector fragile in the need to continuously expand the market through product exporting to achieve economies of scale and increase its profits (Kruja 2020b).

This sector represents full integration possibilities into the supply chain and low-cost labour force. Due to its' favourable environmental conditions and opportunities of competitiveness in European markets, this sector embodies innovative, inclusive capacities in using digital platforms, peer-to-peer (P2P) collaboration, and developed collaboration on a larger scale, including main actors in the economy (industry-academia-government-society). However, despite that, there exist some disorders and a lack of regulations in this sector. Generally, this sector is composed of small-sized farms, which is rather difficult to include in a common collaborative structure. Additionally, there is a lack of a standard quality control system, which again poses some critical barriers. Collaboration is perceived as crucial for the enhancement of innovative processes, minimising the risk that entrepreneurs continuously face, especially for sustainable economic development (Kruja 2020b). The proper existence and a functional quadruple helix model that supports the collaborative economy in agriculture would serve to solve the identification of the clients, the identification of suitable trade networks, supply segments opportunities, and market price adjustments.

## Tourism Sector Vitality

The tourism sector constitutes 26.2% of Albania's GDP (World Travel & Tourism Council 2018). Albania provides a variety of differentiated entertainment opportunities to tourists through mountain tourism, seaside tourism, historical tourism, and religious tourism. It is one of the main socio-economic resources of the country, contributing not only to job creation and employment but also to infrastructure and technological developments. The impact of technology in this sector has been a long-studied subject where researchers try to understand how technology shapes service processes and whether such enactment improves customer satisfaction and sector performance (Sari et al. 2006; Law et al. 2014; Melián-González and Bulchand-Gidumal 2016; Ferizi and Kruja 2018).

Collaborative economy in the tourism sector in Albania, as in other countries, is found to be highly vibrant and relatively competitive. This is due to a globally increased demand for tourism, especially for global tourism. In this context, the digital platforms (online applications allowing participants to interact with each other) are widely used by Albanians and foreigners, for example, Albania Tourism, Albania. al, Info Albania, Smile Albania, and Thema Tourism App. Yet, the tourism sector is characterised by two main sharing economic models, complementary to each other, which makes it quite interesting. The labour market in this sector is mainly short-term contracts or freelance work, otherwise defined as 'gig economy.' The other form of the economic model in tourism is the peer-to-peer economy, when the exchange of goods and services is directly concluded among two individuals, without the intermediation/intervention of a third party.

## Strengths, Weaknesses, Opportunities, and Threats Analysis

This section is devoted to a general strengths, weaknesses, opportunities, and threats (SWOT) analysis evaluation for the Albanian case. As a first step, this study tries to find out the current situation of the agriculture and tourism sectors (given above) and then the main advantages and disadvantages that may arise in general. The best way to have a concrete framework of capacities, opportunities, and barriers is the SWOT analysis of both sectors.

Bakker and Twining-Ward (2018), in their study, have identified the top 10 opportunities and challenges of P2P accommodation from the literature. Accordingly, this study can highlight the selected features of this list of opportunities and challenges to be most evident in the case of Albania: Opportunities: (1) Helps attract new markets and demographics to new and existing destinations. Influences the type and nature of visitor purchases and services; (2) Builds consumer trust to visit a destination in new ways and try new products; (3) Lowers the barriers to entry for entrepreneurship; and (4) Increases access to market, which is particularly helpful for community-based homestays. Challenges cover: (1) Unregistered and unregulated P2P accommodation; (2) Not following tax laws; (3) P2P accommodation may cause housing prices and rents to increase; (4) May put visitors at higher risk; and (5) Providers lack organisation and representation.

As seen, the incorporation of sharing and collaborative aspects within this sector foresees significant progress and enhancement. On the other side, each of the challenges can be offset by a tight collaboration of main actors in the quadruple helix model. For instance, challenge 1, 2, and 4 can be improved by governmental intervention, which needs to be in frequent consultations with businesses, academia, and civil society. The collaboration among these actors should be an ongoing process that functions as a chain giving and getting the support of each other to improve as much as possible the sharing economy.

Figure 17.1 summarises the integrated SWOT analysis of both sectors considered in this study. The strengths are mainly related to the capacities of the existing young age structure and the readiness of academia to widely collaborate. At the same time, weaknesses are mainly related

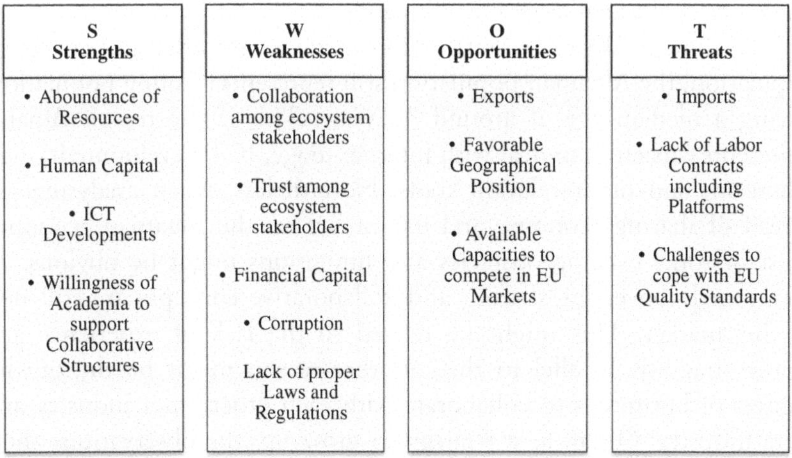


**Fig. 17.1** Strengths, weaknesses, opportunities, and threats analysis of the main sharing economy sectors in Albania (*Source* Own elaboration)

to the lack of appropriate policies to support sharing economy. Lastly, opportunities and threats are clear-cuts with each other, meaning that it depends on how they are managed and surpassed.

## Future Insights for a Solid Foundation of the Sharing Economy in Albania

Accordingly, some suggestions are drawn based on the above-mentioned findings, which support as best as possible the concept of sharing economy. To be in line with the characteristics and features of the Albanian market structures, nature of domestic businesses, and businesses climate and environment, it is proposed the establishment of a solid framework of the 'quadruple helix model.' According to the EC's project 'ECORL Economy Co-responsibility Learning' (2016), online shopping, as one of the indicators related to sharing platforms, it is found to be not a common habit in Albania. Additionally, according to this project outcomes and suggestions, people in this country tend to rely too much on institutions to solve their problems. Inspired by the conclusions of this comparative study, it strongly advocates the collaboration of four main actors of the aforementioned model.

Even though Albania is starting to experience the effects of an ageing population, the Albanian population still represents a young population, having a median age of around 36 years. This is the reason Albania represents capacities to deal with internet usage, ICT development, digitalisation, and other relevant tools. Nevertheless, when analysing the spread of sharing economy and its' impact on the Albanian economy, a list of some existing obstacles and limitations might be obvious. As mentioned above, the sharing and collaborative concepts are still new to this market. This might be related to the lack of experience and market fragility. Parallel to this, another reason might be the unwillingness of businesses to collaborate with each other, inter-industry and intra-industry. Often, as a strategy to grow up, the observations show that the businesses in Albania decide to compete instead of collaborating. Apart from internal structures and decisions are taken by the companies, there are other external factors negatively affecting the sharing economy.

The business environment in Albania is surely affected by the low performance of the sharing economy. As such, one of the external factors is the corruption level, which is relatively high compared to EU countries. Again, and still, important impeding factors to sharing economy is low trust and low reinforcement of laws and regulations. Moreover, the existence of problems with property rights and related issues might emerge as a fundamental obstacle for sharing and collaborative opportunities.

Universities, vocational education, and training (VET) entities, and institutes play a major role in the concept of sharing economy. They can be supporters with the platform conceptualisation and implementation, they can promote entrepreneurial spirit and foster ICT developments, and they can build bridges with the businesses to come up with solutions addressing the market needs. Development in sharing and collaborative economy can be achieved by having a smart combination of labour, capital, land, and entrepreneurship, with investment, exploration, education, and technology innovation (Berhani and Hysa 2013; Vladi and Hysa 2019).

Knowledge is the key element of the innovation systems, and the institutions which have an important role in its development can be stated as universities and academic institutions (develop and transfer knowledge), government organisations, and innovative enterprises (Kruja 2013). To achieve this knowledge in the form of sustainable innovation with an impact on sustainable development, the among and in-between industry-academia-government-society as defined by the 'quadruple helix model' is crucial. This collaboration model is an extension of Etzkowitz and Leydesdorff (1995) university-industry-government triple helix spiral collaboration, which recognised 'media-based and the culture-based public' as a fourth helix of collaboration by emphasising that 'culture and values, on the one hand, and the way how "public reality" is being constructed and communicated by the media, on the other hand, influence every national innovation system' (Carayannis and Campbell 2009, p. 206). Yun and Liu (2019) emphasise that the quadruple helix collaboration model is crucial for social, environmental, economic, cultural, policy, as well as knowledge sustainability necessary to bring about open innovation micro-dynamics and macro-dynamics. Through the synergic collaboration aiming at the advocacy and advancement of a sharing economy, the expected economic developments will be brought up.

Finally, there is an absence of transparent testimony of the quadruple helix support among industry-academia-government-society collaboration. Whenever sharing economy had been stimulated by the support of these actors' synergy, the sharing economy would have driven the economy forward through lower costs, increased consumer surplus, innovation, and exposure to larger markets. Figure 17.2 provides the framework for effective and efficient implementation of the collaborative economy for Albania, but not only. Through a synergic collaboration among the main economy's stakeholders, actors of the value co-creation process, the collaborative economy implementation will turn back to a sustainable development process to the country, enhancing its economic, social, and environmental improvement.

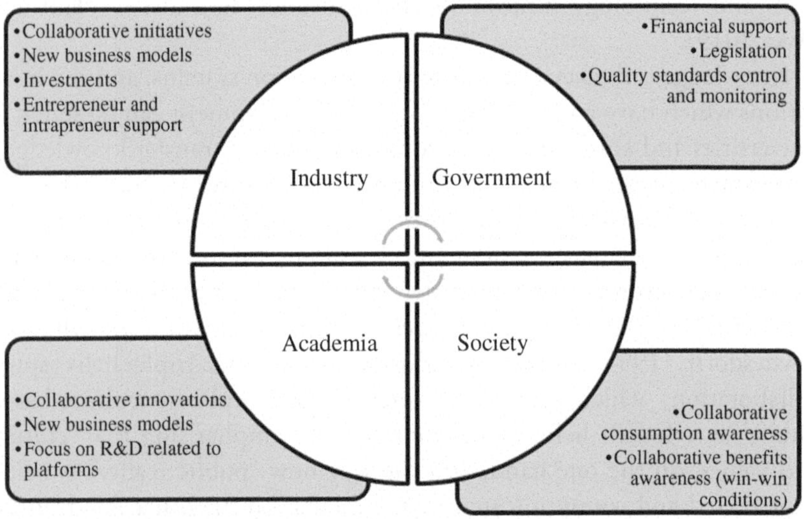


**Fig. 17.2** Quadruple helix framework for the collaborative economy effectiveness (*Source* Own elaboration)

## Discussion and Summary

As one of the post-communist countries, Albania is yet considered a country in transition with respect to economic development and progress. The good news is that Albania is inspiring to join the EU in 2004, and thus, it aims to adopt the EU legislation and frameworks in regard to development. As the technology and innovation formulated policy are the right way to transform the economy into a knowledge-based economy (Alfaro et al. 2019), it can be said that this country has made some progress in adapting some strategies at the national level, which have in focus ICT development and digitalisation. Another positive aspect that helps in the adaption of technology and innovation is the young generation. Being keen on technology, the young generation promises to integrate novelties faster and further, which somehow can be considered as a very first step towards a collaborative or sharing economy.

Having a fragile economy, Albania is representing considerable limitations. First, there is a lack of common understanding of benefits and positive outcomes that might arise from a collaborative and sharing economy. The positive outcomes have to be considered at the micro-level and macro-level. The governmental bodies, non-governmental organisations (NGOs), and other relevant actors have to increase awareness and use the necessary channels to promote collaboration and sharing economy.

This research comes up with many contributions having crucial theoretical implications. First, the study acknowledged that the quadruple helix collaboration among industry-government-academia-society is the main facilitator and coordinator of the collaborative economy. The findings of the study encourage, at the same time, scholars to further research the impact of this collaboration on sharing economy enhancements, developments, and performance on other sectors as well as other developing and developed countries. Aside from the theoretical implications, this research points out also practical implications related to the ecosystem stakeholders—the quadruple helix actors: the government; the industry, the academia; and the society. The study findings highlight the necessity of collaboration among and in between the quadruple helix actors to achieve effective and efficient implementation of sharing economy. Albania, as a country with an abundance of natural resources, has a lot of capacities to serve not only domestic customers but also foreign customers of the agriculture and tourism sectors. These two sectors are decisive in the country's development as they both contribute almost to half of its gross domestic product (GDP). Through the sharing economy implementation, both sectors' entrepreneurs will be able to decrease operational costs, reduce unfair and unequal informality and competition, increase their markets, and better serve customers. For its accomplishment, it is requested a proper governmental policy planning for the sharing economy development; legislation; creating a proper infrastructural and technological support; subsidy and financial support for the sharing platforms developments. Along these lines, the Albanian government should put efforts into arranging the building and implementation of functional platforms and collaborative environments by creating the proper legislative framework in line with the EU directives and processes. Concurrent, academia and research institutions should intensify the urgent obligation of supporting these advancements. The contribution of academia in technological innovation and innovative business models support a vital part of this process. Finally, this process cannot be accomplished without society's support of collaborative consumption. An increase of awareness and trust on reciprocal benefits of P2P consumption is decisive at this point. The continuous communication and synergic quadruple helix supportive collaboration of these stakeholders is necessary for the fragile and crucial sectors of the sharing economy's success in a developing country.

## References

Alfaro, Emigdio, Fei Yu, Naqeeb Ur Rehman, Eglantina Hysa, and Patrice Kandolo Kabeya. 2019. 'Strategic Management of Innovation.' In *The Routledge Companion to Innovation Management*, edited by J. Chen, A. Brem, E. Viardot, and P. K. Wong, 107–168. UK: Routledge.

Bakker, Martine, and Louise Twining-Ward. 2018. *Tourism and the Sharing Economy: Policy and Potential of Sustainable Peer-to-Peer Accommodation.* Washington, DC: World Bank.

Berhani, Riada, and Eglantina Hysa. 2013. 'The Economy of Albania Today and Then: The Drivers to Growth.' In *The 4th International Conference on European Studies*, 598. Albania: Epoka University.

Carayannis, Elias G., and David F. J. Campbell. 2009. '"Mode 3" and "Quadruple Helix": Toward a 21st Century Fractal Innovation Ecosystem.' *International Journal of Technology Management* 46 (3–4): 201–234. https://doi.org/10.1504/IJTM.2009.023374.

Corradini, Flavio, and Barbara Re. 2016. 'The European Digital Agenda and the Impact of ICT on Public Administrations and Small and Medium Enterprises.' In *Proceedings of the 2nd International Conference on Recent Trends and Applications in Computer Science and Information Technology*, Tirana, Albania, November 18–19, 2016. CEUR Workshop Proceedings 1746, CEUR-WS.org, pp. 11–16.

Council of Ministers. 2009. National Strategy of Science, 'Technology and Innovation 2009–2015.' *Technical Report. Council of Ministers. The Republic of Albania*. Accessed June 30, 2019. http://portal.unesco.org/en/files/47499/12677115709STI_english.pdf/STI%2Benglish.pdf.

Economy Co-Responsibility Learning. 2016. 'Comparative Study on Sharing Economy in EU and ECORL Consortium Countries.' *Technical Report. Economy Co-Responsibility Learning*. Accessed June 30, 2019. https://www.ecorl.it/documenti/Risultati/comparative-study-on-sharing-economy.pdf.

Etzkowitz, Henry, and Loet Leydesdorff. 1995. 'The Triple Helix—University-Industry-Government Relations: A Laboratory for Knowledge Based Economic Development.' *EASST Review* 14 (1): 14–19.

Ferizi, Vjosa, and Alba Demneri Kruja. 2018. 'Coastline Hospitality Industry Performance, Challenges, and Opportunities: Evidence from Durres Coastline.' In *Managing Sustainable Tourism Resources*, 14–38. Hershey, Pennsylvania: IGI Global. https://doi.org/10.4018/978-1-5225-5772-2.ch002.

Flora, Cornelia Butler, and Corene Bregendahl. 2012. 'Collaborative Community-Supported Agriculture: Balancing Community Capitals for Producers and Consumers.' *International Journal of Sociology of Agriculture & Food* 19 (3): 329–346.

Gecaj, Merita, Edmira Ozuni Shahu, Drini Imami, Engjell Skreli, and Attila Jambor. 2019. Analysing the Impact of Subsidies in the Albanian Agriculture Sector: A Comparative Approach. *Bulgarian Journal of Agricultural Science* 25 (5): 883–890. https://doi.org/10.22004/ag.econ.271964.

Hysa, Eglantina, and Egla Mansi. 2020. 'Integrating Teaching and Learning in Graduate Studies: Economic Development Course.' *Technology Transfer: Innovative Solutions in Social Sciences and Humanities*, 61–64. https://doi.org/10.21303/2613-5647.2020.001305.

Hysa, Eglantina, Alba Kruja, Naqeeb Ur Rehman, and Rafael Laurenti. 2020. 'Circular Economy Innovation and Environmental Sustainability Impact on Economic Growth: An Integrated Model for Sustainable Development.' *Sustainability* 12 (12). https://doi.org/10.3390/su12124831.

Hysa, Eglantina, Alba Demneri Kruja, and Vera Shiko. 2021. 'Current and Prospective Expansion of the Sharing Economy in Albania.' In *The Collaborative Economy in Action: European Perspectives*, edited by Andrzej Klimczuk, Vida Česnuitytė, and Gabriela Avram. Limerick, Ireland: University of Limerick.

Institute of Statistics. 2020a. 'Përdorimi i teknologjisë së informacionit dhe komunikimit në ndërmarrje, 2019 [Information and Communication Technology Usage in Enterprises, 2019].' *Publication. Albanian Institute of Statistics.* Accessed May 30, 2020. http://www.instat.gov.al/al/temat/shkenc%C3%AB-teknologji-dhe-shoq%C3%ABria-dixhitale/informacioni-dhe-teknologjit%C3%AB-e-komunikimit/publikimet/2020/teknologjia-e-informacionit-dhe-komunikimit-n%C3%AB-nd%C3%ABrmarrje-2019/.

Institute of Statistics. 2020b. *Sectorial Based Labor Force 2000–2019.* Accessed July 28, 2020. Retrieved from http://databaza.instat.gov.al/pxweb/sq/DST/START__TP__AD__ADY/ADY132/table/tableViewLayout2/?rxid=2d582861-bfe1-4141-a7e6-5d95288cbf60.

International Telecommunication Union. 2016. 'ICT Centric Innovation Ecosystem Country Review: Albania.' *Technical Report*. Accessed on June 30, 2019. https://www.itu.int/en/ITU-D/Innovation/Documents/Publications/Albania%20Country%20Review%20Innovation%20June%202016.pdf.

Kemp, S. 2020. 'Digital 2020. Report.' *Hootsuite.* Accessed May 30, 2020. https://hootsuite.com/resources/digital-2020.

Kruja, Alba. 2013. 'Entrepreneurship and Knowledge-Based Economies.' *Revista Românească pentru Educaţie Multidimensională* 1: 7–17.

Kruja, Alba. 2020a. 'Entrepreneurial Orientation, Synergy and Firm Performance in the Agribusiness Context: An Emerging Market Economy Perspective.' *Central European Business Review* 9 (1): 56–75. https://doi.org/10.18267/j.cebr.229.

Kruja, Alba Demneri. 2020b. 'Entrepreneurial Challenges of Albanian Agribusinesses: A Content Analysis.' *JEEMS Journal of East European*

*Management Studies* 25 (3): 530–554. https://doi.org/10.5771/0949-6181-2020-3-530.

Law, Rob, Dimitrios Buhalis, and Cihan Cobanoglu. 2014, 'Progress on Information and Communication Technologies in Hospitality and Tourism.' *International Journal of Contemporary Hospitality Management* 26 (5): 727–750. https://doi.org/10.1108/IJCHM-08-2013-0367.

Melián-González, Santiago, and Jacques Bulchand-Gidumal. 2016. 'A Model That Connects Information Technology and Hotel Performance.' *Tourism Management* 53: 30–37. https://doi.org/10.1016/j.tourman.2015.09.005.

Ministry of Innovation and Public Administration. 2014. 'Cross-Cutting Strategy: Digital Agenda of Albania 2015–2020.' *Technical Report. Ministry of Innovation and Public Administration. Republic of Albania*. Accessed June 30, 2019. https://akshi.gov.al/wp-content/uploads/2018/03/Digital_Agenda_Strategy_2015_-_2020.pdf.

Sari, Yasar, Metin Kozak, and Teoman Duman. 2006. 'A Historical Development of "IT" in Tourism Marketing.' In *Progress in Tourism Marketing*, edited by M. Kozak and L. Andreu, 33–44. Netherlands: Elsevier.

Stahel, Walter. 2010. *The Performance Economy*. Basingstoke, UK: Palgrave Macmillan.

TIMBRO. 2018. 'Sharing Economy Index.' *Technical Report. TIMBRO.* Accessed June 30, 2019. https://timbro.se/app/uploads/2018/07/tsei-version-17_web.pdf.

Tukiainen, Taina, Seppo Leminen, and Mika Westerlund. 2015. 'Cities as Collaborative Innovation Platforms.' *Technology Innovation Management Review* 5 (10): 16–23. https://doi.org/10.22215/TIMREVIEW/933.

Vladi, Eneda, and Eglantina Hysa. 2019. 'The Impact of Macroeconomic Indicators on Unemployment Rate: Western Balkan Countries.' In *International Firms' Economic Nationalism and Trade Policies in the Globalisation Era*, edited by Harish C. Chandan and Bryan Christiansen, 158–181. Hershey, Pennsylvania: IGI Global.

World Travel & Tourism Council. 2018. 'Travel & Tourism Economic Impact 2018: Albania.' *World Travel & Tourism Council*, United Kingdom.

Wosskow, Debbie. 2014. *Unlocking the Sharing Economy: An Independent Review*. London: Department for Business, Innovation and Skills. Accessed June 30, 2019. Retrieved from https://www.gov.uk/government/uploads/system/uploads/attachment_data/file/378291/bis-14-1227-unlocking-thesharing-economy-an-independent-review.pdf.

Yun, JinHyo Joseph, and Zheng Liu. 2019. 'Micro-and Macro-Dynamics of Open Innovation with a Quadruple-Helix Model.' *Sustainability* 11 (12): 3301. https://doi.org/10.3390/su11123301.

## Suggested Readings

Čavalić, Admir. 2017. *Sharing Economy in Western Balkans: Potential for Rural Development*. Bosnia and Hercegovina: International Burch University.

Duli, Manjola. 2019. *Albania: Report on the Preparation of Post-2020 Strategy*. Bosnia and Hercegovina: Regional Cooperation Council.

Kruja, Alba Demneri, and Geri Ruci. 2021. 'Sharing Economy Perspectives for a Sustainable Agriculture and Tourism Development.' In *International Scientific Conference 'Sustainable Agriculture and Rural Development*, Institute of Agricultural Economics, Belgrade, December 17–18, 2020, Belgrade, Serbia.

OECD. 2020. OECD *Tourism Trends and Policies 2020*. Paris: OECD Publishing. https://doi.org/10.1787/6b47b985-en.

## Relevant Websites

Agroquality: http://agroquality.al/?lang=en/.

Digital technologies key to accelerate agricultural development in Albania, United Nations Albania: https://albania.un.org/en/104824-digital-technologies-key-accelerate-agricultural-development-albania.

Innovation Map Albania: https://innovationmapalbania.org/about.

# Part V

## Conclusions

# 18

# The State and Critical Assessment of the Sharing Economy in Europe

Vida Česnuitytė, Bori Simonovits, Andrzej Klimczuk, Bálint Balázs, Cristina Miguel, and Gabriela Avram

## Introduction

This chapter summarises the theoretical and empirical analyses presented in the edited collection of papers 'The Sharing Economy in Europe: Developments, Practices, and Contradictions.' The majority of the chapters' authors were actively involved in the COST Action CA16121 'From Sharing to Caring: Examining Socio-Technical Aspects of the Collaborative Economy' (abbreviated as 'Sharing and Caring') that was a research network operative between 2017 and 2021 and supported by the COST

V. Česnuitytė (✉)
Mykolas Romeris University, Vilnius, Lithuania

B. Simonovits
Eötvös Loránd University, Budapest, Hungary
e-mail: simonovits.borbala@ppk.elte.hu

A. Klimczuk
SGH Warsaw School of Economics, Warsaw, Poland
e-mail: aklimcz@sgh.waw.pl



V. Česnuitytė et al. (eds.), *The Sharing Economy in Europe*,
https://doi.org/10.1007/978-3-030-86897-0_18

(European Cooperation in Science and Technology) Association. This COST Action created a conducive and advantageous space for knowledge sharing and for lively discussion, which resulted in numerous scientific publications (Avram et al. 2019; Bassetti et al. 2019; Bødker et al. 2020; Fedosov et al. 2019; Light and Miskelly 2019; Klimczuk et al. 2021). The present edited collection is one of the final outcomes of the COST Action 'Sharing and Caring.'

The main goal of this book is to provide readers with original and comprehensive approaches to the emerging phenomenon of the sharing economy. As a new conception, it raises plenty of questions. Therefore, authors from sixteen European countries and various academic backgrounds made efforts to answer the following questions: how is the sharing economy understood nowadays? What variations of its interpretations appear in theory and practice? How do harmonious or contradictory interrelations between the sharing economy and various contexts (public policies, legislation, digital platforms and others) occur? What are the specific issues for the functioning of the sharing economy in different economic sectors? What experiences and achievements are inherent for the selected European countries in the process of the integration of the sharing economy measures?

The current chapter, first, reviews the main findings presented in the book's Parts II-IV (while Part I is dedicated for Introduction, and Part V is dedicated for Conclusions). Further, it discusses and critically assess these findings through the lens of existing knowledge on the sharing

B. Balázs
Environmental Social Science Research Group, Budapest, Hungary
e-mail: balazs.balint@essrg.hu

C. Miguel
University of Gothenburg, Gothenburg, Sweden
e-mail: cristina.miguel@ait.gu.se

G. Avram
University of Limerick, Limerick, Ireland
e-mail: Gabriela.Avram@ul.ie

economy in the context of scientific publications, political and legal documents, official statistics, and reports on social surveys. Finally, it provides concluding thoughts on the state of the sharing economy in Europe and includes some future directions.

## Main Findings on the Sharing Economy in Europe

### Development of Conceptualisation and Regulation of the Sharing Economy

Authors of the chapters included in Part II made efforts to review, firstly, the theoretical conceptualisation of the sharing economy since there is still no consensus on its definition (Dillahunt et al. 2017). Building on Wacker (2004), the authors of Chapter 2, Cristina Miguel, Esther Martos-Carrión, and Mijalche Santa, notice that such an 'ill-defined concept' may mislead practitioners and researchers and negatively impact their efforts. By applying the framework for theoretical meaningfulness, the authors identified the 'essential' features of the sharing economy. Based on these essential properties, they proposed the following definition for the sharing economy: 'The sharing economy is a closed socio-economic system facilitated by digital platforms which match peer-to-peer service demand and offer based on the rules and culture of the platform actors.' Then the status and situation of the sharing economy in the context of public policy and legislation were explored. It was noticed that the sharing economy is spreading rapidly and widely in today's European societies. The sharing economy gained popularity because it maximises the efficiency of consumption (Hamari et al. 2016), as well as the redistribution of goods and services (Howard 2015). With sharing economy platforms, people have gained more opportunities to exchange goods with strangers over long distances, to consume a wider variety of goods and services at a lower price and with less formal barriers. At the same time, as an innovative phenomenon, the concept of the sharing economy still raises many disparities and issues such as sharing and exchange for-profit or not-for-profit, monetary or non-monetary transactions, as well as regulated or unregulated activities (Slee 2015).

Moreover, the sharing economy calls for intervention and regulation because of increasing problems related to its functioning, for example, (unfair) competition and (lack of) consumer protection, employment conditions, relations with social policy, or taxation of sharing economy companies (Thelen 2018). The authors of Chapter 3, Błażej Koczetkow and Andrzej Klimczuk, based on the literature review, identified three ways to solve those problems: (1) targeting of interventions and regulations to specific areas (e.g., accommodation, mobility, and agriculture), and avoiding universal regulations (Gautrais 2018); (2) building a set of good practices to regulate the sharing economy at various levels (local, regional, national, EU, and global) (Frenken et al. 2020); (3) interpreting the regulation of the sharing economy through the prism of assumptions of various theories on public policy (e.g., group theories, class analysis, and analysis of transaction costs) (Huising and Silbey 2011).

Kosjenka Dumančić and Natalia-Rozalia Avlona, the authors of Chapter 4, show that, apart from a broad European Commission Communication (2016), the sharing economy still lacks regulation at the European level. The situation creates an obvious opportunity for local, national, and EU legislation to respond to the phenomenon of the sharing economy. Though, the exploration of the cases of Uber and Airbnb reveal legal problems related to distinguishing transportation or accommodation services providers from digital platforms (Colangelo and Maggiolino 2018; Van Cleynenbreugel 2020) by the Court of Justice of the European Union. Such a *laissez-faire* approach left space for sharing and collaborative economy companies to grow globally without proper regulation. The authors of the chapter conclude that the re-opening pan-European consultation engaging the national legislators, the trade unions, and the workers' collectives are a necessity in order to respond to the void of legislation on sharing economy activities.

## Mapping Variety of the Sharing Economy Sectors

In Part III, the authors explored the contribution of the sharing economy in some selected market sectors in Europe. First of all, attention is paid to the mobility sector. Shared mobility is defined as an alternative trip that maximises the utilisation of mobility resources in society (Machado et al. 2018). Authors Agnieszka Lukasiewicz and co-authors (Chapter 5) state that the sharing economy manifestations in the transportation sector promote more integrated transport solutions and environmental sustainability. At the same time, they generate inequality among age generations, and across disadvantaged social groups, as a result of the digital divide and sometimes—even social exclusion. They also create traffic congestion, pollution, regulatory disputes, stakeholder conflicts, and other unwanted effects (UNPF 2015).

Another sector in which the sharing economy has been largely implemented is peer-to-peer (P2P) accommodation. Anna Farmaki and Cristina Miguel, in Chapter 6, identified P2P platforms with business models ranging from paid to not-for-profit, plus based on home exchanges. Authors found that both hosts and guests benefit from such sharing, particularly through obtaining authentic experiences, interaction with locals, and supplementing their income (Lutz and Newlands 2018; Bucher et al. 2018). At the same time, there are many negative impacts on local economies and communities, among which overcrowding from the influx of tourists, increased housing prices, higher pollution levels (Ioannides et al. 2019), as well as the impact on the performance of hotels (Sigala 2017).

Next, authors of Chapter 7, Bori Simonovits and Bálint Balázs, focus on the sharing economy in food supply chains, defined as the use of food surplus via online communities or donating vulnerable groups via food banks. A new way of food sharing is related to the novel, digitally mediated and for-profit iterations (Pottinger 2018). However, food supply via ICT platforms, often related to unregulated marketplaces, also hide from consumers the negative outcomes such as precarious jobs, unfair labour practices, generating overconsumption, and hiding ecological externalities (Frenken and Schor 2019).

The financial sector is further explored in Part III. According to Agnieszka Lukasiewicz and Mijalche Santa (Chapter 8), practices of sharing within the financial sector range from P2P lending to crowdfunding, involve start-ups and incumbent financial service providers and may achieve for-profit or not-for-profit goals. Authors notice that the expansion of the FinTech industry offers a variety of new tools and services to consumers and the financial market, such as donation-based platforms, reward-based funding, equity-based platforms, or lending-based platforms. At the same time, the disruption of the role, structure, and competitive environment for financial institutions, the markets, and societies in which they operate emerge (Löher 2017; Poetz and Schreier 2012).

Education, knowledge, and data sharing are also presented as part of the sharing economy (Pouri and Hilty 2021). Gabriela Avram and Eglantina Hysa, in Chapter 9, discuss the fact that these activities are seldom recognised as being part of the sharing economy due to their intangible, non-material nature. Meanwhile, almost ubiquitous access to the Internet extended the opportunities for learning, knowledge and data sharing, and generation of new information and knowledge, despite distance and professional backgrounds. The authors discuss new models of education supported by online platforms (Reich 2020; Schor et al. 2015): open learning, connected courses, co-creation of open textbooks with students, peer-guided learning, or networked environments learning. According to the authors, collaboration and knowledge sharing create value, while learning and community building contribute to the community and social capital creation, as well as to the common good.

The solidarity and care economy is the last sector discussed in this section of the book. Authors of Chapter 10, Penny Travlou and Anikó Bernát, explored how recent crises, such as austerity after the 2008 economic crisis, the arrival of the numerous refugees/migrants, and the COVID-19 pandemic, interrelated with the sharing economy. The authors found that the crises highlighted the contribution of the sharing economy to the creation of solidarity involving the personal networks to cope with material deprivation: community kitchens, housing squats, and volunteer activist and grassroots organisations were created or repurposed for this reason. On the other hand, the latter activities contributed at a rather different level in various countries, particularly, higher in Greece and lower in Hungary. Identified trends revealed and highlighted the potential of the sharing economy in the face of the crises.

## Diversity of the Sharing Economy at the Country Level

Part IV is dedicated to the exploration of selected country-specific cases. Seven country-focused chapters in which specific sectors of the sharing economy are highlighted were included. First, the case study of the Netherlands was introduced as the pioneering country in the sharing economy with distinguished sectors of mobility (car- or bike-sharing) and gig work platforms. Martijn de Waal and Martijn Arets, authors of Chapter 11, pay special attention to the fact that the sharing economy was initiated with the hope of contributing to social cohesion and sustainability, i.e., from the perspective of society. Though, in the last years, discussions in relation to the spread of the sharing economy started focusing on the safeguarding of public values, as well as on the quality of the services, and the efficiency of the commercial platform operators, i.e., mostly raising economic aspects. Meanwhile, a suitable answer on the regulation of these platforms has not been found yet.

Further, an alternative governance model within the sharing economy, platform cooperativism, is analysed in the context of the French sharing economy. Authors of Chapter 12, Myriam Lewkowicz and Jean-Pierre Cahier, focus on the analysis of platform cooperatives in three emblematic domains: meal delivery service, carpooling, and energy. In order to develop sustainable sharing activities, their initiators needed to match social demand with economic models, legal conditions, appropriate social and organisational forms, as well as software components. As a result, such an economic model created jobs and confidence. It is also economically sustainable in the long run. Even more, shared activities create a natural synergy between public action and public policy.

The third country presented in this part of the volume is Austria, with its well-developed tourism and accommodation. Malte Höfner and Rainer Rosegger, in Chapter 13, discuss the development of the sharing economy in the mentioned sectors and highlight its strong effects on traditional provider structures and the local labour market. As the authors state, alternative business models in the P2P accommodation sector are more important than ever before, especially in the face of the COVID-19 pandemic situation. At the same time, the debates of national regulation's power over global players are in full swing.

Later, regulatory issues of the sharing economy are discussed in the context of the Italian sharing economy environment. Italian legislation, as Giulia Priora and co-authors (Chapter 14) state, is still not adapted to regulate the sharing economy. Legal gaps create uncertainty among all stakeholders and obstacles for future development. According to the authors, the main priorities in a prospective process of sharing economy development in their country are the following: definition of the role and obligations of platforms and service providers; prevention and fighting of discrimination across the involved economic sectors; common taxation system; principles of social sustainability, environmental protection, and community welfare.

The United Kingdom is the home of over 200 time banks, a noteworthy sector of the sharing economy. In Chapter 15, Rodrigo Perez-Vega and Cristina Miguel note that timebanks started as community-led initiatives. They create opportunities for people to exchange and trade their generic and specialist skills. However, the discussion focuses on whether these time banks operate efficiently. The COVID-19 pandemic highlighted the ability of time banks to contribute to providing needed skills (e.g., psychological support to frontline workers) in a historically challenging period.

The sharing economy in Poland is presented in the context of coping with the problems of trust and legal regulation in relation to the sharing economy activities within big, global businesses, but also in smaller, local initiatives. As Agnieszka Lukasiewicz and Aleksandra Nadolska, the authors of Chapter 16, notice, sometimes the local initiatives, especially when it comes to specific niches, are doing even better than global corporations. Though, together with opportunities, the sharing economy creates issues that require solutions, such as competition, labour law, regulation, and conflicts among stakeholders.

Finally, Eglantina Hysa and Alba Demneri Kruja, authors of Chapter 17, describe the role of the sharing economy implementation in Albania, both in the agriculture and accommodation sectors: it will decrease operational costs, reduce unfair and unequal informality and competition, enlarge their markets, and better serve customers. The country has made progress in adapting national strategies focused on ICT development and digitalisation. Moreover, the contribution from academia in innovation and innovative business models support this overall process. Additionally, increased awareness and trust in the benefits of P2P consumption at the societal level are decisive at this point.

## Final Reflection: Critical Assessment of the Sharing Economy

Online platforms for the sharing economy (or collaborative consumption) have been rapidly growing in Europe in various sectors and services. As described throughout the book, the underlying causes are multiple, most importantly related to environmental issues and labour market changes, and the growing demand for sustainable consumption and flexible lifestyles. On the one hand, some scholars view the recently emerged collaborative platforms as a positive paradigm change from the conventional economic business model, with a potential of democratisation of socio-economic relations (Belk 2009; Sundararajan 2016; John 2017). On the other hand, there are scholars who are more concerned about the potential 'neoliberal nightmare' of the sharing economy (Arnould and Rose 2015; Martin 2016) and who highlight how disadvantaged people are excluded from sharing economy activities (Schor 2017).

In the following, we discuss some of the major problems related to the sharing economy. From a legal point of view, the various models provided by the sharing economy can raise certain legal and ethical labour-related concerns. According to Zrenner (2015), the practices of numerous sharing platforms create concerns with regard to market competition, legality, and consumer protection. At the same time, the fact that the sharing platforms claim to only facilitate transactions between people outlines the potential approach of these companies towards responsibilities. Cohen and Sundararajan (2015) stress the relevance of self-regulation issues in peer-to-peer platforms, stemming from the information asymmetry between the service provider and the consumer, negative and positive externalities, as well as the blurred boundaries between the personal and the professional.

From an economic perspective, the spread of sharing economy platforms changed practices related to consumption, displaying benefits as well as potential risks. An essential change in consumption is represented by the shift in consumer choices when it comes to owning assets versus using them on-demand, the latter being facilitated by the sharing economy. According to a comprehensive analysis in the context of the sharing economy (Codagnone et al. 2016), consumer welfare is increased due to the capacity of service delivery and lower prices. In contrast, a widespread critique is that the sharing economy has nothing to do with sharing (Slee 2015; Scholz 2017), as Airbnb is basically a short-term renting platform, and Uber is operating as an unregulated taxi company. Sundararajan (2016) also highlights the way some companies, while considered to be car-sharing platforms, do not have a significantly different business model from traditional car rental companies (e.g., Zipcar and car2go in comparison to P2P Turo). Certain scholars use the term 'sharewashing,' meaning a marketing strategy, where the business is based on an idea of sharing and pro-social behaviour, rather than on profit-oriented principles. According to the 'sharewashing critique,' Airbnb is much closer to a rental agency and Uber to an unregulated taxi service than to sharing economy initiatives (Tu 2017; Schormair 2019). It is worth noting here that other economic models are emerging at the moment, such as the social and solidarity economy, the creative economy, the silver economy, and the circular economy (Klimczuk 2015). It is essential to highlight that some of these concepts are much more focused on justice and equality.

From a social policy and sociological perspective, a series of critiques have been linked to the problems of inequality, discrimination, and social exclusion of certain minorities. Even though in most online sharing economy platforms, racial or any other kind of discrimination are prohibited—either by anti-discrimination policies (e.g., Airbnb, Uber, and Lyft) or by rules of conduct that articulate desirable behaviour (e.g., BlaBlaCar), in practice, discrimination still exists. Simply because there is a built-in selection mechanism that results in unintended consequences, namely discriminating platform users that belong to certain groups or minorities as both users and service providers can choose with whom they want to share their rides or apartments. Several audit studies (based on control field experiments, see, e.g., Cui et al. 2017; Edelman et al. 2017; Ge et al. 2016; Simonovits et al. 2018) have proven that discrimination (primarily based on ethnicity and race) is prevalent, i.e., unequal access to certain services (Airbnb, Uber, and other ride-sharing platforms) remain a serious policy concern.

Yet creating trust is crucial in order to minimise risks within the newest forms of peer-to-peer transactions because the sharing economy does not involve the only direct sale or simple sharing, but mutual participation. To create trust in response to these risks, users tend to provide more robust information on newer forms of collaborative consumption platforms (Ert et al. 2016; Sundararajan, 2016). To sum it up, creating social links and building social capital have crucial roles in the sharing economy organisations, especially in those platforms which offer risky, 'high-stakes' offline experiences, such as ride-sharing companies or Airbnb. Trust signals and the use of digital trust are a required and essential resource for sharing platforms (Botsman 2017). In online interactions, trust has to be approached differently, as the level of trustworthiness is not known (Chen and Fadlalla 2009).

To conclude, from a scientific perspective, the book provides a better understanding of the sharing economy in Europe. It reveals that the sharing economy is still a novel and innovative phenomenon. Hence, it is no surprise that unsolved critical issues encourage the continuation of its investigation, discussions, and debates from various perspectives: economic, legal, political, social, ecological, and others. Meanwhile, considering the comprehensive and up-to-date materials collected and analysed in this book, it may become an outstanding source of knowledge and tool in the process of expansion of the sharing economy in Europe and beyond. From a global economic perspective, it seems that societies are entering an era where multinationals and globalisation are shaping the playing field for industry and business players within the sharing economy. Simultaneously, highly innovative local initiatives are growing and spreading throughout Europe. Will the sharing economy continue to provide new solutions for more environmentally aware consumption and help build more community-based and caring lifestyles? We can only hope so.

## References

Arnould, Eric J., and Alexander S. Rose. 2015. 'Mutuality: Critique and Substitute for Belk's "Sharing".' *Marketing Theory* 16 (1): 75–99. https://doi.org/10.1177/1470593115572669.

Avram, Gabriela, Jaz Hee-jeong Choi, Stefano De Paoli, Ann Light, Peter Lyle, and Maurizio Teli. 2019. 'Repositioning CoDesign in the Age of Platform Capitalism: From Sharing to Caring.' *CoDesign* 15 (3): 185–191. https://doi.org/10.1080/15710882.2019.1638063.

Bassetti, Chiara, Mariacristina Sciannamblo, Peter Lyle, Maurizio Teli, Stefano De Paoli, and Antonella De Angeli. 2019. 'Co-designing for Common Values: Creating Hybrid Spaces to Nurture Autonomous Cooperation.' *CoDesign* 15 (3): 256–271.

Bødker, Susanne, Myriam Lewkowicz, and Alexander Boden. 2020. 'What's in a Word? Platforms Supporting the Platform Economy.' In *Proceedings of the 11th Nordic Conference on Human-Computer Interaction: Shaping Experiences, Shaping Society*, 1–10. https://doi.org/10.1145/3419249.3420167.

Belk, Russel 2009. 'Sharing.' *Journal of Consumer Research* 36 (5): 715–734. https://doi.org/10.1086/612649.

Botsman, Rachel. 2017. *Who Can You Trust? How Technology Brought Us Together and Why It Might Drive Us Apart*. New York: Public Affairs.

Bucher, Eliane, Christian Fieseler, Matthes Fleck, and Christoph Lutz. 2018. 'Authenticity and the Sharing Economy.' *Academy of Management Discoveries* 4 (3): 294–313. https://doi.org/10.5465/amd.2016.0161.

Chen, Kuanchin, and Adam Fadlalla, eds 2008. *Online Consumer Protection: Theories of Human Relativism*. Hershey, PA: IGI Global. https://doi.org/10.4018/978-1-60566-012-7.

Codagnone, Cristiano, Federico Biagi, and Fabienne Abadie. 2016. *The Passions and the Interests: Unpacking the 'Sharing Economy'*. Institute for Prospective Technological Studies, JRC Science for Policy Report EUR 27914 EN. https://doi.org/10.2791/474555.

Cohen, Molly, and Arun Sundararajan. 2015. 'Self-Regulation and Innovation in the Peer-to-Peer Sharing Economy.' *University of Chicago Law Review Dialogue* 82: 116.

Colangelo, Margherita, and Mariateresa Maggiolino. 2018. 'Uber in Europe: Are There Still Judges in Luxembourg?' *CPI Antitrust Chronicle*. Available at https://ssrn.com/abstract=3192086.

Cui, Ruomeng, Jun Li, and Dennis Zhang. 2017. *Reducing Discrimination with Reviews in the Sharing Economy: Evidence from Field Experiments on Airbnb*, 1–35. Harvard Business School. https://doi.org/10.2139/ssrn.2882982

Dillahunt, Tawanna R., Xinyi Wang, Earnest Wheeler, Hao Fei Cheng, Brent Hecht, and Haiyi Zhu. 2017. 'The Sharing Economy in Computing: A Systematic Literature Review.' *Proceedings of the ACM on Human-Computer Interaction* 1, art. 38: 1–26. https://doi.org/10.1145/3134673.

Edelman, Benjamin, Michael Luca, and Dan Svirsky. 2017. 'Racial Discrimination in the Sharing Economy: Evidence from a Field Experiment.' *American Economic Journal: Applied Economics* 9 (2): 1–22. https://doi.org/10.1257/app.20160213

Ert, Eyal, Aliza Fleischer, and Nathan Magen. 2016. 'Trust and Reputation in the Sharing Economy: The Role of Personal Photos in Airbnb.' *Tourism Management* 55: 62–73. https://doi.org/10.1016/j.tourman.2016.01.013.

European Commission. 2016. *Communication to the European Parliament, the Council, the European Economic and Social Council and the Council of Regions: European Agenda for the Collaborative Economy*, 356. Brussels.

Fedosov, Anton, Airi Lampinen, Tawanna R. Dillahunt, Ann Light, and Coye Cheshire. 2019. 'Cooperativism and Human-Computer Interaction.' In *Extended Abstracts of the 2019 CHI Conference on Human Factors in Computing Systems (CHI EA '19)*. ACM, New York, NY, USA. https://doi.org/10.1145/3290607.3311751.

Frenken, Koen, and Juliet Schor. 2019. *Putting the Sharing Economy into Perspective: A Research Agenda for Sustainable Consumption Governance*. Cheltenham, UK: Edward Elgar Publishing.

Frenken, Koen, Arnoud van Waes, Peter Pelzer, Magda Smink, and Rinie van Est. 2020. 'Safeguarding Public Interests in the Platform Economy.' *Policy & Internet* 12 (3): 400–425. https://doi.org/10.1002/poi3.217.

Gautrais, Vincent. 2018. 'The Normative Ecology of Disruptive Technology.' In *Law and the 'Sharing Economy': Regulating Online Market Platforms*, edited by Derek McKee, Finn Makela, and Teresa Scassa, 115–147. Ottawa: University of Ottawa Press. https://doi.org/10.2307/j.ctv5vdczv.8.

Ge, Yanbo, Christopher R. Knittel, Don MacKenzie, and Stephen Zoepf. 2016. *Racial and Gender Discrimination in Transportation Network Companies*. No. w22776. National Bureau of Economic Research. https://doi.org/10.3386/w22776.

Hamari, Juho, Mimmi Sjöklint, and Ukkonen, Antti. 2016. 'The Sharing Economy: Why People Participate in Collaborative Consumption.' *Journal of the Association for Information Science and Technology* 67 (9): 2047–2059. https://doi.org/10.1002/asi.23552.

Howard, Billee. 2015. *We-Commerce: How to Create, Collaborate, and Succeed in the Sharing Economy*. New York, NY: Perigee Books.

Huising, Ruthanne, and Susan S. Silbey. 2011. 'Governing the Gap: Forging Safe Science Through Relational Regulation.' *Regulation & Governance* 5 (1): 14–42. https://doi.org/10.1111/j.1748-5991.2010.01100.x.

Ioannides, Dimitri, Michael Röslmaier, and Egbert Van Der Zee. 2019. 'Airbnb as an Instigator of "Tourism Bubble" Expansion in Utrecht's Lombok Neighbourhood.' *Tourism Geographies* 21 (5): 822–840. https://doi.org/10.1080/14616688.2018.1454505.

John, H. A. (2017). *The Age of Sharing*. Malden, MA: Polity Press.

Klimczuk, Andrzej. 2015. *Economic Foundations for Creative Ageing Policy: Vol. I Context and Considerations*. New York, NY: Palgrave Macmillan. https://doi.org/10.1057/9781137465337.

Klimczuk, Andrzej, Vida Česnuitytė, and Gabriela Avram, eds. 2021. *The Collaborative Economy in Action: European Perspectives*. Limerick, Ireland: University of Limerick.

Light, Ann, and Clodagh Miskelly. 2019. 'Platforms, Scales and Networks: Meshing a Local Sustainable Sharing Economy.' *Computer Supported Cooperative Work* (CSCW) 28 (3): 591–626. https://doi.org/10.1007/s10606-019-09352-1.

Löher, Jonas. 2017. 'The Interaction of Equity Crowdfunding Platforms and Ventures: An Analysis of the Preselection Process.' *Venture Capital* 19 (1–2): 51–74. https://doi.org/10.1080/13691066.2016.1252510.

Lutz, Christoph, and Gemma Newlands. 2018. 'Consumer Segmentation Within the Sharing Economy: The Case of Airbnb.' *Journal of Business Research* 88: 187–196. https://doi.org/10.1016/j.jbusres.2018.03.019.

Machado, Cláudia A. Soares, Nicolas Patrick Marie de Salles Hue, Fernando Tobal Berssaneti, and José Alberto Quintanilha. 2018. 'An Overview of Shared Mobility.' *Sustainability (Switzerland)* 10 (12): 1–21. https://doi.org/10.3390/su10124342.

Martin, Chris J. 2016. 'The Sharing Economy: A Pathway to Sustainability or a Nightmarish Form of Neoliberal Capitalism?' *Ecological Economics* 121: 149–159. https://doi.org/10.1016/j.ecolecon.2015.11.027.

Poetz, Marion K., and Martin Schreier. 2012. 'The Value of Crowdsourcing: Can Users Really Compete with Professionals in Generating New Product Ideas?' *The Journal of Product Innovation Management* 29 (2): 245–56.

Pottinger, Laura. 2018. 'Growing, Guarding and Generous Exchange in an Analogue Sharing Economy.' *Geoforum* 96: 108–118. https://doi.org/10.1016/j.geoforum.2018.07.007.

Pouri, Maria J., and Lorenz M. Hilty. 2021. 'The Digital Sharing Economy: A Confluence of Technical and Social Sharing.' *Environmental Innovation and Societal Transitions* 38: 127–139. https://doi.org/10.1016/j.eist.2020.12.003.

Reich, Justin. 2020. *Failure to Disrupt: Why Technology Alone Can't Transform Education.* Harvard University Press. https://doi.org/10.4159/9780674249684.

Scholz, Trebor. 2017. *Uberworked and Underpaid: How Workers Are Disrupting the Digital Economy*. Malden, MA: Polity Press.

Schor, Juliet B. 2017. 'Does The Sharing Economy Increase Inequality Within The Eighty Percent? Findings From A Qualitative Study Of Platform Providers.' *Cambridge Journal of Regions, Economy and Society, Cambridge Political Economy Society* 10 (2): 263–279.

Schormair, Maximilian. 2019. 'Assessing the Risk of Sharewashing in the Sharing Economy: An Analytical Framework.' In *Academy of Management Proceedings* 1: 18559. Briarcliff Manor, NY 10510: Academy of Management. https://doi.org/10.5465/AMBPP.2019.18559abstract.

Schor, Juliet B., Connor Fitzmaurice, Lindsey B. Carfagna, Will Attwood-Charles, and Emilie Dubois Poteat. 2016. 'Paradoxes of openness and distinction in the sharing economy.' *Poetics* 54: 66–81. https://doi.org/10.1016/j.poetic.2015.11.001.

Sigala, Marianna. 2017. 'Collaborative Commerce in Tourism: Implications for Research and Industry.' *Current Issues in Tourism* 20 (4): 346–355. https://doi.org/10.1080/13683500.2014.982522.

Simonovits, Bori, Iryna Shvets, and Hannah Taylor. 2018. 'Discrimination in the Sharing Economy: Evidence from a Hungarian Field Experiment.' *Corvinus Journal of Sociology and Social Policy.* https://doi.org/10.14267/CJSSP.2018.1.03.

Slee, Tom. 2015. *What Is Yours Is Mine: Against the Sharing Economy.* New York, NY: OR Books.

Sundararajan, Arun. 2016. *The Sharing Economy: The End of Employment and the Rise of Crowd-Based Capitalism.* Cambridge, MA: MIT Press.

Thelen, Kathleen. 2018. 'Regulating Uber: The Politics of the Platform Economy in Europe and the United States.' *Perspectives on Politics* 16 (4): 938–953. https://doi.org/10.1017/S1537592718001081.

Tu, Duy Patrick. 2017. *Sharewash in the Sharing Economy: A First Look on the Phenomenon and Effects of Sharewash.* Karlsruhe, Germany: Karlsruhe Institute of Technology.

UNPF (United Nations Population Fund). 2015. *Transforming Our World: The 2030 Agenda for Sustainable Development. A/RES/70/1.* New York: United Nations Population Fund. Accessed November 15, 2020. https://www.unfpa.org/sites/default/files/resource-pdf/Resolution_A_RES_70_1_EN.pdf.

Van Cleynenbreugel, Pieter. 2020. 'Accommodating the Freedom of Online Platforms to Provide Services Through the Incidental Direct Effect Back Door: Airbnb Ireland.' *Common Market Law* Review 57 (4): 1201–1228.

Wacker, John G., 2004. 'A Theory of Formal Conceptual Definitions: Developing Theory-Building Measurement Instruments.' *Journal of Operations Management* 22 (6): 629–650. https://doi.org/10.1016/j.jom.2004.08.002.

Zrenner, Alexandra. 2015. *The Ethics of Regulating the Sharing Economy* [Online]. Available from Duke Ethics. https://kenan.ethics.duke.edu/wp-content/uploads/2018/01/Sharing-Economy-2015.pdf.

# Index

A

access economy 7, 30, 32
accommodation sector 68, 124–126, 285, 289, 290, 294–296, 307, 310, 394, 395
Albania 8, 14, 103, 147, 152, 365–378, 395
algorithm-led learning 185
attention economy 10, 308
austerity 208–214, 218, 225, 228–230, 392
Austria 8, 13, 97, 152, 196, 285, 286, 289, 290, 292, 293, 295, 296, 393
Austrian tourism 292, 293, 296

B

babysitter 251, 312, 327
bartering 3, 8, 140, 141, 144, 145, 327
benefits 6, 14, 24, 52, 54, 69, 92, 104, 106, 116, 117, 121–123, 125, 138, 140, 142, 143, 163, 165, 166, 168, 182, 195, 198, 210, 242, 271, 272, 275, 276, 292, 312, 326, 327, 331, 332, 336, 355, 369, 377, 378, 391, 395, 396
bike-sharing 10, 12, 13, 99, 101, 247, 248, 309, 353, 369, 393
biobased economy 231
borrowing 214, 306
business model 3, 4, 6, 13, 35, 49, 53, 67, 69, 70, 94, 103, 107, 116, 119, 122, 125, 142, 151, 193, 245, 250, 264, 274, 286, 288, 289, 292, 294, 305, 307,


V. Česnuitytė et al. (eds.), *The Sharing Economy in Europe*,
https://doi.org/10.1007/978-3-030-86897-0

311, 313, 316, 345, 346, 359, 378, 391, 394–396
business-to-business (B2B) 33, 146, 287
business-to-consumer (B2C) 146, 287

C

carpool 264, 270, 274, 275, 393
car sharing 10, 12, 13, 90, 93, 97, 98, 102, 105, 107, 241, 242, 246–249, 255, 309, 315, 353, 356, 396
circular economy 296, 346, 359, 396
civic engagement 217, 334
civic sector 220, 223
co-creation 10, 146, 183, 193, 207, 376, 392
collaborative consumption 6, 11, 25, 33, 35, 77, 106, 140, 153, 287, 290, 378, 395, 397
collaborative economy 3–6, 14, 23, 35, 65–70, 74, 76–79, 91, 101, 104, 181, 182, 245, 255, 263, 265–267, 286, 313, 314, 343–345, 358, 365–369, 371, 372, 375–377, 390
collaborative learning 12
commoning 8, 137, 138, 142, 288, 296
commons 22, 32, 34, 45, 78, 89, 93, 106, 141, 149, 153, 154, 191, 193, 194, 197, 200, 207, 211, 220, 226, 230, 231, 245, 266, 269, 272, 273, 275, 278, 279, 313, 317, 329, 334, 347, 371, 374, 377, 392, 394
community 4, 23, 30, 33, 34, 43, 58, 66, 92, 93, 117, 124, 126, 140–146, 149, 150, 153, 154, 165, 167, 172, 182, 184, 186, 191, 192, 194, 195, 199, 200, 207–209, 211, 220, 226, 229, 230, 249, 255, 264, 267, 275, 277–279, 288, 294, 296, 307, 310, 311, 317, 326–336, 346, 391, 392, 394
conceptual economy 9, 22, 29, 35
conceptualisation 5, 9, 29, 44, 141, 375, 389
conflicts in sharing economy 14, 394
consumption 11, 12, 24, 30, 33–35, 139, 140, 142–144, 153, 155, 200, 277, 285, 286, 294, 346, 378, 389, 395, 396, 398
cooperatives 13, 148, 149, 184, 191, 192, 198, 211, 242, 263, 264, 266–268, 270, 272, 273, 275–279, 297, 357–359
co-production 331, 333
cost-sharing 104
CouchSurfing 6, 11, 115, 116, 119, 123, 125, 356
Court of Justice of the European Union (CJEU) 67, 70, 72–75, 77, 78, 390
COVID-19 11, 91, 98, 104, 105, 124, 149, 150, 155, 171–174, 195, 216, 222, 223, 248, 253, 270, 286, 292, 295, 335, 344, 352–356, 359, 369
COVID-19 impact on the sharing economy 352
COVID-19 pandemic 11–15, 99, 100, 107, 116, 118, 124, 126, 141, 167, 171–173, 186, 195,

208, 210, 212, 215, 216, 222, 223, 225–231, 291, 306–308, 313, 317, 327, 335, 336, 355, 392, 394
coworking 190, 192, 197, 306, 313, 355, 356, 359
creative economy 396
creative industries 15
creativity 194, 334
critical assessment of the sharing economy 395
Croatia 8, 148, 352
crowdfunding 11, 12, 164–174, 312, 354, 355, 357–359, 392
crowdsourcing 165, 171–173, 198, 306
cultural capital 119
cultural industries 223
Cyprus 8, 122, 152, 352

D

Denmark 8, 99, 147, 352
design, designed 43, 57, 120, 184, 186, 189, 190, 193, 194, 196, 240, 245, 269, 340
digital divide 391
digital economy 32, 69, 78, 182, 265, 268, 269, 311
digitalisation 45, 137, 209, 286, 293, 296, 366, 368, 374, 377, 395
digital platform 3, 6, 7, 34, 35, 50, 52, 58, 60, 67, 77, 90, 102, 103, 184, 186, 192, 193, 200, 212, 213, 266, 274, 285, 288, 290, 296, 297, 314, 366, 371, 372, 388–390
disruption 48, 173, 313, 317, 392
donation-based platforms 167, 392

E

economic branch 58
economic perspective 255, 396, 397
economic sector 5, 9, 10, 296, 317, 370, 388, 394
economy of care 208
empowerment 32, 116, 125
entertainment 224, 245, 355, 371
entity 57, 66
equity-based platforms 168, 392
e-scooter sharing 99, 101, 309
Europe 10–12, 49, 54, 68, 77, 90, 91, 94, 97–101, 116–118, 122, 125, 126, 138, 139, 145, 170, 173, 174, 183, 185, 186, 197, 199, 208, 210, 212, 221, 227, 272, 292, 389, 391, 395, 397, 398
experience economy 10, 140, 215, 217, 254, 307, 316

F

fair trade 270
farm-to-table 147, 149
financial services in the sharing economy 11
Finland 150
food bank 139, 146, 152, 172, 391
food sharing 137–148, 152, 154, 155, 306, 310, 391
food sharing initiatives 139, 145
food supply chains 10, 11, 144, 146, 391
food waste 141, 142, 145–148, 152, 153, 311, 359

France 8, 12, 13, 49, 75, 97–99, 103, 104, 147, 149, 169, 263–268, 270–274, 276–279
freelance economy 372
freelancers 192, 251, 268, 279
French cooperativism 264, 279
future research directions 336

G

gamification 189
Germany 169
gift 3, 6, 8, 145, 147, 207
gig economy 13, 66, 223, 228, 244, 246, 250–252, 254, 372
gig worker 251
globalisation 55, 397
goods and services 4, 6–8, 31, 34, 35, 50, 60, 65, 182, 215, 227, 312, 313, 327, 372, 389
governance 42–44, 46, 47, 55, 154, 155, 246, 277–279, 286–288, 393
grassroots 12, 144, 153, 155, 199, 208, 211, 212, 219–226, 228–230, 392
Greece 8, 12, 147, 191, 208–213, 215–218, 220, 222, 224–231, 291, 332, 393
green economy 246

H

hacker spaces 195, 197
home exchange 121, 125, 309, 391
household 140, 142, 145, 149, 174, 242, 312, 354
Hungary 8, 12, 96, 97, 99, 102, 103, 147–149, 152, 154, 192, 208, 217–231, 393
hybrid sharing 293

I

informal economy 215
information 8, 12, 24, 27, 31, 34, 52–54, 67–69, 71–76, 78, 106, 116, 118, 142, 154, 165, 168, 169, 183, 185, 192, 195, 196, 199, 200, 213, 287, 293, 347, 356, 367, 392, 396, 397
information and communications technology (ICT) 142, 144, 152, 154, 211, 212, 347, 351, 367, 368, 374, 375, 377, 391, 395
information economy 8
information society 67, 68, 72–76, 78, 347
infrastructure(s) 7, 91, 92, 94, 100, 106, 172, 191, 193, 200, 209, 212–215, 217, 222, 224, 248, 267, 269, 270, 273, 288, 295, 367, 368, 371
innovation 4, 14, 15, 27, 33, 35, 49, 57, 67, 69, 92, 138, 139, 140, 154, 155, 167, 182, 191, 193, 194, 196–198, 244, 264–268, 294, 310–312, 338, 340, 341, 366, 368–370, 375–378, 395
intermediary organization 245, 309
Ireland 8, 74, 75, 121, 190, 199, 208
Italy 8, 13, 14, 97–99, 102, 103, 150, 171, 208, 306–308, 310, 311, 313, 315–317, 351, 357

J

judgment 52, 67, 75, 77, 78
judgment and Airbnb 67, 78
judgment and Uber 67, 72, 75, 77, 78

K

knowledge economy 8
knowledge sharing 181, 182, 192, 194, 195, 200, 388, 392

L

learning 172, 182–186, 188, 195, 198, 200, 215, 332, 353, 355, 366, 392
learning community 184, 266
legislation 7, 9, 14, 32, 47, 53, 69, 76, 78, 101, 198, 315, 333, 346, 377, 378, 388–390, 394
legislative reform 316
lending 90, 164, 174, 306, 312
lending-based platforms 168, 392
library 195
Lithuania 8, 103, 120, 351

M

maintenance 75
makers 144
market(s) vii, 4, 6, 10–12, 23, 31, 33, 42, 45, 46, 49, 51, 53, 57, 65–69, 71–73, 78, 79, 98, 99, 102, 103, 105, 115–117, 120, 122–124, 138, 140–146, 149, 151, 152, 155, 165, 169–171, 173, 174, 190, 208, 211, 224, 242, 246, 249, 252–255, 266, 268, 269, 271, 274, 276, 278, 286, 288, 289, 291–295, 306, 307, 309, 311–316, 327, 329, 332, 344–346, 353, 354, 357, 359, 366, 368, 369, 371–376, 391–395
market-based viii, 8, 9, 13, 31, 145, 146, 286–288, 296, 297
marketing 23, 189, 271, 295, 331, 355, 356, 396
marketplace(s) ix, 6, 31, 33, 115, 140, 243, 313, 391
Massive Online Open Courses (MOOC) 182, 184–186, 200
meal sharing 151
micro-entrepreneurs 32, 52, 122, 355
micro-mobility 100, 101, 105, 353
mobility platforms 242, 308

N

network(s), networking xi, 5, 9, 10, 24, 30–33, 35, 43, 44, 46, 54, 59, 66, 91, 118, 140, 143, 145, 149, 152, 154, 166, 174, 183, 184, 186, 192, 194, 208–214, 216, 217, 220, 224, 227, 228, 230, 243, 265, 267, 269, 278, 288, 295, 296, 297, 307, 327, 330–332, 366, 371, 387, 392
new economy 4, 12, 139, 144, 154, 250
new manufacturing economy 45
nongovernmental organisations (NGO) 42, 48, 145, 213, 217–220, 377
North Macedonia 8, 190, 212

Norway 150

O

on-demand 31, 91, 93, 99, 102, 151, 346, 396
on-demand economy 67, 140
online community 24, 139, 391
online platforms 54, 66–69, 76–78, 146, 149, 165, 182, 190, 195, 197, 200, 242, 251, 290, 306, 355, 365, 392, 395
open access 182, 186
open education 12, 182, 183, 185, 200
open innovation 375
open source 194, 211, 217
operations 14, 49, 118, 125, 215, 220, 221, 265, 269, 287, 288, 334–336, 353, 356, 378, 395
organization 104, 344
ownership 3, 4, 6, 9, 30, 32, 43, 89, 90, 99, 168, 182, 246, 247
owning 66, 140, 224, 306, 396

P

pandemic solidarity 216
partnership 90, 173, 275, 335, 368
peer-guided learning 186, 392
peer-to-peer (P2P) 3, 9, 12, 25, 31–34, 65, 102, 115, 121, 122, 124, 143, 144, 146, 173, 198, 199, 241, 244, 249, 287, 296, 325, 347, 371, 389, 396, 397
peer-to-peer (P2P) accommodation 10, 11, 13, 115–126, 286, 293, 295, 372, 373, 391
peer-to-peer (P2P) economy 68, 372
peer-to-peer (P2P) learning 146
peer-to-peer (P2P) lending 11, 164, 168, 190, 392
peer-to-peer (P2P) production 11
platform cooperatives 13, 264, 286, 293, 296, 393
platform cooperativism 13, 264, 269, 288, 393
platform economy 66, 242, 243, 245, 246, 250, 252, 254, 255, 271, 279, 286, 293, 296
Poland 8, 14, 102, 149, 170, 344, 345, 350, 352–354, 356–359, 394
policy 10, 14, 15, 32, 41–43, 47, 52, 54, 57, 64, 69, 78, 91, 137, 139, 219, 242, 248, 252, 267, 269, 274, 308, 315, 316, 334, 340, 341, 345, 367, 375, 377, 378, 389, 390, 393, 397
Portugal 8, 102, 103, 149–151, 191
practices 7–10, 12, 15, 22, 29, 32, 33, 35, 42, 43, 47–49, 52, 56, 60, 68, 100, 101, 119, 120, 125, 139, 140, 142, 152–155, 166, 182, 186, 200, 207–209, 211, 215, 217, 224–226, 230, 250, 251, 274, 277, 289, 291, 293, 306, 313, 315–317, 365, 388, 390–392, 395–397
pre-existing solidarity networks 216
produsers 296
prosumers 6, 10, 33, 34
public policy 7, 9, 10, 15, 41–43, 60, 264–266, 269, 388–390, 393
public policy instruments 47

public values 243, 246, 247, 250, 255, 256, 393
pure sharing economy 14, 119

R

real time 32, 104, 106, 107, 353
refugees 12, 208, 209, 212–226, 229, 392
regulation 32, 42–44, 46–49, 51–54, 56–58, 60, 66–68, 70, 72, 77, 78, 97, 100–104, 106, 126, 141, 150, 169, 170, 174, 220, 244–247, 250, 252, 255, 256, 271, 273, 293, 297, 307, 310, 313, 315, 345, 346, 358, 367, 368, 371, 375, 390, 393, 394
regulations and sharing economy 10, 41, 43, 48, 60, 313, 367, 390, 394
regulations in the collaborative economy 67, 70, 101, 313, 358, 390
relationship 23, 42, 44, 46, 50, 67, 72, 75, 76, 91, 93, 116, 123, 140, 143, 182, 198, 265, 268, 271, 286, 287, 312, 314, 315, 331, 332, 346
renting 3, 90, 119, 122, 144, 249, 306
reputation economy 23
reusing 184
reward-based funding 167, 392
ride-hailing 10, 13, 97, 104, 105, 247, 249, 250
ridesharing 11, 90, 91, 93, 97, 103–105, 107, 269, 308, 353, 397
risk 44, 46, 48, 50, 57, 58, 60, 69, 91, 105, 222, 223, 227, 229–231, 246, 253, 255, 279, 297, 326, 345, 353, 371, 373, 396, 397

S

scaling up 267
second hand 31, 242, 358
self-regulation 10, 47, 48, 396
self-regulation in the sharing economy 43, 47
selling 148, 153, 277
service fees 215
services 6, 10–14, 21, 23, 24, 31–35, 49–54, 56, 57, 66–79, 90–93, 97, 98, 101–103, 105–107, 116, 118–122, 139–141, 144, 146, 147, 149–151, 155, 163, 164, 166, 168, 172–174, 181, 182, 184, 195, 197, 200, 213, 215, 216, 241–251, 253–255, 264, 266, 267, 269–275, 277, 287, 290, 291, 293, 306–317, 325–331, 333–335, 343, 344, 346–353, 356, 357, 359, 368, 369, 371, 372, 389, 390, 392–397
sharewashing 396
sharing 4–8, 10, 12, 23, 24, 29, 31, 33–35, 65, 69, 77, 89–91, 93, 97–99, 101, 104, 106, 107, 116, 119, 120, 137–140, 143–148, 150, 151, 153, 155, 169, 181–184, 186, 191–200, 207–209, 214, 242–245, 249, 250, 255, 269, 274, 276, 278, 286–288, 291, 294, 296, 305,

308, 309, 313, 316, 325, 326, 343–347, 353, 356, 357, 359, 365–369, 373–375, 378, 387–393, 395–397
sharing economy 3–15, 21–26, 29–36, 42, 43, 45, 50–54, 57, 59, 60, 66, 69, 91, 93, 94, 100, 104, 106, 115, 116, 121, 123, 124, 138–146, 152, 154, 155, 163, 173, 182, 183, 197, 200, 208, 241–246, 249–251, 255, 270, 276, 278, 286–289, 294, 296, 306–317, 325, 328, 332, 335, 336, 344–348, 351, 352, 356, 358, 359, 365–370, 373–378, 387–398
sharing economy business model 8, 13, 118, 139, 287, 345, 358
short-term-rentals (STR) 54, 56, 116, 118, 288, 289, 308–310, 314, 315, 345, 352, 359, 396
silver economy 396
social capital 200, 288, 330–332, 392, 397
social economy 275
social engagement 344
social innovation 4, 182, 266, 311
social participation 125
soft instrumentum 55
soft law 10, 43, 54–56
soft negotium 55
solidarity 10, 12, 15, 45, 66, 137, 139, 153, 207–213, 215–231, 311, 392
solidarity economy 12, 207–215, 217, 220, 221, 223–231
Spain 8, 72, 99, 120, 170, 191, 198, 208, 332, 351, 357
stakeholders 3, 10, 14, 47, 68, 69, 91, 93, 94, 106, 140, 145, 164, 193, 194, 254, 267, 277–279, 316, 344, 346, 365, 367, 376–378, 391, 394
standardisation 10, 33, 42, 57, 58, 265
standards 43, 45, 47, 52, 56–59, 72, 102, 122, 126, 268, 269, 314, 371
subscription, subscription-based 143, 188, 227, 249
sustainable, sustainability 22, 28, 34, 91, 92, 97, 106, 116, 139, 142, 144, 150, 152, 154, 155, 163, 210, 215, 277, 334, 340, 346, 375, 391, 393, 394
swapping 140, 142, 144, 147, 287, 294, 306, 309
Sweden 150

T

temporary employment 252
the Netherlands 8, 12, 13, 97–99, 152, 169, 170, 241–243, 245–255, 393
the United Kingdom (UK) 8, 12, 14, 54, 96–99, 168–170, 173, 226, 326, 327, 330, 333–336, 394
third sector 144, 145
threats 59, 121, 220, 222, 227, 345, 373, 374
timebanking 149, 326, 327, 329, 333, 334
time banks 6, 12, 14, 31, 35, 211, 325–336, 394
timesharing 196

time-swap 329
Triple-P (People, Planet, Profit) 92
trust 10, 23, 33, 34, 45, 76, 91, 142, 149, 165, 174, 208, 214, 217, 287, 327, 344, 346, 347, 351, 354, 359, 367, 372, 375, 378, 394, 395, 397

U

Uber 4, 10, 11, 13, 14, 49, 50, 60, 66, 70–75, 77, 78, 91, 94, 97, 101–103, 146, 150, 151, 242, 245, 249, 250, 253, 274, 288, 315, 344, 345, 353, 356, 359, 390, 396, 397
uberisation 11, 151

V

value market 12, 169
virtual economy 24
volunteering 148, 330, 331, 334, 335

W

warm-glow giving theory 166, 343

The manufacturer's authorised representative in the EU is Springer Nature Customer Service Centre GmbH, Europaplatz 3, 69115 Heidelberg, Germany. If you have any concerns regarding our products, please contact ProductSafety@springernature.com

Printed and bound by CPI Group (UK) Ltd, Croydon, CR0 4YY
30/09/2026
02225704-0009